Craig Collie is the author of *The Path of Infinite Sorrow* and *Nagasaki: Living in the Shadow of the Bomb*. He is a well-established television producer and director who has worked in senior roles both at the ABC and SBS. He lives in Sydney.

THE REPORTER AND THE WARLORDS

CRAIG COLLIE

ALLEN&UNWIN
SYDNEY • MELBOURNE • AUCKLAND • LONDON

First published in 2013

This project has been assisted by the Australian Government through the Australia Council for the Arts, its arts funding and advisory body.

Allen & Unwin
83 Alexander Street
Crows Nest NSW 2065
Australia
Phone: (61 2) 8425 0100
Email: info@allenandunwin.com
Web: www.allenandunwin.com

Cataloguing-in-Publication details are available from the National Library of Australia
www.trove.nla.gov.au

ISBN 978 17423 7797 1

Map by Darian Causby
Set in 12/16 pt Bembo by Midland Typesetters, Australia
Printed and bound in Australia by Griffin Press

10 9 8 7 6 5 4 3 2 1

The paper in this book is FSC certified.
FSC promotes environmentally responsible, socially beneficial and economically viable management of the world's forests.

Dedicated to Winston Lewis, on whose shoulders
I stood to write this book

Contents

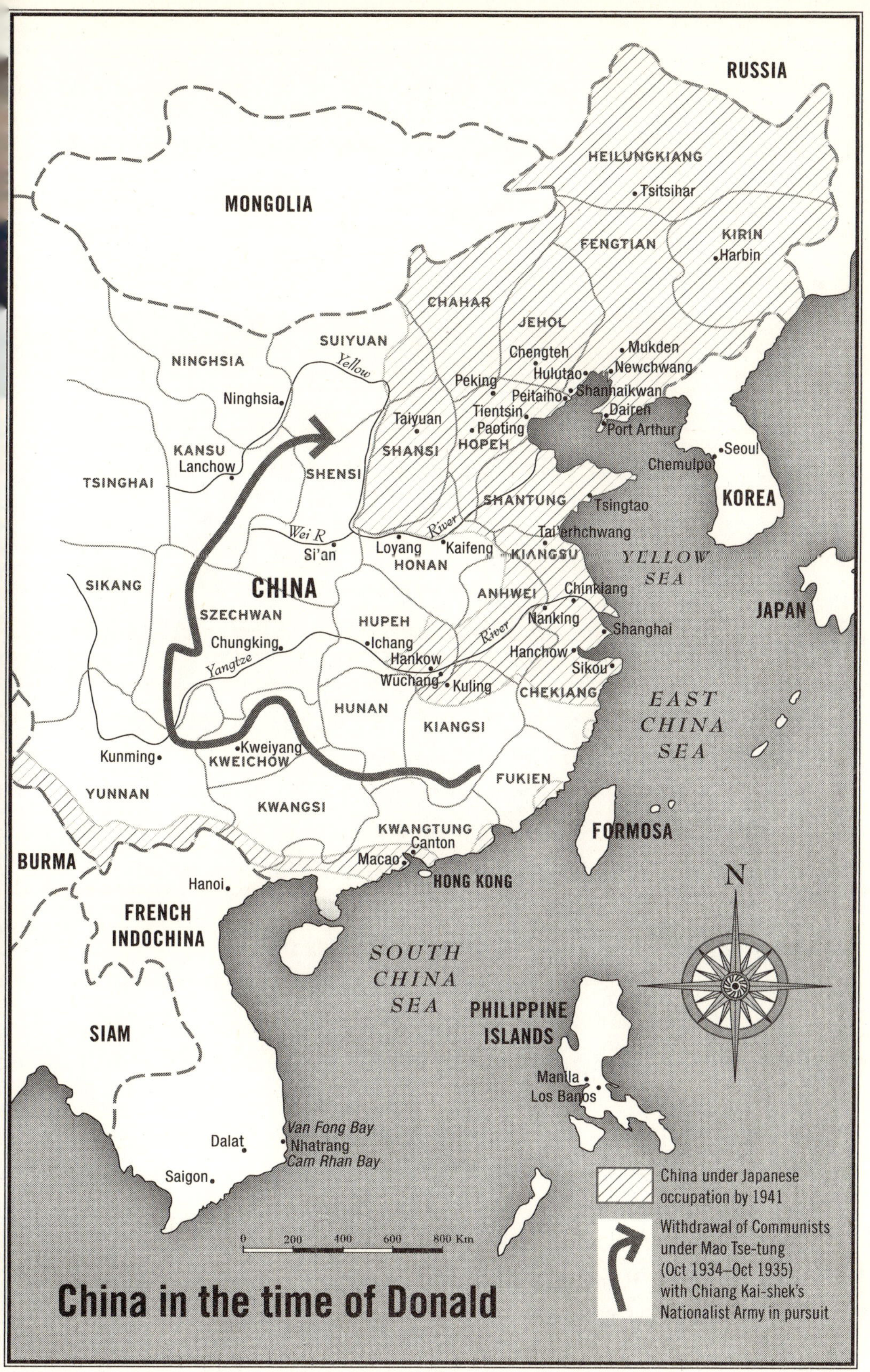

China in the time of Donald

People featured in this book

Anderson, Roy ('The Admiral')—Chinkiang manager, Standard-Vacuum Oil; close friend of WH Donald

Chang Ching-kiang ('Curio Chang') (Zhang Jingjiang or Zhang Renjie)—Shanghai art dealer associated with the Green Gang

Chang Hsueh-liang ('the Young Marshal') (Zhang Xueliang)—Manchurian warlord; son of Chang Tso-lin

Chang Hsun, General (Zhang Xun)—Manchu general; military governor of Anhwei

Chang Jen-chun—Viceroy of Canton; Viceroy of Nanking

Chang Tso-lin ('the Old Marshal') (Zhang Zuolin)—Manchurian warlord; President of Republic of China, 1927–28

Chennault, Captain Claire—American airforce adviser to Madame Chiang

Chiang Kai-shek, Generalissimo—Commandant, Whampoa Military Academy; Commander-in-chief, National Revolutionary Army; President of Republic of China 1928–31

Chow Tzu-chi ('Old Joe')—Minister of Finance under Hsu Shih-ch'ang

De Jonquiéres, Rear-Admiral de Fauquen—second-in-command, French Far East Squadron

Donald, Mary, nee Wall—wife of WH Donald and mother of Muriel Donald

Donald, Muriel—daughter of WH and Mary Donald

Donald, William Henry ('WH' or 'Don')—Australian journalist and editor (*China Mail, Far Eastern Review*), adviser to Sun Yat-sen, Chang Hsueh-liang and Madame and Generalissimo Chiang Kai-shek

Feng Kuo-chang, General (Feng Guozhang)—commander in Peiyang Army; President of Republic of China, 1917–18

Feng Yu-hsiang, General (Feng Yuxiang)—northern China warlord; Vice-president, Republic of China

Fraser, David—Peking correspondent, *The Times*

Fraser, Everard—British consul-general, Shanghai

Ho Ying-chin, General (He Yingqin)—Minister of War under Chiang Kai-shek

Hochschild, Harold—American businessman; friend of WH Donald

Hu Han-min—leading member of Kuomintang (Nationalist Party)

Huang Chih-jung ('Pockmarked Huang')—leader of Shanghai's Green Gang

Huang Hsing (Huang Xing)—Kuomintang (Nationalist Party) founder; first commander-in-chief, Republic of China army

Huang, Colonel JL (Jen-lin)—aide to Chiang Kai-shek

Kung, Dr HH (Hsiang-hsi)—banker; Premier, Republic of China; husband of Soong Ai-ling

Li Yuan-hung (Li Yuanhong)—President of Republic of China, 1916–17, 1922–3

McHugh, James—US Naval Attaché, China; friend of WH Donald

Morrison, Dr George Ernest—Peking correspondent, *The Times*; adviser to Yuan Shih-k'ai

Nebogatov, Rear-Admiral Nikolai—commander Third Pacific Squadron, Russian Navy

Pratt, Lionel—Australian journalist working in Japan and China

Pu-i (Puyi)—last emperor, Ch'ing Dynasty

Rea, George Bronson—publisher of Shanghai journal, *Far Eastern Review*

Reinsch, Paul—US Minister to China, 1913–19

Shepherd, Rev. George—New Zealand-born missionary working in China

Rozhestvensky, Vice-Admiral Zinovy—commander Baltic Fleet (Second Pacific Squadron), Russian Navy

Selle, Earl Albert—American journalist; author of the biography, *Donald of China*

Soong Ai-ling (Madame Kung)—eldest daughter of Charlie Soong; wife of HH Kung

Soong, Charlie—Shanghai businessman; close friend of Sun Yat-sen

Soong Ching-ling (Madame Sun)—daughter of Charlie Soong; second wife of Sun Yat-sen

Soong May-ling (Madame Chiang)—daughter of Charlie Soong; third wife of Chiang Kai-shek

Soong, TV (Tse-ven)—Minister of Finance under Chiang Kai-shek; chairman Bank of China; son of Charlie Soong

Stennes, Captain Walther—security adviser to Chiang Kai-shek

Strawn, Silas—American lawyer; US delegate at Chinese Customs Tariff Conference

Sues, Ilona—Polish typist; hired to investigate Chinese Ministry of Propaganda

Sun Yat-sen, Dr—Chinese revolutionist; first President of Republic of China, 1912

Sung Chiao-jen (Song Jiaoren)—Kuomintang (Nationalist Party) founder

T'ang Shao-i (Tang Shaoyi)—associate of Yuan Shih-k'ai

Togo Heihachiro, Admiral—commander Japanese Fleet (Russo-Japanese War)

Tong, Hollington—Chinese journalist; Minister of Information under Chiang Kai-shek

Tu Yueh-sen ('Big-eared Tu') (Du Yuesheng)—leader of Shanghai's Green Gang

Tuan Ch'i-jui, General (Duan Qirui)—premier, then President of Republic of China, 1924–26

Von Falkenhausen, General Alexander—German military adviser to Chiang Kai-shek

Wang Ching-wei—associate of Sun Yat-sen; president of collaborationist government of Republic of China (Nanking)

Wen Shih-tseng—Canton administrative head

Wen Tsung-yao—chief adviser to viceroy, Canton

Wu P'ei-fu, General (Wu Peifu)—Peiyang commander; north China warlord

Wu Ting-fang, Dr—acting Foreign Minister under Sun Yat-sen

Yang Hu-cheng, General—commander, Shensi Army

Yen Hsi-shan, General—Shansi warlord

Yuan Shih-k'ai (Yuan Shikai)—Commander, Peiyang Army; President of the Republic of China 1912–16

A note on names

Westerners are accustomed to people's names with given name first, surname last, but Chinese and Japanese names are constructed in the reverse order with family name first. In this book, I've adopted the convention I used in previous books for Japanese people and reversed Japanese names so they will be in the order familiar to the Western reader: given name first, surname last.

With Chinese names, that's not so easily done. Western readers are already familiar with a number of them in the Chinese order: Chiang Kai-shek, Sun Yat-sen, Mao Tse-tung (Zedong). I have retained that order for Chinese in this book unless their name has been anglicised (mostly just with initials): TV Soong, JL Huang, Hollington Tong. I hope this schema of names is reasonably intuitive for readers.

In the choice between the older Wade-Giles system of Romanised names and places (Mao Tse-tung, Canton) and the current pinyin (Mao Zedong, Guangzhou), I have opted for Wade-Giles. It is the system in use at the time this story takes place. In any case, some of the main characters are better known in that form. It is more accessible for Western readers even if it is a less accurate rendition of the Chinese. Some place names are given in pinyin as well for readers more familiar with the modern usage.

Chapter I

A different world

May, 1903. Looking out over Hong Hom Bay from the deck of the steamship that brought him here from Melbourne, he has arrived at a different world, his vessel sitting in a floating forest. Tall wooden sail masts, intricately rigged with ropes and crossed with square yards, nod lazily to the blunt masts of steamers and tripod masts on light grey warships. Squat junks with fabric sails bob around the bay among thin sampans loaded with families and their worldly belongings huddled under small awnings. Across the bay, he can see heights draped in green, stately houses here and there on the steep, lush sides almost to the summit. A small city lies prostrate at its base.

He turns his gaze to the shore and takes in what he can with one gulp of a newspaperman's eye. Behind the austere customs offices and warehouses lining Kowloon's waterfront, shanty dwellings cluster and rugged rocky hills rise to a craggy peak. Further behind stretch the blue mountains of Kwangtung, and the vast empire of the Manchus about which Will Donald knows almost nothing.

The rush of berthing SS *Changsha* completed, a gangway is lowered. Sandy-haired with a prominent nose, of medium build and wiry, Donald disembarks into the swarming dark-haired humanity he was watching from the deck. He knew it would be approaching summer this side of the equator but, in a light suit and tie, has seriously underestimated the humidity and heat that now greets him. He feels oppressed and alien. Carrying his cabin bag down the gangway, he spots the bloated body of a dog floating in the water between the ship and the wharf.

The letter from the *China Mail* had said he'd be met by a staff member. All around him is a sea of Chinamen with shaved foreheads and long plaited pigtails, wearing ankle-length gowns and soft black shoes as if they are all just out of bed. There are few women. A European is preparing to get into a rickshaw, another is struggling out of one, suited and hatted; in fact, dressed not unlike Donald despite the weather. No Europeans are walking about. They can't move, it seems, except by rickshaw. The wharf area is surprisingly noiseless, some voices and the shuffle of jostling movement, but not the cacophony he would expect from so many people pushing and shoving. An aroma of wood smoke and incense drifts past his nostrils and, when that eases, there is the damp smell that comes off the harbour.

Finally, he spots a Chinese man standing over to the side with a sign held up on a pole: 'Mr W. H. Donald'. Waiting patiently for the new arrival to identify himself, he too has a pigtail and a shaved forehead. The sign is a sheet of paper pinned to a flat board attached to a wooden pole. It looks like a baker's paddle given a new purpose. Donald walks up and points to the sign. 'That's me,' he says chirpily.

The man welcomes Donald enthusiastically in sing-song pidgin English. The Australian can follow parts of it only. He is being asked, he thinks, whether he has luggage still onboard. He answers, yes, he has a large trunk. The man says it will be brought to the *China Mail* office and says something in another language to a young man standing to one side who then disappears. Donald hadn't noticed him.

A rickshaw boy pulls up alongside them as if already hired. Donald's companion must have hailed him with a wink and a nod, but he didn't notice that either. Things are moving a little faster than he can follow. The subdued sounds on the wharf have been overtaken by the hubbub he was expecting: shouting and clanging and clattering.

'We go ferry.'

The contact picks up the bag Donald has put down and motions for him to climb onboard the rickshaw. Doing so with the intention of making space for a second person, Donald finds there is no room. He assumes a second rickshaw will be called, but before he can claim his bag, the rickshaw takes off with a sudden lurch and bounces along at a slow clip, its iron wheel rims clanking over the stony road. His welcoming committee of one walks alongside, carrying Donald's bag and the pole with his name on it. The Australian, from a culture of aggressive egalitarianism, is uncomfortable, but is too unfamiliar with this culture to do anything about it.

The metal rickshaw doesn't give as smooth a ride as Donald expected. Threading through the clamour of the unending human stream, bumping around obstacles—lumbering wooden handcarts piled high with goods, sellers and buyers fussing over wares displayed on upturned crates, stacked wooden cages of ducks—and dodging past shoulder poles loaded at each end, it arrives noisily at the Star Ferry Company's Kowloon wharf.

The man from the *China Mail* has kept pace with him all the way. Gesturing with a wave of his open palm, the guide indicates that they should board the ferry that can be seen through the wide entrance of a grandiose pavilion. The rickshaw boy is given a coin which he examines closely. The Australian's companion leads the way into the terminal, still carrying his cabin bag. The *Morning Star* is ready to leave, a black cloud billowing from its tall smokestack poking through a fabric awning that shelters the upper deck.

Installed under the sloped cover as the ferry pushes across Victoria Harbour, Donald can now feel himself relaxing into these new and unfamiliar surroundings. He starts to take stock of how he got here.

Will Donald had moved to Melbourne from Sydney a few months earlier to work as subeditor on the *Argus*. Previously with Sydney's *Daily Telegraph*, he'd become frustrated with so few opportunities for advancement. In any case, the *Argus* had offered significantly more money.

A country boy from Lithgow, across the Blue Mountains from Sydney, Donald was still feeling his way with his new employer when a telegram came out of the blue. From Hong Kong, the cable offered the Australian a job as subeditor and eventually editor on the colony's afternoon paper, the *China Mail*. In conclusion, it instructed: 'APPLY AT CHINA NAVIGATION COMPANY MELBOURNE FOR TICKET AND EXPENSE MONEY'.

Something of a jokester himself, Donald thought someone was pulling his leg. He carried the telegram around in his pocket for most of the day before going to the shipping office to confirm his suspicions.

'I think I'm the victim of a leg-pull,' he told the clerk. But he wasn't. The cable order for money and a ticket was waiting for him, as the telegram had said.

'When would you be thinking of going?' asked the clerk.

A flummoxed Donald mumbled that he'd have to get back to him. It was unusual for the convivial journalist to be at a loss for words.

Returning to the *Argus* office, he mentioned the offer to a reporter working at the next desk. 'It's an adventure,' his colleague said. 'Take it.'

Discussing it that evening with Melbourne's correspondent for the *Daily Telegraph*, Donald got the opposite advice. 'Look, you've got your foot on the ladder here,' his friend argued. At the time the *Argus* was a beacon for journalists in Australia and considered a prestigious paper to work for. 'Why throw it away on a paper you know nothing about? In a country you don't know?'

Clearly Donald was going to have to make up his own mind. The next day he went to the editor's desk.

'I'm going to China,' he said and waited.

The editor looked up. In the short time Donald had been there, the editor had already taken note of his new subeditor's blunt manner.

'Isn't it a bit sudden, Mr Donald? You've just started here. I'd hate to lose you. I would have thought the *Argus* is your sort of paper. Anyway, what do you know about China?'

The answer, of course, was not much. But Will Donald had made up his mind. He had been fascinated by the Orient for some time, although precious little that was current could be found about it in libraries. Coincidentally, a journalist from Japan's *Kobe Herald* had passed through Sydney a short time before, on a circuitous visit to Britain via Hong Kong, Australia and America. The Scotsman, Petrie Watson, had come into the *Telegraph* office on Christmas Day. Finding an interested audience in Donald, he had expounded at length about the Chinese and the Japanese.

Watson was highly critical of the Japanese and their turbulent politics, dismissive of their 'so-called culture'.

'Never trust the Japanese,' he had said, 'and don't believe a word they say. They copy Western inventions without getting licences for them.' The visitor predicted the Japanese would soon attack Russia, having already defeated the Chinese six years before and imposed sanctions on them.

As for the Chinese, they were 'a mess', a culture consumed with maintaining 'face'. The Chinese spend so much time acquiring wisdom, he said, they have no time left to use it.

'But there's a power there,' Watson concluded. 'China is a sleeping giant.'

Sleeping giant. Those words would take on immeasurable importance in Will Donald's life, but at the time that conversation was as near as Donald had come to the Chinese. Scattered across market gardens outside Lithgow and in Sydney's markets in Surry Hills, the Chinese were to be ignored or regarded with suspicion. The White Australia policy made sure of that.

In Hong Kong a sort of White China policy is in operation, but it's too soon for Donald to recognise that. What he does see, when he eventually disembarks on the island, are turbaned policemen and pigtailed coolies, everywhere carrying out their duties and plying their harbourside trades.

On the pretext of needing something from it, he takes hold of his cabin bag as a gesture to his own Australian-ness. Otherwise it is the routine as before: a rickshaw journey with his companion walking briskly alongside. Donald is overpowered by the rich stench of smoke, faeces and garlic when he steps onto Icehouse Street Wharf. Everywhere the smells of eating—coriander, dried seafood, anise, fish and soy sauces, barbecued pork—are made richer and more pungent by the hot May day. As Donald moves away from the shoreline, the crowds thin out to reveal the heavy Victorian architecture of colonial rectitude and decorum. Storeys layered like filing drawers, with deep balconies behind repeating patterns of granite arches and columns. What strikes Donald as he travels through the more muted bustle on these boulevards is the lack of horse-drawn traffic. Anything that moves is either human or pulled by humans, always Chinese.

After a couple of blocks they are making their way a short distance up Wyndham Street with flower stalls either side of the roadway, blooming with colour as the street starts to wind its way up the rise towards Victoria Peak. They soon come to a three-storey building which has seen better days. Over the ground-floor colonnaded portico hangs a tailor's wooden sign. Above it, attached to the first-floor balcony is another proclaiming 'China Mail Editorial Offices'. The rickshaw stops and the Chinese man spreads his arms like a ringmaster towards the unprepossessing structure, proud of the honour of being a part of it.

'Master,' he says, apropos of nothing in particular.

Donald climbs a dark staircase and walks into an editorial room on the first floor. As the newcomer enters, a short, squat man gets down from his high chair and approaches him with a broad smile. He is clearly the editor, Thomas H. Reid, who had cabled Donald with the offer of this job.

'You must be Mr Donald,' he says in a distinct Scottish brogue. 'So happy you could join us.' Indicating a desk over to one side, old papers strewn untidily across it, he adds, 'That will be your desk.' It looks like its current occupant has just ducked out for something to eat and will be back any moment.

'How did you come to hire me?' Donald asks.

'In this business, there are too many drunks,' the editor replies. 'I'm sick of them. Too many bad experiences.' He explains that a newspaperman passed through Hong Kong late last year on his way home, via Australia and America, after working in Japan. Reid told him he was looking for a new subeditor and to let him know if he came across a competent journalist who was a teetotaller. 'He found you,' Reid says, shrugging his shoulders. 'Petrie Watson. Do you remember him?'

Donald says he does. After they'd talked for a while, he'd taken Watson to lunch. Unlike most journalists, notoriously heavy drinkers, Donald has never had a drop of alcohol in his 27 years. He'd had a cup of tea with the meal, now that he is reminded of it. Watson had remarked on that, talking about it at some length. Now he understands why.

'I never thought he'd find one, but he did,' continues Reid. 'You don't drink, so you get the job.'

The editor hands his new subeditor a sheaf of telegrams. 'Here are some late telegrams from London, Mr Donald,' he says. 'Caption them for the next edition, if you would.'

In shuffling through them, a couple of sheets slip to the floor. Donald stoops to pick them up, but Reid stops him sharply, calling out, 'Boy!'

A small Chinese man with a grey pigtail sticks his head through the door.

'You want something, Master?'

'Yes, pick up those papers.'

'Yes, Master!'

As the Chinese man hands the papers to an embarrassed Donald, the *China Mail* proprietor, Murray Bain, comes into the room. Without waiting to be introduced he says to the new recruit, 'You must learn not to exert yourself. The climate here is too hot.'

That a man, old enough to be his father, is made to do such a menial task as pick up a few dropped papers will take the Australian newsman some getting used to.

•

So began the extraordinary Chinese adventure of William Henry Donald in a significant and turbulent time in that country's history, in which the Ch'ing dynasty of the Manchus collapses and dies, and the Republic of China grows out of its carcass. Arriving as a local newsman, Donald would become first a foreign correspondent witnessing great events, then a participant in them. But it all began in the editorial office of the *China Mail*.

Donald found he was expected to do everything on the newspaper, to be, as he described, 'chief cook and bottle-washer', but Reid and Bain gave him the editorial freedom to write about subjects as he saw them. He found the British snooty and wrote editorials about Hong Kong life, often with a satirical take on the colony's social mores. This didn't greatly endear him to the British expats.

The Australian had arrived in Hong Kong with his countrymen's ambivalence towards the English. Although of British stock—or they were then—Australians notoriously had a chip on their shoulder from the belief that the English looked down on them, that they were seen as brash descendants of convicts from Great Britain's working classes, unrefined and uncultured. Hong Kong provided ample opportunity to reinforce that prejudice in Donald's mind. It was a staid British entrepot, serving as a way-station for trade with China, and run by mercantile expatriates from Britain with a puffed-up sense of their own importance.

Europeans and Americans came to Hong Kong to do business. The *hongs* (foreign businesses) had made huge fortunes out of opium and were now investing in less tainted enterprises. Shipbuilding, maritime insurance and dry docking were the growth industries of the colony. Tea from China was a source of great wealth, with duty providing 10 per cent of the government's income. At this time, it was also the banking centre of China; the daily rate of silver, long used as the standard of monetary exchange, was set in Hong Kong.

Taipans, as the foreign businessmen were called, did most of their business in the morning, dictating letters before going to the Hong Kong Club for gin and tonic. After a nap in long rattan deck chairs on the club's verandah, they might go back to the office to sign their letters. With that onerous duty out of the way, the evening was theirs to enjoy.

A problem for all the Hong Kong papers was that the colony was small and local news was not very interesting. Foreign stories came by cable, but the high cost of this service limited the reporting of foreign news, for the most part, to English cricket and football. Opinion pieces, light satire and news summaries were added to the mix, but Donald's editorialising was not always well-received. In a close-knit community the dominant interests—businesses, clubs and social cliques—could redirect their advertising or block access to news stories in retaliation for an item against their interests. Power in the colony resided in the Hong Kong Jockey Club, the trading conglomerate Jardine Matheson and Co, and the Hongkong and Shanghai Bank. The governor came a distant fourth.

The city of Victoria spread around and extended up Victoria Peak. Hong Kong's most affluent residents lived on 'The Peak', not just for the superior views, but because the breeze gave some relief from the stifling summer heat. Transport to and from the city below was by the Peak Tram, a funicular railway built late in the nineteenth century. Between 8 a.m.

and 10 a.m., downhill services were reserved each morning solely for first-class passengers. At the lower terminal, liveried chair-bearers would carry passengers to their offices. At the summit, upholstered wicker sedans stood by to carry them home. The Peak Tram's front seat was reserved permanently for the governor, whose summer residence, Mountain Lodge, was up on the slopes. To ensure the protocol was observed, a sign warned: 'This seat is reserved for his Excellency, The Governor'. It was an aspect of Hong Kong life that gave Donald a disdain for the colony's elite.

The *China Mail* featured a series of 'Intercepted Letters' between 'Betty' and 'Nell', light-hearted dissections of colonial life. The pseudonymous author was in fact WH Donald. One of his intercepted letters described a moonlight picnic to end the bathing season, heading out by launch with the women in the stern exchanging domestic gossip and men in the bow enjoying their cigars. The gossip was about the Chinese servants, how the 'boy' of one of them only lived for 'squeeze' (extortion) and washed his feet in the soup tureen, and how the *amah* (nanny) of another wore her mistress's stockings and stole her handkerchiefs.

Although the content of the *China Mail* was not always appreciated, Donald was not a social outcast. Bubbling with friendliness, he confirmed a stereotype by playing the uncultivated Australian, and the Hong Kong gentility put up with it because he was a lively and engaging conversationalist. He may not have been seen at the tea dances and bridge parties up on The Peak, but he did join the bathing parties that set out from Blake's Pier in steam launches for some quiet spot to enjoy tea and cakes and convivial if slightly stuffy company. And he could write about it afterwards. Life in Hong Kong could be fun if you didn't let it irritate you too much.

Bill Donald was a charmer with strong views on certain subjects which he would happily share, but he was more Calvinist than anti-establishment. About six months after his arrival, the East's first association of journalists was formed, its inaugural president being *China Mail* editor, Thomas H. Reid. WH Donald was on the committee. The association's objective was 'the elevation and improvement of the status of journalists in the Far East'. A lofty ideal, but unfortunately Hong Kong was not ready for it. The association petered out soon after it started.

Donald was a member of two yacht clubs, the Royal Hong Kong and the Corinthian. He even joined the silvertail Hong Kong Club, just around the corner from the *China Mail* on Queens Road. The newspaperman probably thought the businessmen who gathered there at noon and in the early afternoon might be useful contacts, but he didn't play cricket or serious tennis and found their conversations dull. Instead, he spent increasing time in the Hong Kong Club's library, reading about China.

Although a country boy, Donald had enjoyed Sydney's beaches and, particularly, sailing on its magnificent harbour in the short time he worked in that city. In Hong Kong, he resumed his love affair with sailing, buying himself a small wooden sailboat which he named *Waratah* after the native flower of New South Wales. While he continued to join the picnic parties from time to time, on most Sundays he took a long sail around the colony's numerous islands, sometimes beaching his boat and walking vigorously up to a lookout point. Will Donald loved the outdoors.

Sailing one afternoon on the harbour on a starboard tack, the Australian noticed a yacht bearing down on him on a port tack. The convention worldwide is that a vessel on a starboard tack has right of way, but the other yachtsman was nonetheless waving his arm, motioning Donald to move out of his path. Donald didn't alter his course. The yachts drew near. The man jumped to his feet, yelling for Donald to stand clear. At the last moment, the man swung his tiller and sheared away.

As Donald shot past him, the wind roaring in his sail, he saw that the man at the helm cursing loudly was the colonial secretary, Henry May. A career bureaucrat in Hong Kong for more than twenty years, May was also the commodore of the Royal Hong Kong Yacht Club. Everyone gave way to him regardless of the rule. May was not used to being crossed, but all he could do on this occasion was shake his fist angrily. Donald gave him a cheery departing wave and sailed on. Anticipating repercussions, he wasn't disappointed. Any entree he might have expected to Government House never seemed to eventuate, but this was a matter of little concern to the knockabout Australian.

The colony of Hong Kong was really two countries ostensibly under the same flag. One country was irredeemably British, with racecourses, parade grounds, barracks, and cricket and polo fields. This was the centre of business, administration and conspicuous wealth. The other was filled with Chinese shops, crowded markets and tea-houses. Although the late nineteenth century had seen the rise of a British-educated Chinese upper class, it was kept in its place by British colonial policies and attitudes. The colony remained racially segregated and polarised.

There was no social contact between Chinese and Europeans. No Chinese played foreign sport and none went swimming. Youngsters kicked shuttlecocks around in back streets or flew kites. Elders took caged birds for an airing on the cricket ground when there was no play. Late afternoons were filled with the clatter of mahjong tiles. Donald was fascinated by all he saw, but he couldn't participate in it.

Chinese ideas of sanitation were deplored by the Europeans, even though the Chinese were personally clean and fastidious. They were crowded together in unsanitary conditions, keeping pigs under their beds and disposing of their sewage in buckets for night soil collectors to carry to Cantonese farms as manure. It was probably a good thing Donald had little access to Chinese life at this stage. Even as a young man, he was a crank about health and hygiene, armed with a range of pills and potions and regularly taking long rambles in the countryside.

To the young journalist, the contrast of dull conservatism on one side with the vibrant strangeness of the other was exciting and appalling at the same time. In exotic Hong Kong, whole families of several generations lived on sampans, moving about constantly in their waterworld and never setting foot on shore, never needing to. That was something you didn't see in Australia, not even in Sydney. In the Chinese quarter of the city of Victoria, the streets were narrow, dirty and crowded with hanging signboards and lines of clothing. The Chinese jostled and pushed in crowds, every man with the shaved forehead and long pigtail which the Manchus made mandatory in China as a symbol of subservience to the Ch'ing dynasty.

The Chinese population of Hong Kong was an overspill from the vast neighbouring Manchu empire. By the time Donald reached Hong Kong, the Ch'ing dynasty was crumbling. Established 250 years earlier when the Manchus had driven down from the north and disposed of the predecessor Ming dynasty, it was showing all the symptoms of slow imperial death.

The Ch'ing dynasty was beset by internal problems and natural disasters beyond the power of its antiquated government and economy to deal with. With no land it could cultivate—it was concentrated in the hands of landlords—and no industrial development to absorb the excess manpower, China struggled to contain a rapidly growing population. Poverty and government corruption were rife. The Ch'ing dynasty's defeat by European colonial powers in the Opium Wars, and the unequal treaties imposed on China as a result, had left the dynasty with diminishing political power. Western ideas sowed the seeds of a consciousness among educated Chinese of their common racial background and a national identity. A New Army was created after China's defeat in the Sino-Japanese War (1894–95), but with anti-Manchu feeling spreading, it gave little loyalty to the dynasty from the north. Secret societies sprang up everywhere.

During the 1890s, advocates of violent revolution plotted to overthrow the Ch'ing empire and establish a republic similar to that in France or the United States. The earliest revolutionaries mostly gathered abroad, but they saw south China as tinder for revolution, and its distance from the imperial capital gave it some independence from Manchu control. In 1895, the Hong Kong–based Revive China Society planned its first uprising in Canton (now Guangzhou). At the helm was Dr Sun Yat-sen, charismatic and full of ideas. After the Opium Wars, public outrage at further humiliation in the Sino-Japanese War created an opportunity. Sun put together a ragtag force to capitalise on the moment, but it was a fiasco with rebels hunted down and decapitated. Sun fled to Macao disguised as a woman and from there to Japan.

More uprisings followed, some in Kwangtung province, but they were either thwarted at the outset through muddled planning or enjoyed a few days of glory before massacre at the hands of imperial forces. The revolutionary clock continued to tick behind the bustle of Chinese life, but it went largely unnoticed as two imperial powers grabbed the limelight in the Far East, facing off amid growing tensions.

Chapter 2

Hide-and-seek

The Japanese were about to get a lesson in the way the Western powers conducted international diplomacy. China had relinquished the Liaotung Peninsula in southern Manchuria to Japan after the 1894–95 war, but tsarist Russia had its own ambitions in the region. Germany and France were persuaded to pressure the victor to give up its claim to the peninsula. Japan agreed, but only after an increase in the financial reparations China was obliged to pay.

With Japan bought off and the tsar's Pacific Fleet sitting pointedly off the coast of Manchuria, Russia negotiated with China a 25-year lease of Liaotung, giving it access to the ice-free seaport of Port Arthur (now called Lushun) and the peninsula's mineral wealth. The Russians immediately began building a new railway through southern Manchuria from Harbin to Mukden and on to Port Arthur. The Japanese had been outsmarted, but they took note.

When the Boxer Rebellion broke out in China in 1900, Russian and Japanese troops were part of the international force sent to relieve diplomatic missions in Peking (now Beijing), the imperial capital. Russia had already sent 177 000 troops to Manchuria to protect its railway under construction. The Ch'ing army was pushed out of the region and Russian soldiers took control, assuring the other powers they would leave when order was restored.

By 1903, Russia hadn't announced any timetable for withdrawal and had, in fact, consolidated its presence in Manchuria. The Trans-Siberian Railway was under construction and nearing completion. Japan became concerned about its bellicose neighbour, and tried unsuccessfully to forge a mutual acceptance of their spheres of interest. With revolution in the air, Tsar Nicholas II wanted to use the threat of war against Japan to spark a revival of Russian patriotism, a time-honoured ruse for leaders whose popularity is slipping. The tsar's advisers didn't want a war. They could see enormous problems trying to get troops and supplies from European Russia to eastern Siberia. The tsar stalled with the Japanese, believing they wouldn't take on his far larger and supposedly superior army and navy. But by 1904, Japan had had enough.

With growing fascination, the world press watched the stand-off between the two imperial powers, Bill Donald no less than the foreign correspondents stationed in the region. In January, a telegram from Reuters landed on his *China Mail* desk reporting that the Japanese fleet under Admiral Togo had put to sea and was heading in the direction of Port Arthur. It was too exciting an opportunity for a newspaperman to let slip by. With his editor's approval, he prepared to go to Tokyo to cover the anticipated war. To offset some of the costs of going there, he cabled several Australian newspapers, including the two for which he once worked, and was duly appointed their reporter on the spot. Donald had graduated from expatriate newspaperman to foreign correspondent.

On 3 February, Donald sailed from Hong Kong, arriving at Kobe two days later. There he contacted Petrie Watson, the journalist who had head-hunted him in Australia for the *China Mail*. After his visit to England, Watson had returned to his English-language daily in Kobe. He told Donald that Japan had just broken off diplomatic relations with Russia over its high-handedness in talks. An outbreak of hostilities had become inevitable and it was a question only of when. Donald hurried on to Tokyo, but Tokyo wasn't where the news was happening.

On a freezing, moonless night, Admiral Togo ordered a torpedo-boat destroyer attack on Russian warships anchored off Port Arthur's harbour. By the end of the night, two of the heaviest battleships in Russia's Pacific Fleet had been badly damaged, but the attack was only a partial success for Togo. Torpedoes hadn't proved to be as decisive as he had expected and one of his destroyers had been sunk in the retaliatory fire. The Japanese ships, several of them badly damaged, limped away.

The attack was over before the Russians had any clear idea of what was happening. The Pacific Fleet's commander, Vice-Admiral Stark, was holding a birthday party for his wife that night on the battleship *Petropavlovsk* and the guests mistook the exploding ordnance for fireworks in her honour. Had they pursued the flotilla, the Russians probably could have destroyed it, but Stark wasn't alert enough for that. Three hours after the attack started, Japan issued a declaration of war.

Both sides had suffered damage, but it was mostly repairable. The Russians were able to do more lasting damage to themselves. With the departure of the attack force, their ships were crammed into the harbour. A converted steamer laid mines across the harbour approaches until it was blown up by one of its own mines. A cruiser, sent out to investigate, hit another of the Russian mines.

The attack on Port Arthur was actually a cover for Japan's main opening move of the war, the occupation of Korea through Chemulpo (now Inch'on). Young, US-trained Admiral Uriu took a flotilla towards the port where several foreign warships were anchored alongside Russian ships. Uriu reasoned that while the Russians remained in the midst of neutral vessels they wouldn't attack his transports. Torpedo boats escorted Japanese troopships up the channel to disembark at Chemulpo throughout the night of 8 February. By morning, the transports had unloaded 3000 troops and left the harbour. The Japanese infantry occupied Chemulpo and moved on to nearby Seoul.

Ensconced in Tokyo's Imperial Hotel along with a number of other foreign journalists, Donald joined the clamour to get to the action at Port Arthur. All they got were sanitised reports from the military's press officers. There was no mention of the sinking of a Japanese destroyer or that their warships had taken a pounding from Russian guns. What they heard was that Admiral Togo had struck a telling blow at Port Arthur and that the Japanese now occupied Seoul, although at the expense of the Koreans, not the Russians.

Newspapermen had been drifting in from around the world, veteran war correspondents with a nose for approaching hostilities. A couple of weeks before Donald arrived, the SS *Siberia* had brought a contingent from San Francisco, among them the young author of a newly acclaimed novel, *The Call of the Wild*. The Hearst group had won a bidding war for Jack London's services. He had limped off the ship at Yokohama with an ankle injury from skylarking onboard. At 28, he was a good-looking, almost pretty young man, obsessed with his own masculinity. He was not going to stand still. Sensing the Japanese would not let journalists report from the front, the new superstar of the literary world decided to sail to Korea and find his way from there to Manchuria. He'd already gone by the time Donald got to Tokyo.

The rest of the press corps of about 30 cooled their heels in a city where war fever ran high. Troops were seen everywhere; boys drilled with bamboo as rifles. Donald noted a group trying on new boots and leggings and they looked proud to be wearing them. Every person old enough to carry a gun wanted to go to the front. Donald asked his room-boy if he would interpret for him and was told, 'No, Sir. I want to be a soldier in the Japanese army.'

The Japanese flag was hoisted on almost every house, Donald reported, although people were restrained in their response to the initial victory in Port Arthur. Tokyo newspapers placed large placards outside their offices with the latest news of the war, 'written in, to me at least, unintelligible hieroglyphics'. On the wall of one house, he saw a large poster of a Russian ship going down while firing a broadside at Japanese torpedo boats.

Trains left Tokyo loaded with troops for ports on the Sea of Japan. The soldiers were to be transported to Korea on ships commandeered by the Japanese high command. Family and friends saw them off in silence, bowing at the trains as they left. The War Office wouldn't tell the foreign press how many men were going to the front. 'The courteous Secretary bows you in with a smile,' Donald wrote, 'refuses you news with a smile, and bows you out again with the same smile.'

The reporters were not allowed to go with the troops so they gathered at the Imperial Hotel's bar and grumbled. For teetotaller Bill Donald—gregarious, chatty and always upbeat—it was another exciting adventure. He revelled in the camaraderie and the tales, tall or otherwise, of the veterans of his craft.

Collier's Weekly star correspondent, the imperious Richard Harding Davis, told the apocryphal story of the Hearst reporter who, prevented by official red tape from getting to the front lines ten years earlier, had covered a naval battle between the Chinese and Japanese fleets without leaving his bar stool. To rub salt in the collective wound, while the international press in Tokyo rewrote official handouts and swapped fables, the story of the attack on Port Arthur appeared in US newspapers two days after it happened, courtesy of an Associated Press stringer in Chefoo, a British treaty port (now called Yantai). It was based on supposed eyewitness reports of passengers and crew on a steamship that had come from Port Arthur. The report added nothing to the Japanese press releases, but it was able to use the magic word 'eyewitness' regardless of whether anyone had actually seen anything of the night battle.

Hotels in Tokyo filled with press seeking accreditation to the Japanese forces in the field. The military said a correspondents' corps would soon be set up when others arrived and they would be allowed to go to the front. In fact, the Japanese suspected many of the foreign journalists were spies. In the meantime, Korea's uninvited guests pushed north and more troops landed at Chemulpo, while a series of actions at Port Arthur kept the Russian fleet distracted.

Within a month, more than 90 foreign newsmen had gathered in Tokyo, anxious to get to the action, but no front opened up in Manchuria and no permission came that they could go there. Captain Tanaka, the liaison officer, was badgered daily by the press men and the answer was always the same: 'Maybe tomorrow.' General Staff kept saying, 'Very soon', and asking them to be patient. At Japanese urging, they hired interpreters, servants, horses and provisions to stand by for when 'very soon' became 'now'. Donald wrote that, to prepare for the icy conditions of Manchuria, one newspaperman slept in a tent on the lawn of the house where he stayed, his tent door facing into the cold wind off Mount Fuji.

The correspondents spent long hours at the bar of the 'Imperial Tomb'. Word came through that Jack London had been arrested taking photos in Moji, not realising it was a naval base. He'd been questioned and eventually released after it was accepted he was not spying for the tsar. Reporters were wined and dined by their respective embassies, but that wasn't what they had come to the Far East for and the novelty wore thin.

Donald managed to avoid that. There was no Australian mission in Japan at that time and he wasn't celebrated enough to be invited to someone else's embassy. His time was devoted instead to his fascination with the way Japanese people reacted to highs and lows in reports from the war. Large demonstrations followed news of victories.

'All of them have disorganised city traffic, upset business, and done other things which in a commercial city are deemed unsatisfactory,' he wrote. 'On Sunday night last, one of the largest demonstrations ever held in Japan took place [about 60 000 marched in celebration and a similar number watched], and unfortunately it ended fatally. More people [twenty] were crushed to death in it than were killed in the first or second attempt to blockade Port Arthur.'

Losses were not bemoaned to the extent victory was celebrated, but merely accepted with a shake of the head, murmuring, 'It might have been worse.' Strangest of all to the newspaperman was the symbolic punning gesture of publicly wringing the necks of black pigeons. Japanese for black pigeon is *kuro bato*, similar in sound to the name of the Russian army commander in Manchuria, Kuropatkin. Donald was trying to understand the everyday Japanese, but both their public rituals and he were a world away from the reality of the war.

In early March, the charismatic Vice-Admiral Stepan Makaroff, known as 'Little Grandfather' with his distinctively parted flowing beard, arrived to take charge at Port Arthur. Two days after his arrival, Japanese small craft moved in and laid mines at the harbour entrance while Russian destroyers chased a decoy flotilla. The mine-layers came under fire from Port Arthur's fort and they headed back to open sea, but on hearing gunfire the Russian destroyers returned to be cut off by waiting Japanese warships. One of the Russian ships had a shell pass through its boiler pipes and four Japanese destroyers closed in for the kill with raking fire. Makaroff came out to try to rescue the stricken destroyer, but grossly outnumbered, he had no option but to turn back, leaving his destroyer to the jackals.

Makaroff was energetic and aggressive. His gesture of attempting to rescue the Russian destroyer raised the sinking morale of his sailors. Under his command, the fleet became noticeably better trained. It started coming out in numbers to meet enemy assaults, inflicting increased damage and casualties on the Japanese. Admiral Togo tried to block Port Arthur by sinking old steamers loaded with stones and cement across the harbour entrance. In two attempts, the steamers were sunk away from their predetermined positions and the harbour remained unblocked.

Tokyo had been colourless and cheerless during the winter, rainy and snowing. As spring approached, cherry blossom flowering en masse signified to the populace the transient nature of life, but not to the visiting newsmen. The boredom of inactivity was getting them down. They called themselves 'cherry blossom correspondents', hanging around bars during the day and in brothels and gambling houses by night. When 'the importance of the great London dailies' was pointed out to the Japanese, it didn't produce 'even an eyebrow tremor'. Frustration and too much alcohol fuelled outbursts of temper and other ugly incidents.

Donald was no wowser and enjoyed the company of these hard-doers during their nights on the town. He renewed acquaintance with Lionel Pratt, a heavy drinker he knew from his Sydney newspaper days, now covering the war for Reuters, and befriended a colourful Adelaide journalist working for London's *Daily News*. A big man with a large moustache and close-cropped hair, AG 'Smiler' Hales sported two missing fingers, and a scar on the side of his head from a Mauser bullet. He was the sort of newspaperman Thomas Reid was trying to avoid when he hired Donald.

On one occasion, the younger Australian had to restrain a drunken, ranting Hales as he staggered towards the British embassy. Convinced the British ambassador was behind his inability to get a pass to the front, Hale bellowed that he would shoot the diplomat. His supposition was actually correct. Sir Claude MacDonald had vetoed Hale's press pass because the English establishment had objected to his reporting of the Boer War.

Time dragged on and still none of the cherry blossom correspondents had seen battle. Rumour-mongers on the China coast were offering stories of battle to the press from time to time and these flowed through the press bars. Official versions were released and written up, but their newspapers were getting sporadic reports from other sources. The Tokyo-based pressmen were learning more from their own newspapers than they were picking up themselves.

By March, the press contingent was told that three groups of correspondents would be allowed to follow the three divisions of the Imperial Japanese Army as they moved into Manchuria. A first group of sixteen—Donald was not one of them—left for Korea, landing at Chinampo (now Namp'o, near P'yongyang), a Japanese outpost where the only foreigner who could speak any English was a German customs collector.

The press had been pressured by the Japanese military to hire a Mr Yokoyama to feed them and transport their baggage, but as soon as they arrived the reporters took off after the First Army marching north to the Yalu River, without worrying about the progress of their supplies. They eventually reached the Japanese forces, but saw no fighting. By the time Mr Yokoyama's canteen arrived with its canned sausages and cheap sugary champagne, they were living in tents among Korean houses.

More was happening at sea than on land in the slow build-up of the Russo-Japanese War. On the night of 13 April, a Japanese squadron drew Russian battleships south from Port Arthur. In driving rain and choppy sea, a Japanese steamer slipped in and laid mines where the Russian fleet had been observed to shelter under Port Arthur's shore batteries. While that was being carried out, Japanese warships had cut off and sunk another Russian destroyer. Admiral Makaroff sent three battleships and three cruisers in pursuit, but the Japanese kept ahead of them. When Togo moved reinforcements in, the Russian ships turned back to the shelter of the shore batteries, led by their flagship, *Petropavlovsk*. They were unaware that mines had been laid overnight.

An explosion rang out, then another. A huge cloud of brown smoke rose from the side of *Petropavlovsk* and its foremast leaned forward. With a third explosion, white steam began to mix with the brown smoke. The boilers had burst. Its enormous rudder rose in the air, its propellers still desperately turning. The rear end of the battleship opened out, belching flames, and its hull disappeared under the water, taking Admiral Makaroff with it. Searchers couldn't find his body, three days later finding only his overcoat.

By the end of April, Japanese forces had gathered along the south bank of the Yalu River, facing entrenched Russian positions on the other side. The Russian strategy was to fight delaying actions to buy time for reinforcements to come by the Trans-Siberian Railway, the incomplete section at Irkutsk slowing delivery. On 1 May the foreign press group was escorted to a high point overlooking a pontoon bridge the Japanese were laying across the river. They watched an exchange of fire between the two armies, but the bridge had been built as a decoy, with reporters part of the pretence. The main Japanese thrust was actually 2 kilometres upstream, repeating a tactic used at the same location ten years before against the Chinese army. Jimmy Hare, a *Collier's* photographer, was the only member of the press contingent to find his way to the main attack point. He watched lines of charging troops rush forward, take cover and raise a flag so gunners on a hill could continue to fire over them, and he captured it with his camera.

WH Donald was still back in Tokyo with the bulk of the foreign correspondents who had come to cover the war. The second press contingent was about to be announced but Donald doubted that a journalist for Australian and Hong Kong newspapers would be high in their priorities. He had found it an invigorating experience even if largely unproductive, but he was beginning to question the usefulness of staying any longer. His mind was made up by the reappearance of the prodigal son of the press corps.

Jack London returned to Tokyo in May, in the process of being deported for knocking out a Japanese groom he believed had been stealing his horse fodder. He had quite a tale to tell. Since leaving Japan three months before, he had chartered a junk and pushed through rough seas, gale-force winds and icy temperatures. He arrived at Chemulpo to find another *Collier's* photographer, Robert Dunn, had somehow got there, too. London and Dunn mustered horses and Korean porters and set out for Seoul, then travelled across frozen fields and through precipitous gorges towards the

Manchurian border. Somewhere out there they had been picked up by the Japanese military and brought back to Seoul, where they were allowed to join the small press contingent already in Korea. But London's frustration began to show, culminating in the incident with the stableboy. The Japanese were happy to be presented with a reason to get rid of him. *The Call of the Wild* didn't cut much ice with them.

The young Californian had come to a jaundiced view of both the Japanese and the Korean people. Donald didn't share that assessment, but he did take some lessons away from London's experience of war reporting. For all his derring-do, the only battle action Jack London had seen was the Japanese decoy advance across the Yalu. The press had been well-managed by the Japanese military. It seemed the way around that was to go it alone as the American had done, but more thoughtfully and without London's posturing impulsiveness. However, now wasn't the time to put that insight into practice. Donald would have to store it up for later. For now, there were matters back in Hong Kong he had to attend to. He returned to the colony on 25 May.

There was a changing of the guard at the *China Mail*. On the day his subeditor returned, Thomas Reid left for England after twelve years in the colony. WH Donald took over as managing editor, as promised when he joined the paper the year before. The new chief continued the editorial line that he had pursued before he went to Japan: a growing interest in China and light-hearted commentary on the peccadilloes of the British colonialists.

Donald continued to eat at Thomas's Grill Room, but his domestic life was about to change significantly. In September, he married Mary Wall, the youngest of six children of a north England bricklayer who had brought his family to Australia when Mary was five. Robert Wall built a successful construction business in Sydney, enabling him to buy a house in then well-to-do Marrickville and send his children to private schools. Despite his success, Robert's wife did not like Australia. After returning to England for a period, she died in her adopted country of acute bronchitis. Mary was twenty years old.

Thirteen years older, Mary's brother, James, spent his life collecting Chinese artefacts which cluttered his home. He'd already been to Hong

Kong and China a few times when he took his younger sister, then aged 21, with him late in 1903. James had numerous contacts from previous visits so, more visitors than tourists, they mixed easily with Hong Kong's expatriate community. Known to friends and family as 'Polly', Mary stayed on with her brother's Hong Kong friends when James returned to Australia to marry.

Caught up in the colony's social whirl, the headstrong blonde met the bon vivant, *China Mail*'s recruit from Australia. A man just returned from reporting the Russo-Japanese War could turn a girl's head, especially when that man had many exciting tales to tell, even without having been to the front. Will Donald was always a good storyteller. A wedding date was set for September, although not with enough notice for either family to make it. No Donalds were there. The Walls were represented by a family friend and an English cousin.

In Sydney, the Wall and Turtle families were close, Mary's older sister, Agnes, having married a Turtle. Sarah Turtle had nursed Mary's dying mother and came to Hong Kong for the wedding with a cousin from the Norwich branch of the Wall family who happened to be holidaying in Australia at the time. Will moved out of his 'bachelors' mess' and into the Peak Hotel where the visitors from Sydney stayed, while Mary remained with her Hong Kong hosts. On 17 September 1904, Will and Mary were married at the Wesleyan Methodist Church.

Work pressures didn't allow the new Mr and Mrs Donald an immediate honeymoon, but three months later they crossed the Pearl River to Macao for a week of rickshaw riding and sightseeing, not unlike what they could have done in Hong Kong.

Mary started calling her new husband 'Don', the nickname used by most of his closer friends. Only his family had called him 'Will', and she hadn't known the family. Associates called him 'Bill' or 'WH', the latter a form of address more common then than it is now.

Despite Donald's iconoclastic views, the couple didn't slum in Hong Kong. Living in Goodwood, a grandiose two-storey apartment building on Babington Path, halfway up The Peak, they were surrounded by a tennis court and lush gardens built on terraces up the steep hillside. Enveloped in columns, balustrades and palm trees, Goodwood provided panoramic glimpses of Victoria Harbour. It was a pleasant base for Mary's new life in Hong Kong's expatriate languor.

•

Since Donald returned from Tokyo, the Russo-Japanese War had plodded on, the Japanese slowly advancing their position but not in any decisive way. In May, two Japanese battleships sank after being lured into a recently laid Russian minefield. By August, with the blockade of Port Arthur already six months old, Russia's fleet tried again to break out, to be met by Admiral Togo's battleship squadron. In the exchange of fire, its flagship received a direct hit on the bridge, killing the new fleet commander, Admiral Vitgeft. Although it had lost no warships, the Russian fleet turned back to Port Arthur and the blockade remained in place.

In a move to break the deadlock, Tsar Nicholas ordered Russia's Baltic Fleet around the Cape of Good Hope to Port Arthur to boost the Pacific Fleet. Under the command of Vice-Admiral Zinovy Rozhestvensky, an armada of seven battleships, along with cruisers, destroyers and support craft, set out in September on the 33 000-kilometre journey from the naval base of Kronstadt, near St Petersburg. Russia had no bases between the Baltic and Port Arthur and neutrality laws limited the hospitality that could be provided by foreign ports. The fleet couldn't use British ports at all because of simmering hostility between the two countries, but as France was friendly it was proposed to use isolated bays in French colonies along the way for coaling and maintenance. The voyage would prove to be a farcical exercise in operatic comedy, more Gilbert and Sullivan than steaming grandly into battle.

Known as 'Mad Dog' behind his back, Rozhestvensky had a reputation for temperamental outbursts, throwing his binoculars at crew who frustrated him. There were plenty of opportunities. Seamen on the fleet's ships were inexperienced. Many had previously been rejected as unintelligent, or for being political dissidents or having a criminal record. Reservists were disgruntled at being called up for a distant conflict. The fleet got no further than Latvia before it was held up by sabotage. Fearful of the long and perilous journey, a reservist had put metal shavings in the propeller shaft of a new battleship and it had run aground.

Meanwhile Japanese land troops carried out several frontal assaults on the fortified hills around Port Arthur. Casualties were high with no progress made until December when they captured a key hilltop position. From there, they could shell the Russian fleet, still bottled up in the harbour below. Four Russian battleships were sunk in a short time, with the last battleship scuttled a few weeks later. Effectively, Russia's Pacific Fleet no longer existed.

On land, attempts to relieve the besieged city had failed and after the Battle of Liaoyang in August, the northern Russian forces retreated to Mukden. The commander of the Port Arthur garrison, believing defence of the city to be a lost cause even though the Japanese were suffering devastating casualties and the garrison was still well-supplied with food and ammunition, surrendered to the surprised Japanese on 2 January 1905 without consulting his senior military staff or Russia's high command.

The Baltic Fleet, now designated the Second Pacific Squadron, had rounded the Cape and arrived at Madagascar. It anchored off the island of Nossi-be, while the Russian Navy Ministry worked out its next move. Instructions and news were telegraphed through the French colony: a third Pacific squadron under Rear-Admiral Nebogatov would leave the Baltic to join them. Rozhestvensky didn't want this—the new squadron was made up of ships he had rejected for his fleet—but he was getting it anyway and it would arrive in eight to ten weeks.

News of the loss of the original Pacific Fleet and the fall of Port Arthur spread through the ships like a disease. Morale began to collapse and insubordination became more blatant every day. Below deck was a cauldron of seething resentment with the coming revolution brewing in the crew. The mission had lost its purpose with no Pacific Fleet to join and no Port Arthur to rescue. Instead the officers acquired all manner of exotic beasts while they waited; a captain had a python and a young crocodile, others had tortoises, lemurs and chameleons.

After more than two months off Madagascar and with Nebogatov's squadron still approaching, Admiral Rozhestvensky's armada suddenly weighed anchor and headed eastwards 8000 kilometres across the Indian Ocean, without going near a port. Wanting his ships to be battle-ready at all times, he wouldn't wait until the coal bunkers in his ships were nearly empty. The fleet stopped every four or five days for colliers to come alongside in the swell of the open sea. As well as replenishing the bunkers, coal was stacked in baskets on deck, in passageways and on mess decks. The crew were permanently covered in coal dust.

The world press had kept a distant eye on the Baltic Fleet while it was at Nossi-be, but information was unreliable and after a couple of months, interest had waned. The Russians slipped away from Madagascar unnoticed. No-one reported seeing them. If any passing ships had, they were still at sea. The armada would have been heading east, but no-one knew exactly where. Around Australia? Towards the South China Sea? No-one knew.

After he returned to Hong Kong from Tokyo, WH Donald had been engaged by the London *Daily Express* as an occasional correspondent in the region, while continuing his editorial duties at the *Mail*. Late in March, a cable arrived from Britain: 'RUSSIAN FLEET REPORTED LOST SINCE LEAVING RED SEA STOP MAY BE SOMEWHERE YOUR AREA STOP GO FIND IT'. The fleet had actually not come through the Red Sea, but Donald had no more idea than the *Express* where it might be, so short of chartering a ship to scour the Indian Ocean there was little he could do. As it happened, it didn't matter—the puzzle soon resolved itself.

In the early afternoon of 8 April, wisps of black smoke appeared to the west of Singapore. Coming up the Strait of Malacca, the 47 ships of the Baltic Fleet were burning soft coal from Germany—Japan's ally, Britain, wouldn't sell them its high-quality Welsh coal—so their smoke was visible far in the distance. Thousands of excited folk lined the shores and piers of the British island colony as the ships steamed past, one by one, a few kilometres offshore, Admiral Rozhestvensky's flagship leading the Russian fleet to war. All the spectacle lacked was a band playing the Grand March from *Aida*.

The Japanese consul in Singapore went out by launch to take a closer look at the enemy fleet. Through binoculars, he noticed seaweed above the waterline and the decks of the warships laden with coal. On another launch, Russia's consul met the fleet as it passed and called out news of interest through a megaphone: Japanese warships had been seen off Singapore three days before; Mukden had fallen; and Admiral Nebogatov had left Djibouti on Africa's Somali coast on 18 January. A satchel of official papers was handed over by pole while the vessels were moving. Rozhestvensky was too restless to stop for any reason apart from his own. By five o'clock, the armada had disappeared to the east, its streams of black smoke still visible long after the ships had gone out of sight.

When Rozhestvensky opened the dossier, he found it contained new orders from St Petersburg. His squadron was to go to Cam Ranh Bay in French Indochina and wait for Nebogatov and the Third Pacific Squadron. They were then to go to Vladivostok and hand over the combined fleet to Admiral Birilev, the newly appointed commander of the Baltic Fleet. Birilev was known as 'The Fighting Admiral' although he'd never actually seen battle action. Rozhestvensky became even more irritable and went from ship to ship, finding fault and issuing new orders.

The fleet sat at anchor in Cam Ranh Bay for several days, waiting for Nebogatov's squadron. Ships coaled as fast as they could. Supply ships went down to Saigon and came back with fresh food and personnel. Crew and officers occasionally went ashore to exercise their animals and to experience the bright birds, exotic flowers and vicious ants of the tropics.

Neither the world's press nor the Japanese knew with any certainty where the Baltic Fleet had moved, but Indochina's colonial administrators knew. On 15 April, the second in command of the French Far East Squadron arrived at the bay on the cruiser *Descartes*. Rear-Admiral de Jonquières paid a courtesy visit to the fleet's flagship and offered the opinion that Japan's attack on Russia was the first step towards expelling all Europeans from Asia and installing a pan-Asiatic league under the Rising Sun. Clearly de Jonquières was not intending to create any problems for the Russians, but problems were lurking anyway.

Back when the fleet was off French Madagascar, Tokyo had raised objections. If France was going to provide shelter to a belligerent in the Russo-Japanese War, it could be regarded as a participant in the war. Madagascar was too far away for the Japanese to do much more than protest, but French Indochina was a different matter. When advised by St Petersburg that the fleet would probably stop at Indochina, French Foreign Minister Delcassé hoped it would take a week or more for official notice to get from Saigon. Then he could send a formal order to leave French territorial waters—after the fleet had taken on supplies.

Trading ships were starting to arrive in Singapore with reports of sighting the Baltic Fleet coaling in Cam Ranh Bay, but this intelligence got buried in the white noise of other reports that had the fleet heading towards Sumatra, towards Formosa (Taiwan), and in other directions across the South China Sea. Cam Ranh seemed to feature prominently in the sightings, so Japan stepped up the diplomatic offensive through its newspapers. If the Russian fleet stayed in an Indochinese port, they declared, Japan would have to consider that port as a Russian base and deal with it accordingly.

Rozhestvensky was still waiting to be joined by the third squadron and move to Vladivostok. He knew that Admiral Togo's Japanese Fleet was somewhere between where he was and where he was going. Increasingly despondent and rattled, he telegraphed St Petersburg: 'SHALL NOT TELEGRAPH AGAIN BEFORE BATTLE. IF BEATEN, TOGO WILL TELL YOU; IF VICTORIOUS, I WILL ANNOUNCE IT'. At noon on 21 April, de Jonquières arrived again on *Descartes* and came onboard the Russian flagship. He was profoundly apologetic. The French Government was demanding the fleet leave Indochinese territorial waters, he said, and he was required to give 24 hours notice.

Throughout the night, Russian ships emptied the colliers, and provisions brought by steamer from Saigon were transferred. By 1 p.m. the next day, when the deadline expired, all the fleet's warships went to sea, leaving only supply ships and auxiliaries in Cam Ranh Bay. The men-of-war remained near the bay but outside territorial waters, waiting for Nebogatov's squadron. Rozhestvensky believed—and de Jonquières agreed—that if he wasn't carrying out operations with the vessels still in the bay, then he wasn't using French waters as a base. A day later, however, word came of an agreement between Paris and St Petersburg that no ship of war or commerce under a Russian flag should remain in French territorial waters.

Paris claimed the Russian fleet left the Indochinese coast on 20 April, but with reports in the world press of sightings of the fleet still in Cam Ranh Bay that day, Tokyo stepped up its public outrage. Foreign Minister

Delcassé lamely protested that instructions had been sent to the fleet via Saigon but it was hard to enforce strict neutrality in such a remote region. Especially, he might well have added, when those instructions are being forwarded through a sympathetic local admiral.

From the bridge of his ship Admiral de Jonquières had watched Russia's support ships leave Cam Ranh Bay, then he returned to Saigon to report to higher authority: 'The Russian squadron left the coast of Annam [now central Vietnam] in an easterly direction; its destination was not known.' Once again the world's press was left to guess what had become of the Russian fleet. Warships were sighted south of Luzon in the Philippines, although their nationality was uncertain. Chinese officials claimed part of the fleet was coaling at Hainan off the coast of south China. They were seen steaming past Nhatrang, up the Indochina coast from Cam Ranh. They could be anywhere around the South China Sea.

•

Donald decided this was the time to act on the *Daily Express* request. He handed responsibility for the *China Mail* over to his subeditor and on 2 May joined the French steamer SS *Armand Behic*, bound for Saigon. Before he left, Donald published a facetious article in the *China Mail*, claiming it was not written by a 'special representative in search of Baltic Fleet news', so that the reader would know it was. Recounting a tale of Captain McLiar of the *Slippery Eel* and his nightmare experience of meeting the Baltic Fleet and Admiral Rozhestvensky at sea, the story was not revealed to the reporter until the captain's third whisky and soda at the bar of the Hong Kong Hotel, and not in full until the seventh. It was vintage Donald journalism: forthright, aggressive and flippant. It related to a second reason for Donald deciding to hunt the Russian fleet.

The Hong Kong daily, *South China Morning Post*, had patted itself on the back for its 'exclusive' announcement that the Baltic Fleet had passed by Singapore and that it was bound for Saigon. Although not a direct competitor—the *China Mail* was an afternoon paper—there was sufficient rivalry among the Hong Kong press for the *Mail* to thunder its outrage in an editorial on 12 April: 'It is not our policy to refer to the actions of our contemporaries, but we cannot refrain at present from remarking that the junior morning paper is endeavouring to take credit for itself which is neither deserved nor just.'

The fleet's passage by Singapore had been widely observed and in all newspapers. The destination of Saigon was pure speculation and a few days later seen to be wrong—the fleet had headed straight to Cam Ranh Bay. But the *Post* didn't let up. It published a succession of reports by 'our special correspondent', named as 'A. Cunningham', and datelined from Singapore, then Saigon and finally Haiphong in what is now northern Vietnam, well north of where the fleet actually was.

On 21 April, Cunningham wrote, 'I am proceeding to Kamranh Bay at the first opportunity but it is a difficult matter to obtain transport.' On 8 May, he complained, 'I find it so impossible to send further messages relating to the Baltic fleet owing to French censorship of telegrams. My despatches are coming forward by steamer.' In an editorial on 22 May, when it was all over, the *Post* claimed its correspondent had seen the fleet in Cam Ranh Bay, although it didn't report that at the time. Either those reports were censored or Alfred Cunningham was unable to get to Cam Ranh before the fleet moved on. It's even possible that he didn't get any nearer to the fleet than Singapore and the reports were contrived to drum up reader excitement.

This was all too much for the new editor of the *China Mail*. Apart from fulfilling his assignment from the London *Daily Express*, here was an opportunity to upstage a cheeky rival. Bill Donald grabbed it with both hands.

By early morning on its second day at sea, the *Armand Behic* reached the Annam coast. On deck, Donald spotted a thin column of smoke rising above the lone towering rock of Cape Varella. As they got nearer, he made out the three yellow funnels and black hull of a laden collier of the Hamburg-Amerika Line. It was anchored about 9 kilometres from shore.

As *Armand Behic* continued down the coast towards Van Fong Bay, Donald noticed a packing case floating past and, soon after, saw another column of black smoke rising from behind the rocky headland of an inlet running well inshore. In time, the French passenger ship came to a channel entrance where he could see a four-funnelled man-of-war and smoke rising behind another headland.

By nine o'clock, Van Fong Bay had opened to reveal a broad stretch of water and a most extraordinary sight. Between an island and the mainland were the yellow funnels of a cluster of warships. Their nationality soon became obvious. A group of Russian nurses and soldiers, returning home on Donald's ship, rushed open-mouthed to the rails, their eyes dimmed with tears. A pretty girl in a Red Cross uniform held her arms out imploringly in the direction of the warships. At first they said little, but as *Armand Behic* passed the little island, they cheered.

At the end of the bay waited the entire Baltic Fleet, bathed in sunshine. All its hulls were painted black. Black smoke drifted up from its distinctive yellow funnels with black tops. Sheltered from land gales by the high hills that surround Van Fong Bay, the fleet waited ominously.

A small warship, patrolling the entrance of Van Fong Bay to ward off intruders, approached *Armand Behic*, dipping its Russian flag as it passed. A mail steamer flying the flag of France, its ally, was not a concern. The Russian warship came close enough for a few men on its deck to wave vigorously to their compatriots on the French ship.

Armand Behic steamed on towards Saigon, the Baltic Fleet slipping into the distance off the stern until it was lost from sight. After that, they saw small coastal steamers and a few fishing junks, but no more warships.

The sight of Russian naval might had put new life into the returning soldiers onboard. They held a religious service on the lower deck. Donald reported that a man in a white coat and blue pants had walked up to them with a jug and glass. He made a 'staccato speech' and filled the glass, holding it aloft with a signal for the assembled soldiers to shout while he drank a toast, presumably to the tsar. Periodic cheers continued for some time, interspersed with the sombre passion of Russian songs.

Donald got into shouted conversation over cheers and singing with a Captain Roberts, a shipping pilot from Shanghai with more than 25 years working China's coast. Engaged to pilot the Russian fleet to Vladivostok, Roberts would be escorted from Saigon to Admiral Rozhestvensky.

As they berthed in Saigon's dimming evening light, Donald noticed two French torpedo-boat destroyers heading out at full speed to investigate new sightings of the Russian fleet. After Cam Ranh Bay, it had moved 100 kilometres up the coast and set up in Van Fong Bay where

Donald had seen it earlier in the day. A small local steamer made monthly runs along the Annam coast bringing supplies and buying up the local fishing catch. Unfortunately for Rozhestvensky and his men, this milk run coincided with their ships settling into their new anchorage. On returning to Saigon, the steamer's crew reported what they'd seen in Van Fong Bay and the administrator at nearby Nhatrang was sent to demand the fleet leave within 24 hours.

De Jonquières had come up from Saigon and watched the entire fleet go to sea the day before Donald came past in *Armand Behic*. Having told the Russians he would cruise along the coast to ensure they didn't enter another bay, the Frenchman reported: 'Sailed in an easterly direction, destination unknown.' That night Rozhestvensky brought his fleet back to Van Fong Bay. No longer caring about diplomatic niceties and close to breakdown, he was heartily sick of the whole venture.

Before looking for transport to take him up the coast, Donald sent a cable to *China Mail* describing what he'd seen in Van Fong Bay. Later, he received a curt note saying the telegram could not be despatched. He was allowed a meeting with the Director of Telegraphs, but that august official couldn't or wouldn't explain why the telegram was refused or what type of message would be permitted. Donald's request to meet the unnamed censor was refused and he was politely told he could recover the HK$65 fee he'd paid for the telegram.

Overnight, Donald devised a plan to get around petty officialdom's intractability. He got a copy of *ABC Telegraphic Code*, a widely used codebook of the time, and composed a coded message to Murray Bain. A business acquaintance in Saigon signed the message and took it to the telegraph office, but the ruse didn't work. A few hours later, a note came requiring the friend to produce the codebook. He named the book, but was instructed to bring it to the office as they didn't have a copy. Each word was looked up, the message was deciphered and Donald's friend left with his book.

The following day, another note came requesting the book be left at the telegraph office until authorities were ready to return it. They were politely refused and asked to buy their own copy. The cablegram was not sent and the form containing Donald's message was never returned.

Coincidentally, the friend was passing Government House a day later and noticed a servant going through the gates with a copy of *ABC Telegraphic Code* tucked under his arm. The censor Donald was not permitted to meet must have been the Governor-General of French Indochina, Paul Beau.

Donald confronted telegraph officials, suggesting the suppression of his telegrams could imply the French had something to hide: that they were assisting the Russian fleet. That warning must have had some impact because when Donald later sent the same coded message at three different times—to see if it had been edited as well as to increase the chances of it getting through—one went through immediately and the other two were delayed but sent. His report was forwarded to the London and Australian papers Donald serviced.

The diplomatic war heated up again and the Tokyo press had a field day. They described the expulsion of Admiral Rozhestvensky from Cam Ranh Bay as a farce and claimed that the whole Indochina coast was now a Russian base. Editorialists loudly demanded Japan respond to France by 'taking up arms' against it and called for Britain to enter the fray under the Anglo-Japanese alliance. The British were not going to do that, but it made great copy.

The French assured the world that the Russian admiral had left French territorial waters off Indochina on 6 May after they had pressured him. The Russians had been instructed not to re-enter their waters and police measures had been put in place to prevent belligerent ships using French Indochinese waters for any purpose. They denied that the French were passive onlookers of Russian coaling and provisioning at Cam Ranh Bay, as newspapers everywhere were suggesting. Admiral Rozhestvensky had been repeatedly requested to leave and when this was unheeded, Admiral de Jonquières had backed the request with a small naval force. The French assurances were all pure fiction.

Diplomacy in both France and Russia was desperately trying to recover the initiative from the press onslaught. Paris newspapers were indignant that the Japanese press did not trust the solemn pledges of France. St Petersburg protested that it was all outside its control. The Russian admiral was acting independently of his orders.

As the Russian fleet continued to move out of one bay every few days and into another the next day, de Jonquières' mood changed. He no longer asked the fleet to leave with a wink and a nod. With the Russian admiral becoming more truculent and obstinate, the Frenchman became more terse and his instruction was that the intruders—they were no longer visitors—should leave. He now stayed to make sure they went. He could no longer read between the lines in his instructions from Paris that he should merely go through the motions. Now they were blunt and unequivocal: get rid of the Russian fleet.

When Rozhestvensky anchored his fleet on 6 May at Thunghoa, opposite Van Fong Bay, de Jonquières arrived the next day and summarily ordered the fleet to quit. The Russian promised to leave the day after that and de Jonquières, when he returned, did in fact find the fleet ready to sail. Rozhestvensky didn't actually depart until the following morning, 9 May, but now he had a second reason to go to sea apart from getting the increasingly irritating de Jonquières off his back.

In the semi-light and haze of 5.30 in the morning of 5 May, Admiral Nebogatov's squadron of four dilapidated battleships and a cruiser, having crossed the Indian Ocean and passed Singapore, was heading towards the Annam coast. Word got through to Rozhestvensky who sent four scouts out to locate them. They couldn't find the Third Pacific Squadron and returned next morning as the Baltic Fleet was going to sea once more. Eventually in the afternoon, the two fleets made contact off the Indochina coast. Nebogatov boarded his commander's flagship. After the two embraced, they went to Rozhestvensky's quarters and got into deep discussion. An hour later, Nebogatov was dismissed with no campaign plan and no advice or instructions. Nebogatov's ships moved into Port Dayot, tucked behind an island adjacent to Van Fong Bay, to coal and run repairs. The main fleet stayed at sea.

While Donald was hunting for transport to take him up the coast, he snooped around Saigon's wharf precinct asking questions, talking to anyone who would talk to him. When told by the Australian that he'd seen the Russian fleet anchored in Van Fong Bay, local Frenchmen insisted indignantly that the fleet was nowhere on the coast and hadn't been seen since it was ordered out of Cam Ranh Bay.

Donald heard of steamers being cleared to travel to distant ports, but instead unloading onto the Russian fleet and returning with no questions asked. Colonial officials would satisfy themselves with a cursory glance at papers and a casual walk around the ship. The steamer *Eridan* loaded stores described in its customs papers as ship's provisions cleared to Hong Kong. Just before it left, Donald saw a Russian tender openly transferring the English pilot Roberts and a Russian to the boat. *Eridan* left on a Saturday and returned the following Wednesday with Roberts onboard but without the 'ship's stores' or the Russian.

Eventually Donald found a trader that would take him up the Annam coast. On 16 May, *China Mail*'s 'special correspondent' filed a story from Quinhon, past all the bays and inlets in which the Baltic Fleet had been sheltering. He had not seen the Russians on the way up. Returning south to Nhatrang during the night, he reported passing Van Fong Bay with no signs of the fleet.

The reason was simple: the expanded fleet had now gone. Although international law allowed a belligerent nation's warships to stay no longer than 48 hours in neutral waters, Rozhestvensky's armada had stayed in Indochina for a month, flitting from bay to bay, playing hide-and-seek with the colonial authorities and with passing ships and the international press. This all ended early on the morning of 14 May when Nebogatov took his squadron out to sea to rendezvous with the main fleet. The combined fleet then followed the most direct route towards Vladivostok—across the East China Sea and through Tsushima Strait separating Japan and Korea. This was the only path to Vladivostok short enough to avoid the need to coal at sea, which would expose the fleet to attack. With no reason now to stay on in Indochina, Donald made his way back to Saigon and caught a mail steamer to Hong Kong.

The Japanese Combined Fleet, down to four battleships but supported by cruisers, destroyers and torpedo boats—three times the number of warships they would face—had been repaired and refitted to meet its Russian counterpart which was travelling at night to avoid discovery. The two Russian hospital ships, to the rear and burning lights as required by the rules of war, were spotted through the thick night fog by a Japanese armed merchant cruiser as the fleet steamed into Tsushima Strait. Togo directed his ships to 'cross the T' of the Russian ships moving in two lines through the straits in early morning mist. Japanese ships positioned themselves either side during the morning and hoisted battle flags.

Both sides went through a series of avoidance manoeuvres and U-turns to place themselves to advantage. The Russian ships moved more slowly because their bottoms were heavily fouled from their long voyage. Shortly before 2 p.m., the Russian flagship opened fire, its armour-piercing shells mostly falling either side of its target, the Japanese flagship *Mikasa*. On the other hand, the Japanese response with high-explosive shells was extremely effective. Hit in its magazines, a Russian battleship exploded and sank with its crew trapped onboard. Rozhestvensky's flagship was badly damaged and the admiral was wounded. With his ship sinking, he was transferred to a destroyer and command passed to Admiral Nebogatov.

Within an hour the battle was decided. Four of the eleven Russian battleships were put out of commission by the concentrated fire of enemy warships and had sunk by nightfall. The Russian ships scattered and the battle degenerated into a melee throughout the afternoon.

Overnight, Togo rested his battleships and threw his destroyers and torpedo boats at the remaining Russian vessels. Before midnight the enemy, seeming to have slipped away, switched on searchlights to spot the attackers, revealing their own positions. More Russian ships were lost to torpedo attack and in the light of morning, Togo's battleships were able to surround the six remaining ships. Realising his situation was hopeless, Nebogatov was unwilling to sacrifice any more lives of his sailors and officers simply to save his own honour. He ordered XGE, an international signal of surrender, be hoisted.

In less than 24 hours of battle, 21 Russian warships had been sunk, seven of them battleships. Three more battleships had been captured after surrender. Only one small coastal battleship actually got to Vladivostok, to be scuttled by its crew. Of more than 10 000 Russian casualties, 4300 were killed in action. On the other side of the ledger, 117 Japanese soldiers had died in the battle and three torpedo boats had sunk. It had been a devastating loss for the Russian Imperial Navy and for the country's international prestige—the first defeat of a European power by an Asian nation.

Safely and comfortably returned to his Hong Kong editorial office, WH Donald cobbled together from various wire services a comprehensive account of the Battle of Tsushima a few days after it happened. It was circulated to client newspapers in England and Australia, as well as run in *China Mail.* Although it had the ring of direct observation about it and indeed was labelled in London's *Daily Express* as an 'eyewitness account', it was nothing of the sort. It was as genuine as, Donald suspected, the reports by Alfred Cunningham for the rival Hong Kong paper a few weeks before had been. Journalism is just the serious face of the entertainment industry.

Chapter 3

The viceroy

He didn't need the incentive, but Bill Donald was moving anyway to run even stronger on his growing obsession—the sleeping giant. In 1906, Murray Bain converted the publisher of the *China Mail* into a private limited company, with members of his family as shareholders. Bain became chairman of the new enterprise and WH Donald was made managing director, giving him a role in the company that produced the newspaper in addition to working on it editorially.

Donald had an inkling of a new China trying to crawl from the crumbling wreck that was the Ch'ing dynasty, but he had no inside knowledge. The Chinese in Hong Kong might have been a source of the insights Donald sought—they were mostly transients: merchants and traders from Kwangtung, workers from Fukien on their way to the tin mines and rubber plantations of southeast Asia, coolies and wharf labourers from Swatow—but there was an impenetrable social wall between Hong Kong's Chinese and the colony's interlopers from more distant parts.

In any case, Hong Kong Chinese was a vassal culture, there to serve the needs of the colonists. It wasn't the real China, whatever that might be. That lay next door. The failure of the Hong Kong British to pay any attention to China and the lack of information about the place increasingly bothered Donald. If it was a sleeping giant, why did people take so little interest in it? He decided to do something about that.

Canton was southern China's largest city, situated 120 kilometres up the Pearl River from Hong Kong at its mouth. Young men being groomed for government jobs would be sent from Hong Kong to Canton for a few months to learn the Cantonese dialect. They would come back and never return to China. Although it was only a few hours away by steamship, China might have been on another planet.

Wanting to get under the skin of a Chinese city that had not been rendered unauthentic by British rule, Donald booked a ticket on the overnight steamer up the Pearl, arriving at Canton as dawn washed away the night. With winter approaching, it was cool at this hour, but the air was still heavy and close. In the pale light, dark figures moved about, jabbering and cackling to the Australian ear, clearing throats and spitting noisily onto the pavement. As he strolled off Canton Wharf, Donald was struck by the reek of night soil collected a short time before. Carried in noisy metal 'honey pots' slung at each end of shouldered poles, it was dumped into pushcarts and wheeled away to be spread on vegetable patches on the outskirts of the city.

An immaculately dressed foreigner was walking in the midst of the crowd, a solitary figure oblivious to the humanity streaming around him. Donald recognised him as Canton's Commissioner of Customs, an Englishman named Paul King. They had met in Hong Kong, but here on the waterfront King was in his realm. He stopped when he saw the vaguely familiar face.

'What are you doing here?' asked King with some surprise and a modicum of suspicion. Newspapermen didn't come to Canton.

'I've come to see the viceroy,' was the reply.

Donald was warned he would need to have an appointment to see the viceroy and that was made through Mr Robert Mansfield, the British consul.

'I have to go to the British consul to get an appointment with the Manchu viceroy?' spluttered Donald, himself a colonial. 'What's the matter with this damned country?'

'Well, that's the way it is, old boy,' said King tapping a Chinese man on the shoulder with the knob of his cane and motioning him out of the way. The commissioner of customs strode off, leaving the astounded Australian to his outrage.

Undeterred, Donald hired a sedan to take him into the walled city, to the viceroy's *yamen*, as the office-residence of a public official was called in China. Long signboards of shops hung everywhere, looking down on the visitor, insignificant in his open chair with two plodding carriers. Past the incongruous Sacre Coeur Cathedral they trudged, through four intricately carved towering archways along Chung-hwa Road, past a mosque and a pagoda until on top of a rise they reached the viceroy's residence.

Entrance to the *yamen* was blocked by gatemen in round white hats with red tassels. With no language in common, Donald tried to bluff his way past them on foot with his chatty conviviality, but the gatemen would have none of it. They gesticulated, they chattered and, as he moved towards the entrance, they jostled him out of the way. Finally, one of them pointed sharply at a tier of steps nearby. Donald sat down with his back against one of several large pillars, fanning himself with his homburg. The cool of the morning had given way to tropical humidity, the sun beating down with growing intensity.

An hour passed and then another. The gatekeepers left him alone. Men in gowns and women in trousers passed by in all directions, carrying loaded shoulder poles, pulling carts piled high. Some glanced at the foreigner with the homburg hat, most seemed not to notice him. Sedan chairs carrying the affluent pushed through the crowds, although here the customers were always Chinese. The day got hotter, accentuating the smell of human excrement that drifted out of the narrow laneways. Donald watched in fascination as men came up to two large earthenware urns either side of the main gate. Casually and without embarrassment, each lifted his gown and urinated in one of the urns, adding to their acrid stench. Donald was unaware the *yamen* did business only in the afternoon, the reverse of Hong Kong, where businessmen did most of their work in the morning before going to the club. Determined to meet the patience that circumstances demanded of him, he went without lunch and he sweltered but he was not going to be beaten.

The activity of the morning eventually eased off. Coolies snoozed in the shade beside emptied rice bowls, but the courtyard of the *yamen*, behind the gates, behind the gatekeepers, began to stir. Figures moved in and out of doorways carrying teapots and pails of hot towels. The gatemen became noticeably more alert.

In the early afternoon, a young man pushed through the crowd towards Donald.

'What do you want?' he asked in clear English.

'I've come to see the viceroy. I want to get the Chinese view on important issues. They seem to be ignored.'

'Have you got an appointment from the British consul?'

'What's the matter with this blasted country?' Donald complained again. 'The British push you around and yet you let them control who sees your officials!'

The young man shrugged and went inside.

As other officials came by, some tried to engage Donald in conversation, but none spoke English. Finally a venerable-looking gentleman stopped and said in perfect English, almost caricature, 'Well, my hearty, and what do you want?'

He was Admiral Wei Han, although in mandarin coat and with grey beard and shaggy eyebrows he didn't match any image Donald might have of what an admiral should look like. Trained in Britain at the Royal Naval College, he had picked up the vernacular of that institution. Donald explained his mission once again. The admiral shook his head, said he'd see what could be done, and went inside.

Soon after, a servant came out and motioned Donald to come in. He was taken to a large reception room where various Chinese officials were seated at a long table. At the far end was the young man Donald had first spoken to. He was Wen Shih-tseng, an administrative head (*taotai*). Next to him was Captain Wu Kwang-yen, the commander of Canton's naval squadron and the viceroy's secretary. Also present was a thickset man in his 30s, Wen Tsung-yao, the viceroy's chief adviser, and alongside him the administrator of salt tax in south China. Next to an empty chair at one end and directly across from Donald sat Admiral Wei.

The viceroy, Chang Jen-chun, entered in pale blue official robes, wearing a pillbox hat with big red buttons and peacock feathers. Dangling from the robes were long strings of beads which he fingered constantly. About 70 years old, the viceroy had a heavy appearance with a big domed head, a drooping white moustache and good-humoured eyes, exuding an air of dignified ancient wisdom.

A cork could be heard popping and a servant entered with champagne and glasses. To the horror of the functionaries at the long table, Donald politely but firmly refused to drink.

'I have never drunk champagne in my life,' he explained patiently. 'I don't want to start now.'

Wen Shih-tseng said he must drink. Protocol couldn't accommodate refusal, no matter how politely put. Captain Wu suggested the visitor pretend to drink.

Donald said to the *taotai*, 'Please tell the viceroy I have never drunk champagne or any liquor in my life and do not want to fool him by pretending to drink now.' Turning to the viceroy, he continued, 'Tell him that I came to find out about China, that the outside world knows nothing about China and I want to be able to tell the truth, and that I hope I can come often to see him and we can become true friends who will never fool each other, regardless of whomever else we may fool.'

The room was tense as Wen translated Donald's words. At first the viceroy looked perplexed, and then his eyes lit up. When the translation was finished, the old man let out a roar and slapped the table.

'Here is the first honest foreigner we have ever met,' he guffawed in his own language.

Delighted, he leaned back and chuckled, the peacock feathers on his hat darting about.

'I like it,' he said to himself quietly, as if he was alone in the room. 'I like it! No matter who we fool, we will not fool each other.' He savoured the enjoyment, then turned to Donald. 'Proceed, proceed!' he said, slapping the table again and Wen translated.

Donald explained that he wanted to know what was happening in China, to educate foreign readers so they could be aware of and understand the Chinese viewpoint. These were extraordinary ideas to the viceroy. He had heard no foreigner utter them before. Indeed, it had been a matter of indifference to him whether the loathsome foreigners cared what China thought or not. But the young journalist talked so earnestly and persuasively, the viceroy began to wonder about the possible merits of foreigners.

When Donald had finished his speech, the viceroy announced that the *yamen* would be open to him any time he came to Canton. He looked forward to their conversations and invited him to return soon.

Elated, Donald caught the night ferry back to Hong Kong. The next day, he reported his progress to his chairman. They had obtained an entree to information about the mysteries of China through the stubbornness that would characterise Donald throughout his career.

A few days later, Donald received a letter from Viceroy Chang through the British consul, the same diplomatic official he'd determined not to approach for an appointment. It offered Mr WH Donald a role as adviser to the viceroy on 'all matters pertaining to government in south China'. Here was a chance to consolidate the opportunity presented by his visit to Canton, with easier access to news from the region. He could report on China from the inside, not from without.

Donald replied immediately, accepting the viceroy's offer with gratitude. 'As to your question of what remuneration I require for my services,' he added, 'the answer is that I require none. I want no reward. If I may be of service at any time, that alone would be enough.' It would prove to be an extremely pragmatic decision. In a country where public corruption and venality overflowed, serious notice was taken of the man who seemed above it.

Donald started making weekly trips to Canton. He suggested to the viceroy his lack of contact with the common people and the foreign press was not working to his advantage. Viceroy Chang Jen-chun controlled the two neighbouring provinces of Kwangtung and Kwangsi, but he wasn't from the region as it was Manchu policy to move high officials around so they didn't develop local roots. Chang had very few close contacts there as a result. The task Donald set for his local advisers was to try to rectify that. As for the foreign press, Donald could help there and help himself at the same time.

The Australian's advice to Chang was mostly on foreign relations. Although he made no pretence of expertise and much of his advice was in the form of homilies, it was lapped up eagerly by his client. Donald sought no payment, and shared his opinions with such a mix of bluntness and fearlessness that the viceroy put great store in them, convinced they were genuinely held.

In a culture in which 'face' played a conspicuous role, the forthright nature of Donald's advice was refreshing. Such candour would have created the impression it was astute even if it wasn't, but much of it no doubt was. Donald was both a pragmatist and an idealist, one of the many contradictions that made him a charming but elusive personality.

In return for his opinions and advice, the newspaperman was told in detail what was happening in Canton and more widely in China, and about how China worked. Able to interpret the nuances, he could now see the dormant power that Petrie Watson had talked about a few years before, the sleeping giant. Within a short time, he understood China better than many who had lived there for a decade or more, driven by his desire to understand the country and its people.

China Mail readers were immediately made aware of Donald's new enthusiasm. 'AWAKENING CHINA' headlined the editorial of 13 November 1907. 'There are those who refuse to admit that China is really awakening,' it cautioned. That assumption was drawn from the failure of previous attempts at change and a return to the status quo, but it was a mistake to think that was the end of change. Reforms by Peking were mostly restricted to Peking and designed to discourage foreign intervention, but in reality the Chinese people desperately wanted reform. Some were wanting more than just reform.

On 5 February 1908, the Chinese gunboat *Bopik* drew alongside and boarded an old, weather-beaten Japanese freighter off the coast of Macao, a Portuguese concession across the river mouth from Hong Kong. *Tatsu Maru II* had been chartered by a Nagasaki company to take coal from Japan to Hong Kong, but the boarding party found also in the hold 94 cases of rifles and 40 cases of ammunition. With a Portuguese permit to land them in Macao, the Chinese suspected the arms were to be smuggled into Kwangtung and they were right. They had been consigned from Osaka on Sun Yat-sen's instruction, although nothing in the paperwork made that connection.

The commander of *Bopik* was the same Captain Wu Kwang-yen who had been present when Donald first met with the viceroy of Canton a few months before. Expecting a confrontation with a Portuguese police launch hovering nearby, Captain Wu hauled down the Japanese flag on *Tatsu Maru* and hoisted in its place the double-dragon emblem of the Manchus. As it happened, *Bopik* was able to escort the large merchantman up the Pearl River without further incident. The arms cargo was confiscated and taken ashore at Canton. *Tatsu Maru* was impounded.

A week later, the Japanese government protested the seizure of its vessel, denying it was involved in arms smuggling. Viceroy Chang notified the Japanese consul in Canton that Admiral Wei Han and Commissioner of Customs, Paul King, would investigate the incident. Japan was offered a role in the inquiry, but it was not interested in that or arbitration by a neutral party. It was uncompromisingly on the warpath, incensed at the insult to its national honour and the 'act of war' of the *Bopik* captain in lowering the Japanese flag.

Meanwhile, the ministry of foreign affairs in Peking had asked the inspector-general of maritime customs, 73-year-old Sir Robert Hart, to advise. A ministry telegram to the viceroy in early March listed seventeen points on which Hart held China to be in the wrong. The British commander-in-chief in Canton paid a visit to Viceroy Chang's *yamen* and offered the view that China couldn't take the action it took if the arms were legally imported. Nothing was going to distract the British from their ardour for the emerging power of Asia.

The Japanese codified their outrage and on 13 March issued a list of demands to settle the matter. They required a formal apology and a salute of the Japanese flag in front of Japan's Canton consul, the unconditional release of *Tatsu Maru*, payment of the (inflated) cost of the firearms detained, an investigation by China into the circumstances of the seizure with measures against those responsible, and indemnity for their actual losses. Privately, the Japanese agreed to help stop the traffic of arms into Kwangtung through Macao, but this was about public face. They had been humiliated. For all its desire to imitate the region's dissembling colonialists, Japan remained steadfastly oriental.

Two days after the ultimatum was delivered, Peking agreed unconditionally to Japan's terms. Canton was aghast and Donald was called. At the *yamen*, the viceroy sat in his usual position at the head of the long table, but he showed none of his usual jollity or authority. His eyes had lost their sparkle; the drooping moustache now set the tone of his face. The functionaries seated around the table looked suitably chastened as if they were the cause of his misery, not just sharing it.

'Adviser,' the viceroy said despondently, 'we are in great trouble over the *Tatsu Maru* and *Bopik* incident. The Japanese are hammering on the table in Peking. Now my empress has ordered me to kowtow to the Japanese flag and pay them a huge indemnity.' The mandarin waved his hand loosely in a gesture of despair. 'We have no choice but to obey.'

Viceroy Chang Jen-chun handed Donald a scroll whose calligraphy presumably spelt out the command, although the Australian had no way of confirming that. He stared at it anyway to give him time to gather his thoughts.

Finally he said, 'You cannot humble yourselves or China like this. Tell her you can't do it.'

'If I do that, you'll find my head in the gutter.'

'You forget there is more to China than this *yamen* and all its niceties and your peacock feathers. There are the people.'

'What are the people?'

Donald gave a short speech extolling the virtues of ordinary Chinese. They were the sweat in China's rivers, the bones in its mansions, the blood in its wines, the meat on its tables, and so on in an inspired flow of rhetoric and metaphor. By the time he had finished, Chang was lost in thought, his face blank with puzzlement.

'Well, adviser, what do you suggest?'

'Give me 48 hours and I'll show you.'

Donald made a rapid tour of the ancient city with an interpreter in tow, calling on as many of Canton's 72 trade guilds as he could locate, explaining to their officials the humiliation proposed by Peking and pressing them to stir their members into energetic protest. He made a speech to the chamber of commerce.

'In a war thirteen years ago, the Japanese sought to grind you underfoot,' he said. 'Now they want to make you feel their hard heel again.'

Public opinion in Canton became strident in its opposition to buckling to Japan's demands. The Self-Government Society of local merchants telegraphed the foreign affairs office imploring it to protect China's sovereignty and not be 'cowardly', but to no avail. Peking had already capitulated and on 17 March the settlement terms were made public. *Tatsu Maru* was returned to its owners.

Despite intermittent heavy rain, 20 000 gathered the next day at a protest meeting organised by the Self-Government Society, many of them clad in mourning robes. A petition was signed denouncing Japanese intransigence and foreign affairs' disloyalty. Carrying funeral banners inscribed 'Recover Our National Rights', the throng marched to the courtyard in front of the viceroy's *yamen*.

Chang Jen-chun spoke to the restless crowd, banners quivering above their heads, from the *yamen* steps. Chang condemned the weakness that accepted defeat, adding with a nod to his own safety, 'but as loyal Chinese, you and I must obey now that the Emperor has spoken'.

The viceroy no longer had his adviser beside him, Donald having returned on the night steamer to Hong Kong and the *China Mail* after stirring up the hornet's nest. Chang received a delegation of seven and was handed the petition, reportedly signed by 15 000. The viceroy explained to the delegates that a nation's ability to combat pressure depended on that nation's strength. Where that was non-existent, the nation had no choice. Nonetheless, he agreed to pass their concerns on to foreign affairs.

The next day, a large crowd in Hua-lin Temple drew on the groundswell of the *yamen* protest, declaring a boycott of all Japanese goods. Importers cancelled orders with their agents in Japan and insisted goods bought elsewhere not be shipped on Japanese steamers. Firms cancelled policies with Japanese insurers. Many traders would lose money, but the response was so strong that not joining the boycott was an equally difficult choice.

Japanese goods were burned on 'patriotic bonfires' at National Humiliation meetings where specially composed 'hymns of national disgrace' were sung. Led by schoolgirls, the women of Canton held their own National Humiliation meetings, from which males were barred. All women were urged to wear a ring engraved with 'National Humiliation' and housewives and cooks were called on to not use 'indigestible' Japanese foods.

The boycott didn't spread in China much beyond Kwangtung Province and Hong Kong, but was remarkably successful there. By mid-April, Japanese firms in Hong Kong were reporting heavy losses. Two Japanese insurance companies lost US$20 000 a month, and Japanese vessels struggled to find passengers or cargo. The boycott was picked up by Chinese communities abroad, particularly where there were significant numbers of Cantonese. Chinese operators of the fish markets in Hawaii refused to buy fish from Japanese fishermen. The protest had generated its own momentum.

In the wake of the *Tatsu Maru* affair, the publisher of the *New York Herald*, James Gordon Bennett, wired Donald: 'YOU ARE THE ONLY MAN WHO CAN MAKE SENSE OF CHINA STOP PLEASE ACCEPT APPOINTMENT AS SOUTH CHINA CORRESPONDENT FOR NY HERALD'. Bennett wanted to challenge the dominance of reporting about China by *The Times* and its legendary Peking-based correspondent, Ernest Morrison, and someone had drawn Bennett's attention to Donald's articles about the stoush over *Tatsu Maru*. The offer included a generous salary and an open expense account. Donald readily accepted. It was an opportunity to expand his growing enthusiasm for the role of foreign correspondent with a new and important readership while continuing to edit the Hong Kong paper. He had found a wider audience for his prognostications about the sleeping giant.

The son of the *Herald*'s founder, Bennett devoted his life to spending an inexhaustible fortune on himself and his newspaper. Eccentric and mercurial, he was both a dandy and a devoted newspaperman, a one-man band hiring and firing on whim. At one time, he asked for a list of 'indispensable' men on the paper and dismissed them all. However, he had a high regard for the people who brought out the paper, paying his composing room foreman and editors well and providing them with the best tools available.

James Gordon Bennett had an innate sense of news as entertainment, long before the era of tabloid journalism, a recognition of the value of immediacy and sensation. In 1899, he hired an experimenter called Marconi to set up a system for transmitting news directly to the *Herald* by wireless. He sent Henry Morton Stanley with an unlimited expense account to find the missionary, Dr Livingstone, lost in unexplored central Africa. Never a man to take a backward step, Bennett was destined to find Donald's blunt conviviality appealing. The two hadn't met, but they soon would.

The American newspaperman was a keen sportsman, and particularly an enthusiastic yachtsman, for whom money was no object. For some years, he had been commodore of the prestigious New York Yacht Club. In 1900, the 100-metre *Lysistrata* was built as his personal cruising yacht, with a crew of a hundred on permanent stand-by. Onboard, a padded stall with a Jersey cow provided fresh milk, and a De Dion Bouton automobile was stowed below for excursions at ports.

In the summer of 1908, the 68-year-old proprietor was cruising the Far East, sending regular instructions to the *Herald* by telegraph. Anchored off Singapore and anxious to know weather conditions before venturing north with the intention of stopping over at Hong Kong, he cabled Donald: 'WHAT ARE THE FOGS LIKE ON THE CHINA COAST'.

The reply came back: 'THEY ARE JUST LIKE OTHER FOGS'.

Bemused, thinking the question had been misunderstood, Bennett clarified, 'I MEAN HOW ARE THEY'.

'THEY'RE VERY WELL THANK YOU WHEN THEY ARE HERE BUT THERE ARE NONE HERE NOW'.

Donald met his new client on the wharf at Hong Kong and the two dined at the Hong Kong Club. The American sampled authentic Chinese cuisine and Donald settled for his preferred bacon and eggs. Bennett remarked in passing that he was interested to learn about the East, proposing the two of them meet each morning for a news conference on *Lysistrata*.

'We'll do no such thing,' replied Donald. 'I'm editor of a paper. It's just as important to me as the *Herald* is to you. You come and see me.'

So, James Gordon Bennett, millionaire American publisher, trekked up past the flower stalls of Wyndham Street each morning for his daily news conference, cabling instructions from there to his staff in Paris and New York. Donald had chanced his arm in a battle of wills and it had paid off. He was now the golden boy.

The new correspondent had a broad brief to write what he chose about Chinese affairs. Like his employer, he had an eye for novelty. One morning, he was finishing a dispatch to the sound of heavy footsteps labouring up the stairs.

'Well, Don, what are your bright ideas for today?' Bennett asked as he entered the office.

Donald waved his copy in the air. 'You could print this in Chinese on page one with an English translation inside somewhere.'

The American loved the idea. Donald telegraphed his dispatch to New York with instructions to take it to the Chinese consulate for translation, then to the printer of a New York Chinese newspaper to set it in Chinese characters. It was the sort of excitement that kindled Bennett's love of newspapers. Readers might well have been mystified by the inscrutable article, but it confirmed to Bennett the wisdom of his South China appointment.

America was immersed in a presidential campaign at that time, but Bennett commented that he favoured neither of the contenders, William Howard Taft and William Jennings Bryan. Donald suggested the *Herald* occupy its front pages instead with promotion of an alliance between China and the United States, the 'linking of the oldest country in the Eastern World with the youngest and most vigorous in the West', as he would come to write when Bennett bought the idea and allocated $40 000 to cover expenses. It bound up romance of the Orient, American pride and mercantile adventurism in one tantalising package. Among other things, it drew attention to investment opportunities opening up in the Far East. An alliance would lay 'the foundation for a sound commercial connection with America', Donald wrote, with 'her immense richness in undeveloped resources and her magnificent potentialities in commerce'.

To add an exotic touch, Bennett took back with him to the US and Europe the editor of *Wah-tze-yat-po*, the Chinese edition of the *China Mail*. In his long black pigtail, black silk gowns and silk slippers, Li Sum-ling created a sensation in the salons of Paris and New York.

He was rumoured to be a Chinese prince. 'Japan wants to keep Europeans out of trade in Asia,' he told them. But the show couldn't run forever. With the election over and Taft chosen as president, the alliance dropped off the *Herald*'s front page as quickly as it had appeared. It was time for the circus to move on.

In southern China, however, the boycott of Japanese goods and businesses hadn't moved on. It continued to be effective throughout 1908 with very little promotion, making it hard to pin down its instigators. Viceroy Chang assured his Manchu bosses there was no boycott in Canton at all, just the city's merchants promoting local industry.

By the end of summer, the boycott was waning. Its leaders tried to get the guilds to act against waverers with limited success. Then boycott leaders in Hong Kong staged riots over two nights in November. Chinese godowns and stores with Japanese goods were looted. In a smart tactical move, no Japanese firm was touched. The British army was called in to help police stop the riots and Canton's Self-Government Society condemned them as 'uncivilised'. The Japanese and British called on the Ch'ing government to suppress the groups responsible. Viceroy Chang responded that the Hong Kong riots were the result of Japanese provocation and British failure to prevent them, not of anything done in Canton.

The Hong Kong riots were the last hurrah for the anti-Japanese boycott anyway. It revived briefly, but had dwindled by the end of the year. It had served its purpose for the viceroy, however. In the end, he didn't have to kowtow to the Japanese flag and Canton didn't pay any indemnity. Peking paid it instead. The Japanese decided against fanning the flames of the boycott. Having saved face with the Chinese announcement that all Japan's demands would be met, they didn't risk a new loss of face by making public that some capitulation terms had not been carried out. Better to look the other way. By January 1909, Japan's trade with Canton and Hong Kong was back to normal.

However, in the China of the Manchus there was now no such thing as 'normal'. Change or the threat of change permeated every activity and normal was only a temporary lull on the bumpy road to disintegration and rebirth.

Chapter 4

Fall of the Manchus

Donald continued to take periodic ferry-rides up the Pearl to advise Viceroy Chang Jen-chun and his officials, receiving insights into life in China in return. A subject of constant interest was the unrest bubbling below the surface—and only just—of Chinese society. Although they supposedly represented the Manchu regime, the target of the revolutionists, the Canton administration was surprisingly detached in its view of the growing threat to its hold on power.

In particular, the viceroy's principal secretary, Wen Tsung-yao, whom Donald had met at the *yamen* on his first visit, showed signs of having moved beyond detachment in his more unguarded moments. His assessment of the cause revealed considerable sympathy and that he was prepared to talk with this candour to the foreigner indicated how much Donald had gained their trust.

Back in Hong Kong, Donald's editorialising in the *China Mail* kept to the party line of reform, not revolution, but the seeds of change had been planted in his mind from the discussions upriver with the nominal targets of revolt. He needed to find out more. Knowing Sun Yat-sen's T'ung-meng Hui, or Revolutionary Alliance, had its headquarters in the colony, he made cautious contact late in 1908. In the absence of Sun, Donald met Dr Hu Han-min and was welcomed even though he was known to be advising the viceroy of Canton. It's quite probable Hu also knew about his informal discussions in the viceroy's *yamen*.

The Manchus were in serious trouble. Empress Dowager Tsu-hsi, concubine to a previous emperor, had been de facto ruler of China for nearly 50 years. Her nephew, Emperor Kwang-tsu, had instituted wide-ranging political and social reforms despite his limited power, seizing the initiative after China's defeat in the Sino-Japanese War. Aware his aunt was plotting a coup to regain control of the empire, he got the backing of Yuan Shih-k'ai, commander of the Peiyang Army, the largest division of China's modernised New Army.

Yuan began to have doubts about the counterplot and the day before the coup was to be staged, he told the empress's supporters of the moves to thwart it. In September 1898, troops surrounded the Forbidden City. Kwang-tsu was placed under house arrest and kept in a small palace on a lake island, guarded by trusted court eunuchs.

By now, the elite of Chinese society and much of the populace believed European powers were driving China's domestic and foreign policy in their own interests. In 1900, rebellion by a secret society dubbed the Boxers broke out in northern China where German interests made huge profits while the Chinese continued to live in abject poverty. When the German ambassador was murdered in the streets of Peking, an Eight-Nation Alliance of foreign powers entered Peking. After classic occupation-force looting and atrocities for the best part of a year, the invaders withdrew, their authority in China re-established.

The Boxer Rebellion may not have succeeded in its intended aim of ridding the country of its foreigners, but it provided the first stirrings of national pride. That chicken would hatch at a later stage. The more immediate effect on China was a weakening of the dynasty, temporarily propped up by foreign interests, and a growing ideological divide between northern Chinese anti-foreign royalists and southern Chinese anti-Manchu revolutionists. One of the latter had plotted the failed 1895 uprising in Canton.

Sun Yat-sen, born to a peasant family in a village near Canton, had been educated in Hawaii where his older brother had emigrated, then studied medicine in Canton after converting to Christianity. Licensed as a medical doctor by the Hong Kong College of Medicine for Chinese, he practised in Macao where he came into contact with members of anti-Manchu secret societies. Frustrated with the refusal of the conservative Ch'ing government to adopt ideas from the technologically advanced West, Sun quit medical practice and devoted himself to transforming China into a Western-style constitutional monarchy.

At first a reformer, he took a blueprint for change to Li Hung-chang, viceroy of Tientsin and a reformer in the Manchu court. Not trained in the classics, Sun's measures for strengthening China were disregarded by the intelligentsia and his proposal made no impact on Li. Moving from reform to revolution, Sun began to call for the abolition of the monarchy and establishment of a republic.

After the 1895 failure, he escaped to Japan where the Manchu reformers had encouraged young Chinese to go for military and other studies. He found young men sympathetic to his revolutionary aims there. By formulating a simple ideology, which later became his Three Principles of the People—nationalism, democracy, socialism—Sun attracted these overseas students to the cause, appealing to their growing disenchantment with China's imperial rulers. In 1905, the Revolutionary Alliance was formed in Tokyo, bringing Sun, another refugee from a failed uprising in China, Huang Hsing, and the overseas students and intellectuals together in joint pursuit of revolution.

Sun's stratagem was that armed uprisings in China's southern border regions would eventually result in the seizure of one or two provinces in the south. Following that, either similar revolts would succeed in other provinces, hastening a Ch'ing collapse, or a republic would be established in the south and, with foreign recognition, it could become a base to overrun the north.

From 1908, Sun was conspiring to finance his planned uprisings through a retired New York banker, Charles Beach Boothe. American investors were guaranteed a 10 per cent return from concessions in railways, banking and minerals granted by the resulting republican government. The revolutionist lobbied with breathless sincerity. He had doubts whether US capitalists would 'commit commercial suicide' by investing in China's development, but saw nothing lost in laying out the lure. The new China would probably sever any demeaning ties to foreigners anyway, but that was their concern and no price was too high for the gift of power. For Sun Yat-sen, the end always justified the means, but nothing came of the American venture and, by April 1909, Boothe had conceded his fundraising had failed.

Unfortunately for Sun, his vision was slowly unravelling on other fronts. In 1907 and 1908, he and Huang attempted several revolts near the China-Indochina border and in Kwangtung. With a price on his head, Sun orchestrated these insurrections from outside China, but because of insufficient funding all were short-lived with considerable loss of insurgent lives. What's more, the Japanese government had turned reactionary, unfriendly to the Chinese revolutionaries in its midst. Sun's Japanese supporters were losing influence and the Revolutionary Alliance was weakening with some of its members becoming dissatisfied with his leadership. They turned to Huang's alternative strategy of revolts organised in central China along the Yangtze River, striking directly at the Ch'ing dynasty's heartland.

As if in support of Huang's strategy, the dynasty was simultaneously delivering fatal blows to its own heart. Empress Dowager Tsu-hsi died in the Hall of the Graceful Bird on 5 November 1908, one day after the death of her nephew, Emperor Kwang-tsu. She had proclaimed her grand-nephew, the two-year-old Pu-i, as the new Ch'ing emperor the day his predecessor died. It appears rushed through to meet a tight deadline. Forensic tests years later reported that Kwang-tsu died of acute arsenic poisoning, the level in his remains being 2000 times higher than average. It seems Tsu-hsi ordered the murder of her nephew, knowing her own death was imminent and that he would reintroduce his reforms when she died.

The death of Tsu-hsi signalled the end of the Ch'ing dynasty, if it wasn't already signalled. The toddler, Pu-i, was crowned in December, screaming and resisting attempts to pick him up. When his father, Prince Ch'un, became prince-regent, his first move was to punish Yuan Shih-k'ai for betraying his brother's counter-coup. Dissuaded from having Yuan assassinated, Ch'un settled for dismissing him from all his posts and banishing him to his village in Honan province.

Prince Ch'un tried to bring in the economic and political reforms that had eluded his brother, but trapped between conservative Manchu factions at court and progressive officials in the provinces, he was too inexperienced to find a path through his dilemma. Provincial assemblies were set up and became largely platforms for dissent. A national assembly was convened in October 1910, half of its 200 members elected and the other half appointed.

The Manchu court felt power slipping away from it as the new assembly pressed to speed up constitutional reforms. The Grand Council, long the policy-making body with equal representation of Manchus and the majority Han Chinese, was replaced by an imperial cabinet led by the prime minister and with no accountability to the national assembly. Its thirteen members included seven imperial relatives and only four token Han Chinese. Through it, more power was concentrated in the hands of the Manchus than since the early years of the dynasty. The next day, the government announced its intention to nationalise China's major railways. It was a move that would finish the Ch'ing dynasty.

•

While China was in a state of flux, Bill Donald was going through his own changes, both personal and professional. In April 1909, he resigned from the *China Mail*, although the reason for this is uncertain. It's claimed he left following a disagreement with a director of the company, although this claim is not made by anyone who knew Donald at the time. A forthright personality like Donald was always disputing one point or another, so memory may merge those altercations into other events.

Significantly, Murray Bain had died shortly before. More likely is that Donald could see the writing on the wall, that the freedom to plot his own course for the newspaper could be curtailed by an incoming chairman of the family company. The independent-minded Australian had become very confident of his own views. In any case, he was tiring of stories from Westminster and Lord's. With ongoing work for several papers in Australia and Britain and a particularly remunerative client in the *New York Herald*, he could devote more time there to his obsession with China and its revolution in the making. To Donald, this was the most important story of the new century.

Opening a small office in Queens Road Central alongside the two new department stores, Sincere and Wing On, he serviced his client newspapers and co-edited with Lionel Pratt an annual publication they had started in 1906, *Who's Who in the Far East*. Pratt, an Australian, had joined *China Mail* after the Russo-Japanese War. At the same time, Donald kept up his contacts with both the Revolutionary Alliance in Hong Kong and the viceroy of Canton, until the latter was moved by his Manchu masters to Nanking in 1909. Opportunities surfaced in business and investment, immersing Donald in the dynamics of Asian economics, although not always profitably.

Home life for the Donalds had its ups and downs. Goodwood, with its surrounds of lush vegetation and harbour views and its servants, provided a gracious colonial life, but Mary was away from her family. Don had always worked long hours, often late into the night, sometimes to one or two o'clock. Leaving the *China Mail* hadn't changed that. It was in his nature.

Life was relatively easy with domestic help, but they had different attitudes to the Chinese. Don saw them as the embodiment of a great dormant social and political force which he had a mission to report to the world and maybe even contribute to its emergence in some small way. To Mary they were useful but alien.

'I must say,' she commented once, 'the little ones do look very chimpy.'

There were arguments between them, but the issues were conventional and domestic: the time Don spent at work and socialising with his colleagues and not with his wife who had sacrificed a return to the comfort and security of Sydney life for him. From time to time, the main hall of Goodwood echoed with raised voices, the strident Australian vowels of one and the diluted northern English accent of the other. For all his immense charm, Don had a quick temper when things didn't go his way. The headstrong Mary was equally fiery and quick to respond.

However, there were good times as well, especially in the early days of their marriage. As both had done back in Australia, Don and Mary would take a picnic hamper, sometimes on his yacht, *Waratah*, sometimes by ferry, and set up tiffin—the colonial word for a light meal—in a remote scenic spot. Mostly, though, Mary felt isolated despite all the indulgences of Hong Kong life.

Bill Donald was unenthusiastic about children. They interfered with the daily routines and pleasures of adult life. Nonetheless, Mary became pregnant late in 1908 and on 22 July 1909 a baby girl was delivered by midwife to the Donalds at their home in Babington Path. They—or perhaps, Mary—named her Muriel. She might have hoped that the baby would constrain Don to spend more time with her, but it only gave her less opportunity to be with him. Always an enthusiast for the great outdoors, the country-raised Don sailed more with Lionel Pratt as Mary became less available to join him.

About this time, Donald became a director of a joint Indochina-Hong Kong venture to make quality paper from bamboo pulp. An American from Manila's Bureau of Science investigated the feasibility of the project and, on his recommendation, Société des Pulpes et Papeteries du Tonkin (Tonkin Pulp and Paper Co Ltd) set up a mill in northern Indochina. With highly engineered machinery needed if it was to tap into the Japanese market for fine paper, Donald left for England in June 1910 to purchase equipment from James Bertram and Sons.

Having worked on the *Advocate* in Bathurst before moving to Sydney, Donald caught up with its former editor, Thorold Waters, in London. Full of excitement about his new venture, he was keen to enlist Waters, reminding him of the younger Donald he'd known in rural New South Wales.

'Join me on a raft trip,' the would-be entrepreneur enthused. 'It'll be a really great picnic and a handy experience.'

Comfortably relocated in England, Waters declined . . . and just as well for him he did. Donald got back to Hong Kong in the new year of 1911 to find Tonkin Pulp and Paper's paper-making enterprise had fallen through. The company cancelled the order with Bertrams and went on to manufacture pulp-board instead, but Donald had moved on by then.

•

By July 1908, after the *Tatsu Maru* travesty and with his support fading in Japan, Sun Yat-sen had moved his headquarters to Penang, in what is now

Malaysia, and went fundraising among southeast Asian Chinese. On offer in the future republic for a price were citizenship, business concessions, parliamentary offices, even statues and parks named after major beneficiaries—whatever it took.

Sun set up a conference in Penang towards the end of 1910. Several leading figures of the Revolutionary Alliance, including Huang Hsing, still supporting Sun despite his different strategy, and Hu Han-min from Hong Kong, gathered and mapped out yet another uprising in Canton. This one, they convinced themselves, would be decisive.

Soon after, under pressure from Peking, the colonial administration of Straits Settlements pushed Sun out of Penang. He sailed to Europe, hoping to impress French politicians by staying in expensive hotels, but none came to see him. Moving on to Canada, his luck changed dramatically.

Sun might have been a shameless operator in his dealings with people whose support he needed, but as a public speaker he was inspirational, wooing his audience with conviction and persuasion. Over four days, crowds of immigrants from China came to hear him speak in Vancouver's Chinese theatre. They loved him; they loved his passion and his sincerity. Enough funds were raised to finance another uprising in Canton.

Planned for early April, the revolt was thrown into disarray when, in a fit of revolutionary zeal, a Singaporean recruit to the cause assassinated the city's garrison commander. The local Manchu response was immediate and decisive: security was locked tight and untrusted army units confined to barracks. Huang Hsing hurried to Canton to take charge of the mess, but the rebels deliberated for two weeks, talking of postponing their action before finally deciding they couldn't disappoint the overseas supporters who bankrolled their ambitions.

On 27 April, Huang led 130 men in an attack on the governor's *yamen* with pistols and homemade bombs. The subversives broke into the inner courtyard where, nearly four years before, Donald had first met the viceroy and his circle of advisers. This time, with a different viceroy, all Manchu officials had disappeared. Revolutionaries battled fiercely with imperial forces in the streets of Canton, but the rebels were outnumbered, badly organised and ill-trained. No-one had thought to notify potential mutineers in the New Army so the expected support didn't materialise.

The uprising was another bloody failure, producing 72 new martyrs. Those taken prisoner were strangled or decapitated; those already dead in the streets were beheaded as well. Huang was wounded, but changed into civilian clothes and slipped into the night. But all wasn't lost. Despite the apparent miserable failure of the action, the scales of history had shifted a little in favour of the revolutionists. Many imperial troops had defected to the rebels; not enough to be decisive, but enough to augur well for future revolts. What's more, some of the gentry and the merchants had switched their allegiance, too.

Unknown to the Manchus or to Sun, dissent was smouldering just as threateningly elsewhere in China. Students brought back from Japan and secret society members had formed a new radical group called Kung-chin Hui (Co-progress Association) in the middle Yangtze province of Hupeh. Early in 1911, a study group from the new class of young intellectuals in the province's New Army grew increasingly political and started stock-piling weapons for the imminent revolution. Wen-hsueh She (Literary Study Society), like the already established Kung-chin Hui, worked assiduously to recruit soldiers of the New Army to the revolutionary cause. At the same time, the Revolutionary Alliance was moving into the Yangtze valley, in the continuing absence of Sun—still overseas—and after yet another Canton failure, giving more serious thought to attacking the dynasty in central China. In July, it established a central China headquarters in Shanghai under 29-year-old Sung Chiao-jen.

After the Penang revolutionary conference, Donald had been sent a telegram in London letting him know that moves were afoot. By the time he returned to Hong Kong in the new year of 1911, he'd decided to move to Shanghai. Hong Kong had become too colonial and too British for him, and in any case he wanted to be at the centre of the action when the Chinese revolution actually got going. Hong Kong would inevitably be on the periphery.

Donald cabled James Gordon Bennett advising him he was leaving the colony and therefore resigning as south China correspondent for the *New York Herald*. Bennett would hear nothing of it and installed him instead as the paper's Shanghai correspondent, with the added inducement of an increase in salary. The Australian's knowledge of China's current affairs was too valuable for the *Herald* to let slip out of its clutches. For him, it meant some financial security with the family's relocation. With a baby girl to care for, it was not a move that Mary would have welcomed.

The Donald family arrived at Woosung Bars by steamer from Hong Kong in February 1911. The shallowness of the Yangtze at that point, from the Whangpoo River flowing into its tidal estuary, prevented a large vessel getting to Shanghai. In the wintery northern morning, much colder than they were accustomed to, the anchored ship unloaded its passengers and their baggage onto a tugboat that took them on the two-hour journey to the Whangpoo customs jetty. Moving along the river towards the centre of Shanghai, junks, sampans and tugs scurried and chugged in all directions. In mid-river, foreign gunboats and light cruisers lounged at anchor. Inshore, four or five hulks sat darkly, bond storage for opium awaiting sale. For Donald, it seemed reminiscent of the day nearly eight years before when he arrived at Kowloon's harbour, but he would soon discover this was a different world again.

The family disembarked with their fellow passengers onto a jetty alongside the Bund, an old towing path converted into a vehicular esplanade. Opposite, the Chinese-style customs house was among the few Chinese *hongs* and bungalows not yet pulled down to make way for the riverside row of Western-style commercial buildings, mostly banks and trading houses. Customs formalities out of the way, the Donalds were taken in rickshaws along the Bund, Don out in front, Mary and the baby just behind. Coolies followed, pulling the family's trussed luggage in handcarts.

Even in this early exposure, it was clear Shanghai was more cosmopolitan than Hong Kong. The Shanghainese placed more emphasis on appearance and dressed ostentatiously. An air in the hustling citizens and self-important buildings suggested progressiveness. As their rickshaws passed by Nanking Road, Donald glanced at the sea of red and gold signboards and banners hanging like washing all the way up the long thoroughfare. They were taken past the Italianate Shanghai Club with two turrets in the front corners. Its grand opening the previous month had all the pomp and ceremony the city's expatriate elite could muster.

At the end of the Bund, they passed between the cast-iron fence of the British Consulate and the Public Garden opposite. Behind a small, neat lawn, the consulate was a jumble of office buildings and residences, including that of the consul-general, Everard Fraser, who would play an important role in the next phase of Donald's absorption into China.

The Public Garden, landscaped around a pavilion and tennis courts, was a peaceful retreat of pathways and seats, but it wasn't really a public garden at all. One of its regulations said, 'No Chinese are admitted, except servants in attendance upon foreigners.' Another said, 'No dogs or bicycles are admitted.' Chinese mythology has since combined these into a sign to symbolise China's national humiliation at the hands of the foreign powers. While no sign advised, 'No dogs or Chinese allowed', it nonetheless reflects the colonial mentality in which WH Donald lived and operated.

The family's two rickshaws trundled over the steel Garden Bridge across Soochow Creek. Taking care around the hazardous tramlines, they travelled into the northern sector of the International Settlement, to their destination located just over the creek. A favourite with foreign correspondents, the magnificently restored Astor House Hotel had re-opened only a few weeks before the Donalds arrived.

On entering the five-storey building, the newcomers found themselves in a spacious lobby with cane and leather chairs. Across from the entrance was a grand, marble-sided staircase leading up to electric passenger lifts. For the Australians, the intangible excitement of the Astor's lobby made the Hong Kong Club seem provincial—although chatting patrons kept their voices as low as they would in a cathedral, people moved briskly in all directions as if called to some important meeting.

Don and Mary were shown to a room with its own telephone, a 24-hour hot water supply and an ensuite bath. Such luxuries were the height of modernity. Donald was interested in seeing China improve itself, but he wasn't a revolutionary and he wasn't averse to a few colonial comforts. On the other hand, there was no contradiction for Mrs Donald. She wanted to continue to enjoy gracious surroundings as she had in

Goodwood and to look after their child with ease until they found their own place with *amah* and cook. The Astor, too, had its attentive service, a 'boy' in white shorts and blue jacket standing by every second door awaiting the guests' instructions.

Courtesy of the *Herald* stipend, the Donalds dined in elegance in the main dining hall. Running the length of the building, it sat 500 in three lines of tables, each with white linen tablecloths hanging almost to the floor. A gallery and verandah overlooked the diners from the second level. Sunlight filtered through an arched ceiling of glass, adding a magical touch. Although his wife had developed patrician tastes, Donald preferred the plain cooking of his Scottish heritage, embodied in steak or bacon and eggs.

While Mary might visit the prettily furnished ladies sitting room, her husband was often in the reading room, settling into leather-upholstered chairs with the room's magazines and newspapers. He had long conversations in the lobby with another guest, the *New York Times* correspondent, Tom Millard, in the process of setting up the *China Press* as competition for the more right-wing *North-China Daily News*. Slightly-built and nattily-dressed, Millard had covered the Boxer Uprising and the Russo-Japanese War for the *New York Herald*, so the two journalists had the experience of James Gordon Bennett as a common point of reminiscence and gossip.

Donald's most important contact, however, was outside the newspaper world. From his Hong Kong friends in the organisation, he made contact with the Revolutionary Alliance in Shanghai, operating its new headquarters out of a print shop on Shantung Road, owned and run by Charlie Soong. A Hainan merchant's son, Soong had gone to Boston to work with an uncle and returned as a convert to Christianity with wealthy American Southerners as patrons. In time he would become a patron himself—of China's revolutionary movement—and give birth to a powerful political dynasty in the scramble after the Manchus had gone.

A Methodist preacher in Shanghai working as part-time bible salesman for the American Bible Society, Soong acquired printing presses and produced cheap vernacular translations of the Bible, and technical books on commission. From the profits he bought a rundown warehouse in the

French Concession and built a grand, two-storey house in the Hongkew district. In 1894, he met a secret society rabble-rouser with several aliases, one of which was Sun Yat-sen. It was a meeting that would set Soong's course for long into the future.

Soong invested in tobacco and cotton factories, importing industrial machinery for them, and launched the Commercial Press of Shanghai, printing mass commercial orders, Western textbooks for China, and a variety of religious material. He became a very rich man, at the same time discreetly publishing political tracts for the Revolutionary Alliance. Bibles went out the front door and revolutionary pamphlets went out the back. In 1905, Soong sailed to the US to raise funds for Sun from wealthy Chinese-Americans and from his benefactors of earlier days in America. Returning to Shanghai with two million dollars, he was officially appointed treasurer of the Revolutionary Alliance.

By the time Donald met him, Charlie Soong had put on weight and habitually wore crumpled trousers and a loosened striped tie. A battered fedora sat low over his sagging eyes. The Shanghai revolutionists met daily in a flat over his print shop to swap views about the shape they envisaged for the new China. Sometimes, Donald was there as an observer, listening to the political discussion where it was in English and chatting to Soong's twenty-year-old daughter assisting her father's revolutionary work. Ai-ling was the eldest of the six Soong children. The other two daughters, Ching-ling and May-ling, as well as the eldest son, TV (Tse-ven), were away at school in America.

The visitor gleaned an understanding of the issues that fired the group's political zeal and discreetly incorporated them into articles written for the *Herald* and his other overseas newspapers, but over time his relationship with the revolutionists changed. The cell included two former members of the viceroy of Canton's inner circle: Wen Tsung-yao, his journey from Manchu functionary to revolutionary complete, and Wen Shih-tseng, who had translated for Donald on that first visit to Canton. Word got around that the Australian could be a source of useful advice in dealing with the foreign press and maintaining relations with foreign interests in China. Donald became adviser rather than observer, contributing to the group's policies and plans.

April's massacre in Canton came and went. Donald arrived in the middle of a discussion about what went wrong and listened, disturbed at the windy rhetoric and the absence of practicality.

'What will you do when you take power?' he asked. 'Government is a big task and needs to be run like an efficient business. It needs men who are trained and capable, who can make it operate democratically.'

'Oh, those are practical matters,' was one response. 'I suppose someone is looking after the details.'

'It needs to be more than a dream and a hope,' Donald added.

The point went unheeded, but the activists did take notice of his advice on how they should deal with the foreigners in their midst. They must be protected, the Australian said, not antagonised. They should not be given any reason to take steps for their own protection. To insure against foreign intervention, Donald suggested approaching either the British or the American consul for support if any foreign power, and in particular the increasingly belligerent Japan, threatened to play a role in China's internal affairs.

Donald also recommended a figurehead known outside China be recruited for dealings with the foreign powers. None of the revolutionaries fitted, apart from Sun Yat-sen and no word had come from him since he had left for the United States. His reputation overseas, in any case, was mixed. On the other hand, the Singapore-born lawyer, Dr Wu Ting-fang, had practised in Hong Kong and London and had been China's consul-general in New York. He had represented the Manchu court there, but had returned to Shanghai with a growing sympathy for the revolutionary cause. Among other pursuits, he had become a business partner of Tom Millard in setting up the *China Press*. Donald argued he was the best man to represent the republicans in their foreign dealings. The alliance leaders agreed and Dr Wu accepted the post when it was offered to him.

The ways and means of setting up an alternative form of government excited his interest, but there was more for Donald to report to his client newspapers overseas than the antagonism smouldering in China's people towards their Manchu rulers. By the middle of 1911, the vast rural population of the Yangtze valley was in the grip of famine and flood. The great river that twisted and turned through thousands of kilometres of central

China had burst over levees built long before to hold back the monsoon floodwaters. The whole valley was devastated, farmlands west of Wuhan resembling a vast inland sea. Crops were washed away, but grain speculation had already started the famine before the monsoon floods began. Floods didn't cause the problem, they simply added to it.

Centuries of silting had raised the river level above much of the countryside, requiring extensive embankments to define its course. Manchu money allocated to flood control ended instead in the pockets of provincial officials and although canals, levees and dredging would have eased flood destruction, little of these measures had been put in place. The new viceroy, Chang Jen-chun—Donald's old friend who had been transferred from Canton to Nanking—was ordered by Peking to investigate. He found a Shanghai *taotai* had used the conservancy fund to buy up anti-government newspapers and shut them down. Unsure how to deal with this beneficial misappropriation of their funds, Peking officials did nothing.

Upriver in August to observe and report on the inundation, Donald was brought into Nanking by sampan. He visited Chang in his new *yamen* and found him surveying conservancy requirements, powerless without the funds to do anything about them.

'Well, adviser,' said Chang, looking every bit of his 70 years, 'what do you think of the state of things now?'

Donald smiled and told him to keep his trunk packed.

'Ah, but it's all receding.'

'It is, old friend,' Donald replied. 'That, I'm afraid, is the unfortunate truth. Soon it will all be gone.'

Donald returned to Shanghai to file his reports and the Yangtze floodwaters did recede as the viceroy had predicted, but the journalist's play on words would also prove correct. Soon the political change he had hoped to witness would explode up the valley from which he had just returned. The overthrow of the Ch'ing dynasty was about to be achieved not by military power or the eloquence of the revolutionaries, but through the Manchus' nationalisation of China's railways and their treatment of provincial investors.

Railways built with foreign capital had begun to appear in different parts of China at the end of the nineteenth century and, although the first line, between Shanghai and Woosung, had been dismantled by the provincial government and shipped to Formosa, lines like Peking–Hankow and Shanghai–Nanking soon became profitable. The US-owned China Development Co had been given the right to build a Canton–Hankow line through central China, but construction fell far behind schedule when the contractor secretly sold its rights to a Belgian–French consortium. Gentry and merchants in the three provinces through which the line would run agitated to build the railway themselves. In 1905, Hupei's provincial government bought back the right to the line from the American company for US$6.75 million, paid from a Hong Kong government loan, so that local capital could build the Canton–Hankow line and another from Hankow into Szechwan.

Companies were formed and shares were sold, but the provinces couldn't raise sufficient funds to complete their sections of the lines. The Szechwan company was further hamstrung by a US$600 000 embezzlement by its directors and none of that line was built. Desperate to rescue the project, Peking put the viceroy of Wuhan in charge of the Canton–Hankow line and the Hupei section of the Szechwan line. In October 1909, in mid-negotiation of a US$30 million loan from four foreign banks, the viceroy died. Still needing to repay bank loans for the Boxer reparations, the project was taken over by the Board of Communications. In May 1911, the imperial government ordered the nationalisation of the two lines and, shortly after, the widely distrusted head of the board signed a 40-year loan agreement with the four-bank consortium.

Gentry and merchants in the affected provinces were furious. 'Railway protection societies' were set up; delegations were sent to Peking to protest the invasion of foreign capital undermining the considerable if insufficient funds they had invested themselves. By June, Peking was offering to indemnify the investors: full compensation for those in Hunan and Hupei; for Kwangtung, part compensation and part recoup from operating profits of the line; but Szechwan, with its proven embezzlement, was offered only government bonds at 6 per cent. Local newspapers accused the Ch'ing dynasty of 'selling Szechwan to the foreigners'.

The Yangtze floodwaters might have been receding, but as Donald had advised the viceroy in Nanking the mood of the people was not.

Szechwan's Provincial Assembly organised a huge rally on 24 August to demand postponement of nationalisation of the railways. More than 100 000 people gathered in the provincial capital of Chengtu in a compelling show of mass emotion. They wailed and they screamed, resolving to strike and to stop tax payments, mourning at a poster of the late reformist emperor, Kwang-tsu—and posing a threat to good order.

Szechwan's recently appointed viceroy, anxious not to displease his masters in Peking, demanded the arrest of the protest leaders. Following detention of the president of the Szechwan Railway Protection Society, who also chaired the Provincial Assembly, another large rally was staged in front of the viceroy's *yamen*. The viceroy ordered troops to quell the protest and, in the course of doing so, 32 civilians were killed.

Szechwan's gentry had only been interested in protecting their own interests, not in overthrowing the Manchus, but things were getting nasty and they looked to the local Revolutionary Alliance for support. On 8 September, the day after the shootings, another rally, more like an uprising, surged through the provincial capital with further spot-fires in the surrounding region. Realising that Chengtu was under siege, an alarmed Ch'ing government moved part of its Hupei New Army to Szechwan to suppress the uprising, leaving their Wuchang garrison under-defended.

The units of the New Army that had gone to Szechwan were those whose loyalty to Peking was more certain. The units remaining in Wuchang were those where the two newer radical groups had been successfully recruiting. These groups had met in June to agree on joint action, inviting Huang Hsing and Sung Chiao-jen from Shanghai's Revolutionary Alliance to join them and exchange views. By September, the two Wuchang groups with their local New Army supporters were building towards an October uprising, with a command post set up in Wuchang and a supply base in Hankow. Wuchang and Hankow were two components of the triple city of Wuhan, provincial capital of Hupei. The date decided for the Wuchang revolt was 16 October.

Once again, events overtook plans. A week before the Wuchang uprising was scheduled, a bomb accidentally exploded in the Russian concession in Hankow. Sun Wu, a leader of the Kung-chin Hui or

Co-progress Association, had been preparing explosives for the coming revolt and was injured, but he managed to escape before police came to investigate. Weapons, explosives and banners were seized, along with documents naming New Army soldiers who had crossed over. The Wuhan viceroy imposed a curfew on the city so police could track down and arrest revolutionaries.

The command post in Wuchang was discovered and 32 people were arrested, three of them publicly executed in driving rain the next morning. It was decided not to delay the uprising any longer. That evening, a New Army squad leader ordered soldiers to stand before their beds for ammunition inspection. One soldier was found to be three bullets short and a fight broke out on the floor with the squad commander. A comrade of the wrestling soldier fired a handgun, shattering a lamp, the opening shot in the uprising that would bring down the Manchu empire. It was a little after 8 p.m. on 10 October, propitious as the 'double tenth day' in the Chinese love of numerical harmony.

Word got out that the revolution had begun. Units of the Hupei New Army still stationed in Wuchang mutinied, the rebel force swelling during the night to 3600, taking on a 3000-strong loyalist Ch'ing force. An engineers' battalion led the first wave of attack, capturing the Wuchang armoury without difficulty with the defenders changing sides. In the cool autumn evening, artillery was pulled up Snake Hill on the edge of the city and trained on the viceroy's *yamen*, while another group attacked it. Hundreds were killed overnight before the *yamen* surrendered after the viceroy had fled with the military governor under cover of dark.

By noon, rebels controlled the city. They set up tactical headquarters and announced formation of the 'Military Government of Hupei of the Republic of China', the first entity of Chinese government to be labelled the Republic of China. Embryonic departments were created—tactical, military, political, foreign affairs—in the abandoned Ch'ing administrative buildings and a banner of eighteen stars was adopted as the military flag.

Li Yuan-hung, a brigade commander who had been in dispute with the departed military governor, was reportedly dragged from under his wife's bed and forced at gunpoint to come to the Provincial Assembly where he was proclaimed the new military governor. Han, not Manchu, and unradical enough to be acceptable to the gentry, 46-year-old Li accepted the appointment with some reluctance. The chairman of Hupei's assembly, T'ang Hua-lung, was made administrative head, so that neither of the leaders of the new revolutionary government were actually revolutionists, but people co-opted into those roles because they were acceptable to the gentry and the merchants.

The plotters of Wuchang had given more thought to how to structure their administration than Donald had seen in the Shanghai Revolutionary Alliance. They also made use of advice he had given to the Shanghai group and passed on to them via Huang Hsing. The new leaders sent telegrams to other provinces encouraging them to declare their independence, and to foreign consuls urging them to stay neutral, assuring them that their interests would not be harmed. The agreement with the consuls worked. A request by the escaped viceroy for foreign gunboat bombardment of rebel strongholds in Wuchang was politely refused.

Donald was still in Shanghai when the news from Wuchang came through. At Dr Wu Ting-fang's house on Avenue Road to find out more, he found only uproar. The suddenness of the Wuchang coup had exposed the revolutionaries' unpreparedness. Wu had heard a lot about the absent Sun, but never met him. Striding up and down the living room, his hands clasped behind his back, he muttered to himself, 'Where is this fellow, Sun Yat-sen?'

The long-awaited revolution seemed to be underway, but happening outside their control, and still there had been no word from their supposed leader. Huang and Sung were more sanguine about developments, having been in contact with the Wuchang rebel groups.

'You should carry out your recommended action,' Huang told Donald, 'and make sure the foreigners here don't feel their interests are under threat.'

The Australian did as suggested. A British regimental band played in the Public Garden while he paced up and down the Bund in autumnal twilight, trying to decide which consul in Shanghai he should approach: Amos Wilder in the US consulate across Garden Bridge or Everard Fraser in the British diplomatic quarters across the road? The decision came down to the foreign presence that held the greater sway in China, and at that time it was Great Britain.

Donald walked past a sentry clicking his heels together to a reception desk in the British consulate lobby. Handing over his card, identifying him as WH Donald, Shanghai correspondent for the *New York Herald*, he asked to see Everard Fraser and was ushered into the plush Victorian decor of the consul-general's room.

'Well, Mr Donald,' Fraser greeted him, 'I suppose you've come about something to do with this revolution.'

'How did you know that?' Donald asked.

'It's my job to know what's going on in these parts.'

'Then you will know that I'm British, not American, even though I work for an American newspaper.'

Fraser nodded. He would have recognised his visitor's strident accent even if he hadn't already known, although he may not have called it British.

The two men chatted about the events of the last couple of days, Donald saying he wanted to be where the machinery of revolution could be found. The consul offered him a letter of introduction to General Li Yuan-hung, if that was of use to him.

'I came here with a purpose,' Donald continued. 'I've been in Shanghai since February and have been in contact with the revolutionaries here.'

Fraser nodded again. He knew that, too, although he wasn't sure what that contact entailed and he wasn't sure what connection the Shanghai revolutionists had with the Wuchang rebellion apart from a common objective.

Donald explained he had persuaded the revolutionists to keep Fraser informed of events as they were developing, but this was only for his government's information and was not to be published in the consulate's Blue Book, its official report to Britain's embassy in Peking. The information had to be passed through more informal channels so it couldn't find its way into the hands of the Manchu court. If these conditions were agreeable to Fraser, Donald was prepared to tell him who the leaders were and bring them to meet him the next day.

After further discussion, Everard Fraser agreed and was given the names of the leaders. When told that Wu was one of them, he exclaimed, 'My God! He owes everything he has to the Manchus.'

Early the next afternoon, Donald returned to the British Consulate with five senior men of the Revolutionary Alliance. The tone of the meeting was formal and Fraser was cautious.

Wu began by saying, 'We have come to present our respects and to confirm the arrangements Mr Donald has made with you.'

The revolutionaries and the foreigners conversed for a while and some of the stiffness went out of the meeting. It finished with each side feeling more comfortable with the other. After the Chinese left, Donald stayed behind briefly.

'There's one thing I didn't tell you yesterday,' he said, 'and I should tell you now. It's why I've made this arrangement.'

Donald paused to assemble his thoughts. Fraser watched and waited.

'Frankly, I'm afraid the Japs might try to take advantage of the turmoil. If that happens, I hope Britain will use its position and its clout to keep them at arm's length from what's going on.'

Fraser laughed. 'I thought there was something behind it,' the consul said, 'but best just to wait and see.'

Donald visited the British Consulate regularly in the days that followed, keeping Everard Fraser abreast of developments. They were passed on to Sir John Jordan, Great Britain's minister (as ambassadors were then called) in Peking, but not through the Blue Book. Fraser would learn to trust Donald and become a strong advocate of the revolution among the diplomatic fraternity.

The next day, New Army units marched into Hanyang and Hankow, the other two cities comprising Wuhan. Over the following days, Manchu functionaries who could be located were slaughtered.

Revolts were staged in provincial capitals around central and southern China by groups made up of New Army dissidents and local Revolutionary Alliance members, merchants and gentry, establishing provincial military governments of the not-yet-existing Republic of China. The Ch'ing dynasty's hold on China was slipping away. By the end of October, eight provincial capitals were no longer under Peking control. With much of the revolt coming from the ranks of its own modernised army, the Ch'ing court was paralysed by indecision, not knowing what move it could make to stem the tide running against it.

Chapter 5

How we took Purple Mountain by stealth

After betraying the late emperor's counter-coup, General Yuan Shih-k'ai was retired to his home province on the public pretext that he was suffering a 'leg ailment'. When the viceroy of Hunan and Hupei deserted his post during the Wuchang uprising, the Manchu court offered the position to Yuan, but hearing that Peking's negotiation of a foreign loan had fallen through, he turned it down on the grounds that his leg ailment had not recovered.

Towards the end of the month, as losses and defections mounted against the Manchus, they begged Yuan to resume his post as commander of the Peiyang Army. His military expertise was desperately needed to turn the tide of revolution. The Ch'ing still had support in the north, including in the Manchu homeland of Manchuria where newspapers reporting the revolution were suppressed, but the south was slipping out of its control.

Yuan put conditions on his return, designed both to mollify the public and the revolutionaries and to consolidate his own power. He wanted command of all the Imperial forces, not just the Peiyang Army, and he wanted some political reforms. Peking had little choice but to accept, and Yuan was officially appointed head of the New Armies on 27 October. However, he stayed in his province and bargained to increase financing of the Ch'ing military response, meanwhile ordering the First Army to strike at the revolutionary army in the three cities of Wuhan. The defending force had grown to 6000, but was no match for Yuan's 15 000 troops. The rebels withdrew with heavy losses and Hankow returned to Ch'ing control.

In the meantime, some army leaders were demanding a rapid transition to a constitutional monarchy, expecting rejection of it to provide an excuse to march on Peking. Instead the Manchu court acquiesced, with Prince Ch'ing resigning as premier. Yuan was appointed in his stead and finally came out of retirement to take up the reins of government on 1 November. By installing a government of ten Han and only one Manchu, Yuan sent out a clear message that things were not going to stay the same.

When news arrived of the initial uprising, Shanghai pulsed with expectation. Primed for revolt, people lapped up word of political action anywhere in China, crowds milling around newspaper offices for the latest reports. The English-language press was having difficulty making sense of conflicting reports telegraphed from the provinces. Reports were glossed optimistically by those temporarily in control. In Shanghai, journalists came to Bill Donald for an insider view of what was happening. As Carl Crow, a reporter for Tom Millard's *China Press*, commented later, 'He was possibly the only foreigner in Shanghai who had the remotest idea of what the revolt in [Wuchang] was all about.'

Millard had just launched his paper and gave the uprisings limited coverage until Donald persuaded him to increase it. At the same time, Donald kept Everard Fraser and the American consul regularly informed, assuring them that treaties with the foreign powers would be respected and political change was welcomed even by moderates in China's business community. Convinced the Ch'ing dynasty was in its death throes, the foreign powers remained neutral in the conflict, depriving the Manchus of support they desperately needed.

The Shanghai insurrection was set for 3 November by the Revolutionary Alliance. The day before it would take place, Donald drafted a letter to the British consul from the 'Military Government of the Republic of China' formally announcing it would assume control of Shanghai to restore order and business confidence. How much order needed to be restored was questionable, but it came as no surprise to Everard Fraser who was kept informed by Donald. On the same day, shops in the Chinese quarter of Chapei stayed closed with their shutters locked. A fire next door to the police station was mistaken for the start of the uprising and the Chapei police took it as the signal to mutiny. Their chief fled to the International Settlement, followed by various Ch'ing officials.

A local revolutionary leader, Ch'en Ch'i-mei, had built a power base with Shanghai's businessmen and its secret societies and underworld, particularly the notorious Green Gang. Taking advantage of the distraction, he entered Shanghai's Kiangnan Arsenal in the dockyard area to persuade its occupants to surrender, but he was held by them instead and threatened with execution. After a tense night of debate between the revolutionist and his captors, a rebel assault force arrived. Mostly workers with rifles, not soldiers, some of them were known to be gangsters, standover men from the Green Gang. On their appearance, the arsenal commander slipped downriver. Left leaderless, the arsenal's three-man guard needed little persuasion to surrender after a few desultory shots, and put on white badges, the symbol of support for the anti-Manchu forces.

Having written his letter, Bill Donald kept his head down, in part to maintain a separation of local politics and foreign interests, and partly because the Australian had no experience of revolution and was unsure how it might pan out. He remained with his wife and daughter in the apartment they had acquired in Hongkong Road. Mary wanted no part of it for either of them. She had married to start a family, not to participate in a revolution.

By morning, with the stand-off at the arsenal settled, Donald ventured cautiously outside and found a city festooned in white: white flags hung from the windows and rooftops of Chapei; Nanking Road was strung from end to end with white cloth; police wore white armbands inscribed 'Restoration of the Han people'. This was a city solidly behind the republicans.

The week ended with the establishment of the Shanghai Military Government of the Republic of China. Ch'en Ch'i-mei was elected its military governor, but he was already looking to maintain the momentum.

At a military school in Japan, he had befriended another student from Chekiang province, a salt merchant's son called Chiang Kai-shek. The two had participated in an expatriate political group in Japan. Ch'en had sent a coded telegram to Chiang before the Wuchang uprising, urging him to return to China and join the revolution.

Chiang answered the call, returning to Shanghai to take command of 83rd Brigade with 3000 men, many of them on loan from the Green Gang. He organised a force of 100 men in Hangchow in his home province. On 5 November, two days after the revolt in Shanghai, Chiang's force stormed the local governor's *yamen* behind two young women throwing homemade bombs. After the *yamen* had been set on fire, the insurgents moved on to the garrison camp by West Lake. Once again, it was an untroubled assault, with the defenders quickly disarmed.

The recovery of Hankow was the sole gain for China's erstwhile rulers. Local revolts were springing up all over the vast Ch'ing empire. By late November, seventeen of the 22 provinces would be controlled by military governments 'of the Republic of China', even though there was not yet any Republic of China. The instigators were mostly mutinous soldiers and disaffected merchants and gentry. Only in a few of the uprisings did Revolutionary Alliance operatives play a dominant role.

On 9 November, the new viceroy of Canton fled when its merchants turned against the Ch'ing, and Hu Han-min—Donald's first contact with the Revolutionary Alliance back in Hong Kong—persuaded the local army and navy leaders to change sides. In Szechwan, the newly proclaimed governor had his predecessor decapitated and rode through the streets of Chengtu with the severed head on display. Just about anywhere the republicans had taken over, pigtails were decreed to be cut off as a show of defiance to the Manchus. In some cities, police roamed with scissors looking for pigtails not yet removed.

Yuan wasn't greatly perturbed by the direction China's fortunes were taking. He had other plans, sending emissaries to Li Yuan-hung, the reluctant military governor of Wuchang, to suggest peace talks. For good measure, his son went to Hanyang to discuss collaboration with Huang Hsing, but both missions failed. Yuan was not trusted by the revolution's leaders, so he took a different tack. On 27 November, he ordered an attack on Hanyang, the second of the three cities of Wuhan. The garrison succumbed, but having made his point Yuan pressed no further with his attack. Instead, he decided to send a new peace emissary, T'ang Shao-i, to Shanghai to negotiate this time with Dr Wu Ting-fang, the nominal foreign affairs minister in the yet-to-be-formed government of the Republic of China.

While Yuan pursued his Machiavellian plan, the new governments were trying to establish a structure for the future republic. In early November, Li Yuan-hung, as 'Head of Wuchang Military Government', telegraphed the provinces that had declared their independence of Peking, asking them to send representatives to a conference in Wuchang. Clearly the reluctant governor was starting to revel in his new authority. Two days later, Ch'en Ch'i-mei cabled the provinces asking for delegates to a similar conference in Shanghai. Provincial representatives met in Shanghai on 15 November as others were arriving in Wuchang. As Huang Hsing and Sung Chiao-jen, two of the leading organisers of the Revolutionary Alliance, were in Wuhan at the time, the Shanghai group had to yield, but it highlighted the need for a consensus capital of the embryonic republic. The ancient capital, Nanking, was the logical choice, although it was still in tenuous Manchu hands.

After the Wuchang uprising and fuelled by police rumours, the people of Nanking expected a revolt in their city at any time. Hundreds left for Shanghai every day, by train and by river steamer. Baggage that the trains couldn't carry was stacked on the railway platform, waiting for someone to claim it. Tension and mistrust coursed through those who stayed behind. Viceroy Chang Jen-chun, the former viceroy of Canton, had breach blocks removed from the guns of New Army soldiers. Five thousand troops were brought down from Peking to patrol Nanking's streets. The garrison commander, Tieh Liang, stationed 1500 of them at T'ai-p'ing Gate, from where they pointed guns and shone searchlights at groups of revolutionary soldiers, distinguishable by their white armbands, camped on the plain below. The viceroy stayed calm, but the unnerved Tieh had field guns moved into both his *yamen* and Chang's.

Six hundred Manchu soldiers had been positioned around an ammunition storehouse in Chinkiang, 65 kilometres down the Yangtze from

Nanking, while republican forces camped on the flat farmland around the city. Chinkiang's local Standard-Vacuum Oil manager sent worried telegrams to the US consulate in Nanking about the unrest in the city with troops gathering on its outskirts, but the authorities in Nanking had their own problems.

In early November, the commander of Nanking's New Army troops, who were unable to defend themselves, demanded their breach blocks be returned and ammunition supplied. With General Tieh jumpy and threatening to react if the viceroy agreed, the request was allowed on condition the troops left the city. They marched out the South Gate and camped nearby, making their allegiance even more uncertain.

Leadership in Nanking continued to unravel. General Chang Hsun, in charge of the Imperial troops brought down from Peking, began a spree of decapitations with nine looters. Squat with a big head and protruding ears, Chang was an old Manchu retainer, once a successful bandit but now a barely competent military commander. More looters went through the empty New Army barracks in heavy rain and were summarily shot on Chang's orders. Because there was a shortage of funds, the director of the mint was personally beheaded by the general. House to house searches for revolutionaries and their paraphernalia, and summary executions of Chinese who'd cut off their pigtails, were the order of the day.

Pandemonium reigned supreme in the hands of the visiting general. Viceroy Chang and garrison commander Tieh were restricted to quarters, all other government officials having fled by mid-November. William Gracey, the US consul, organised the evacuation of American citizens, but his vice-consul and some missionaries refused to go. After the Chinkiang garrison changed sides and joined the republicans, trains ceased to run between Nanking and Shanghai. Three kilometres of track was pulled up so it couldn't be used by the insurgents if and when they attacked.

Donald decided to go up the Yangtze valley to observe and report on the build-up of republican forces at Chinkiang, poised to overpower Nanking. Although a confidant of the revolutionists, he was still primarily a journalist and it was for that purpose that he made the journey. Moving up the low, flat Yangtze Valley, he noted that the floods of three months before had gone. In their place, under the grey sky, was snow the colour of pale dirt where it had mixed with slush. Even with weary figures trudging across it, bent into the knife-edged wind, the landscape looked desolate and abandoned.

Arriving at Chinkiang station in the rain with Wen, his interpreter, Donald found troops had pitched camp nearby and were waiting, although why they were waiting was far from clear. Standing at the end of the platform, a tall Caucasian in his mid-30s with a clipped bristly moustache and greying hair was looking up and down for someone who apparently wasn't there. Even in his crumpled raincoat, it was obvious to Donald that the blue-eyed stranger was a large man as well as tall. He came over to Donald—they were the only foreigners on the platform—and said he was waiting for someone to come from Shanghai. In a strangely lilted American accent, he introduced himself as Roy Anderson, local manager of Standard-Vacuum Oil. Donald introduced himself in turn, but the American seemed to know who he was.

'I can't sell any oil,' said Anderson, 'and I can't get any peace with the military moving all over the place. Would you like me to interpret for you?'

Donald said he had an interpreter and introduced Wen, standing alongside him. Anderson hadn't noticed him, but now made a great show of meeting him, pumping his hand.

'I don't know if you could be of much use,' Donald said bluntly. 'Do you know the garrison commander here? I'd like to find out why nothing's happening.'

'Oh, something's happening all right. They're always on the move. But they're not going anywhere.'

Words poured out of the hearty American like a burst water pipe. He explained that the garrison commander, General Ling, was pulled out of nowhere by the local businessmen and made military governor when they changed sides. Anderson was going to see Ling, inviting Donald to go with him.

The three of them took sedan chairs into the city to General Ling's headquarters. The streets were swarming with soldiers and civilians going about their daily business in the rain, but there was a buzz of excitement in the crowd that contrasted with the bleak landscape Donald had observed from the train. They made an odd couple, the sandy-haired Australian with a prominent nose and the bulky American, as they entered Ling's *yamen*. The general came to meet them in the drawing room, drowsy from smoking opium.

'Headquarters is wondering why there's no move on Nanking, why you're just sitting on your backsides,' Donald said without any preceding niceties.

Ling was taken aback, but in his mildly opiated state didn't respond immediately. He wasn't sure if the Australian was an emissary of the Shanghai leadership or yet another arrogant blustering foreigner. He mumbled a near-incoherent reply anyway: 'I have done nothing to interfere with the orders of the generalissimo. It is the confusion existing and only when the confusion is smoothed out can orderly progress be made.'

Even with two interpreters, Donald couldn't make much sense of that. In fact, as the military governor of Chinkiang, General Ling was insisting on being the senior general in the coming battle for Nanking so he could claim the honour of victory. He was obstructing, whenever he could, the advance of the senior Chinese commander, the generalissimo General Hsu Ko-ching, who had come up from the lower Yangtze. Hsu had attacked Nanking with little ammunition and been driven back. Withdrawing with his men to Chinkiang, he'd expected to get backing from Ling, a former junior officer, but Ling had refused to see him.

'Maybe you could lend a hand to abolish the confusion,' said Donald.

Ling nodded blearily.

The three left Ling and went to Anderson's office where Donald filed a report via Shanghai for his newspapers. It was one in the morning by the time Donald and Wen returned to the railway station, rain dripping off the newspaperman's hat, his coat collar pulled up against the downpour. They waited in the stationmaster's office for the shuttle to Shanghai, drying by the fire. Donald lay his head against an iron safe and fell asleep, to be woken two hours later by a Chinese with a handwritten note.

'Come to my office at once,' it said. 'Hell's a-poppin'. Anderson.'

Walking to Anderson's office through the slush, Donald could hear rifle fire in the distance. In the main office of the Standard Oil building, a pyramid of cases was stacked halfway to the ceiling. A Chinese man was squatting silently on top of the boxes

'What's in these boxes?' Donald asked the American, now dressed in khaki and riding boots.

'The generalissimo's money.'

'And who's that on top?'

'That's the treasurer.'

Anderson explained that about 45 minutes before, soldiers had rushed into his office with the boxes in a state of panic, insisting they be allowed to store them there. They claimed that Ling had tried to bomb the generalissimo, although it could have been anyone or a false alarm. Probably reasoning that no-one would risk attacking the office of a foreign business, Hsu had sent the money to Standard Oil for safekeeping and fled to a rebel gunboat on the river. The money was to pay expenses in the assault on Nanking.

Donald burst out laughing. The whole debacle was splendid: the generalissimo somewhere out on the river in the cold and the dark, his money packed in boxes in Anderson's office, and the local military governor stupefied on opium.

With no idea where all this was leading, Donald and Anderson took matters into their own hands. Getting General Hsu back on land and into Anderson's office first thing in the morning, they assured him they had spoken to General Ling and he had agreed to cooperate. His army could move forward immediately. The fact that Ling had given no assurances of anything, indeed hadn't made much sense, didn't concern the two foreigners. However, when told of the promising development, Hsu would not budge. Perhaps he knew better, but the reason he gave was that the railway track between Chinkiang and Nanking had been mined and his troops would be blown up.

Donald and Anderson decided to call Hsu's bluff by taking a locomotive along the line to see if any mines were attached to its tracks. Anderson donned a pith helmet to meet with the Shanghai-Nanking Railway manager. Looking like a big-game hunter, the bulky American cut an even more comical figure than he had the evening before. The manager was not interested in lending a locomotive to anyone to test the tracks, not even to the republican army. It took some talking before he reluctantly relented.

'If you sign a chit for it, I'll let you have it,' the manager said.

'If the locomotive is blown up,' Donald pointed out, unable to let sleeping dogs lie, 'I'll go with it and the chit becomes invalid.'

The manager ignored the witticism and accepted the chit, giving rudimentary driving instructions and assigning a couple of his men to operate the engine while Donald sat on the projecting ledge over the cow-catcher at the front, ready to raise his hand if he saw any metal object attached to the track. Anderson took control of the regulator and brake handles in the engine cabin, closely watched by one of the railwaymen. The other was to keep an eye on the water level and stoke the fire. With the American playing engine-driver and the Australian as front-end lookout, the locomotive crawled hesitantly down the line.

The railway ran alongside the Yangtze and wound into the foothills approaching Nanking. Their progress was cautious and stuttering. They questioned anyone they saw along the way; some said there were no guns ahead of them, some claimed there were many, others weren't sure what answer to give. Interpreting, Anderson told them to stay where they were or they would be killed. The enormous American was not someone they wanted to test their courage against. At one point, the foreigners dragged two men into the locomotive cabin, opened the firebox and threatened to throw them in. Cowered by Anderson's sheer size, they said the only guns were on a spur of Purple Mountain on the eastern edge of the city, and there were no contact mines.

The adventurers pressed on until the engine rounded a corner to find two hand-cars on the line, loaded with rice for General Chang back in Nanking, Anderson ordered the operators to lift their trolleys off the line so the locomotive could pass. It could proceed from there confident the hand-cars would not have been pushed along a track known to be mined.

Approaching Nanking around Purple Mountain, they spotted through binoculars five gun emplacements up on a spur, but no-one fired at them. Donald said, 'They're so surprised to see us, they've forgotten to shoot.'

Within sight of Nanking's city wall, they saw men further up the line dismantling the tracks. Having found no mines to that point, the engine was reversed. Steaming back to Chinkiang after dark, Donald advised the general and his senior officers that it was safe to advance along the railway to Nanking, at least as far as the dismantled tracks.

In the morning, Donald heard bugles playing and soon after spotted soldiers marching towards Chinkiang's railway station. There were barked orders; there were salutes; there were clicked heels; a military air of precision and resolve. General Ling's troops, ordered to advance, got into empty carriages and steamed off towards Nanking. Donald and Anderson followed in a caboose hooked to a later troop train, expecting to go straight to Purple Mountain or Yaohuamen railway station to its north, but instead the train stopped after travelling less than 10 kilometres. The earlier troop trains stood on a siding, emptied of passengers, drained of resolve. Soldiers were busily digging gun pits in the small hills either side of the line.

Donald was there to report on the coming battle and Anderson had merely come along for the ride, but both were being drawn into the revolution. Irritated by the lack of purpose, the two outsiders returned to Chinkiang and told General Hsu the vanguard was holed up 60 kilometres from the objective without an enemy soldier in sight. The commander from Chekiang thanked them and waited politely until they got the hint to leave. With nowhere else to go, they went to Anderson's home to wait until they got word, shortly after noon, of troop movements again at the station.

The generalissimo had ordered his own troops to advance around Purple Mountain and past the Ming Tombs towards Nanking's East Gate. They rolled past the camped army of General Ling, arriving at Yaohuamen late in the afternoon, and marched to a village among paddy fields at the near end of Purple Mountain. An auxiliary force was sent on to attack the Tiger Hill forts, about 4 kilometres downriver from Nanking.

Following the main force, the American and the Australian stayed in a large house the revolutionary generals had set up as their headquarters. The two civilians sat on the porch, rugged up, overlooking the glowing spots of cooking fires and Chinese chatter as soldiers went about their tasks, their unfussy routine contrasting with the posturing drill of Ling's officers, while wheelbarrows squealed as ammunition and rations were rolled up and down the temporary camp. A friendship grew in the first unpressured time the newspaperman and the oil salesman had been able to share since meeting on the platform. They chatted, swapping backgrounds.

The loquacious Donald grew up in a country town in recently federated Australia, the son of a Scottish stonemason turned builder. Because of a childhood injury, he wasn't able to follow into his father's trade, working instead as a typesetter on a local newspaper and graduating to reporter. He had worked his way up from roundsman on the Lithgow *Mercury* to Shanghai correspondent for a number of overseas papers, most notably the *New York Herald*. Anderson was the son of an American missionary. Born in Soochow, he learned Chinese before English and now spoke seven or eight of its dialects. Completing his education in America, he had married and returned to China, joining the Standard Oil Co (now Exxon) in Shanghai and was later made Chinkiang manager of a joint venture with Socony-Vacuum (now Mobil).

The generalissimo arrived during the night and, even later, two Japanese reporters who'd been detained were brought in before being sent back to Shanghai. Donald got very little sleep—the two shared a double Chinese bed in the house, not easy with a man of Anderson's size, the disturbances of constant comings and goings, and Anderson's excitement at it all.

The next morning, rain clouds gathered while the two foreigners—one in khakis and pith helmet, the other in coat, tie and hat—took a morning walk around the south side of Purple Mountain towards the Ming Tombs and Nanking's city wall beyond. Along the way, they came across two dapper officers who, on closer examination, were girls in military uniform, officers of the Cantonese army following behind General Hsu's force and extremely serious, with none of the giggling usual in Chinese women of their age. But when Donald said, 'I'll take your photos', and got out his Kodak, they ran away shrieking.

'If they run from a camera, what do you think they'll do in front of guns?' he asked Anderson.

Purple Mountain loomed over them. Literally 'Purple-Gold (Tsuchin) Mountain' from the mysterious purple and gold clouds that gather around its peaks at dawn and dusk, the forested feature stood over the east side of Nanking, a perfect site for artillery attack.

As they got within sight of the wall, they could see smoke rising from several houses. It had triggered an overnight rumour that the city was in flames, but it turned out to be a local fire. Troops of the Imperial Green Banner Corps watched through narrow openings in the stonework battlement, but there were no republican troops to be seen anywhere.

With no experience of war, Donald and Anderson assumed the inactivity meant they were ahead of the military. In fact, they had unwittingly wandered onto a recent battlefield. While they were settling into the house in the paddy-fields the evening before, an advance party had moved in the gathering darkness on the city's eastern side. A junior Manchu general led an exploratory probe out East Gate, but his men soon found themselves surrounded on three sides and under fire. Shots were exchanged throughout the night and by morning the counterattack had retreated inside the city wall with its dying commander.

Arriving with the skirmish finished, Donald had drawn the wrong inference. The Australian was never short of an opinion, but he wasn't always right. As he and Anderson walked back, they came across two rebel generals on ponies who looked as if they were out on a pleasant ride, but in fact were surveying the scene of the recent battle. One of them was Hsu's chief of staff. Like sightseers wanting a souvenir, they asked Donald to take a photo of them on an arched stone bridge with Purple Mountain behind.

'Are you planning to set up on Purple Mountain?' asked Donald through Anderson.

'It's already held by enemy soldiers,' was the reply.

Donald scanned the ridge with his field glasses but saw no enemy activity. He thought he was starting to get an insight into the military thinking here: look for any reason to not take risks, and hold your position until something on the other side changes. The Australian didn't have the patience for that and decided once more to call their bluff, once again crossing the line between observing and participating. He decided he would go over the mountain to Yaohuamen rather than around it, and told Anderson, who had no physique for mountain-climbing, he would meet him on the other side. That would settle, one way or the other, whether the ridges of Purple Mountain were occupied by enemy troops or not.

The drizzle had stopped and the sun shone weakly, but the air remained chill, the track still muddy underfoot. Climbing up a rough path in coat and tie, Donald's gnawing hunger reminded him he hadn't eaten since breakfast the day before. He found a vegetable garden near the top and scoffed a small cabbage he pulled from the soft soil. In the arched brick hall of a nearby Buddhist temple, a priest responded to his hand gestures with eggs and tea. Further signals, and a smattering of Chinese words picked up over eight years, established there were no soldiers about on that part of the mountain.

Walking later along the ridge, Donald heard distant shouting and saw far below on the flat Yangtze plain the train that had brought him from Chinkiang. Absorbing this panorama in late winter light, he spotted from the corner of his eye two heads peeking between the rocks about 500 metres away. He froze and then waved his white handkerchief, the colour of the revolutionists. A couple of bullets screamed past. Heart pumping, the intrepid correspondent-cum-republican scurried down the north side of Purple Mountain, his face running with sweat despite the evening cool. Eventually he realised the two soldiers had lost interest in him, mystified at what a foreigner in a homburg hat was doing up there in the first place.

After a long, slow twilight descent, picking his way down a rough track between shrubs and rocks, an exhausted Donald reached the railway. A local farmer came across him and brought him in the dark on the back of a donkey, following the railway track. When they got to Yaohuamen, an army doctor ordered Donald to go to bed and not try to get to the generals' headquarters. After another meal of eggs, the Australian climbed wearily aboard the first carriage he came to, into an empty compartment. Lying down on its berth, he fell instantly into deep sleep.

When Bill Donald woke, he sensed something was amiss. There was no sign of Roy Anderson. Through the wall he could hear chatter in Chinese. Looking out the window, all he could see was water, the Yangtze River flowing steadily past. This wasn't Yaohuamen. The train had been brought back to the river during the night. With a discreet tap on the door, a Chinese 'boy' poked his head in and Donald asked what was happening. The boy explained in an awestruck gabble the Australian had difficulty following. It appeared the headquarters had come under artillery fire from somewhere and the generals had retreated to the carriages at Yaohuamen which then came under fire. The train had been moved back, out of range of the artillery.

'Mr Andy, he go Chinkiang.' said the boy. 'He b'long very sick.'

'Where is the generalissimo?' asked Donald, unsure what his friend's illness was.

'He b'long next door.'

Donald opened the door and looked in. The generalissimo was indeed in there, planning moves with the two officers he'd photographed earlier on their ponies. None of them spoke English any more than Donald spoke Chinese. Anderson wasn't around and the boy had already disappeared. Donald pulled the door shut and went outside.

While Hsu had been setting up below Purple Mountain for the assault on Nanking and trying a few exploratory probes, Tiger Hill fort had been taken. The next day, white flags were up on Tiger Hill and its big guns had been turned around to bombard the northern end of Nanking city. Fire was returned from Lion Hill, just inside the city's North Gate, and from the guns on Purple Mountain that Donald had seen when he was testing the line for mines. Foreign warships stood in the river off Nanking's port, but took no part. Their instructions were to evacuate only foreigners.

At a safe distance, Donald could hear the continuing artillery exchange between Tiger and Lion hills. In one of these crossfires, Yaohuamen had come in range and the generalissimo's train had been moved overnight. A shell from Tiger Hill exploded on the North Star Tower in Nanking where General Chang watched with the two officials in his protective custody, the viceroy and the garrison commander. Unhurt but shaken, the two took refuge in the Japanese consulate.

The Purple Mountain fort was still in the hands of Imperial troops, but they were cut off from their main force inside Nanking's city wall. Rebels were attacking East and South gates although both had resisted them up to that point. Their cannons were not strong enough to break down the wall or the gates. A couple of heavier cannons were being brought by rail from Shanghai.

Unexpectedly, Roy Anderson appeared. He hadn't been taken sick back to Chinkiang at all, but in his exhaustion had found somewhere to lie down in the locomotive cabin and slept till mid-morning. The two foreigners jumped onboard the trains getting up steam to shunt back to Yaohuamen.

•

Thousands of rebel soldiers swarmed up the north side of Purple Mountain on a bright, sunny but cold day, 30 November 1911, their objective to position themselves above the fixed loyalist cannons. A ridge protected them from the guns on the western spur, so rifle- and gun-fire passed over their heads. Buglers playing on crags built the drama, along with crossfire in the air. White flags indicated progress of the front line up the slope, while field pieces and trench guns were dragged up behind. Shells from the fort and ramparts inside Nanking fell wide of their target and shrapnel burst high in the air. Donald and Anderson followed like a couple of excited schoolboys, oblivious to the danger.

In the afternoon, the two heavy cannons arrived at Yaohuamen on flatcars, along with a carload of sleepers. They were shunted along the line towards Nanking to a bank where the guns were rolled along the sleepers until they were able to be set up pointing at T'aip'ing Gate, north of the city's East Gate. On the city's south side, General Ling arrived with his Chinkiang troops, having advanced from their distant camp, and directed heavy fire at Manchu units moving forward to meet them before they got to the city wall. Another Manchu unit tried to break through to the isolated outpost on Purple Mountain.

By dark, four or five thousand rebel troops were positioned along the craggy top overlooking the outpost, its whitewashed floor shining in the starlight. When Donald and Anderson got to the ridge, they sheltered behind a stony outcrop and scanned the scene with field glasses. Guns could be seen firing from the fort below; beyond the spur they could see Nanking.

Gunfire rang out through the night, flashes springing from rifles along the top of the mountain. Shells fizzed around in the dark in all directions. With defenders in the whitewashed fort easily spotted, Manchu dead could be seen lying around their big guns. Crimson bursts from the cannons brought from Shanghai were followed by the thudding of bombardment of T'aip'ing Gate and its adjacent walls and fort. It was what a foreign correspondent dreams of being part of, but not usual for an oil trader.

Skirmishes between the two armies continued the next morning just outside the walled perimeter of Nanking. The T'aip'ing Gate had taken a battering and only riflemen positioned inside it kept rebel soldiers out of the city. The Manchu general, Chang Hsun, had joined his soldiers trying to force a path through to their outpost on Purple Mountain, but to no avail. They were driven back and the fort was overrun by revolutionaries. An increasingly irrational Chang was forcibly carried back from the spur shortly before its capture.

By this stage of the battle, most loyalist soldiers outside the wall had either retreated or been shot. Chang's subordinate officers inside the city were ready to surrender, but their commander wouldn't hear of it. Called to his headquarters, US vice-consul Alvin Gilbert found the walrus-moustached Chang in tears, rejecting the pleas of his generals to give up. He wanted Gilbert to agree to put him on an American gunboat so the city could be handed over and his life saved. Gilbert, by then at loggerheads with departed consul William Gracey over his refusal to leave Nanking, was unable to help.

General Chang was running out of options. Reluctantly he agreed to offer to surrender with conditions. He and his officers must be given safe conduct to Peking, Chinese and Manchu residents must not be harmed, and soldiers and officers left in the city must not be killed. The vice-consul was asked to carry the message out to the republican commander.

Donald and Anderson returned from breakfast to their observation post up on Purple Mountain in time to see far below a large American flag emerge through South Gate about midday. Underneath the flag was another flag, this one white. A European in silk hat and frockcoat, mounted on a white horse, was carrying the two flags. It was the American vice-consul, accompanied by Reverend Bowen of the Methodist University and a representative of General Chang. Gilbert had decided to show two flags because in the past Chang had sent out a white flag then fired on the rebels. He thought the American flag was more likely to be respected.

Chang's delegation met with General Ling, the senior officer on the south side. Later in the afternoon, it came back with Ling's reply: Chang must surrender and remain in his quarters where he'd be protected; all troops must lay down their arms and come out of the city, but they will not be harmed; and government funds of US$800 000 must be handed over. The defenders were given till eight the next morning to agree to the terms. Word went up to Purple Mountain that surrender was in the wind. Hostilities ceased for the time being—there wasn't much left outside the city to shoot at anyway—and everyone on the republican side, including the two foreign observers, waited.

With Chang refusing to listen to his men, the vice-consul left the Manchu generals to work out their impasse during the night. Word came to him at 3 a.m. that Chang's generals had decided to surrender anyway. Told of this, Chang had fled, taking 4000 troops with him across the Yangtze and north by rail from the other side.

Asked again to mediate, Gilbert met General Ling, this time outside T'aip'ing Gate accompanied by a Canadian medico and an American missionary. Once again Gilbert carried an American flag as well as a white one. Ling was told that Colonel Chao, now in command of loyalist forces, had agreed to Ling's terms with the proviso that Chang Hsun was beyond his reach.

Shortly after, the battered remnants of T'aip'ing Gate groaned open and loyalist troops led by General Chao—his instant promotion a consequence of Chang's departure—marched out, laid down their arms and saluted the revolutionaries. With martial music playing, General Ling rode at the head of his army entering the city through T'aip'ing Gate. White flags flew everywhere and the rebel soldiers were greeted with enthusiasm by the people of Nanking. Five hundred Imperial soldiers with reversed rifles paraded to welcome the conquerors and to honour General Ling, a commander who had entered the fray only at the last moment after sulking in a dispute over who was the rightful senior commander.

Ironically, his weren't the first rebel troops to enter Nanking, although none on that side of the city knew it at that time. The commander of Lion Hill fort had agreed some days before to hand over to the rebel force from Tiger Hill if his commander, Tieh Liang, could be guaranteed protection. Viceroy Chang Jen-chun and General Tieh had been sheltering in the Japanese consulate and, on the night General Chang made his dash north, fled to a Japanese cruiser anchored above Nanking. They sailed the next day to Japan via Shanghai. With Tieh no longer requiring protection, the Lion Hill commander opened North Gate and allowed the enemy troops into the city, a few hours before General Ling entered T'aip'ing Gate with such pageantry.

Bill Donald returned to Chinkiang with his new friend Roy Anderson, bid him farewell and caught the train to Shanghai. Provincial representatives were gathering there for another conference at the same time as a similar conference in Hankow, each electing leaders of the provisional military government of the republic. Delegates from both conferences moved to Nanking on 11 December and started to debate a mutually acceptable provisional constitution. Three days later, they began to elect a consensus president of a new central government. The meeting was deadlocked in two factions, one supporting Li Yuan-hung, the other Huang Hsing, but with the suggestion that Yuan Shih-k'ai might be moving to support a republic, the decision was delayed until his position became clearer. Sun Yat-sen wasn't raised because his whereabouts were still unknown.

Meanwhile in Peking, Prince Ch'un, deprived of power when Yuan took over as prime minister, stepped down as regent and was replaced by his sister-in-law, the new empress dowager. He'd never greatly relished power anyway and was relieved to have left office. One of the empress dowager's first moves was to instruct Yuan to negotiate peace with the revolutionists without sacrificing the Manchu position.

•

Donald had taken up a vantage point across the Bund in the dining room of the Palace Hotel to watch T'ang Shao-i arrive by steamer at Whangpoo jetty. With an elaborate gown for warmth and a coterie of attendants, Yuan's peace negotiator stepped onto the wharf with all the splendour of a grandee, but his ostentation was wasted on China's new order. The onlookers appeared unmoved, though they would have quietly noted with interest that his pigtail had been lopped off. It sent a signal that despite the Imperial flourish, he was representing Yuan Shih-k'ai in the talks, not the Manchu court.

Dr Wu had sought Donald's advice before the meeting and discussed issues as they arose with him over the several inconclusive days in which the negotiations took place. Among the reporters covering the conference was another Australian, the Peking-based reporter for *The Times*, Ernest Morrison, thirteen years Donald's senior and already something of a legend among foreign correspondents. As he did for other journalists, Donald provided Morrison with inside information from the republican side of the debate. A friendship grew between the two Australians, each with the reassurance of the certainty of his views.

While the republican conference continued its debates in Nanking, peace talks took place in Shanghai's Municipal Council building, the first sessions devoted to procedure, then discussion beginning in earnest. T'ang was not a Manchu himself, but Cantonese like many of the men across the table. The two parties hammered out an agreement that both had silently supported from the outset, but needed nonetheless to go through the process of appearing to make concessions. Eventually there was agreement to a four-point peace plan proposed by Dr Wu: abdication of the Manchus, establishment of a republic, a generous pension for the emperor, and relief for aged and poor Manchus.

The elephant in the room as the Nanking constitutional conference proceeded was the one-time driving force of the Chinese revolution and still, in the minds of many, its spiritual leader. Through over two months of tumultuous change in the crumbling Manchu empire, there had been no word from Dr Sun Yat-sen, supposedly raising funds in Europe and North America for a revolution that had now taken place. People had stopped asking 'When will Dr Sun be returning?' No-one, not even his closest associates, had the slightest idea.

Sun slipped off the agenda, until on the way to a meeting of Dr Wu and his advisers part-way through the Shanghai talks, Donald picked up a copy of an English-language paper. Tucked away towards the bottom of the overseas news page was a small item date-lined Singapore. It was already a couple of days old, but the single paragraph riveted the Australian's attention. Dr Sun Yat-sen, it said, had arrived in Singapore, en route to Shanghai, 'accompanied by American generals'.

Chapter 6

The unshining Sun

In putting together a list of great packing blunders, this would have to come into consideration: when Sun Yat-sen went to Europe and North America in 1911, he left his codebook behind. As a result, he was unable to decipher any of the coded telegrams from his comrades including one telling him an uprising was about to take place in Wuchang and another telling him it had succeeded.

The first Sun knew of Wuchang was from a newspaper over breakfast one morning in Denver. The report suggested he was a potential leader. Rather than return belatedly to take over the reins of revolution, he decided it would be more politic to go to Washington, London and Paris and seek assurances that the Western powers wouldn't be providing arms or loans to prop up the dying Ch'ing dynasty.

He caught the train to Washington, but Secretary of State Frank Knox refused to meet him. The British Foreign Secretary, Sir Edward Grey, wouldn't see him either, but lobbied by Sir Trevor Dawson of the arms manufacturer, Vickers Sons and Maxim, he relented slightly. Having an assessment of Sun by his advisers as 'an armchair politician and windbag', Grey sent a message through Dawson that Britain would remain neutral and that there was 'a good man on the opposite side, Yuan'. Sun was unaware of Yuan's growing equivocation, and it's unclear how accurate a perception the British government had either, but it bore out a view Dr Morrison put to China-based journalists: Yuan was the only man who could persuade the foreign powers to recognise the republic.

In Paris, Sun was greeted warmly by ex-premier Clemenceau, but he got no support from the French government and no loan from French bankers. Travelling by steamer from Marseilles via the Suez Canal and Singapore, Sun arrived at Shanghai on a grey, cold day. It was Christmas 1911, a day of significance to much of the foreign community there and to converts to Christianity like himself, but not to the vast mass of Chinese. No-one was on hand in the howling gale at Whangpoo wharf to welcome home the returning visionary of the Chinese republic. Instead he had to hire a motorcar to take him to a house in the French Concession.

While other republican leaders were at the Nanking conference, Wu Ting-fang and Wen Tsung-yao were negotiating with Yuan's emissary, T'ang Shao-i. Bill Donald was with them when Sun rang Wu's house and proposed a meeting. Wu, Wen and Donald went to the address Wu had been given and were shown into a gloomy drawing room where Sun sat dejectedly on one side of a weak fire burning in a small grate. On the other side sat an American in full military regalia with large shining buttons and a set of medals, but the gaudy uniform failed to distract the callers from the obvious. He was a hunchback, less than 5 feet (1.5 metres) tall. This was the 'American generals' the English newspaper had reported accompanying Sun Yat-sen back to China. Sun breathlessly introduced 'General' Homer Lea to his visitors as a 'world brilliant military talent'. Lea's story failed to live up to that description.

A hunchback since he was dropped as a baby, and dismissed from West Point military academy for health reasons, Lea had travelled to China during the Boxer Rebellion. He was made a lieutenant-general by the sidelined emperor, but the small volunteer force he led to restore Kwang-tsu to power was routed by the empress dowager's Imperial army. Lea had fled to Japan where he met Sun Yat-sen.

Back in the United States, Homer Lea built a volunteer army of Chinese immigrants using American instructors, but it didn't go anywhere. He wrote two geopolitical works, one predicting the rise of

Japanese militarism to forge a Japanese empire in the Pacific, the other predicting a German Reich based on national supremacy and ethnic purity. Although both books would prove quite prescient 30 years later, they didn't sell well at the time.

In the US in 1911, Sun had reconnected with Lea and brought him back as his military strategist and adviser. It was not a wise choice. In Chinese folklore, hunchbacks are omens of bad luck. Lea's presence as an adviser to a senior figure of the revolution was immediately shocking to Sun's Chinese colleagues. On top of that, as if to make up for his diminutive physical stature, the American was a boorish loudmouth. Both Wu and Wen refused to talk to him, or to Sun about him. Sun Yat-sen's first meeting in the emerging republic of China was rapidly becoming not a meeting at all. Silence settled on the group. Wu and Wen shuffled uncomfortably.

Having great difficulty seeing the magnetic personality he'd heard so much of, Donald persisted.

'Doctor,' he said, 'the question you will need to address is what form of government China will take.' He told Sun that, in his opinion, the Manchus were finished as a governing force, but the shape and substance of the new government had not yet crystallised. It was important it do so as a matter of urgency.

'We'll have a republic,' Sun announced.

Donald waited, expecting the political strategist to elaborate, but no more was offered. His dreaming had gone no further. The Australian moved on, asking Sun what he intended to do about Yuan Shih-k'ai.

'Yuan Shih-k'ai? I'll drive him across the Gobi Desert,' piped up 'General' Lea, possibly recalling Yuan as the betrayer of his sponsors last time he was in China.

'Will he wait until you walk up and whack him?' asked Donald. 'He has an army, you know.'

'So have we! So have we!' Lea retorted, but by then the puff had gone out of the conversation. Soon after, the three visitors rose, offered formal farewells and departed.

The next day, with Sun planning to join the leaders of the new China in Nanking, Donald suggested he do so without the hunchbacked general.

Homer Lea remained in Shanghai, ignored. Ernest Morrison sardonically wrote that 'his claim to the title of "General" appears to be based on the fact that when resident in Los Angeles he taught the goosestep to some Chinese laundrymen'. Six weeks later, the self-styled military man fell down unconscious. A diabetic, he returned to his homeland where he had a stroke later in the year and died at the age of 35.

With its constitution drawn up by the end of December, the provisional parliament returned to the issue of provisional president. Torn between Li Yuan-hung and Huang Hsing, the supporters of both turned to Sun as a compromise now that he was back in China. Although conspicuously absent during the uprisings, he was still widely admired by the people. By the time the vote was taken, sixteen of the seventeen participating provinces supported him and Dr Sun Yat-sen was elected first Provisional President of the Government of the Republic of China.

Sun came by special train from Shanghai on 1 January 1912 with a large entourage and bodyguard. He was greeted enthusiastically at many stations along the way, reaching Nanking at 5.30 in the afternoon amid loud cheering. Met at the station by prominent revolutionaries, he was escorted to Government House along a route lined with soldiers, the gates of the inner avenues decorated with multicoloured electric lights. The president-elect was saluted by a salvo of cannon-fire from the nearby forts on Tiger and Lion hills and Purple Mountain, sites of very recent memory for Donald, who had come with Sun's contingent. He noted that what was now Government House had been the viceroy's *yamen*, last occupied by his old mentor from Canton, Chang Jen-chun.

The party reached the former *yamen* at seven. As Sun entered its main hall, all present bowed their heads and he stepped onto a central platform to take the oath of office in a simple and dignified ceremony. The newly inaugurated president then moved on to what he did best. In an address to the assembled gathering, he promised to oust the remaining Manchus, to devote energy to the Chinese nation and its people. It was vintage Sun Yat-sen, with the wide-eyed conviction of a man with a mission.

When the Manchus had abdicated and peace was restored, he said, he would resign from the provisional office he now held. It wasn't clear whether he was referring to a deal being worked out with Yuan Shih-k'ai or if his statement was intended to give parliament an opportunity to elect him unprovisionally. He may not have known himself.

Meanwhile, Yuan was busy playing the incompetent Manchus against the naive republicans. He cancelled the peace talks in what appeared to be a response to Sun's inauguration, but actually resulted from a long audience with the empress dowager, unhappy with the deal T'ang Shao-i had arrived at in the Shanghai talks. It didn't appear to her to preserve the Manchu position as she had instructed.

The next day, Yuan publicly dismissed T'ang and announced he would continue negotiation with Wu by telegraph. However, he secretly cabled T'ang to continue discussions with Wu, no longer to save the Ch'ing dynasty but to find the best way to secure peace.

With the army demanding money to continue the war and Yuan appearing prepared to resign, the empress dowager was cornered. She agreed to draw on palace gold and the Imperial princes' hoarded wealth to keep the campaign afloat. Instead of resigning, Yuan announced he would fight on for a constitutional monarchy, saying he believed the republican movement in the southern provinces would soon disintegrate. Events elsewhere said otherwise and Yuan probably knew that. In Hankow, troops were saying they had been fighting for the Manchus, but were now fighting for Yuan. It was a delicate balance to maintain, but Yuan was well in control.

Sun, meanwhile, considered the composition of his cabinet. He thought Wu Ting-fang, who was 69, too old for the post of foreign minister and wanted instead his former legal adviser, 30-year-old Wang Ch'ung-hui, who 'can receive instructions at my convenience'. Sun wasn't sure where he stood with Wu after the incident with the hunchbacked general, but he was confident he could control Wang, a Kwangtung delegate to the provincial assembly in Nanking.

Cabinet appointees were made known on 3 January and included the unsurprising appointments of Li Yuan-hung as vice-president, and Huang Hsing as premier and war minister. General Hsu Ko-ching, of the battle for Nanking, was named chief of staff. (His rival in that campaign, General Ling, had fallen out of favour and was in hiding in fear of his life.) Most unexpected was the naming of Wang as foreign minister and Wu as attorney-general.

The Cantonese Guild in Shanghai cabled Sun protesting the treatment of Wu, and threatening to withdraw its proposed loan of US$400 000 to the Nanking government, arranged by Wu and Wen Tsung-tao. Wang demurred, saying he wasn't qualified for the position, but Sun would hear none of it.

'We have to get rid of these so-called bureaucratic qualifications,' he complained to his chief secretary, Hu Han-min. 'As for foreign affairs problems, we can solve them ourselves.'

Sun insisted publicly he had a high regard for Wu's past law reforms, assuring the Cantonese Guild that Wu and Wen would continue the peace talks, notwithstanding they appeared to be derailed by the dismissal of T'ang, and the loan came through. While the issue of the foreign ministry was debated, Wu continued to act as foreign minister.

Donald had been in Nanking for the inauguration. He filed a story for the *New York Herald* and returned to Shanghai. The next day was bitterly cold and Donald was up at the Revolutionary Alliance's headquarters when Wang Ch'ung-hui arrived from Nanking. Excited and breathless, he said the new president was being pressured to produce a manifesto, a document outlining for the foreign powers the reasons the Ch'ing dynasty had been overthrown, and providing key policy positions of the new government. Sun wanted the Australian journalist to write it. He was already familiar with the new republic's policies and he could give the document the right tone for its intended audience.

'Well, we'd better get cracking then,' Donald said, sitting over a battered typewriter. 'There's no time to dilly-dally.'

In the wintry air his fingers grew stiff and numb. He had to give himself regular breaks to recover from typing, but he needed the pause anyway to marshal his thoughts. Wen Tsung-yao joined them, asked by Donald to assist in the manifesto's creation. The three debated the content, drawing extensively from Sun's speeches of the evening before, already paraphrased by the journalist for the *Herald*. Donald would type out sections which they would all look at, discuss and argue about. Then they would be rewritten.

Evening became night and the cold cut even deeper. They drank tea and walked around the room in heavy coats to get warm. Ideas were tossed up, discussed and discarded, or worked into the text. When the first draft was produced late in the night, all three went through it, pencilling in alterations, arguing their merits, before Donald commenced to write again.

With Donald surrounded by Wang and Wen who were pacing and debating, and kept awake and warmed by further pots of tea, four drafts had been prepared by six the next morning. As the dawn light poked weakly into the room, they saw with some satisfaction that out of this process had come a crisp, unambiguous statement of the aspirations of the new China, written to persuade non-Chinese readers. Donald had curbed his habitual verbosity in favour of economy and eloquence. The fourth draft was agreed by Wang and Wen to be the final draft and was cabled to Nanking. The 'Manifesto from the Republic of China to All Friendly Nations' in English was signed by Provisional President Sun Yat-sen, countersigned by the acting foreign minister, Wu Tingfang, and sent to consulates on 5 January for transmission to their home governments.

A week later, the debate about the foreign minister had run its course. Wu handed over to Wang who saw the manifesto had been signed by his temporary predecessor and issued another communiqué under his own signature. There was no response from the foreign powers, even though it was issued three times, several days apart. They were cautious about any move that might imply recognition of the new government.

The new cabinet met in Nanking around a large rectangular table in the former viceroy's *yamen*, but its authority was limited by its uncertainty. Sun tried desperately to keep a tight grip on the reins of power. Some of the senior figures like Wu, Li and Ch'en had emerged while he was out of the country. He'd brought in his erstwhile adviser Wang to shore up his position, but much took place outside his control. Sun went his own sweet way while the new ministers tried with little success to work together. Without consulting cabinet, he issued military bonds repayable in three months, but made no provision for their payment. Adding to the confusion, a stream of overseas Chinese poured into the capital for positions and other rewards promised when Sun was on the fundraising trail.

Even more alarming to Nanking's political circles and Shanghai's business leaders was the growing influence on Sun of foreign advisers, especially his old Japanese cronies. In a letter to Morrison in Peking, Donald complained, 'Every day the trains disgorged new hordes, among them scores of Japanese who settled down in the *yamen* as if by right. They brought their bedding, their cooking and eating paraphernalia and milled and wandered about like herds of sheep.' Eventually the army ejected the squatters.

Wu continued to deal with T'ang Shao-i at Shanghai's peace talks, as if his resignation had never happened. The uncertainty of T'ang's authority didn't seem to worry Wu, but it unsettled Sun. He demanded Yuan appoint a peace delegate to replace the dismissed T'ang and cease semi-official dealings through him. Yuan ignored the demand and work continued in Shanghai on a number of treaty documents and interim agreements. Outlines were taken away for drafting, drafts were discussed, revised and redrafted. It was agreed Yuan would force the Ch'ing emperor to abdicate in return for southern province support for Yuan as president of the new republic. Among the considerations in republican thinking was the possibility the new regime might be defeated in a protracted civil war or by foreign intervention. Yuan's northern army was still a formidable force, whereas the ability of the southern alliance of mutineers and volunteers to sustain a campaign was extremely doubtful.

At one stage, Sun had been talking about personally leading an army to Peking.

'What about finances?' asked Donald. 'It costs money.'

Sun swept his arm grandly and looked straight at Donald as if this was to be a revealing moment of great candour.

'Finance is the last thing I think of,' he said.

The Imperial family had decided it wouldn't abdicate, that the throne had made enough concessions, the empress dowager declaring that a war to the death was more honourable than meekly handing over power. General Chang Hsun, having regrouped after retreating from Nanking, began to rattle his sabre, announcing that even if the throne abdicated, he'd fight on. But Yuan was leaving the Manchus isolated. He now seemed disinclined to aggression and said he had no desire to kill his fellow Chinese.

He told the press, 'The Imperial military is weaker than when I was persuaded by the British with promises of financial support to agree to an armistice.'

'That support,' he added, 'hasn't come.'

Yuan's position had become virtually unassailable. Even an assassination attempt in Tientsin came to nothing. He controlled the powerful Peiyang Army. He had supporters in the provisional government and all the powers given to him by the Manchu court. He had foreign backing as the powers saw him as the only person in China strong enough to maintain law and order. With an inexperienced and disunited cabinet without clear legitimacy, Sun had no option but to agree that he would hand the presidency of the republic to Yuan if Yuan was able to force the Manchus to abdicate.

Yuan was sounding more like a politician than a soldier, declaring he was inspired to serve the best interests of the Chinese people, not of republicans or monarchists. His one unswerving desire, he said, was that China enjoy peace and a government of substance as soon as possible. Having got that off his chest, he started working on the Manchu emperor's abdication. Yuan told the empress dowager that if the revolutionaries came to Peking, he did not believe the lives of the royal family would be spared, but if they agreed to abdicate he was confident the terms of abdication would be honoured.

Shortly after, 47 generals from the Peiyang Army requested the royal family announce the abdication of the emperor and let the republic assume control of the nation. The revolution had spread across China's provinces and the Peiyang Army could no longer defend the Ch'ing government because it lacked reinforcements. It was a public statement arranged by the Peiyang Army's supreme commander, Yuan Shih-k'ai.

On 12 February, after being successively pressured and persuaded by Yuan, Emperor Pu-i, his sixth birthday the week before, and the empress dowager accepted terms for the Imperial family's abdication, the empress dowager proclaiming the edict with tears streaming down her face. It said, in part, 'The majority of the people are in favour of a republic. From the preference of the people's hearts the will of heaven is discernable. How could we oppose the desires of millions for the glory of one family? Therefore, we, the Dowager Empress and the Emperor, hereby vest the sovereignty of the Chinese Empire in the people. Let Yuan Shih-k'ai organise to the full the powers of the provisional republican government.'

That same day, Sun Yat-sen resigned in favour of Yuan, who was inaugurated second provisional president of the Republic of China, pending national elections. Sun had wanted the symbolism of him bestowing the presidency on Yuan, but he'd been outsmarted. At Morrison's suggestion, Yuan had arranged it so his legitimacy was authorised instead by the abdicating Manchus, avoiding any suggestion of treachery in his actions, as well as having the advantage of sidelining Sun. Formal continuity made recognition easier for the foreign powers, particularly the British.

Yuan was to come to Nanking to take up the presidency, but he was reluctant to leave his power base of Peking. A delegation of republican leaders went to the old capital to escort the new president back, but he had set up a phony mutiny there, then insisted he had to stay for security reasons. He was allowed to be inaugurated in Peking and never left. By April, he had persuaded parliament to approve its retention as the national capital.

No longer the provisional president, Sun Yat-sen was at a loose end. He claimed he no longer had an interest in politics and worked instead on a vision for China's railway future. 'Transportation is the mother of industry,' he wrote, 'and the railway is the mother of transportation.' Sun was convinced railways would be the key to China's economic development. America had 200 000 miles of railway and had become the world's wealthiest nation. By Sun's calculation, China was five times as large as the US—it would seem geography wasn't his strength—so it would need a million miles of railways to become the strongest power. He believed this could be done in ten years, even though China had less than 6000 miles of line at that time.

Donald had reservations about Sun from the Homer Lea incident, but after the success of the manifesto Sun was keen to continue involving him in policy discussions. He sought the newspaperman's views on a variety of issues, especially on what could be done to develop China's railways and how, although Donald had no particular experience or expertise in that area. There was never a formal arrangement and no salary as such—Donald continued to earn income from writing for various foreign newspapers—merely payment of expenses as they arose, but the Australian was always more interested in being influential than in making money. In any case, it kept him in touch with useful sources for his journalism.

Donald regularly exchanged letters and candid views of Chinese politics with his fellow Australian, Ernest Morrison. Visiting Peking, he was encouraged by Morrison to consider working for *The Times*. The Peking correspondent was about to resign, sick of China and wanting to marry his secretary and go back to Australia, but Donald decided to stay where he was for the time being, close to his sources and wanting to see what developed with Sun.

At the time he resigned, Morrison was offered a lucrative position as adviser to President Yuan. The salary of £3500 was three times what *The Times* had been paying him. On top of that, he would get travel expenses, a house allowance, and secretary and interpreter supplied. It was too tempting to turn down. The Morrisons married in England and returned to China so Ernest could take up his new post.

Yuan had made Sun the Director for Construction of All Railways in China on a salary of 30 000 Chinese dollars a month, with full powers to plan a national railway network and negotiate financial backing from foreigners. Set up in Shanghai for his new post, Sun made Charlie Soong treasurer of the Chinese National Railway Corporation and hired Soong's eldest daughter, Ai-ling, as his secretary. The Soong family were identified publicly with Sun Yat-sen for the first time. Operating from Shanghai also meant Donald was on hand when needed.

•

The new railway chief decided he should make a lengthy tour of inspection of the existing rail system. Waving presidentially to an enthusiastic crowd of office-seekers, courtiers and onlookers, but no-one of any significance from the new government, he set out from Peking belching steam and trailing banners and bunting. The train included two dining cars, several saloon cars and sleepers and a personal Pullman coach for Sun's private use that had belonged to the late empress dowager. Among the crowd of hangers-on, staff and pretty secretaries onboard were Sun's wife, his personal secretary and his foreign adviser, WH Donald.

As the train puffed and rattled through the northern provinces from one whistlestop to the next, Sun had long conversations with Donald about developing China, always in his characteristic confidential whisper, his voice filled with breathless excitement. In an opulent carriage with imperial yellow silk drapes and leather chairs on a blue velvet rug etched with gold designs of peony and phoenix, the revolutionist talked and his adviser listened. Once more, Sun ran through his calculations of the extent of new railway lines necessary to make China a great power, promising he would divulge details of his scheme in due course. Sometimes Ai-ling sat on a chair nearby and scribbled notes.

Ideas came pouring out of Sun's fertile imagination. He would solve the Yangtze's silting problem by building a stone wall from Hankow to Shanghai, about 1000 kilometres. The river would wash the silt along the wall so silt would not bank up. Since the river rose some 15 metres between Hankow and Nanking when flooding, this didn't sound very practical to Donald, but he let it go.

Sun said he'd decided to devote himself entirely to railway development, but to the crowds that gathered when the train stopped at the larger cities, he behaved as if he was running for office. He greeted local dignitaries, had tea and made speeches, always full of the visionary rhetoric that had worked so well for him in the past. China's political circles might be growing disenchanted with him, but he still managed to inspire the masses.

At gatherings with provincial officials, Sun insisted Donald sit beside him. When the adviser suggested locals might want the seat of honour next to the great leader, Sun was adamant.

'No, I want you to sit here,' he insisted. 'I can't talk to these up-country fellows. I don't know what they're saying half the time.'

It would be difficult to converse in dialects that kept changing as they traversed the provinces, especially for someone who'd been absent from

China as much as Sun, but Donald wondered whether there was another explanation. A sizeable bodyguard accompanied them, so Sun clearly had concerns about his security. Perhaps he thought a political bomb-thrower might think twice with a foreigner alongside him, because of the international complications that would result.

Back in the luxurious Pullman, Donald would try to explore the plans to rectify China's economic backwardness, but it was to Sun's advantage that his adviser was more inclined to talk than listen. Sun's expressionless gaze would fix on the Australian for a while, then surreptitiously transfer to the scribbling Ai-ling and rest there without the flicker of an eyelid.

In his whistle-stop speeches, Sun sometimes raised points that Donald had canvassed, but the people wanted to hear passion from the national hero, not details, and provincial officials were only interested in what was in it for them. Newsmen would push their way to the front of the adulatory crowds, one asking Sun if he was a socialist. Looking bewildered, he turned to his adviser.

'Am I?' he asked.

'You are everything that is required of you as a nationalist,' said Donald.

Throughout the nights, as the train roared past small stations, bugles blared a welcome and a farewell, with the train's horn responding. Undisturbed sleep was difficult. In the unending evenings, the staff, guests and pretty girls had to find ways to occupy themselves.

The Australian had a strong sense of propriety, sometimes to the point of prudishness. With the frequent sounds of sex behind curtains in the sleeper booths each night and new crackpot ideas during the day as they continued their benighted journey, Donald was starting to wonder where this circus was going and how it could help China's embryonic republic.

The schemes kept coming. When money was short, Sun would simply print more, rather than raise a foreign loan. Donald asked where he would get the bullion as collateral for this money.

'Oh, we'll melt down all our silver teapots,' Sun explained.

He would create huge department stores with branches all over China and they would issue paper money in the form of scrip. When the paper wore out, they would print more.

Sun proposed to divide the country into areas according to the types of metal mined there, be it gold, silver, copper or whatever. In each area, the stores would issue paper money against the district's metal, buy and sell its produce and destroy the paper money as it was paid for in commodities. Ai-ling continued making busy notes.

One day, after Donald had been pressing him for more detail about his railway scheme, Sun spread out a large map, about 2 metres square, on the carriage floor. With his brush and ink stick, the director of railways had filled every province with as many lines as he could squeeze in, double lines to indicate trunk railways, thin lines for laterals and less important connections. Straight lines had been drawn everywhere with no rhyme or reason, and without consideration of topography, as a child might fill in a puzzle book. One trunk line swept across Mongolia, skirting the Gobi Desert. Who would need to use that track? Another crossed from Shanghai to Szechwan and on to Lhasa, straight across the mountainous terrain of Tibet.

Donald stared at the map and at its creator proudly sitting crosslegged on the floor beside it. A realisation was dawning on the Australian that had been nagging for some time . . . The great revolutionary thinker was, in fact, a complete ninny.

Pointing to Tibet on the map, the adviser said quietly, 'That line circling Tibet can never be built except with brush and ink. Some of the passes your railway will run over are fifteen thousand feet high.'

'There are roads there, aren't there?' insisted Sun.

'Not roads. Just rough narrow tracks. They're so steep a strong yak can barely climb them.'

'Where there's a road,' said Sun with absolute assurance, 'a railway can be built.'

Later, Donald raised again the subject of Sun's railway scheme, pointing out that it may not be possible to build 55 000 kilometres of railway lines in ten years. It would take a lot of money.

'It's very simple,' said Sun with certainty. 'We can get all the money we want. I'll build some lines with British capital, some with American, some with German, some with Japanese, and so on.'

'The Manchus tried the same thing,' Donald replied. 'They tried to nationalise the railways and run them on foreign capital. They got a railway revolt instead and now they're gone.'

But Sun wasn't interested in naysayers. The grand tour was coming into the major rail junction of Fengtai where a meeting with the foreign press had been scheduled. Here was an opportunity to find an appreciative audience.

'I wouldn't show your railway map,' advised Donald, convinced Sun was about to undermine whatever credibility he had left. 'You'll be giving away your ideas.'

Sun would have none of it. 'No, I don't mind. I want people to know about them. My map will save China.'

Donald suggested they stroll on the platform at Fengtai so Sun could gather his thoughts for the press. The adviser excused himself 'for a minute' and left Sun in the fresh air brimming with satisfaction. Reporters boarded the train, admiring the Pullman's lush decor, perhaps even making a mental note of the irony of it, and were seated when Sun entered. He stood behind a lectern to deliver his 'railways vision' speech, working up to the pièce de résistance, the first public showing of The Map.

'Gentlemen,' Sun announced, going to the drawer where he kept it, 'I have something that might interest you.'

But the map was not there. Perplexed, he asked, 'Don, have you seen my map?'

Before Donald could reply, a secretary walked across to Sun with a look of concern on her face. While the two engaged in animated Chinese, Donald addressed the journalists.

'Gentlemen, Dr Sun Yat-sen is working on a railway plan. His map will set out the detail for you. I'm sure—'

An agitated Sun said something aloud in Chinese, then in breathy English addressed the gathering. 'I'm sorry, gentlemen, but the engineer has been warned of a possible bandit attack. He says we must start the train at once.'

The newsmen left and the train was away within a few minutes. A few hours later, the map was discovered elsewhere in the coach. There were no further meetings scheduled with the foreign press and by the time the train reached Shanghai, Sun was absorbed in making fine adjustments to his map.

The grand tour was over and Donald had become completely disillusioned with Sun, seeing no ability in him beyond making stirring speeches and now believing him to be a political liability. Donald wrote to Morrison complaining that Sun 'is absolutely impractical without common sense and devoid of the most elementary ideas he professes to be now fathering'.

Sun, said Donald, recalling his stated disdain for finance, 'thinks he can preach anti-foreignism, socialism and a dozen other isms in this benighted country and then think all the financiers of the world will pull open their purse strings and scatter their sovereigns about the burnt face of China because he, Sun Yat-sen, lifts his hand'.

Although Sun feigned indifference to politics, Donald's Shanghai contacts were telling him the Revolutionary Alliance was secretly preparing to stand Sun against Yuan in the coming elections under a new constitution. By now, Donald was persuaded by Morrison that Yuan was the key to China's political stability and actively campaigned against the Revolutionary Alliance. The owner of the *Shanghai Times* had fallen ill and Donald's old Hong Kong mate, Lionel Pratt, had put his problems with alcohol on hold and taken over. Donald fed him stories of the revolutionaries' campaign to destabilise Yuan, undermining Sun Yat-sen by association.

Sun and Huang Hsin had been trying to persuade Wen Tsung-yao, a revolutionist who had worked with but hadn't joined the Revolutionary Alliance, to dissolve his faction and form a new wider-reaching party with the alliance. Wen had known Donald since his days as an adviser to the viceroy of Canton and, coming to him for advice, was told to give the Revolutionary Alliance a wide berth. A week later, Wen argued at a faction meeting against joining with the alliance and its leaders decided not to dissolve. Despite that setback, the alliance absorbed four other revolutionary groups in August 1912 to form the Kuomintang (Chinese Nationalist Party) under the leadership of the young Shanghai revolutionary, Sung Chiao-jen. It was to become the vehicle for the next phase of China's transition from empire.

Donald continued his tirade against Sun in his correspondence with Morrison. 'I think Sun Yat-sen is an imposter—he has never done anything to me, and we are good friends,' he wrote. 'But politically I won't stand for his imbecility, his downright wideness, and his attempt to bluff foreigners as well as Chinese.'

It was a perception of Sun that was getting a toehold. Since his short term as first provisional president, his reputation had taken a battering. His propensity to go it alone with hare-brained schemes, his insistence that his authority be unchallenged, his overweening self-belief, all contributed to a nickname of 'Sun Dapao' ('Big-gun Sun').

His reputation among the upper echelons as a womaniser might have been hypocritical, but it, too, was part of a waning influence. Sun had left his wife in Hawaii with their three children while he traipsed around the world, consorting with prostitutes in south-east Asia and fathering a daughter in Japan. Donald noted: 'That was the trouble with the old boy. Couldn't keep him off the women.' The number of beautiful Chinese women invited to join his railway inspection tour had not gone unnoticed.

Despite his low opinion, Donald continued to give advice when Sun sought it, mostly relating to his railway plans. On one occasion when he was in Sun's Shanghai office, Ai-ling brought in some papers and left. Leering after her, Sun whispered to his visitor that he wanted to marry her.

'You'd better kill that idea,' said Donald. 'You're already married.'

'I'll divorce my wife first.' Their marriage had been arranged by his home village.

'Ai-ling is Charlie Soong's daughter. Your best friend,' protested Donald. 'Without him, you'd have been in a pickle many times. You've been an uncle to his children. They've almost been your children.'

'I know. I know,' said Sun with feigned solemnity. 'But I want to marry her just the same.'

Sun coerced Donald to go with him to Soong's house to ask for Ai-ling's hand. Concerned at the repercussions—for himself as much as for anyone else—Donald took a lot of persuading and then insisted he would go only as an observer.

In Charlie Soong's drawing room, Donald stood back trying hard to emphasise his role as chaperone not supporter, while Sun put his request to his old benefactor. As a stunned Soong leaned back in his chair, the colour drained from his face.

After a long silence, he said, quietly and deliberately, as if there was some prospect of being misunderstood, 'Yat-sen, I'm a Christian man and I thought you were, too. I didn't bring up my children to live in the sort of looseness you propose. I won't accustom myself with people who trifle with marriage. We are a Christian family and, Lord willing, we will stay that way.'

Sun was confused and embarrassed, looking around for support as if this was the last response he had imagined. Donald stayed motionless in the background.

'I want you to go, Yat-sen,' said Charlie Soong. 'I want you to go and I never want you to come back. My door is closed to you.'

The two visitors left in silence. They were driven back to Sun's office without discussion, the rejected suitor shaking his head and muttering to himself from time to time, 'I don't understand. I don't understand.'

As soon as they got out, Donald said, 'Goodnight', and walked off without waiting for a response.

Chapter 7

21 Demands

George Bronson Rea was a lanky Irish-American with fading red hair, the son of a wealthy New York banker from a family of refugees from the potato famine. He had gone to Cuba as the engineer he had trained to be, but the war of independence there intervened and he became special correspondent for the *New York Herald* instead. Rea stayed in newspapers. In 1904, he started a monthly devoted to engineering, finance and commerce in the Far East. Published in Manila, it was called the *Far Eastern Review*.

In 1907, US War Secretary WH Taft visited Shanghai and called for an 'open door' to prevent European and Japanese monopolisation of China's economic development. Five years later Taft was president of the United States and, already convinced Manila was on the outskirts of the Far East, Rea took note and relocated his publication to Shanghai. Talking big and talking politics, although not with any consistency, it wasn't long before he came across a fellow raconteur journalist, WH Donald, with an impressive array of contacts within China's new elite and past experience as managing editor of a Hong Kong daily.

Rea offered Donald joint editorship with himself of the *Far Eastern Review* and equity in the company that published it. Because the *Review* came out monthly, there was no suggestion Donald should stop working for the *New York Herald.* The partnership brought other benefits at the same time. With his engineering background, Rea had an unshakeable belief in the importance of railways to economic development. His new partner came with connections in the Chinese National Railway Corporation, as well as links to British and American finance not available to the recently arrived American. It might be that Donald was hired more for his railway contacts than his newspaper experience or it might have been just serendipitous, but whatever the truth—and it was probably a bit of both—it presented a window of opportunity to the two enterprising foreigners.

Bronson Rea had a vision of America as a benevolent empire and used the *Review* for diatribes against foreign competitors. Like Sun Yat-sen, he saw railways as key to the development of China, as it had been in the US. 'The civilising factor of a great network of railways could secure the consolidation of China, the development of her industries, the growth of her agriculture, the exploitation of her mineral wealth, and her political future,' he wrote. Such gushing prose was irresistible to Sun. Rea was hired as an adviser on railway development in conjunction with Donald.

A volatile man, Rea was capable of finding a conspiracy whenever something didn't work out for him, but after eight years of reporting business and industry in the region, he was shrewd in the commercial ways of the Orient. Empowered by Sun to negotiate contracts on behalf of the Railway Corporation, he was not prepared to act without knowing what financial arrangements were already in place. He didn't have to look far.

Sun rented his Shanghai office in a building owned by two dubious operators. Reiss, a Brazilian, had appeared out of nowhere and very little was known about him; Spielman was said to have been dismissed as an agent of the Russo-Chinese Bank for speculating privately with the bank's funds. The pair had manipulated shares together in the 1908 Shanghai rubber boom. To finance Sun's railway scheme, Reiss and Spielman had issued bank notes, already in boxes in his office. Since the railway scheme was compromised, Rea and Donald tendered their resignations, forcing Sun to squeeze Reiss and Spielman out of the picture, but to little avail.

The two advisers accumulated engineering and costing data, using it to detail key lines that would connect the more economically critical centres, taking note of topography and other restraints so cavalierly ignored by Sun in his map. Rea and Donald worked with Sun to find partners with capital for the various sections of the network, at the same time trying to keep him within the bounds of prudence, but Donald's prediction to Morrison was proving correct. They could find no foreign investor that didn't see Sun and China at that time as too great an investment liability.

Sun was meanwhile meeting with Huang Hsing and other political cronies, planning to oust Yuan from office. Donald was once again commenting sourly to Morrison that 'Sun has no brains to develop his own solutions and is the instrument of wire-pullers with nothing to lose and everything to gain'. Sun's clique bought Shanghai's *China Gazette* and renamed it *China Republican*, aiming to glorify their man and denounce Yuan, but Sun was losing ground while the Nationalist Party and its young leader were out on the hustings in preparation for the parliamentary elections mandated by the provisional constitution.

Major moves were in the air for Bill Donald, however. James Gordon Bennett, the proprietor of the *New York Herald*, cabled him in November: 'AM THINKING OF RECALLING OHL [Peking correspondent for the *Herald*] TO AMERICA STOP HOW WOULD YOU LIKE TO SUCCEED HIM IN PEKING BENNETT'. Donald stalled, replying that it would be good to know the salary and when he would be expected to move. He wasn't prepared to drop the *Far Eastern Review* when there were good prospects of building his equity in it, but if the *Herald* was happy for him to retain his role on the *Review*, he would look seriously at going to Peking.

Donald was better at giving advice than consulting to get other views, a trait he carried into his domestic life. Mary was not greatly enamoured of Shanghai, a city lacking in gaiety for all its sophistication. Inhabited by people with hard, bitter expressions, she much preferred the provincial pretensions of Hong Kong, more like the Sydney she grew up in, with the added benefit of Chinese servants.

With her husband hobnobbing with the movers and shakers of the new China, and joining Dr Sun on his grand tour with a retinue of pretty women, Mrs Donald was seeing less and less of him, uncertain how he was occupying his time so fully. But it wasn't with pretty women. Donald's time was mostly filled with talk; talking about what he was doing, talking about what others should be doing, talking about all the things in China that weren't being done as well as they should.

Unlike in Hong Kong, Mary had made few friends in Shanghai and much of her time was taken up with three-year-old Muriel, even though they had an *amah* to assist. Had Donald asked what Mary thought about a move to Peking, he might have detected her apprehension, but he didn't. He told her what a great opportunity it was—for them. For him.

The Donalds moved to Peking at the beginning of 1913 with none of the excitement of entering an exotic new world that had accompanied their move to Shanghai. Donald was already familiar with Peking and his wife was not sure she wanted to be. Through his connections in the Chinese government, Donald was able to purchase one of a pair of two-storey redbrick houses in the foreign quarter of the capital, but as Westerners could only rent in Peking, it had to be bought in the name of a Chinese. The other house was acquired by Roy Anderson, Donald's compadre in the storming of Purple Mountain. Anderson was still working for Standard Oil, but had been moved to its Peking office.

The two 'gingerbread' houses were contained within a walled compound surrounded by modest Chinese dwellings. A bond might have formed between the two women, but Anderson's wife, described by a fellow American as 'vapid and pretty-pretty', was not the sort to appeal to the feisty Australian. They weren't unfriendly, but were never close. Mary spent much of her day in the roof garden or with the three servants: an *amah*, a cook and a coolie. Outside, the cobbled *hutung* (lane) rattled and echoed with the alien chants of hawkers and pedlars.

Donald spent his days—and much of his evenings—in the press bureau he set up in a dusty little office in the old Russo-Asiatic Bank building with an American, Rodney Gilbert, the Peking correspondent of the *North-China Daily News*. Donald would file reports for the *Herald* and prepare copy for the coming edition of *Far Eastern Review*, travelling to Shanghai each month by train or steamer to publish the *Review*.

The two worked with the sound of camel bells outside as cargo-laden lines wound their way through Peking's back streets, and with the shouts, drums, gongs and rattles of street vendors trying to attract customers. The odour of Peking wafted into the office, the smell of dung, cooking and wood smoke, the stench of dust.

With so little investment response to the railway scheme and having moved to Peking, Donald's involvement with Sun Yat-sen waned, but in any case the political ground was moving dramatically in China. In the mandated national election, the Nationalist Party won 45 per cent of seats in both houses of parliament, positioning Sung Chiao-jen to become premier with alliances with a few smaller parties, and displace Yuan's premier, Chao Ping-chun. Sung was not opposed to Yuan as president, but was an advocate of government by cabinet responsibility and a functional opposition, neither of which suited Yuan's ambitions. Attempts to win Sung over with bribes failed and other methods to neutralise him had to be found.

On 29 March, Sung was with a group of friends at Shanghai's crowded North Railway Station, about to board a train to Peking to join the new parliament. As they pushed their way along the platform, a figure in black rushed towards him and shot him twice in the stomach with a Browning revolver. The victim was rushed to hospital but was told they had to wait for official permission from Peking before they could operate. By the time permission came, peritonitis had set in and Sung died the next morning.

Police tracked down the perpetrators, one by one, and trials got underway, but all those implicated died before the courts could reach any clear verdicts. Given the task by the premier of arranging the execution of Sung, a disaffected revolutionary called Ying had hired the assassin. Police found telegrams and a letter implicating Premier Chao and possibly President Yuan. The assassin was caught and, after a preliminary hearing in the Shanghai Mixed Court, was found dead from poisoning in his prison cell. Ying escaped after being arrested in a brothel, and fled to Peking only to be stabbed to death in a railway compartment soon after. The premier stood down, claiming debilitating toothache, and refused a subpoena on grounds of illness. He was made military governor of Chihli, where he died of poisoning a year later.

Widely suspected of having ordered the assassination, but never brought to court, Yuan set about consolidating his power, intent on absolute rule. In April, he arranged a 'reconstruction loan' of US$125 million from five foreign banks to strengthen his Peiyang Army. With vehement objections by parliament that a loan of that size would put China under foreign control, Yuan refused to submit the contract for its approval, in defiance of the constitution. On the president's instructions, the acting premier surrounded parliament with troops, claiming the agreement with the banks was completed and there was no need for parliament to meet.

Donald wrote to Yuan's adviser, Morrison, 'It's the worst thing China ever did. China has signed her death warrant.' But both knew Morrison had little influence over Yuan and on this issue would have none.

Within a few months of taking up his appointment, Morrison was sick of it, complaining he was enmeshed in 'intrigues, lies and incompetence'. 'This is a rotten damned country to be in,' he grumbled, 'and a putrid people to serve! Suspicious of me because I'm friends with Donald . . . '

Morrison's moods swung between railing against Yuan and his 'cohort of unscrupulous Chinese jealous of the foreigner' and feeling driven by the issues he regarded as important to China. With a new family to support and debts to clear, he had no choice anyway; he was stuck with it. He and Donald swapped notes about who to trust and who not to trust, and about what was needed for China.

A prolific letter-writer, Donald confided with an old friend at Sydney's *Daily Telegraph*. 'I see Dr Morrison daily, and he does not know whether to be tired of his job or not,' he wrote. 'The Chinaman listens to advice, but will do what he thinks he wants to do. Morrison feels that, frequently. During the revolution, he asked me, in Shanghai, why I did not enter the service of the Government. They were then offering me £250 a month. My reply was that, once a man entered the paid service of a Chinese, his influence was gone. Morrison scoffed—now he admits it. Bitter proof. As *Times* correspondent he had twice the prestige and three times the influence.'

Morrison's advice on the reconstruction loan was not sought. In response to it, parliament impeached Yuan but that was of no effect. Sun returned from wooing investors in Japan to denounce him and was dismissed from his railways post, accused of using railway funds for rebellion. The president sacked the military governors of Kiangsi, Kwangtung and Anhwei who had criticised him. On 12 July, Kiangsi seceded from the new republic, followed by six other provinces in quick succession. Dubbed the 'Second Revolution', it did not fare well. Within a few months, Yuan's army had defeated the poorly equipped southern armies and Yuan's generals took control of the Yangtze area as warlords, a development that within a few years would have profound repercussions on political power in China.

By the end of October, parliament had drawn up a constitution with a cabinet system of government, not a presidential one. The president brought pressure to bear, including the presence of troops, but the parliamentarians stood firm. Yuan, growing hungrier for absolute rule, responded by dissolving the Nationalist Party and revoking its members of parliament for their supposed involvement in the Second Revolution. Troops surrounded the party's Peking office, and its MPs were prevented from entering parliament. Without a quorum, parliament could not function.

The Nationalist Party leader in the National Assembly, CT Wang, had known Donald since his days with the YMCA in Shanghai. He phoned his Australian friend in fear of his life and babbled in terror that Yuan's gunmen were outside his house and would kill him as soon as he stepped outside. 'What should I do?' he pleaded to Donald.

While he pondered the options, Donald advised Wang to destroy all his papers and stay calm. Then he told Wang he would call him back.

A few minutes later, Donald phoned back and instructed the leader to disguise himself as an old lady. Wang was to wear the black headband that elderly Chinese women wore and allow himself to be guided unsteadily by servants to a carriage Donald would send round. It would take him to the front door of the Methodist Mission which he should enter, hurry through to the back door, and out and across to the US Legation.

Wang did as instructed and the escape went as planned. Donald had arranged with his American contacts to get the Yale-educated Wang to a Peking railway station so he could be smuggled, still in disguise, to the foreign concessions in Tientsin—and safety. Donald's ability to work effectively in China revolved around the contacts he had made.

With orders out for his arrest, Sun fled to Japan, to be joined by his new protégé, Chiang Kai-shek. Chiang had fallen in with a Shanghai financier known as Curio Chang from his lucrative antique business. Chang had underworld and secret society connections. Chiang's fiery temper had resulted in him quarrelling with and shooting a rival of his old comrade, Ch'en Ch'i-mei. Fleeing to Japan, he published a military magazine that promoted centralised military power. China, the magazine argued, should be ruled by enlightened despotism, combining 'Washington's ideals' with 'Napoleon's methods'.

Chiang returned to help Ch'en whose Shanghai revolutionary administration, unpopular through high taxes and corruption, had been ousted by Yuan. In the Second Revolution, Chiang had futilely attacked the Shanghai Arsenal, with heavy losses. By the time Yuan had disposed of the Nationalist Party, there was a price on the heads of both Chiang and Ch'en. They had every reason to follow Sun to Japan.

Charlie Soong was another. He and Sun had been working together again, the incident over Ai-ling patched up with apologies, and all were carrying on as if it had never happened. Seeing no safety for his family in Shanghai, Soong closed up his house in Hongkew and took those living there—Ching-ling had returned to China during the year, but Mai-ling and TV were still in America—downriver to board a steamship to Kobe.

The Soongs later moved to Yokohama where Ai-ling resumed work as Sun's secretary and Ching-ling hung around the party offices. Soong visited the Chinese YMCA in Tokyo and met HH (Hsiang-hsi) Kung, who came from a rich Shansi pawnbroker family. A Yale graduate and recently widowed, the 33-year-old had guided the finances of Shansi's military governor before taking up the post of YMCA administrator.

Kung and Ai-ling were married in the spring of 1914 and Ching-ling took over as Sun's secretary. Where Ai-ling was hard-nosed and calculating, Ching-ling was a romantic. She was infatuated with Sun for the same reason her sister was not: because he was a dreamer. Returning from the US full of passion and idealism, she saw Sun, plotting and organising, as a heroic figure. She believed in the unfinished business of his revolution and a romance blossomed between them despite a disparity in their ages of nearly 30 years.

The stampede of revolutionists to Japan had drained Bill Donald's pool of political contacts, but he'd never been a revolutionist himself, merely an idealist about China's potential as the sleeping giant. The group in which he'd placed great faith had proved in many ways to be as inept and as venal as the regime it had replaced. Circumstances required him to build a new network, which he set about doing with characteristic single-mindedness. Increasingly he saw the key to China's growth in the right foreigners working with those Chinese capable of implementing necessary reforms.

First and foremost was the other Australian, Dr Morrison, who was a source of inside information about the workings of the new bureaucracy. They exchanged candid views about the people operating the machinery of China's government, but their relationship had its ups and downs. Donald's letter to Jennie Morrison congratulating her on the arrival of their first child and wishing happiness 'for ten thousand years' indicates its closeness. 'If you can't manage the little chap,' wrote Donald, 'hand him over to his father, who will no doubt be able to set him to work on his library catalogue. He needs brainy assistants.'

On the other hand, Donald's letter to his friend at the *Daily Telegraph* about Morrison's disenchantment with his position made its way to an article in *The Bulletin*. The article quoted Donald as saying that Morrison found his job impossible and that his connection with government had reduced him to a non-entity. Donald tried to downplay its significance without success. Morrison's nose was mightily out of joint, but the two needed each other, if for no other reason than they both required an audience and each provided that for the other. They soon resumed their regular exchange of letters and opinions. Although he chose to be ingenuously mystified how a letter to a journalist could appear in a journal, Bill Donald learnt a lesson about indiscretion and after that incident was more cautious—or calculating—about what he passed on.

There were others he cultivated at the same time. His neighbour and close friend, Roy Anderson—dubbed 'the Admiral' by Donald for no apparent reason—was looking beyond Standard Oil to become more embroiled in China, and made himself available to visiting American businessmen with advice on China's inner circles.

Donald also connected with America's new ambassador, Paul Reinsch, an inexperienced diplomat with little capacity to delegate and a readiness to take up cudgels on anyone's behalf. They formed a mutually useful partnership with Donald able to source information where the American would only get diplomatic waffle, and to bring pressure through Reinsch where his own influence was negligible.

The Australian got to know David Fraser, a blustery Scotsman who had taken over from Morrison as Peking correspondent for *The Times*. A newspaper veteran of the Boer and Russo-Japanese wars, he carried the vestiges of a wound inflicted on the Baghdad Railway. Fraser wrote to his London masters recommending a replacement for when he was out of Peking for any significant period. Donald, Fraser reported, was joint editor of an 'excellent engineering magazine ... a bit of a rough diamond, with an awful Australian accent, but a very nice fellow and one of my best friends'.

Donald's most active contact, though, was Bronson Rea. Following the dismissal of Sun Yat-sen from his railways post, Rea had taken overseas a multinational version of the rail network proposal he, Donald and Sun had worked on. With US President Woodrow Wilson receptive to the plan, Rea returned to China and persuaded Yuan to back it and appoint him Technical Adviser (Railways) to the Minister of Communications. He set out with Donald to attract foreign engineering firms to a consortium that would finance, construct and equip future government railways in China. The Chinese wanted the contractors to arrange finance of the project, in return for a stake in profits, so they didn't have to deal with legations or big banks. Without their scrutiny, China's high officials could more easily direct some of the funds to themselves.

Conscious of Japanese demands for railway projects and the pressure by British firms to operate exclusively, the new American ambassador agreed there was an urgent need to keep competition at bay. Donald wired New York engineers JG White & Co to interest them in the project. Proposing to secure an option for them, he assured them it would not commit the company, but would hold the railway until Rea could get to the US and establish a Sino-American construction company. White & Co replied: 'WE AUTHORIZE YOU TO SECURE RAILWAY OPTION ON OUR ACCOUNT AS PER YOUR TELEGRAM TODAY'.

Donald wrote to selected international partners—South African firm Pauling & Co, through its London office, Sociétè Construction des Batignolles in Paris, and Frankfurt's Philipp Holzmann AG—that he was authorised by the Chinese government to form a consortium of leading railway construction firms, inviting them to join JG White & Co, tentatively already onboard. The participants were to meet with Rea in Paris and exchange powers to act on behalf of the respective principals.

From humble origins in a New South Wales coalmining town, Bill Donald had become a player on the global business stage, recruiting international partners to a major national development project. It was exhilarating, even more than being a foreign correspondent. At the same time, Donald continued to bring out *Far Eastern Review* each month, commuting between Peking and Shanghai, while his business partner travelled to the US and Europe with Dr Ch'en of the Ministry of Communications to finalise arrangements with the participating construction companies. Investor backing was to be discussed, but instead of consolidating, the grand scheme fell apart.

Rea was unpersuasive in the United States. The state department produced a long memo opposing the consortium as a monopoly perpetuating the principle of spheres of influence. The practice of foreign powers allocating parts of China to each other as a trade priority was strongly opposed by the US. Conversely, the British foreign office and the French government were opposed to a plan that would see an international consortium operating in their sphere of influence, undermining their monopoly. JG White & Co was prepared to commit if it had a formal invitation by the Chinese government, necessary to appease the US state department, but by June the company was writing to Rea that they'd received no official letter from Dr Ch'en.

There was a good reason for that. The construction company was to be floated with one-third Chinese interest, but senior ministry officials told Minister of Communications Liang and President Yuan that China would have only 20 per cent of the capital, intending to divert the 13⅓ per cent difference to themselves, the widespread practice in Chinese business of 'squeeze'. Unfortunately, Rea's interpreter told Liang's vice-minister the actual figure, whether accidentally or deliberately is not clear. Rea's contacts in the ministry lost their jobs and the Chinese cancelled the mission. On 29 June, Rea received a registered letter from the minister: 'Under present conditions, the Ministry has determined to stop all negotiations concerned with the organization of the International Railway Company, and direct Rea to return to Peking at once. Letterheads of the Ministry have been improperly used by Rea.'

By September, Rea had resigned his post, claiming the long silence and cancellation of the railway project had made financiers and construction companies in Europe wary of doing business with China. He complained to the minister that his expenses had not been reimbursed and to others that he had been treated 'as if I had been a coolie'. A month later, Liang resigned.

Rea wrote to his ambassador, Paul Reinsch, that he had been dealt an injustice, speculating it was the result of British scheming to get all China's advisers to be British. Warming to his theme, Rea launched an attack through the pages of the *Far Eastern Review* claiming that Dr Morrison and the British Engineers' Association were working to undermine American commerce in China and describing ex-minister Liang as an 'opium sot'.

Donald's venture into a major construction project had been a fizzer, as he might have put it himself, but he seems to have remained sanguine while his partner became obsessed. The railways would be built anyway, one way or the other, although not necessarily efficiently or corruption-free. The Australian could comfort himself that the failure stemmed more from his partner than himself. In any case, other issues would soon overshadow the railway plan. Donald would have a role to play in them and his doggedness would be an important factor in their outcomes.

•

With parliament without a legal quorum and unable to convene, nearly half its members being from the expelled Nationalist Party, President Yuan formally suspended it in January 1914 and set about to refashion the government structure to his own needs. A conference of hand-picked representatives from the provinces extended the presidential term to ten years, renewable for a further ten and with the right of the president to nominate his own successor. The incumbent was well on his way to absolute rule and establishing a new dynasty. The provincial body had revised the Provisional Constitution of the Republic of China, under Yuan's guidance, allowing him to declare war, sign treaties and appoint officials without seeking the approval of parliament. Even if parliament had been able to convene, it now had little purpose.

A decreasingly democratic system of government, as China became more and more a republic in name only, was less of a long-term threat than the other growing issue. Since the Russo-Japanese War, Japan had become more belligerently assertive of its role in Asia. Its government had fallen under the control of a militaristic clique, with the left, many of them Sun's former supporters from his revolutionist days, fighting for survival.

When war broke out in Europe in 1914, Japan saw an opportunity to advance its territorial ambitions while the Western powers other than America were preoccupied. While China stayed neutral, Japan declared war on Germany in support of the Allies, landing a force of 21 000 in Shantung and, joined by 1000 British troops, laying siege to Tsingtao (now Qingdao) in the German leasehold there. Premier Okuma announced to the West: 'Japan has no ulterior motive, no desire to secure more territory, no thought of depriving China or other peoples of anything they now possess.'

The Japanese seized the Shantung Railway between Tsingtao and Chinan, mostly outside the leasehold area, despite China's protests. The Chinese told Dr Reinsch they planned to ask both US President Wilson and the British government to pressure Japan to restrict its military activity to within its assurances, but the US ambassador advised against that, persuaded the Japanese were acting in good faith and would respect China's rights. Throughout 1914, Reinsch considered Japan to be merely assuming Germany's economic responsibilities in Shantung. It would take him some time to recognise his error.

After the Germans were defeated in November with heavy Japanese losses, Tokyo decided to retain control over Shantung, at least until the war was over. Japan had made 'no promise whatever', Foreign Minister Kato told his parliament, 'regarding the ultimate disposition of what she has acquired in Shantung'.

By January, the Japanese were still there, even though German soldiers had been inactive for two months and British troops had gone. China demanded Japan withdraw its troops from the province and that Tokyo pay for all damage caused by the fighting. Japan feigned outrage at this 'insult'. The time for withdrawal had not arrived, but when the right moment came it would consult with China. In other words, Japan would decide when and what it did in China. It was an attitude Japan would take for the next 30 years, attracting Bill Donald's increasing acrimony, but where he saw a sleeping giant the Japanese saw only bumbling cousins.

•

On 18 January 1915, Japan's ambassador to China, Eki Hioki, back from protracted leave, met in the afternoon with Yuan Shih-k'ai. The diplomat told the president that Japanese public opinion was hostile, regarding him as anti-Japanese, although if he agreed to proposals in a document the ambassador presented, that might help calm things down.

The document contained 21 demands set out in five sections. Hammering the table with his walking stick, the dapper Hioki insisted the demands be accepted immediately. Unless they were kept absolutely secret, particularly from Britain, Japan might find itself 'unable to exercise any control over the revolutionaries who fled to its territories and were seeking to overthrow the present administration of China', an unsubtle reference to Sun Yat-sen's continuing presence in Japan plotting Yuan's downfall. Sun had not returned to China since he fled from arrest.

Yuan initially kept the 21 Demands to himself, prompting a game of cat-and-mouse. The next day a Japanese reporter called on Reinsch to ask if he knew what Hioki had discussed at the meeting with Yuan, as he'd been told nothing. The American was aware of the meeting and knew no more, but suspected the reporter's real purpose was to find out if the Chinese had confided in him.

The president hadn't even confided in his own ministers at that stage and, meeting with his foreign affairs adviser, Dr Morrison, talked through Japanese trade in Manchuria, but didn't mention the ultimatum served by Japan two days before. At a dinner at a Japanese diplomat's home, China's minister of finance, Chow Tzu-chi was taken to a large map of the world hanging on the sitting room wall. He hadn't noticed it there before.

'I'd like to explain the real reasons we have made these demands,' the diplomat said, 'and in such a form.'

'What demands?' asked the minister.

Tatsuichiro Funatsu missed the significance of the question, explaining that the greater part of the world was held by the white races, now weakened by fighting each other. This was the time, he said, for the Japanese and the Chinese to unite and win back a share of the world's territory. The documents were in reality a proposal for an alliance in a form that would deceive the foreign powers.

Donald had left for Shanghai on the morning of the Yuan–Hioki meeting to get the next issue of *Far Eastern Review* out. He, too, heard of the meeting and, suspecting it might be over more than Shantung, left instructions for his staff to do some digging. Little had been unearthed by the time he returned, apart from the rumour that Japan had made demands while the Allies were tied up in war. Donald called on both the American and British ambassadors, but they could tell him nothing.

In fact, now that Yuan had briefed his cabinet, one of his ministers had told the US ambassador in confidence that serious unspecified demands were being made by Japan to make China a vassal state, but Reinsch wasn't going to pass that on to a journalist, not even one with whom he was friendly. Advising Washington of this threat to American interests, the only response he had got was that the matter was being looked into. It's doubtful there had been any similar confiding by the Chinese with the British.

Rumours ran hot for a couple of weeks, with leaks adding tinder to what little was known or thought to be known: the Japanese were demanding more territory, even a footing in the Yangtze Valley; they wanted extended railway and mining leases; they were threatening to remove restraints on the Chinese rebels sheltering in Japan. The Japanese international news agency, Kokusai, stated on highest authority that reports of negotiations between Japan and China were absolutely without foundation.

On 3 February, the emphatically denied negotiations got underway at the foreign office in Peking, but no information was released about what was under discussion. It might have been Shantung; it might have been much more. Frustrated, the Australian journalist decided to pursue another tack.

Friendly with Chow Tzu-chi since arriving in Peking, he paid the minister an evening call at his home and was ushered into a room with a disarmingly cosy fire. His friend came in, moon-faced and flustered, his trim moustache quivering. He had guessed what Donald's visit was about. Never one to waste time on pleasantries, Donald got straight to the point.

'What's that overdressed Jap, Hioki, twirling his moustache about now, Old Joe? No-one's talking.'

'I can't say, Don,' replied the minister in an agitated state. 'It's a terrible, terrible business.'

'So what is it?'

'Talking is dangerous.'

Chow was clearly too afraid to reveal any more, so Donald tried a different approach. Proposing to write down all the things he could think of that Japan might try to squeeze out of China, he asked his friend to cross off anything that wasn't in the demands.

'Very well,' responded the minister without enthusiasm.

They sat down at a table near the fireplace and Donald pondered what might be there: increased control of Shantung and Manchuria; extended railway, mine and industry privileges; preferential treatment over other foreign powers. He wrote them down, one by one, refining them as he went, until he ran out of possibilities.

Believing he'd put together a fairly harsh set of demands, Donald presented the list to Chow for deletions. A few items were crossed off. Knowing he now didn't have in his list any demands that weren't, in fact, demands, Donald thought he had a list he could work with. He didn't know how short of the full set of demands it was, but he imagined he had most of them. As it happened, he had a précis of only half the actual demands.

At the time acting Peking correspondent for *The Times*, Donald wrote a detailed story from the version of the demands he'd gleaned from Chow and sent a long telegram to London. The *Times*' foreign editor, Wickham

Steed, showed Donald's set of demands to the Japanese ambassador in Great Britain for confirmation. Their existence was initially denied, before the ambassador conceded generally some of the less objectionable claims, describing Donald's cable as 'wilfully exaggerated'.

Japan was already working on friendly governments through diplomatic channels, and particularly on its ally Britain, providing them with a heavily pruned version of the demands that omitted anything they might object to. The document was insouciantly described as the basis of friendly discussion of outstanding problems between the two countries.

The diplomatic onslaught reaped rewards for the Japanese. An independent report of the demands, provided by 'Putnam Weale' (nom-de-plume of Bertram Lenox-Simpson) to the London *Daily Telegraph*, was suppressed in England. Donald had given his version to Frederick Moore of Associated Press (AP), who wired it to New York without naming his source. A cable came back from Melville Stone, AP's aging general manager, that it had been shown to the Japanese ambassador who categorically denied any demands had been made. Unless they could name and quote Donald as a source or name his Chinese sources, Associated Press would not publish. Having given an undertaking to Donald and not knowing who his Chinese source was anyway, the AP correspondent refused. Later, Frederick Moore would be fired and, even later, Melville Stone would work for the Japanese.

The Times had been shown a copy of a confidential note from Japan's Foreign Minister Kato, the architect of the 21 Demands, to his British counterpart, Sir Edward Grey. It made no reference to most of the demands listed by Donald and claimed the Chinese were trying to inflame opinion in America against Japan. *The Times* deleted any demands not mentioned in Kato's note in its version of Donald's report, along with an editorial that accused China of trying to stir up discord among the Western powers.

Steed cabled Donald that it was thought Peking was exaggerating the Japanese position and *The Times* required verification of his information, to which Donald wrote a furious response. Meanwhile, Japan used the *Times* leader to argue that the British government regarded the demands as reasonable and compatible with existing conventions.

Bill Donald was on the warpath. He showed Steed's cable to the British Legation in Peking. They agreed to confirm to the foreign office in London their belief that Donald's story was substantially correct and to advise *The Times* to publish it in full. He also showed the cable to his Chinese cabinet contacts to make clear that the Japanese were stopping publication. Asked for an exact translation of the 21 Demands, the Chinese were too fearful to respond directly, proposing instead that Donald contact Dr Morrison with his request. As a result, Morrison finally got the translation of the demands he had been requesting for some time from the government he served.

The next day, Donald's rickshaw pulled up in the noisy, crowded street in front of Morrison's spacious Chinese house. Entering through a small postern door in a high masonry wall, across an open courtyard and through a large lobby, Donald was shown into a dimly lit wood-panelled room lined with books. As in the rest of the house, valuable Chinese pieces were displayed on stands and in corners—screens, porcelains, bronzes—many of them picked up in looting after the suppression of the Boxer Uprising. Under a heavily draped window, a carved lumber desk was covered with papers and writing paraphernalia.

Morrison entered, a Chinese gown over his soft flannel shirt and linen trousers, and greeted his compatriot. Tall, somewhat ungainly and blue-eyed, he was as taciturn as his guest was loquacious. Like Donald, he had at best a sketchy knowledge of Chinese, surprising perhaps in an avid collector of Chinese books.

'Good to see you, Don. To what do I owe this pleasure?' said Morrison, although he knew exactly what Donald's pleasure was on this occasion.

'I'm fine, Doctor,' was the reply, 'but China isn't. I'm having the devil's job trying to find out what that Jap dandy is demanding of the poor blighters.'

'They're keeping very silent. Won't tell me much at all.'

'They tell me you've got a translation of Hioki's paper. You might be able to show me a copy.'

'It's risky, Don. Very risky.'

Morrison had wandered over to the window and was pushing papers around on the desktop as he spoke. He seemed to be agonising over a decision, then suddenly looked up and excused himself.

'I'll be back in a minute, if you could just wait on,' he said and, after straightening some of the papers once more, left Donald alone in the room.

Donald wondered whether it was his imagination or was there a message in his host's pantomime with the papers. He stepped toward the desk to investigate, glanced at the papers Morrison had fiddled with before leaving and, seeing enough to excite his hopes, folded them into the inside pocket of his jacket.

'Sorry to keep you waiting,' said a voice behind him.

Donald turned.

'That's all right, Doctor, but I must be hurrying off. Things to get done.'

Without batting an eyelid, Morrison called for a boy to see his guest out and they parted cordially as if after a satisfyingly productive meeting.

Returning to his office, Donald scanned the document he'd grabbed. It was indeed a translation of the demands, of which there were 21, about double the list he had worked out with Old Joe. He read through them carefully and with increasing alarm. These were much more audacious, more aggressive than anything he had imagined.

The objective of the 21 Demands was to control the direction of China's administration. Tokyo was to expand its hold over Shantung and Manchuria and to have investment priority in Fukien. China's key officials were to have Japanese 'advisers'. Coal, steel and armaments works in the Yangtze valley were to be run jointly with a ban on competitors, the Chinese police would be under effective Japanese administration, China was to buy its armaments exclusively from Japan and to grant Japan further railway concessions in south China. No further coastal concessions were to be granted to other foreign powers. Small wonder the Japanese wanted to ensure the details were not disclosed to the West. Apart from curtailing any expansion of the spheres of influence, the demands would effectively establish a Japanese protectorate over all of China.

Donald seethed with outrage as he read and re-read.

He then gave copies of the 21 Demands to the US and British ambassadors, to compare with their versions received from the Japanese, as well as to some Peking-based correspondents. After the response to his earlier report he didn't feel he owed *The Times* exclusivity, but he produced a report for it as well. The London paper cabled back that his message was held up pending an enquiry, but it mattered little. The full text of the 21 Demands appeared meanwhile in the *Manchester Guardian*, Chicago *Tribune* and English-language Peking papers.

With publication of the full set of demands, Japan had to explain the discrepancy between the eleven demands notified to friendly governments and the longer, more draconian list revealed by the Australian newspaperman. A distinction was drawn between 'demands' and 'requests' in the document. The demands, those shown to the diplomatic circuit, were simply the wash-up of issues already under discussion, the Japanese said. Several additional matters, presented as requests for separate consideration and mutual discussion, had been designated as such when raised with Yuan in January.

While this fiction was presented to the West, Hioki continued in the unreported Peking negotiations to demand acceptance of the whole document. On 8 March, Japan told China it was dissatisfied with progress and if the concessions weren't granted *en bloc*, 'means outside diplomacy might be resorted to'—in other words, force.

China's foreign office contacted Donald and asked him to advise and draft a reply.

Donald asked, 'Why me? Surely you have Dr Morrison.'

The office explained that Dr Morrison was now a paid officer of the government in China. They believed that paid officers only said 'Yes' to whatever the government proposed, and they wanted independent advice which the government had not bought and paid for.

Although he shared China's hostility towards Japan, Donald could see no alternative to submission. China's deep sense of humiliation after the war with Japan and the Boxer Rebellion, along with Japan's likely backing from its wartime allies, Britain and France, made sustained resistance pointless. However, he suggested stalling on the 'Group 5' demands, the most contentious in the document's presentation in five blocks, and asking for a revision of the list there.

The Japanese threat of force was a hollow one, although China wasn't to know that at the time. Sensing the US had concerns about the negotiations, Japan wanted to conclude them as soon as possible. After a note from the US government asked for clarification of the demands that impacted on its interests—China's own interests weren't of great concern—Japan advised it was holding off the Group 5 demands for the time being. Ambassador Reinsch was instructed to tell the Chinese that America had expressed concern to the Japanese about the 21 Demands in discussions that were continuing.

This information put steel in the spine of China's negotiators. They told the Japanese they wanted to see a revised list of demands and it was duly delivered on 26 April, but the Japanese were in no mood to be stalled further. The delays were damaging the Okuma government back home.

On 7 May, Japan issued an ultimatum to the Chinese to accept the modified 21 Demands (five of the seven articles of Group 5 were to be held over and there were minor changes to the other groups) by 6 p.m. on 9 May or Japan would 'take steps she may deem necessary'. Japan, for its part, would return the German-leased territory in Shantung to China. It was similar to the threat of a month before which didn't materialise, but this time the *Lusitania* had been sunk and America's attention was turning towards Europe. China replied the next day that 'with a view to preserving the peace of the Far East', it accepted the amended demands.

Negotiations over the 21 Demands might have come to an end, but the undercurrents they created had not. Britain and the US pressured Japan to drop the postponed requirement of advisers to China's government. On the other hand, the Treaty of Versailles, signed between Germany and the Allies at the end of World War I, granted to Japan control over the former German leaseholds it had relinquished with the demands.

The issue was eventually redressed at the Washington Conference (1921–22) with Japan agreeing to withdraw its forces from Shantung and restore China's sovereignty. It was a belated achievement at the end of a patchy performance of diplomacy. Not caught up in war, America was well-placed to take a firm position with an increasingly aggressive Japan. Instead it prevaricated, setting up a climate of appeasement towards Japan and its militaristic clique that would continue and grow to no-one's benefit, not even Japan's. For the next 25 years, policy towards

Japan would pull in two opposing directions: China wanting to confront its bellicose neighbour and its allies seeking to appease it.

Donald was now a part of China. From this time on, he would regard any action by Japan with mistrust. As far as he was concerned, it was a nation with belligerent and dishonest leadership, despite the regard he had for ordinary Japanese people from the time he was reporting the Russo-Japanese War. This would colour all his future advice to the Chinese where Japan was a factor in the issue. The feeling was mutual. The Japanese had worked out Donald's role in the 21 Demands and would continue to keep a close eye on him as he became involved on the edge of their affairs.

Chapter 8

The day of the warlord

Mary Donald's dislike of China was increasing. Peking hadn't grown on her as Hong Kong and to some extent Shanghai had. It seemed even more alien to her now than when she arrived. Don was always out and about trying to save China. *God knows it needed it!* Roy Anderson's wife had fallen ill and gone home to the States. *No great loss there!* Don was always writing to and visiting Dr Morrison. Maybe she should make an effort to see more of his young wife, who she quite liked, but Jennie Morrison had a baby to look after and another on the way.

Mary, too, fell ill in early 1915 and spent a few weeks in the Peking Union Medical College. From time to time, she suffered wrenching abdominal pain, but the doctors seemed loathe to give her morphine, saying she was progressing 'satisfactorily' and they still wanted to keep her under observation. Don would visit her in hospital and try to buck her up in a clumsy male way. The Morrisons sent her flowers which brightened the room. Finally discharged, she went by train with Don, Muriel and the *amah* to the seaside resort of Peitaiho, but its enjoyment was fleeting. Far too soon, she was back in the house on Tsung-pu Hutung and her husband was once again out saving China.

China had succumbed to malady as well. Yuan Shih-k'ai and his supporters were advocating revival of the monarchy, arguing that the republic was only a transitional phase to rid China of the Manchus. Yuan invited Professor Frank Goodnow, an American constitutional expert, to prepare a paper comparing the merits of republic and monarchy for China. His naive treatise, theoretical and abstract but endorsing a monarchy, was used by the president to promote his interests. Following on the heels of the American's paper, numerous 'petitions' called on the government to return to the old system.

While Sun Yat-sen remained in Japan reorganising the Nationalist Party under his strict control, many of his supporters drifted back to China. Charlie Soong returned with his family, including the recently married Kungs—HH and Ai-ling—and a reluctant Ching-ling. He purchased a modest mansion in Shanghai's French Concession and through the Green Gang's aging leader, Huang Chih-jung—known as 'Pockmarked' Huang—arranged Ching-ling's engagement to the son of a good family. She fought the proposal. Confined by her father to her room upstairs, a letter was smuggled to Sun Yat-sen, who replied with a declaration of how much he needed her. Ching-ling escaped through the bedroom window, sailing that night to Kobe and on to Yokohama. The revolutionary hero and Soong's star-struck daughter married soon after she arrived.

Sun told Ching-ling he had divorced his first wife, but in fact he only considered himself divorced, sufficient for a Confucian. To a Christian, as he professed to be, this was bigamy and Ching-ling was his mistress. Charlie Soong went to Yokohama to confront the couple, but Sun remained stubbornly silent. Soong returned to Shanghai consumed with bitterness, vowing he'd have nothing more to do with Sun. It turned out to be a vow he could easily keep. Sun's supporters blotted Charlie Soong from the revolutionary movement. With no prior indication of poor health, he died in agony of 'stomach cancer' three years later, at the relatively young age of fifty-five.

Yuan Shih-k'ai was determined to press ahead with his imperial ambitions. After the National Assembly endorsed the monarchy with an overwhelming majority, the provinces were prompted to petition in the name of the people that he consent to be emperor. In an ostentatious display of self-effacement he declined, citing lack of virtue, then 'reluctantly' agreed the next day, announcing a new era of the Chinese empire to commence on 1 January 1916 under the unintentionally ironic banner of *Hong-hsien* (Constitutional Abundance).

Yuan's proclamation didn't excite the popular imagination as he expected. It became instead a clarion call for opposition to rally as his sons squabbled over who would be crown prince and his subordinates deserted him to form their own factions. A National Protection Army was formed in Yunnan under its military governor. On 25 December, with Yuan refusing to cancel the monarchy, the province declared itself independent of Peking. As the new army marched north, several other provinces followed Yunnan's lead and a second anti-monarchist army was formed in Shantung.

Delaying his enthronement, Yuan offered two of his generals command of a force to confront the National Protection Army. Both declined. The foreign powers sensed Yuan's weakening popularity and their support for his regime evaporated. The central government's finances were deteriorating, with a soaring gap between expenditure and revenue. With the war drying up European finance, Chinese domestic bonds were issued at 73 per cent discount and funding for the coronation was cut.

Although he hadn't met with Dr Morrison for six weeks, the president received Donald on 18 March, with Roy Anderson translating. In the red, gilded presidential palace inside the Forbidden City, they were shown into a gloomy salon where Yuan was already waiting. Standing in an old velvet coat he'd taken to wearing at all times, their arrival was barely noted. He looked puffy and ill, his breathing asthmatic. Below the coat was a pair of ill-fitting khaki pants and common Chinese slippers. Suffering from toothache, he constantly rubbed his teeth with alcohol-soaked wool wrapped around a chopstick. Grey-haired at 57, he didn't look much like the president of the Republic of China or its would-be emperor.

Sitting with arms spread on a solid wooden table, his stumpy body slouching forward in a shabby ornate armchair, Yuan motioned feebly with one hand towards two chairs opposite. After a brief exchange of platitudes, Yuan wheezed that his military and political opponents were retreating. He would soon be able to resume his enthronement plans.

Donald wasn't one to mince words, even with a president. With Anderson translating, he corrected Yuan: the provinces were in open revolt and China was in danger of breaking up.

'Only seven of the provinces are unhappy,' the president replied.

The Australian corrected him again. 'Seventeen. You must abdicate if you care about what happens to China. You have to stop this make-believe.'

Yuan Shih-k'ai stared into space.

'I am tired,' he said, getting up and shuffling out of the room.

Three days later, Yuan proclaimed the end of the three-month monarchy, reinstating the republic with himself as president. Having made his bid for greatness, many were not interested in him resuming the more modest role of president. Further provinces rebelled as he tried to reassert his authority.

Summer was rolling in. Yuan announced he was too unwell to continue and decided to retire to Tientsin. A request for safe conduct by the British, with their long-standing concession there, got no response. The American ambassador offered guards to accompany him to Tientsin and a destroyer to take him from China, but by then Yuan had changed his mind,

Donald was asked to contact the Shanghai revolutionists, the people creating most of Yuan's problems, and request safe conduct to Tientsin. In Shanghai, Donald found Sun Yat-sen had slipped back into China under cover of an alias and was living with Ching-ling in the French Concession, their house bought from donations to the revolution by overseas Chinese. The Shanghai Nationalists agreed to the president's request, but Donald returned to Peking to the news that Yuan had been found dead in his bed that morning from kidney failure.

Yuan Shih-k'ai had been such a powerful and cunning leader at a crucial point in China's transition from empire to republic, that it's hard to see his contribution to China's political and social development as anything but negative. Historian Immanuel Hsu sums up one view: 'His mockery of the constitution, his illegal manipulation of the parliament, his methods of bribery, coercion, murder, and enslavement were an irreparable affront to public character and morale, and laid the groundwork of lawlessness and disorder in the decade that followed.'

In the long run, however, perhaps Yuan was the strong-man China needed. At the time, Donald, and Morrison even more so, could see the shortcomings in his character, but both being pragmatists, they believed only Yuan could hold together a cohesive enough central government to start China on its journey to nationhood, eventually, as it turned out, to the emerging superpower we see today. To Donald, the end justified the means.

After Yuan died, China was plunged into political chaos. Li Yuan-hung, the reluctant military governor in the wake of the Wuchang uprising, became president. Tuan Ch'i-jui, one of the two generals who declined to lead Yuan's army against the southerners, became premier; the other general, Feng Kuo-chang, was made vice-president. Peking's ability to function as a national government waxed and waned as military governors commanding local armies jostled for dominance. These warlords were mostly commanders in Yuan's armies who had remained in the provinces after dealing with the Second Revolution. Fighting each other for power and prestige—often without much other reason—they created a national instability that would continue for more than a decade as they flexed their various muscles, formed coalitions with other warlords, expanded their territories and were finally pushed back and replaced by rival commanders by either military defeat or, more commonly, betrayal.

•

Early in 1916, Bill Donald and Rodney Gilbert had set up the Pacific Press Agency in their dusty joint office, producing articles about China for America and Britain. Funding from wealthy Chinese exiles through a Japan-based American, BW Fleischer, came in a trickle. Donald and CC Wu of the foreign office, the American-educated son of Wu Tingfang, had each loaned US$3000 to the venture, relying on assurances money was there to repay them, but by the end of the year Pacific Press closed with all involved losing money except Fleischer.

Money was never a high priority for Donald personally and sometimes he would be scratching to make ends meet. While he often provided economic and business advice, it's questionable how much he understood of how money works. Politics and political connections were his strength, requiring a willingness to surf the political waves. The skill was in spotting the right wave.

With the country in turmoil and Donald's political connections lying low, he concentrated on servicing his remaining clients and bringing *Far Eastern Review* out each month. Of concern was his partner's emerging irrational behaviour. Rea turned on the American ambassador's German descent, accusing him of sympathy with Germany in the European war, and of colluding with another German-American looking for trade opportunities and with the WF Carey Company for railway concessions against the interests of Russia, France and Britain. Rea was clearly still smarting from his own failed bid to secure a railway project. Donald threatened to resign if an editorial with Rea's claims was published by the *Review*. It was dropped.

Rea made a special trip to Peking to confront Reinsch, complaining that his ideas had been stolen. The ambassador duly informed the US state department. He'd actually been unable to help the German-American and, as he pointed out, any railway proposal is likely to draw objections from other powers. The publisher, Reinsch said, was 'crazed with hatred and jealousy, because he believes himself overlooked and discarded'. That this was Bill Donald's principal working partner didn't auger well. Donald had a warm friendship with the American ambassador and he didn't want Bronson Rea messing it up.

With World War I in full swing, China sent a labour force of 10 000 to the Western Front to dig trenches and carry out other non-combatant duties for the British Army. A few weeks later, Germany announced its submarines would sink all ships near Britain, no matter what flag they sailed under. The United States, with its public still up in arms about the sinking of the *Lusitania* two years before, broke off diplomatic relations and encouraged other neutral powers to do the same. Paul Reinsch enlisted his friend's help to get the Chinese government to respond to President Wilson's call. In a two-pronged attack, Reinsch met with China's officials and leaders to propose breaking with Germany and aligning with the US, while Donald and Anderson, with close contacts in the Nationalist Party, would put the case to its parliamentary leaders. Prompted by Donald and Reinsch, Dr Morrison spoke to President Li, who he now advised, and found him vacillating on the subject, convinced by German propaganda that the Allies would be defeated.

Premier Tuan was persuaded, however, severing relations with Germany on 14 May without the approval of president or parliament, and seizing all German shipping off Shanghai. When Li dismissed him, several provinces that backed Tuan declared their independence and an army assembled at Tientsin to march on Peking. The embattled president sought help from Chang Hsun, the Manchu general who had been driven out of Nanking in the revolution, but whose pigtailed soldiers had retaken the city in the Second Revolution. Now military governor of Anhwei, Chang and his army of 20 000, funded and armed by Germany, came to defend Peking. Parliament was forced to dissolve, but the old warlord had other plans in mind, old scores to settle.

On a sultry summer night, he attended a banquet with some of his officers, followed by a visit to the theatre. Out-of-towners looking for a good time, the revellers returned late and drunk to their temporary quarters. The time had come, Chang decided, for a return to Manchu rule. After sending some of his men to force Li to sign a decree restoring the Ch'ing dynasty, the 60-year-old general struggled into his old court robes. At 3 a.m., Chang went to the Forbidden City to demand admission to the Imperial quarters.

'There is to be a restoration today,' he slurred, 'and I have to ask the Young Master to come to the audience-hall without delay.'

After some argument, the Grand Guardian appeared with eleven-year-old Pu-i and helped him up onto the Dragon Throne. With the old warrior prostrating himself before the confused boy, voices called out: 'May He reign for ten thousand years!'

Escaping the height of the oppressively hot summer of 1917, Morrison had moved with his young family to the seaside at Peitaiho. On the evening of 1 July, the adviser was dining with Dr Wu Ting-fang, who had briefly succeeded Tuan as premier but had been replaced when he refused to countersign Li's dissolution of parliament. Wu favoured declaration of war so that in the aftermath China would have a voice in the fate of Shantung. During the meal, a telegram arrived: 'EMPEROR RESTORED TWO O'CLOCK DONALD'.

This was impossible, Wu said to Morrison, adding, 'Badness for China if true.' It was true and it might have been badness had it lasted, but it didn't.

The presidential palace had been surrounded by Chang's men, Li having served his purpose. The president managed to slip away to the French Hospital on Legation Street for safety, but the night sister wouldn't admit him. Going on to the home of Japan's military attaché, he was allowed refuge if he didn't involve himself in any political activity. Li agreed because it no longer mattered. He had sent a message to Tuan Ch'i-jui reappointing him premier with instructions to lead the northern army against Chang Hsun.

While Chang busied himself in the capital, General Tuan marched on Peking from Tientsin with an army that had grown to 50 000. Bombs were dropped on the Forbidden City from one of Tuan's aircraft, Asia's first aerial bombardment. Soon after the ground attack began, most of Chang's forces deserted with only 3000 offering resistance. After wild artillery fire for twelve hours, but little fighting and few casualties, the defenders surrendered and Chang sought refuge in the Dutch legation. Restoration of the monarchy had lasted only twelve days.

Pu-i was returned to the Imperial quarters in the Forbidden City, barely comprehending what he'd been through. Li resumed as president and General Tuan as premier, but Li soon stepped down in favour of General Feng. Tuan called a new parliament, rather than reconvene the one dissolved by Li and, on 14 August, China went a step further and now declared war on Germany and Austria-Hungary, this time endorsed by the president and ratified through parliament.

Outraged at Tuan's disregard for the constitution, Sun Yat-sen and deposed members of parliament united six of the southern provinces to establish a military government in Canton. Underpinned by a newly formed Constitutional Protection Army with Sun as its Grand Commander of the Armed Forces—Generalissimo in the Western press—it was no more based on the Provisional Constitution than the Peking government.

Donald watched developments in Peking and Canton with consternation. The dream of a unified China was unravelling in the pursuit of power. The *Far Eastern Review* tried to stay abreast of the changes, but to his overseas clients it was all too untidy and confusing. The focus of their international news was on the war in Europe. His business partner was increasingly in conflict, not only with ambassador Reinsch but with much of the party in power in Peking. Having gone to Washington to put some space between himself and his growing army of detractors, Rea wrote to Donald to announce he'd joined the Intelligence Department of the US Army and was stationed in France. He'd given a Colonel Van Deman access to the *Review*, instructing Donald to provide any information the colonel might request.

Although it meant an increased workload, Donald was quite happy to have a break from Rea. The American had become stridently pro-Japanese, reflected in the articles and opinion pieces he wrote, while Donald had moved in the opposite direction. Nearly half their advertisers were Japanese. Donald had no argument with that—the *Review* needed revenue—but he saw no editorial obligations flowing from it.

In negotiation with the United States regarding China at the time, Japan resisted a secret arms deal with the Tuan government. On 2 November 1917, the Lansing-Ishii Agreement was signed, pledging to uphold an open door policy and recognising Japan's 'special interests' from its proximity to China. The open door was only ajar.

The Chinese felt betrayed by the US priority for Japan's interests over China's, encouraging Japanese ambitions in Manchuria and Shantung. Soon after, Japan reconsidered Peking's furtive request and agreed to supply weapons and military advisers in return for an iron mining concession. Britain's diplomats in China and Japan picked up on the arms deal, but could do little about it. Britain was preoccupied with the war in Europe.

Donald also got a sniff of the clandestine arms deal and applied to the British ambassador, Sir John Jordan, for a letter of introduction to take to Tokyo. Although he knew the Australian was commissioned by the *Manchester Guardian* as an occasional correspondent, the ambassador didn't discover until later that the trip was connected with the arms question. As Donald was inclined to be very outspoken about Japanese policy, his visit was unlikely to be welcomed there. However, that could serve the British desire to unsettle Japan's intentions. 'Any embarrassment caused by his visit,' an internal embassy note said, 'is welcome and we have no responsibility for it.' The newspaperman did manage to irritate a few Japanese officials, but could learn little about the arms deal.

Let off the hook for the time being, Tuan dispatched two of Feng's former officers to conquer Hunan. One of them, Wu P'ei-fu, supported Feng's position and refused to fight, forcing an embarrassed Tuan to resign, but his influence and support in Peking was sufficient for him to remain in cabinet as minister of war, and the government's instability continued.

Heartily sick of the power-grab shambles that China's politics had become, Morrison went to Australia to see his family, staying in touch with Donald through frequent letters. Stopping over in Shanghai, he tried unsuccessfully to contact fellow-Australian, Lionel Pratt. A pathetic letter had come the next day, reading like the end of a long binge and acknowledging the truth of Morrison's earlier reproach for allowing beer to rule his life. Pratt said he would soon cease to trouble friends and enemies, a prediction of imminent death that didn't eventuate. Donald was concerned, with none of Dr Morrison's sanctimony, at the decline of an old Sydney newspaper friend and sailing buddy from Hong Kong days, but he had his own worries to deal with.

Soon after, he went to Japan again to chase up advertisers for the *Far Eastern Review* with spectacular success, although most expected or were led to believe that in return the paper would promote their nation's political and trade interests. Staying on in Japan for treatment of his increasing eyesight problems, he was joined by Mary, glad to get away from Peking for a while. Much of their time was spent at Atami, the hot springs resort on the coast below Mount Fuji. Donald saw several oculists with no discernible improvement and was told he needed a change of climate, outdoor exercise and no reading. He wasn't going to take any notice of the last instruction, managing the *Review* in the continuing absence of Rea and dealing with a rival paper being set up with Japanese assistance by BW Fleisher, his nemesis from the Pacific Press Agency. After six weeks, the Donalds returned home.

The scramble for power in Peking continued to seesaw unabated. General Tuan formed an alliance with yet another warlord, a former bandit from Manchuria, Chang Tso-lin. By February 1918, the pair were prevailing over Feng with the Manchurian's army surrounding Peking, when Feng fell ill. He died later that year.

Resuming his military campaign against the southern government in Canton, Tuan found a growing tide for unifying China through negotiation, not only with Feng's henchmen, but increasingly among his own supporters. With widespread disquiet at Japan funding his army's fight against internal enemies and hiring its officers to train his troops, and with rumours of his secret arms dealings finally surfacing widely, his position was further weakened.

Over this period, Donald was in constant contact with Paul Reinsch, swapping notes on who was doing what within China's hierarchies, reporting conversations, recommending stenographers, delivering parcels to the ambassador's friends in Shanghai. Both were particularly interested in the Consortium of Banks in China, an overseeing body being set up by five foreign powers, including Japan, to strengthen China's credit control and prevent reckless borrowing and misappropriation. Its underlying objective, apart from more profitable trade, was improving conditions in the vast country; a stable, orderly China being less dangerous politically than the opportunistic free-for-all then in play. The Americans also wanted to see reform of industry and railways, a system of open bidding by the powers with abolition of spheres of influence, and reconciliation of the north and the south.

If Tuan's Peking government had its difficulties, Sun's government wasn't faring much better. Many in Canton felt Sun's authority needed trimming and reorganised the administration as a seven-member elected cabinet. Finding himself sidelined by political opponents and military strongmen, Sun moved back to Shanghai. By then he had been joined by Chiang Kai-shek as a military aide.

Erratic and self-centred, despite his insistence on Confucian respect for elders and superiors, Chiang had seen ups and downs since the Shanghai uprising as an associate of Ch'en Ch'i-mei. Ch'en's star had waned as his Shanghai administration became unpopular and by 1916, having engineered assassinations of political rivals, he, too, was assassinated.

Without the anchor of his mentor, Chiang slipped out of control with a debauched life on the fringes of the Shanghai underworld, eventually finding a new patron in the crippled art dealer, Curio Chang. Chang had set up a stock and commodity exchange in Shanghai as a front for Green Gang activities under its new strongman, Tu Yueh-sen, known as 'Big-eared Tu'. Chiang was given a job as a 'broker' on the exchange, involving no real work. He took the opportunity to make quick money and squander it just as quickly, overspeculation losing him US$20 000. It was paid out with the help of Curio Chang and the Green Gang, and the debt was left to be recouped in kind at a later date.

Chiang fell for a Shanghai prostitute working for Big-eared Tu. A friend of 'Pockmarked' Huang's wife, the seventeen-year-old married Chiang in November 1917 after he divorced his village wife. The next month, Chiang went to a Christmas gathering hosted by TV Soong at Sun Yat-sen's Shanghai house and met Soong's vivacious younger sister, May-ling, recently returned from America. Entranced with her and with her connections, Chiang asked Sun to arrange an introduction to his sister-in-law, assuring him he had put his personal affairs in order. He mentioned his divorce, but not his new bride.

'I have no wife now, Teacher,' the would-be suitor said. 'Do you think Miss Soong could be persuaded to accept me?'

Sun said he doubted it, but he would raise it with his wife, May-ling's older sister. Ching-ling was outraged at the suggestion.

•

At the end of World War I in 1918, China believed it should regain its territories leased by Germany in Shantung Province. Having sent the Chinese Labour Corps of eventually 140 000 to the Western Front, China had a seat at the Paris peace negotiations that culminated in April 1919 in the Treaty of Versailles, but the German rights in Shantung were handed to Japan. Promoting the ideals of self-determination, President Wilson was no match for the resistance of the British and French leaders, Lloyd George and Clemenceau, or the US congress.

The May Fourth Movement was ignited, a demonstration in Peking on that day by more than 3000 students voicing its anger at the 'spineless'

Chinese government and America's betrayal. A boycott of Japanese products was called and the home of a cabinet official was set on fire. With protest spreading to Shanghai workers and businessmen and widening to strikes and withholding tax, the Peking government was forced to release arrested students. The Chinese delegation at Versailles refused to sign the peace treaty.

Japan still retained control of Shantung, but the movement radicalised many Chinese intellectuals, turning them from Western liberal democratic ideals to Marxism. It became a fork in the road for China's republicans. Chiang Kai-shek and Sun Yat-sen were not among those swept up in the events, criticising the movement for corrupting the morals of youth. Like many of the Westerners operating in China, Donald was not drawn down the path of Marxism, but remained a staunch supporter of the Western model.

Bronson Rea had been at the Paris peace talks as an unofficial adviser to the Chinese delegation, but remained with the US Legation in Madrid after the war rather than return to China while Reinsch was still ambassador. After the talks he fell out with the Chinese, complaining they hadn't paid him for his work, went to New York and disappeared from sight. When he resurfaced, it was clear why the Chinese were not happy with him in Paris.

At the Paris talks, Rea met privately with Yokohama Specie Bank's Masunosuke Odagiri, who he had previously known as Japan's consul in Shanghai. Rea's attitude towards Japan was already changing before the war, after attacking it in *Far Eastern Review* over the 21 Demands, but by 1919 his conversion was complete. Denouncing America's befriending of China at the expense of Japan, he wrote a monograph, *The Breakdown of American Diplomacy in the Far East*, defending Japanese policy, and sent it to all and sundry.

Rea began filing strongly pro-Japanese articles, the first of which Donald dropped. Rea argued that the *Review* should change its support since Fleischer's rival paper, the Japanese-financed *Trans-Pacific*, had Chinese government advertising and US government endorsement. The *Review*, he said, would be doing no more than adopting the policies of these two governments. Donald published some articles under Rea's byline with a disclaimer by the paper, and some went unpublished.

A *Peking and Tientsin Times* journalist traced Rea's about-face to his meeting with Odagiri in Paris, noting 'his views have undergone a very remarkable change—a tribute indeed to the persuasive powers of Mr Odagiri'. Others concluded Rea was on Japan's payroll to turn America around, observing that he was under considerable financial pressure from alimony payments and little income from either his newspaper or the Chinese in Paris. A US state department China-watcher wrote, 'Rea's own statements to me and to others in my office left no room for doubt that he has simply been seeking a more generous paymaster.'

Dr Reinsch resigned late in 1919 and Rea returned to Shanghai. It was a tense time for Donald while he remained editor of *Far Eastern Review*, but that wouldn't be for long. The joint editors were quite different personalities, one a rambunctious bull-at-a-gate, the other a brooding intriguer. When they worked productively together, each was able to harness the other's boundless energy and single-mindedness, but when they went in different directions, it couldn't continue. Donald's increasing distrust of everything the Japanese did was at irreparable odds with Rea hitching his wagon to Japan and promoting its imagined destiny.

For three months in a row, Rea's pro-Japanese articles appeared in the *Review*, attacking ex-ambassador Reinsch and US policy in the Far East. Donald had cabled Rea that he would resign if he insisted on publishing such articles. In February 1920, he put a disclaimer on the front page: 'The Editor does not necessarily accord with or support opinions expressed in signed articles appearing in the *Far Eastern Review*. Any expressions of opinion on subjects dealt with by this paper will, if signed by the writer, be published.'

By the March edition, Donald had decided it was time to part ways. A statement on the front page notified readers: 'The complete reversal of the policy of the *Far Eastern Review* effected by its publisher, Mr. Geo. Bronson Rea, in the course of recent months compelled its editor—the undersigned (in the February issue) to disclaim responsibility for views expressed by writers of signed articles. The receipt of further similar articles which the undersigned cannot endorse cause him to withdraw from his position as editor of the *Far Eastern Review*. W.H. Donald.'

Bill Donald's life was in turmoil. He had become something of a man about town but, far from joining in, Mary rightly or wrongly felt excluded and had grown resentful of the expatriate community. She would claim, late in her life and embittered about the marriage, that Don became 'a ladies' man' and his women 'spoiled him', whatever that might mean. Her husband did a great deal of work for no recompense and that added to her chagrin. She felt people used him.

Mary continued to dislike Peking and its foreign-ness, yearning to be somewhere she could feel she fitted in, somewhere more British perhaps. She wanted the family to move, at least to Hong Kong if not back to Australia, but Don wasn't listening. He saw his mission and his future in China and remained steadfastly on that course.

'If you're not happy with China,' he told her, 'perhaps you should leave it.'

And she did. With ten-year-old Muriel in tow and stopping briefly in Shanghai, she stayed in Hong Kong for several months with old friends she hadn't seen for nearly ten years. Probably Mary hoped that her husband would wake up to himself and follow her there. Perhaps he thought a break in the colony would dispel her rancour and she would return. Either hearing or imagining he had 'made a fuss to his lady friends' that she had robbed him of his child, Mary sent Muriel from Hong Kong for a visit. In three weeks she was back, with Donald saying he 'couldn't stand her fussing for her mother'.

Donald didn't come to Hong Kong and Mrs Donald never returned to Peking. On 25 May 1920, Mary Donald and Muriel boarded SS *St Albans* for Sydney.

•

After James Gordon Bennett died in 1918, the *New York Herald*, already distracted by the war in Europe, lost all interest in China and its incomprehensible politics. Donald was still friendly with David Fraser, through whom he'd developed an interest in horse-riding, but he was still mightily put out by *The Times* distrust of his reports on the 21 Demands and, three years later, after another report about Japan's aggressive behaviour, the cabled reprimand: 'YOUR ATTACK ON ALLY HIGHLY INDISCREET

STOP OBLIGED SUPPRESS GREATER PART OF MESSAGES STOP AVOID WASTING MONEY ON DIATRIBES UNPUBLISHABLE PRESENT CONDITIONS TIMES'. On top of that, *The Times* quibbled endlessly about payments.

He'd abandoned his Australian newspaper clients—or they'd given up on him—and of his other overseas papers only the *Manchester Guardian* provided a trickle of reporting commissions. Apart from three servants, Donald now occupied an empty house, which he was thinking of selling to move back to Shanghai. He might have been planning to follow Mary or he might have thought Shanghai a better city to revive his career, but it never happened anyway. The Chinese government asked Donald, through its minister of finance, Chow Tzu-chi—Donald's friend 'Old Joe'—to set up a Bureau of Economic Information. He'd always complained about the lack of facts and figures about China and here was an opportunity to rectify that.

The bureau was backed by China's Maritime Customs and the Ministry of Finance with monthly funding of 2000 Mexican dollars, a currency then in circulation in China, but soon after, Old Joe lost office and the ministry never paid its part of the funding. However, it was an enterprise to which Donald could give wholehearted commitment and handpick his staff. George Sokolsky, the American son of a Russian-speaking rabbi, had joined the Russian Revolution as a supporter of Kerensky and fled to China a bitter anti-Communist. Herbert Elliston was a different kettle of fish, a young Yorkshireman who had left the British Army and come to Shanghai in 1919 to work for the *Shanghai Times*, but left when he found it was Japanese-funded. Elliston would edit the *Chinese Economic Monthly* for the next seven years. Donald also recruited a number of attractive European women to the staff. It was a new challenge giving him a new lease of life. 'Get the facts' said a sign he put up on the office wall.

Although into middle-age—he was now 45—Donald put his domestic discord behind him and soaked up the bachelor life, meeting regularly for drinks with his American friends, Rodney Gilbert and Roy 'the Admiral' Anderson. He became a conspicuous social figure within the expatriate whirl of Peking. Although still teetotal, Donald was a gracious host, providing French wines, Scotch whiskey and Cuban cigars for his guests, along with a collection of records for dancing or listening.

In the late afternoon, he was often at the Wagon-Lits Hotel or the Hotel de Pekin, where the band played the fashionable two-step and Boston. The greying sandy hair and prominent nose of the Australian was a familiar sight on the dance floor, always gliding, as if he hoped the music would never stop, like some latter-day Nero while China burned. When the music inevitably stopped, he would continue its momentum with chat, recounting things he'd done and places he'd seen, tales of extraordinary happenings in the new China . . . But where was the new China going?

Donald and Anderson had developed an interest in the Far Eastern Republic, set up in 1920 as a buffer between the new Soviet Republic, which controlled it, and territory occupied opportunistically by Japan during the Russian civil war. Nominally independent, it forestalled a Japanese intention for a similar puppet state and Japan instead pulled back its troops. Through a Russian journalist, Donald met the head of the Russian Far Eastern mission, Ignatius Yourin, in its reception room.

'Mr Khodorov says you're from the Far Eastern Republic, not Bolshevist Russia,' said Donald, getting characteristically straight to the point.

Yourin nodded.

'No matter which,' his visitor continued, 'it's significant in the new politics.'

Donald offered an informal exchange of any inside information that either he or they might come across. The Australian's ability to keep abreast of the changing shape of China's politics depended on such arrangements, but he was also interested in business opportunities for himself and Anderson in the new republic. Yourin introduced him to Marc Kasanin as his contact at the mission.

Donald brought his American friend to discuss oil exploitation in the Far Eastern Republic. They visited the republic in mid-1921 looking at opportunities for the Admiral's American contact, the Sinclair Oil Company. Anderson, with Donald's assistance, was constantly advising Americans on potential mining ventures, but little came of the Sinclair venture, or of Oriental Mines' iron prospect, or of Newmont Mining's interest in Yunnan tin.

A frequent visitor to the republic's mission, Donald sometimes dropped by for no purpose other than staying in touch and reminding them of his existence. Once, he arrived at the reception room with the exquisitely gowned Princess Ghika of Romania, soon to return to the salons of Paris and share her impressions of Asia. Donald, it seemed to the fascinated Kasanin, appeared everywhere. He would often see him on horseback with a Chinese society lady and if spotted by the Australian would be greeted with an upraised palm like an Indian in a cowboy movie.

Since the fall of the regime in 1917, tsarist envoys had no formal authority in China, but it was convenient for a while for both governments to operate as if they did. Prince Kudashev, a pompous former tsarist diplomat, occupied the embassy quarters with his staff as representative of the Provisional Government of the Soviet Union, although he no longer appeared much in public. It couldn't last and it was useful to the Far Eastern Republic's representatives to know as soon as it was terminated.

Kasanin caught sight of the ubiquitous Australian one evening on the Hotel de Pekin dance-floor. Donald nodded and raised his hand in the familiar greeting. As he circled the floor and passed Kasanin's table a couple more times, he repeated the gesture behind his dance partner's back.

'Strange behaviour,' thought the Russian.

A Chinese waiter came to his table, fiddling with bottles and glasses and, screened by his body, slipped a note in front of Kasanin. Handwritten in English and unsigned, it said, 'An hour ago the President signed an order depriving Prince Kudashev of recognition.'

Kasanin glanced up and once more Donald glided past, palm raised behind the young lady's back.

After the death of Dr Morrison in May 1920, his widow decided to sell up and return to England. Knowing the Far Eastern Republic was expanding its mission, Donald dropped by to interest them in taking over the lease of the Morrison house and buying its sumptuous furnishings. Yourin gave the Australian cheques for US$15 000 to be handed over when the police in conjunction with the foreign office approved the mission occupying the house. Donald meanwhile hunted around on Jennie Morrison's behalf for a buyer for her late husband's valuable book collection.

For more than two weeks, Donald was given the runaround by both police and the foreign office, one claiming the request had been passed to the other and the other denying it. He even had lunch with the latest foreign minister, Dr Yen, but nothing came of it. The Japanese had objected and no-one in the foreign office was prepared to stand up to them. Two months later, Yourin moved his mission into a different house where the rent was lower and the owner had more political pull.

In the shifting sands of Peking political fortune, the Manchurian warlord, Chang Tso-lin, switched allegiance from Premier Tuan to Wu Pei-fu, the northern general sidelined by Tuan. The premier found himself caught between Wu's army marching on Peking from the middle Yangtze and the Manchurians coming from the north. His army quickly overcome, he fled to the Japanese concession at Tientsin.

Campaigns between northern warlords were mostly fought on the north China plain outside Peking, whose size and foreign legations prevented it from becoming a battleground. But the signs of fighting were familiar in the city: distant cannon fire, and soldiers marching out in uniforms of varying shades of grey-green. Supplies and communications were disrupted. Newspaper hawkers shouted out the latest rumours. When they saw shuttered shops and empty marketplaces but streets crowded with refugees and defeated soldiers, foreigners knew hostilities had temporarily ended and a new regime had been installed.

Donald's personal life post-Mary was also one of shifting fortune. Apart from cementing his reputation as a man-about-town by chaperoning society ladies, the middle-aged bureau head became infatuated with a young American on his staff and intensely jealous of her male friends. Through Anderson, Donald had met Harold Hochschild, sent by his father's business, the American Metal Co, to collect a defaulted payment for silver shipped to the Canton Mint. On a night out at the Hotel de Pekin with Anderson and Donald, Hochschild met the young woman and offered her a lift home in his taxi. When they got to her house, she invited him in, suggesting he let the taxi wait. They chatted for an hour and then he departed. She later told him Donald had followed them and paced up and down on Peking's old city wall above her house until Hochschild left in his taxi.

The Australian was acting for David Fraser when Lord Northcliffe, owner of *The Times*, came to Peking in November 1921. Summering with his family at Peitaiho, Fraser was talking of retiring and Northcliffe sounded out Donald's interest in the position over dinner. The newspaper proprietor had picked up British concerns in China about Japanese intentions and commented that Donald hadn't kept his paper informed. Shown the telegram from the foreign editor's office instructing Donald to cease criticising Britain's ally, Northcliffe made a show of cabling Wickham Steed to sack the man responsible. It didn't matter. Donald declined the position, agreeing instead to write occasional pieces as a special correspondent, and David Fraser continued in Peking for several more years.

The administration of *The Times* in China was more settled than the administration of China. In 1922, Wu turned on Chang Tso-lin and drove him out of Peking back to Manchuria, which stayed independent of the northern capital under its warlord. Li Yuan-hung was restored as president, but by the end of 1923 he'd also been driven out of office.

In the south, the progressive warlord Ch'en Chiung-ming forced the militants from Canton and invited Sun Yat-sen to return as president. Ch'en respected Sun's inspiration and writing, but considered him an impractical idealist and his planned military expedition to Peking to unify the country ill-conceived. Sun's military aide, Chiang Kai-shek, was regarded as an upstart. Ch'en favoured a federation of warlord provinces with Kwangtung as the model.

With neither Ch'en nor the Western powers interested in supporting his military campaign, Sun turned to the Soviet Union, fresh from its own revolution. The Soviets provided scathing attacks on Western imperialism and, as an insurance policy, offered support simultaneously to both Sun's Nationalist Party and the newly formed Chinese Communist Party (CCP).

Leaving the Canton administration in the hands of corrupt incompetents, Sun headed north with the Northern Expedition armies. The title generalissimo didn't necessarily make him a military strategist and progress was slow. In any case, word came that Ch'en had moved his forces into Canton and dismissed Sun's officials.

Scurrying back to their hillside residence in Canton, the generalissimo and his wife were bombarded during the night by Ch'en's troops. Sun escaped to Whampoa fort down the Pearl River, while Ching-ling had to flee on foot across the countryside to join him. Their house was burnt down, destroying all his manuscripts except his letters to the Soviets asking for aid. They were passed to the *Hong Kong Telegraph* to worry Sun's conservative backers in the overseas Chinese community.

After cabling Chiang Kai-shek to come to his assistance, Sun sent gunboats up the Pearl to shell the Bund, following in his own boat into a barrage of shore guns before turning back. For the next six weeks, Sun, Chiang and their wives lived on a gunboat moored just off the British concession while Chiang organised a few half-hearted sorties ashore. With little achieved, they were given safe conduct by the British back to Shanghai, Chiang now established in Sun's mind as his loyal right-hand man.

A mercenary army, hired with funds solicited from overseas Chinese, drove Ch'en's army from Canton. Sun returned, settling into a fortified cement factory on Honam Island opposite the Bund, but his troubles were far from over. The mercenaries camped in and around Canton demanded to be paid. Insurance against a Ch'en counterattack, they were encouraged to steal and run gambling and protection rackets. Merchants were forced to provide 'loans', jobs were auctioned, and special duties were put on every enterprise. When they attempted to seize customs revenue, with which the Peking government paid foreign indemnities and loan interest, Sun found himself confronted with warships brought in by the foreigners who ran China's customs service.

Rebuffed by the US and Britain, Sun took up a Russian offer of more money and arms. Now a general, Chiang Kai-shek was sent in August to Moscow where he inspected Red Army units, military schools and Kronstadt naval base. He met Leon Trotsky and bought a Chinese translation of *Das Kapital*. Impressed by the discipline of the Red Army and the fear instilled by the state security organisation, Cheka, he got a surfeit of revolutionary advice but resisted joining the Communist Party, finding Russia drab and alien. The Communists were bitterly fighting each other. Comintern (Communist International) would not provide military aid to Sun's northern campaign, believing the Nationalist Party had first to develop an army and win over the masses. Chiang returned to China and told Sun the USSR would provide advisers and funding, but their aim was to legitimise China's Communist Party. His warning fell on deaf ears.

By the time Chiang returned, Comintern's Mikhail Borodin was already in the south organising Sun's party along Leninist lines and helping set up an army. The 39-year-old Borodin—his real name, Mikhail Gruzenberg—was a charismatic personality, tall and thickset with a heavy moustache, scarred face and deep bass voice. In a cautious alliance, Borodin thought Sun matched poor political judgment with high self-esteem, calling him an 'enlightened little satrap [provincial governor]'.

The Russian proposed a military academy at the fort on Whampoa Island, 15 kilometres down from Canton. Set up with money and arms from Moscow, it would give the Nationalist Party muscle and free it from the plague of mercenaries. Chiang was a driving force in setting up the academy, basing it on Red Army training, Japanese military strategies he had learned as a cadet, and Chinese tradition. Where once the object of war had been to make a lot of noise and reach a settlement, the prime strategy to be taught at Whampoa was killing enemies.

Chiang headed the new academy and became chief of staff of the Nationalists' southern army. Military instruction was combined with ideological instruction, with party leaders like Wang Ching-wei and Hu Han-min as political instructors. A young Communist named Chou En-lai, recently returned from France, was appointed deputy political director, but Whampoa proved less revolutionary than the Russians had hoped. Many of the cadets were sons of landowners and officials, nationalistic but not always leftist. A strong anti-Communist group grew within the academy which would in time become grist for the mill of Chiang's ambitions. His leadership at Whampoa would enable him to cultivate a cadre of young officers loyal to both the Nationalist Party and him.

Having set up business operations in Peking without even the Shanghai paper to bring him regularly to that city any more, Donald had lost contact with Sun Yat-sen. Events unfolding in the southern republic would eventually roll north and draw the Australian into them, but Sun would be gone by then. Donald was occupied with the Bureau of Economic Information and the occasional pursuit of mining ventures with his corpulent American friend, none of which seemed to go anywhere.

He got more return on his ventures into Peking social life as a 'confirmed bachelor'. Renowned as a host, Donald rented a former Imperial hunting lodge in the Western Hills, a rugged mountainous area on the outskirts of the city from where he could gaze at sunlit dust, smoky white, lifted from unpaved Peking streets by a hot midday wind. He bought a Locomobile roadster to get out there, when the few with motorcars owned a sedan or a limousine. Sleek and spacious, with a dicky seat in the back and a roof that could be folded away, Donald's car had two chauffeurs: a driver, and a coolie as footman and car-watcher.

American journalist, Edna Lee Booker, was one of several at a house party hosted by Donald at the 'temple', as he liked to call it. She wrote that the guests dined by candlelight in evening dress, beautifully served dishes complemented with 'appropriate' wines. The 'four-day picnic' included daytime rides on donkeys over the hills, trundling along paths cut through forested rocky slopes, past staring children in smocks and tall layered pagodas buried inside high-walled villages.

At home, Donald was looked after by a wizened little Chinese *amah*. They spoke in pidgin English, common enough in Hong Kong and even Shanghai, but rarely heard in Peking. She bossed him around ferociously and he always obeyed, generally making a joke of it. He had a cook as well who was rarely seen about the house, but the meals always appeared, even at the lodge in the Western Hills.

But an edge to Donald's good humour is revealed in letters to the Rathvons in rural New York, friends from his married days in Peking. In November 1923, he wrote he'd run his car into a lamp-post avoiding a boy with a rickshaw and tram tracks were being laid in Peking's streets. As an afterthought, he confessed he would 'be out on the hills as of yore on Christmas, alone, of course, but still in the good company of memories and thoughts of the might have been'.

In the first half of 1924, Donald went to the US and Britain on a business and medical trip, both his teeth and his eyes needing the attention of Western specialists. He had met Kermit Roosevelt, son of former US president Teddy Roosevelt, in Peking and travelled with him and his mother on the Trans-Siberian Railway. In London, *The Times* had been notified of his intended visit by Fraser. Donald, he said, was 'one of the cheeriest of fellows, adored by the Chinese although he doesn't speak their language and is a severe critic of their faults', but he had close contacts on both sides of China's political fence and was a 'warm empire patriot', always ready to help, often at inconvenience to himself. David Fraser might have seen him as a colleague to be treasured, but to the mandarins of *The Times* he was just a colonial blow-in to be patronised.

Over several weeks in New York with China friends, including Harold Hochschild, Helen and Peter Rathvon in New Rochelle, and the Roosevelts on Long Island, Donald had his long-neglected teeth repaired in a sequence of visits and his eyesight problems treated by further specialists. By the time he returned to Peking, the Manchurian warlord Chang Tso-lin was vying for control of the capital and its government, and Anderson was in Moscow discussing oil rights in North Sakhalin for Sinclair Oil. Nothing stood still in Donald's world.

The northern government continued its game of alliance and betrayal through 1924. While Wu led an army from Peking to do battle with Chang's army in Manchuria, the commander of Wu's Third Army, General Feng Yu-hsiang, mutinied and took over Peking. Tuan, brought back to head a provisional government, invited Sun Yat-sen, now in failing health, to come to Peking to discuss peace and the unification of north and south. Although Sun arrived to a warm welcome from a huge crowd, he thought Tuan insincere in seeking unity and made contact with Chang to offer an alliance in his ongoing war with Wu. The Manchurian wasn't interested, referring to the Nationalist Party as 'the cancer of China'.

Sun was complaining of abdominal pains when he got to Peking and, after fainting, entered the Rockefeller-funded Peking Union Medical College (PUMC) on New Year's Eve. Diagnosed with terminal liver cancer, he was moved to the home of Wellington Koo, a diplomat and Nationalist Party associate who had briefly been premier in the Peking regime the year before.

Sun wasn't the only Chinese politician in bad health. In February, Chow Tzu-chi returned to Peking with an abscess in the groin which Hong Kong doctors had discovered and recommended lancing. He was met at the railway station on a bitingly cold day by Donald and Anderson, the health-conscious Donald in a heavy overcoat, but Anderson without a coat. Up at his lodge in the Western Hills, Donald later phoned Anderson to find him in bed with a cold and a fever.

Doctors at PUMC lanced Chow's abscess but a few days later it grew worse and he was treated at the insistence of his dominant concubine by a Chinese herbal doctor. Donald came down from the hills to see Old Joe, bringing a box of cigars with him. They smoked together, mostly in silence. Chow was clearly in a bad way.

As his visitor got up to go, Chow said weakly, 'You take the cigars, Don. I won't be needing them.'

Next morning, Chow's nephew rang Donald to tell him that Old Joe had died overnight.

It was the beginning of a bad month. Calling next door to pass on the sad news, Donald arrived as Anderson was leaving, wrapped in a big blanket and looking pale and haggard.

'Pneumonia,' the big American wheezed. 'I'm going to the French Hospital.'

Having heard Sun had been brought back to the PUMC and was sinking, Donald hurried there and chatted to the dying man for a short time, at the same time concerned that Anderson seemed to be making little progress. He rang the French Hospital and was told doctors held little hope for the American. Horrified, Donald rushed down to the Catholic hospital, opposite the American Legation, to the bedside of his close friend of fourteen years. Although only 46, Anderson looked old and tired, his breathing, never easy, even more laboured than usual. A doctor was trying to bleed him to relieve the pressure on his lungs, the blood coming out sluggishly, almost congealed.

'That finishes me,' said Anderson, lapsing into unconsciousness. He died a few minutes later. It was twenty past six in the evening.

Donald stood by the bed, stunned. His brain numb, his body immobile while medical staff fussed over their lost patient, he wasn't even sure what to feel, so devastating was his loss. The duo—Don and the Admiral—had finished their adventuring, pulling down the shutters on their business. He walked slowly out of the ward, out of the hospital and over to the home of Wellington Koo.

On 12 March 1925, nine hours before Roy Anderson's laboured breathing ceased, Sun Yat-sen succumbed to his cancer at the age of 58. He had been an ineffective administrator and a frustrated dreamer who believed he had failed in his mission to unite post-Imperial China. In many ways, he was the victim of his personal shortcomings. Like Yuan Shih-k'ai, he was a political manipulator and a hypocrite, but also like his nemesis he held China on the path fate had determined for it when it was in danger of falling apart and collapsing backwards into the old dynasty or worse. For all his faults, Sun provided inspiration for the republican movement when no-one else was able to do that. Ironically, he is now one of the few figures well-regarded in both Communist and Nationalist China. WH Donald is another.

Bill Donald was inconsolable. Working feverishly at the Bureau of Economic Information, he wouldn't go anywhere for some time, making no attempt to maintain his status as Peking bon vivant and man-about-town. The gloss and excitement had gone out of his world, leaving him with a leaden greyness, his friend's death a salutary reminder of his own mortality. About to turn 50, his eyesight was troublesome, his teeth in bad shape. He had been treading water for a few years as the China on which he'd pinned so much faith fell into the hands of the venal and the incompetent. Nothing seemed to hold much attraction.

However, the dark clouds slowly separated and Donald recovered some of his spirit, though never all of it. He got about business, made new contacts, found new friends, discovered new recreations, but he'd left the Peking *beau monde* behind. He was an older, greyer man now with older, greyer pursuits.

Intruding into his greyness came a spectre from the past that still wandered ambivalently on the perimeter of his thoughts. When Roy Anderson's widow came to China to settle the Admiral's affairs, she told Donald she had run into his estranged wife on the ship to Shanghai. Arriving in March 1925, Mary wrote to her husband that she wanted to see him. She didn't explain why, but he assumed it was to seek a divorce and had decided to agree to it. In mid-May, she wired that she was about to return to England and asked if he could come to Shanghai.

'I have not come out in a belligerent mood,' she wrote, 'nor do I wish to seek a reconciliation or rake up unpleasant things.'

Donald responded that he couldn't get to Shanghai at that time and thought it unnecessary and inadvisable. Mary left China without pursuing the matter further and her husband got on with re-immersing himself in China's public life.

The US delegation to the Chinese Customs Tariff Conference was headed by Silas Strawn, a Chicago lawyer with a letter of introduction from Harold Hochschild. Strawn saw the Australian regularly and valued his advice about Chinese matters. At that time, Donald had taken under his wing a young Naval Academy graduate, Jimmy McHugh, in China to learn the language. In his mid-twenties, McHugh had become honorary secretary of the Peking Golf and Country Club and Strawn, a keen golfer, gave Donald a set of golf clubs. The three of them played most afternoons, sometimes going out to the Western Hills course in Donald's roadster. It was an opportunity for Donald to rediscover some of life's delights even if, as Strawn reported to Hochschild, 'he whacked around the fairways in a pretty horrible manner'.

McHugh went home in May 1926 and returned six months later to work with the US Naval Attaché, Captain George Pettengill, a grizzled old destroyer commander. Silas Strawn had gone, but Donald, Pettengill and McHugh became the new afternoon regulars on the golf course. For Pettengill, Donald was a fund of inside information about Chinese politics and he paid him informally for it.

The Australian also befriended newcomers to Peking from his homeland. Harold Timperley, a journalist from Western Australia with bright blue eyes, wavy blond hair and refined tastes, had joined Reuters in Peking. His association with Donald would last for the next decade and longer. Henry Gullett, a former immigration head for Australian prime minister Billy Hughes, and with political ambitions of his own—he would eventually become minister of external affairs in the first Menzies government—came to China and was taken to Manchuria and western China by Donald, by then on good terms with the warlord Chang Tso-lin.

The northern government continued to play musical chairs. By 1926, Wu had made a truce with Chang and the pair joined forces against the turncoat Feng and drove his army back through the Nankow Pass to the north-western provinces. Feng announced his 'retirement' from public life and took the train to Moscow. Chang stayed in Peking consolidating his position with alliances with warlords from Shantung and central east China.

Funeral ceremonies for Sun Yat-sen had been held around the country and, after lying in state in a traditional carved hardwood coffin for two weeks, his body was carried in procession through the streets of Peking to the Temple of Azure Clouds in the Western Hills. With no clear heir as the southern republic's leader, there were three main contenders, all powerful figures on the Central Committee of the Nationalist Party: Wang Ching-wei, a dashing orator with wavy pomaded hair; Hu Han-min, slim and bookish, without Wang's magnetism and indifferent to corruption; and Liao Chung-k'ai, the leftist political commissar at Whampoa and governor of Kwangtung. Hu had worked closely with Sun, but Wang had Borodin's backing and became leader. Hu had to settle for foreign minister and Liao was minister of finance. Chiang Kai-shek, considered rough and provincial with no ideology to guide him, wasn't thought to be a contender despite his military power.

•

In May 1925, a striking worker at Shanghai's Naiga Wata cotton mill was shot and killed by a Japanese foreman, triggering a summer of labour unrest and anti-foreign demonstrations. Two weeks later, at a large Communist-run protest about the municipal council's failure to arrest the foreman, a junior British police officer—his commander was in the Shanghai Club—ordered his Sikh police to fire into the crowd, killing eleven. The unrest escalated as strikes, boycotts and demonstrations spread to other cities. In Canton, 52 protestors were killed by French and British machine guns, leading to a protracted general strike in Hong Kong, a siege of Western concessions on Canton's Shameen sandbank and a boycott of British products.

On 20 June, five gunmen stepped from behind the columns of a Canton building and shot Liao as he got out of a motorcar for a Central Committee meeting. The rumour mill pointed at Hu Han-min, even though he had been a close friend of Liao for twenty years, and he fled from Canton with his family, leaving only Wang of the leadership triumvirate but room for a new contender to emerge.

The CCP-dominated General Federation of Labour had become a threat to Shanghai's workers' guilds, operated by the Green Gang. Big-eared Tu, very anti-Communist, sent Curio Chang to Canton to manage a bid for power with Chiang Kai-shek as the frontman. Now confined to a wheelchair with creeping paralysis of the spine, Chang cut a sinister figure with gaunt face, hollow cheeks and thick-lensed glasses, but he was an effective operator.

The reconfigured Canton government, now controlled by Wang, Chiang and Borodin, used Russian money and arms, but Chiang had reservations about Soviet intentions, unearthing what he claimed was a plot to kidnap him and take him to Moscow on the gunboat *Chungshan*. His response was swift: political workers at the Whampoa academy were arrested and Soviet advisers in Canton were put under house arrest. Borodin was out of town at the time. When Chiang declared martial law, the Central Committee tamely passed a resolution that it hoped he would realise his mistake. Wang took no chances, announcing that he had 'taken ill' and leaving for Hong Kong and exile in France.

Several days later, Chiang apologised and released all his prisoners, calling it a 'misunderstanding' for which the responsible officers would be reprimanded. The scenario bore a disturbing resemblance to an extortion method of the Green Gang. By the time Borodin returned from Moscow, he found a new power structure in place and no option but to go along with it. Chiang Kai-shek was named head of the party by the leadership of the Nationalist Party and deputised Curio Chang as chairman of the Central Executive Committee. More importantly, on 5 June Chiang became commander-in-chief of the National Revolutionary Army (NRA), an appointment that would ultimately bring an end to the warlord era and fulfil Sun Yat-sen's unrealised dream of a united China.

Chiang launched the Northern Expedition with the stated aim of ridding China of its warlords and implementing Sun Yat-sen's Three Principles of the People: nationalism, democracy, socialism. The NRA was outnumbered by warlord troops and looked unthreatening in ill-fitting uniforms of grey and dusty yellow, but it was a well-structured army, well-equipped with Russian and German weapons, well-trained and well-led. The Nationalist Party had become a tightly organised political force with public appeal, even if it was fractured internally into left and right. It was now a formidable foe.

With Communist forces in support, Chiang's army drawn from the Whampoa Academy advanced on the northern warlord Wu and his allies in Hunan, capturing the capital of Changsha, then taking the supposedly impregnable bridge across a steep gorge at Tingsiqiao, with peasants guiding the soldiers along a hidden path. Wuchang was besieged for five weeks before capitulating to the NRA in October, while the general defending Hanyang took a bribe and surrendered.

Canton's left-leaning politicians moved their government to Wuhan and were joined by Borodin. They proposed to continue their advance towards Peking, but Chiang turned his army towards Nanking and Shanghai. Pockmarked Huang of the Green Gang came up the Yangtze to meet with him in November, wanting him to eliminate the Communist-led Shanghai trade unions threatening his opium and other criminal enterprises. Soong Ai-ling (now Madame Kung) came by steamer a few weeks later and offered Chiang the support of Shanghai business through her family connections if he appointed her brother, TV Soong, as finance minister and her husband as premier. She warned that without their backing, the left would soon dispose of him. As an added incentive, she would engineer a marriage to her vivacious younger sister, May-ling.

Chiang's determination for a political union—and there was none more advantageous than the Soongs—required his second wife, Chen Jieru, known as 'Jennie', to accept it for the good of China. 'Ai-ling has struck a very hard bargain,' he argued. 'Her offer is the only way for me to achieve my plans to unite China. I now ask you to help me. True love is measured by the sacrifice one is willing to make.'

He proposed Jennie go on a five-year 'study trip'—the pretext used to remove China's failed politicians and bureaucrats from the machinery of government—and he would wed May-ling only as a 'political marriage'. After that, they'd resume their life together. Jennie was shocked, but in no position to bargain. All she could offer was to go back to Shanghai and think about it.

In the New Year, a mob seized the British concession in Hankow, forcing a return to Chinese control and creating a panic in Shanghai's foreign community over the approaching National Revolutionary Army. It was a city on edge with foreign troops rushed in, trenches dug, barbed-wire barricades erected and sandbags laid along the border between the foreign and Chinese quarters. Leaflets fluttered down on Nanking Road and Nationalist flags were hung from balconies in the foreign areas.

An attempt by workers to liberate Shanghai from the warlord Sun Ch'uan-fang in October 1926 had been dispersed with twenty suspected leaders beheaded. The following February, with Chiang's army having entered nearby Hangchow and seeming imminent in Shanghai, 350 000 workers were mobilised. While Chiang's army stayed pointedly in Hangchow, the warlord's execution squads roamed the streets of Shanghai with broadswords. Strikers and leaflet distributors were shot or decapitated indiscriminately. Victims were marched to a prominent square, forced to kneel and were beheaded. Heads were put in bamboo cages hung on telegraph poles. Around them relatives moaned and crying women banged their heads on the ground amid the growing stench of unclaimed decapitated bodies lying in the square.

When it was all over, the National Revolutionary Army resumed its slow progress down the Yangtze, scattering the warlord's army. The Communists still hadn't worked out what was going on and planned a repeat action when the army was on the outskirts of the city. Union members fortified themselves in buildings, raided police stations for weapons and executed suspect employees of foreign firms.

Chou En-lai had come from Canton after the disastrous February strike to take control of the Communist underground, calling a strike of 800 000 workers for 21 March. Shanghai was shut down and workers' militia took over police and military stations, but there were moves afoot to hamstring the planned action. Shanghai's businessmen offered Chiang $3 million to suppress the labour movement and set up a Nationalist government in Nanking. Pockmarked Huang offered the added assistance of the Green Gang.

In a bid to curtail Chiang, the Wuhan government had revoked his emergency powers, but it had little effect. After meeting Huang on the southern outskirts and being introduced to the new Green Gang strongman, Big-eared Tu, as someone who could help the cause, Chiang entered Shanghai on 27 March. He didn't stay long, leaving General Bai in charge while he steamed back to Nanking, now under Nationalist control. Bai's order to the strikers to return to work was ignored. Instead a major rally was called to welcome Wang Ching-wei, opportunistically returning from exile.

Chiang might not have been in town, but he'd made his arrangements and left his instructions. On the evening of 11 April, the labour leader Wang Shou-hua was invited to Tu's house and told to call off the pickets. When he refused, he was beaten up and buried alive. Just before dawn, a siren on a gunboat on the river rang out. Fifteen hundred men in blue uniforms and white armbands inscribed 'LABOUR' fanned out across the city in trucks and armoured vehicles supplied by the British military, attacking trade union strongholds, gunning down pickets and arresting labour leaders.

Prisoners were taken out on the street and shot or beheaded or else marched to Nationalist headquarters for execution. The next day, a huge protest march converged in pouring rain on the Nationalist commander to be met with machine-gun fire. Soldiers pursued the fleeing protesters, bayoneting them and smashing their heads with rifle butts. Tu's men and Nationalist soldiers made house-to-house searches for suspected Communists and labour leaders. For days, trucks rumbled along Shanghai's roads ferrying prisoners. In the three weeks of the purge, known as the White Terror, an estimated five to ten thousand people were killed. If the Communists didn't know before what was happening, they certainly knew now.

Chou En-lai was arrested, but escaped with the help of a sympathetic Nationalist officer he had known at Whampoa, said to be Chiang

Kai-shek. If true, it repaid a debt from when Chou had saved Chiang from violent leftists some years before in Canton. Chou and his wife hid in Astor House for two months, dressed as other guests, until they could be got safely out of Shanghai.

With a Nationalist government in Nanking, there were three capitals and three governments of China: the internationally recognised warlord regime in Peking, the weakening Communist and left-wing Nationalist administration under Wang in Wuhan, and now the right-wing of the Nationalist Party ruling from Nanking. To try to gain the ascendancy, Chiang extracted further funds from Shanghai businessmen to pay his troops and continue the military campaign against the other two governments, applying extortion and intimidation to any who refused. Big-eared Tu and the Green Gang worked to consolidate Chiang's position, with a Tu associate appointed head of the Opium Suppression Board to ensure the Green Gang's monopoly of opium traffic.

While south and central China went through rapid change and the southern armies pressed north, Bill Donald remained in Peking, for once not involving himself in the confusion of China's politics. Although growing more and more disillusioned with the venality and incompetence of the northern government's administration, he didn't have high hopes for its rivals from the south. He wrote to Bert Elliston, by then back in England: 'The Kuomintang [Nationalists] are now trying to settle their differences but it will not last. Nothing can last in China. Even graft will come to its end when everybody is bled white . . . You are lucky to be out of this mess here.'

The Nationalist Party settled its differences to the extent that the militarily weak Wuhan government came to an end with Wang and the left wing of the party surrendering to Chiang and joining him in Nanking. Threatened by the army of Chang Hsueh-liang, son of the Manchurian warlord Chang Tso-lin, Wang made a deal with the northern warlord, Feng Yu-hsiang, who had reappeared in China's power play, to drive them back in return for the demand that Wang expel the Communists from his government and dismiss his Soviet advisers. The Russians in Wuhan were sent home, with Borodin predicting the Communists would go underground for a while, and eventually resurface, but for the time being the main bone of contention between the party's left and right had been removed.

Reconciliation of the factions didn't work as Chiang expected. Many party members were shocked at the bloodiness of the purges and had secret talks with Wang about a new administration, coming to a head with a Military Council meeting proposing to restrain Chiang's command. He left the room, took a train to Shanghai to confer with key supporters and retreated to his home village in Chekiang. Soon after, the Green Gang stopped its funding of the Nanking government.

The deposed leader used the respite to pursue his entrée into the Soong dynasty. A week after he left Nanking, Jennie and two of Curio Chang's daughters sailed to America. Newspapers there reported that Chiang insisted she was not his wife but a former concubine. Finding herself blocked from the Chinese consulate in New York and preparing to throw herself in the Hudson River, she was talked out of it by a passer-by.

Charlie Soong's widow disapproved of her daughter marrying a soldier of humble birth who was not a Christian and was already married; she had an inkling as well of his earlier debauched life. Chiang had to smooth over this obstacle to his ambitions and went to Kobe where Madame Soong was staying at a hot spring resort. He showed her his divorce papers for his first wife, dismissing the allegations about Jennie, and undertook to read the Bible, although he couldn't guarantee to become a Christian from doing so. The matriarch still wasn't enthusiastic but it was sufficient to get her reluctant blessing.

The wedding of Chiang Kai-shek and Soong May-ling on 1 December 1927 took the form of a Christian service at the Soong house followed by a Chinese ceremony in the ballroom of Shanghai's Majestic Hotel, its walls festooned with white roses. The groom entered in formal tail-coat and striped trousers, the bride on the arm of her brother, TV Soong, to the 'Wedding March' played by a Russian orchestra. May-ling wore a silver and white georgette gown, long lace veil and silver shoes and stockings. The couple bowed three times to a portrait of Sun Yat-sen on a platform beside a Nationalist flag. Chiang had achieved his ambition of joining his name with those of Sun and Soong in a political union of seeming limitless possibilities.

In Peking, Bill Donald was aware of the wedding and its general implications, but it didn't greatly affect him. With no idea that this was a union that would come to play a major role in a later chapter of his life, all he could see for the present was China's more immediate political changes that seemed to be achieving very little. In June 1928, Peking was wrested by Chiang's forces from the alliance of warlords controlling it. By December, the Manchurian warlord had pledged allegiance to his government, completing Chiang Kai-shek's nominal unification of China and ending the warlord era. By then, Donald was back in the thick of it. The cavalcade of China's national politics had rolled in and immersed him once more.

Chapter 9

The Young Marshal

Like a scene from a spaghetti western, the father of the Manchurian warlord, Chang Tso-lin, went into a tea-house in a village near his home and watched local men play cards with two strangers. Before leaving, he told one of the locals, 'Don't play for money with these men; they're cheating.'

The strangers followed Chang's father out of the village and killed him. Gathering vigilantes from nearby hamlets, Chang sought out and executed the strangers in retaliation, the gang fleeing into the mountains to avoid further retribution. Manchuria was the wild northern frontier of China.

The Japanese used Chang's brigands to harass Russians during the 1904–05 war and, when it was over, helped him set up headquarters in Mukden. Japan took over Russia's leases in the region, annexing the Kwantung Leased Zone and installing a garrison to protect its interests. It wanted to extend its railway in southern Manchuria to compete with the Russian-operated Chinese Eastern Railway, but Chang wouldn't support the plan. During the 1920s, the Old Marshal, as Chang was called, was governor of the three eastern provinces (Fengtian, Kirin and Heilungkiang), turning his attention to northern China and Peking in the succession of alliances and betrayals that had him alternating between controlling Peking and being driven out.

Despite his failure to support its railway ambitions, the Japanese continued to back the Old Marshal with money and advisers, and Mukden grew into a prosperous industrial centre with an arsenal, power stations and factories. By the late 1920s, they were again pressing for railway concessions, and although his minister assured them he would, Chang wouldn't budge. The Japanese were asking themselves whether the Old Marshal had outlived his usefulness.

Compared with his father, Chang's eldest son was a sophisticate. Educated by private tutors and at ease with Westerners, Chang Hsueh-liang had considered a career in medicine, but either out of respect for his father's ambitions for him or pressured into it, he entered the Fengtian Military Academy instead, graduating as a colonel. He was appointed commander of his father's personal guard at the age of nineteen.

Slim and broad shouldered with deep-set eyes, Chang cut a debonair figure when in Peking. He wore Western clothes with loud ties, played tennis and golf, and was often seen at the races by day and at the Wagon-Lits Hotel on dance nights. One of the first Chinese to wear tweed suits and shirts with a folded collar, he made small talk at cocktail parties and witty banter about women. Chang was a dandy whose decadence should have been more at home in Shanghai than Mukden, but his heart was nonetheless set firmly in Manchuria.

Dismissively called the Young Marshal, the name stuck although its disparaging connotation faded. The Young Marshal shared delicate features with his father but not a great deal else in their sometimes stormy relationship. Often speaking out on policies his father opposed, he was threatened with execution after a failed rebellion by one of the Old Marshal's commanders who happened also to be one of the Young Marshal's friends. His father's older comrades talked him out of it.

Chang Tso-lin's sons spent much of their time in Peking when their father controlled the city. Finding himself short of money, Donald rented his house to one of the younger sons. When he complained to the Old Marshal about the damage caused by his son's frequent wild parties, the eldest son was sent to sort it out and the Australian and the Manchurian became friends. With Donald also a Peking social gadabout at the time, they had much in common, but he could also see character in the young warlord-in-waiting.

By the age of 26, Chang Hsueh-liang was a major-general leading an army across the Yellow River to halt the Northern Expedition marching to unite China. Forced back across the river with substantial losses, he was not happy as a military commander and took to smoking opium. The drug had been previously prescribed by an old-style Chinese medical man for food poisoning. A military doctor tried to wean him off opium with the 'opium cure' pavemal, but instead the Young Marshal became addicted to the cure, a derivative of morphine.

Declaring himself Grand Marshal of the Republic of China, Chang Tso-lin was forced back to Peking by Chiang Kai-shek, then withdrew his troops to Manchuria. It was an opportunity for Kwantung Army officers plotting to assassinate him and install a more amenable warlord. In response to the inevitable Chinese outcry, they would move troops across from the leased zone.

Chang left Peking on 3 June by the night train, reaching the outskirts of Mukden the next morning. As is the Chinese custom when men of rank approach one's city, General Wu, acting governor of Manchuria during Chang's absence in Peking, met the Old Marshal a few stations out of Mukden to accompany him in to his destination. Some Japanese had tried to talk Wu out of it, but wouldn't give reasons. On the outskirts, the line ran under the Japanese-operated South Manchuria Railway. At that point a bomb exploded, killing General Wu instantly and tearing off Chang's leg. The warlord was loaded on a motorcar and taken, bleeding profusely, to his home in Mukden where he died.

The bomb had been planted by junior officers of the Kwantung Army. The Japanese blamed the incident on Chinese nationalists, but the anticipated public outcry didn't materialise. For two weeks, the Old Marshal's death was kept secret while his successor was decided, depriving the Japanese military of the excuse to move in.

When his father was killed, the Young Marshal was stationed near the Great Wall. In the scramble for a successor, the ambitions of his father's chief of staff, General Yang Yu-ting, were held in check while the warlord's son returned secretly to Mukden. He emerged eventually as the new leader of the Manchurian political and military clique with its factional plots and disloyalties. There was much to reform and people to watch closely. Rather than accuse Japan of complicity in his father's murder and provoke a military response, Chang went about a quiet reconciliation with Chiang's Nationalist government.

At this time, things were not going well at the Bureau of Economic Information. It was bad enough under the warlord regimes where one foreign minister had wanted a monthly 'squeeze' of $5000, which Donald declined to pay. Now, China's unified Nationalist government operating from Nanking wanted the bureau to be a propaganda vehicle, unacceptable to its high-principled head. He resigned and escaped to the resort of Peitaiho, where he ran into the new Manchurian leader and Wellington Koo, who had served as foreign minister and premier under Chang's father. Discussing political developments, the three agreed the new central government under Chiang was worthy of support.

Donald moved on to Shanghai. A minister tracked him down, but couldn't entice him back to the bureau where he'd been biding his time while China went through the upheavals of the warlord era. Ready to move on, he wrote to Bert Elliston back in England, 'I am going to do what the average Chinese official does when things get beyond endurance—flee. I shall go to Mukden.' In Peitaiho, the Young Marshal had offered him a position as adviser.

It was winter, December 1928. Donald took a steamer to Dairen and the train on to Mukden. From the ornate South Manchurian railway station, he crossed the large Great Square with its wintery emptiness to look for a car and driver. Having been here several times before, the shoebox trams, the wide streets and Russian Revival architecture of the commercial district were familiar to him, less so the huts and narrow lanes around it. Outside the old walled city, Mukden now had extensive industry built by the Old Marshal with Japanese money. His son lived on the inside with wife, concubine and four children.

Hunched in the chill air, soldiers guarded all approaches to Chang Hsueh-liang's palatial residence, its outer courtyards surrounded by Chinese buildings. Donald was taken through a rough-walled garden alongside two tennis courts to the imposing Western-style edifice built for his new employer's father. The decorative columns of a grandiose portico were repeated in the wall between each window on all three of its floors. On the edge of a rooftop terrace, a balustrade ran along the parapet.

Donald met Chang in the Tiger Room, which had two stuffed Manchurian tigers dominating its dark decor. Since returning to Mukden, Chang had consulted foreign doctors about his drug addiction and was playing tennis and golf daily on their advice, but with little apparent improvement. He looked worse even in the few weeks since Donald had last seen him in Peitaiho and certainly since his Peking days. Emaciated, with sunken cheeks and furtive eyes, Chang was now jumpy with a cold, unresponsive handshake. He spoke with clarity, however, about the problems that plagued his new leadership.

Japan had its sights on the whole of Manchuria, the Young Marshal said. Already holding Dairen and Port Arthur, and 700 miles of railway line in the south which they wanted to extend, they would be watching his moves closely. Russia owned a half interest in the thousand miles of the Chinese Eastern Railway to the north and controlled its operation. Communist union leaders had come in with Soviet workers on the line and Chang sensed trouble from that quarter. The Nationalist government in Nanking was pressing Manchuria to submit to its authority. Equally as problematic were the intrigues within his own government. General Yang Yu-ting, his father's chief of staff, was being groomed by the Japanese, but events had overtaken them.

Donald's sense of the mountain in front of him remained sketchy since, after twenty minutes of talk, Chang left for his daily morphine injection—but it wouldn't stay sketchy for long. Although addiction was starting to take its toll, the Young Marshal's other challenges had their own momentum.

In Shanghai, preparing to move to Mukden, Donald had been visited by an emissary from General Yang and Governor Ch'ang Yin-huei of Heilungkiang who wanted him to raise a £15 million development loan in Britain. Since Manchuria could offer no acceptable security on the loan, he declined. His visitor then produced from his pocket a bank draft of £2000 for the fare to London, thrust it on him and left. Donald had arrived in Mukden with a suspect cheque and cautious of Manchurian political intrigue.

Leaving the Young Marshal, Donald called on Yang to get to the bottom of the proposed British loan. Disinclined to talk and vague about how much the new warlord had been told, the general said Governor Ch'ang wouldn't be down for some months from his headquarters at Tsitsihar in the far reaches of northern Manchuria.

Frustrated by this lack of progress, Donald decided to take the initiative on the elusive matter. He caught the next day's train to Tsitsihar.

Arriving with an interpreter at Harbin, more than halfway to his destination, Donald found a cable waiting for him. Tsitsihar was in the midst of celebrating the New Year, it advised, and he should break his journey until 6 January. While he waited in Harbin—an icy city of émigré Russians, onion domes and tall tented roofs—he wrote down reasons he would not expect a loan or any other assistance from London.

At General Ch'ang's *yamen* with his memo and Chan, his interpreter, Donald was shown into a deserted reception area. They waited, looking around for some sign of interest in their arrival. Angry voices shouted outside in Chinese. Since his arrival in Tsitsihar, everything seemed strange and disconnected to Donald, although Chan was unconcerned. A crash outside suggested something metallic had been knocked over. The governor came in puffing on a cigar, gaping in a disassociated manner and seeming at a loss what to do next.

Donald asked, 'Should we sit down?'

Translated, the question mobilised Ch'ang enough to gesture agreement.

'This says all I have to say about the British loan,' Donald began, handing over his memo.

'I have to go to Mukden,' was Ch'ang's non-sequitur response. 'I waited for you so you could go with me.'

Surprised by Ch'ang's sudden statement, Donald agreed to go, but wondered where the meeting had taken him and what had prompted the unexpected Mukden trip. As the pair left, Ch'ang casually set fire to the memo with his cigar.

The Tsitsihar experience was so disorienting, the Australian was now questioning the wisdom of working in Manchuria. As he had to interrupt his journey at Harbin to pick up his luggage, he told Chan to stay on the train with Ch'ang and find out in Mukden what was going on.

Met by Chan when he reached Mukden's railway station, Donald walked across the Great Square to be sure no-one was eavesdropping. Ch'ang, the interpreter said, was a different man now, very quiet and sober, as if something was troubling him. In his quarters at the Hotel Keining, Donald dictated letters to Yang and Ch'ang, asking to meet the next day and intending to tell them he'd decided to return to Shanghai. Events were moving strangely beyond his comprehension. Donald smelt danger and didn't like it.

At six the next morning, Chan arrived at the hotel full of excitement.

'General Yang's house is surrounded,' he said. 'So is the house where Ch'ang's staying.'

Speculation was rife, with rumours both men had been arrested, but the issues ran deep and their resolution had been final. The two generals had both built private armies and now had Japanese backing. Warned that they were planning a mutiny and that if he didn't move quickly he would soon be disposed of, the Young Marshal decided to confront the alleged conspirators, wiring Ch'ang to come to Mukden for a meeting with him and Yang. That cable had arrived just before Donald arrived in Tsitsihar and the governor had been worried about its implications.

The Young Marshal had ordered production at the Mukden arsenal be scaled back. At a preliminary meeting with General Yang, Chang asked for a report on the arsenal and was told offhandedly it would be brought to the next meeting. Yang's tone and demeanour were disturbing, but that didn't necessarily mean anything. Two days later, Generals Yang and Ch'ang met as arranged at the warlord's grand residence within the walled city. Asked again over dinner for a report on reduction of the arsenal, Yang retorted, 'I'm running the arsenal.'

When the Young Marshal questioned Ch'ang about railway accounts, he was asked scornfully, 'What do you know about accounts?'

Increasingly and aggressively dismissive of their host, the pair demanded he create a position for Ch'ang to take control of the Chinese Eastern Railway, then jointly managed by Chinese and Soviets. Chang said he would have to think about that and, with dinner over, took his guests to a table set up for mahjong.

He excused himself for what the visitors assumed was his morphine injection—as they were supposed to think. As soon as he had gone, his bodyguard barged into the room and summarily shot the two generals. Whatever doubt there might have been about their intentions—and Chang had little now—no longer mattered. A possible problem had been short-circuited with utmost finality and needed no further discussion.

By the next afternoon, it was widely known the two men had been shot at the warlord's home, but all was eerily quiet in Mukden as if nothing untoward had happened. Donald met Chang in the afternoon and went with him to see one of his officials. Nothing was said of the previous night's extraordinary events, but as they passed the house Donald had visited two weeks before, Chang said, 'Poor General Yang!'

On the way back from their meeting, the comment was made again. This time, Donald chose not to ignore it, trying to come to grips with a side of the dandy he'd not seen before. His young friend was a man of contrasts and contradictions, it seemed.

'I've heard a lot of talk about General Yang this morning,' he said. 'Now tell me about it.'

When the Young Marshal had finished his account of the previous evening, Donald told him of the plan to raise British investment, for use after Chang had been assassinated, he now realised. He showed Chang the bank draft for £2000.

'What will I do with this?' Donald asked.

'Keep it.'

'If I keep it,' the Australian said, 'it will be an advance on my salary as your adviser.'

No more was said in Mukden about the deaths of the two generals. It was as if they had never existed, although Donald, ever the newspaperman, cabled a report to David Fraser in Peking to pass on to *The Times*.

Having decided, despite his unease, to stay with the Young Marshal for the time being, the new adviser had to find a way of working with the genial and balding Jimmy Elder, a boyhood friend and confidant of Chang and fluent speaker of Chinese. Born in China of Scottish parents, Elder's father had worked as an engineer, building the Peking–Mukden railway. Initially the younger man resented the intrusion of the newcomer, but over time Elder and Donald forged a working relationship built around their mutual regard for Chang and concern for his wellbeing in the plunder of addiction and Chinese politics.

The Young Marshal also had a Japanese military adviser, but that was to appease Japan. Doubtless his mission was to keep an eye on the warlord for the Kwantung Army. The agreement with his father had been that only Japanese advisers would be appointed. When he was pointedly reminded of this, he responded, 'Mr Donald is my friend, not my adviser.'

It was a quite accurate description. Donald was coupled to the Young Marshal's family, frequently at their residence for work and retiring to the Hotel Keining at the end of the day. It was family life unlike any he had experienced, but he'd been in China long enough to have some understanding of how it worked.

At sixteen, Chang had been married by arrangement to Yu Feng-chih, two years his senior and the daughter of a landowner friend of the Old Marshal. They had four children, three sons and a daughter, but Madame Chang was now addicted to the opium given by her father-in-law to prevent further children. Also living in the mansion was his concubine, Chao Yi-ti, whom Chang had met as a teenager in 1927 at a ball in Tientsin. Wife and concubine accommodated each other, but the set-up was complicated by a second wife. In 1922, Chang had met Ku Jui-yu in Tientsin where she helped with negotiation of a purchase of aircraft from the British. They married two years later and she lived separately in a house he bought opposite the family residence, but the relationship had become strained by the time Donald arrived in Mukden.

Donald added to the puzzle by hiring a striking, dark-haired Russian as his secretary. He had met Irina with her mother on the train to Moscow in 1925, her father and brother having been shot and their land confiscated during the Russian Revolution. Mother and daughter escaped to China, then lived in the US off the sale of family jewellery. Irina returned to Mukden soon after the Old Marshal's death and wrote to Donald asking about work possibilities. Her timing was good, joining him when he set up in Mukden. She spent much of her time at the Mukden mansion, or wherever else Donald and the Young Marshal went, but she had her own separate home.

With internal threats neutralised for the time being, Donald looked into the external threats, starting with the Soviets. Tsarist Russia had built the Chinese Eastern Railway (CER) to shortcut across Manchuria from the Trans-Siberian Railway to Vladivostok. Following the Russian Revolution, agreements were struck between the Soviets and the Peking and Mukden governments, with the railway jointly owned and operated by the Soviet Union and China, although senior management positions were held by Russians. By 1929 there was no longer a Peking government, but Chang Hsueh-liang and Chiang Kai-shek agreed to coordinate their dealings with the USSR.

Profitable for most of its 25 years of operation, the railway had started to lose money through mismanagement and graft. Chinese employees, resenting their junior role, were intent on pushing the Russians out, but Donald advised against the provocation of confiscating the line. If the Russian management was bad, China should propose to manage the railway as trustee for both Russia and China. In the end, the softer option of more equal management of CER was refused by Moscow.

A May raid on the Soviet consulate in Harbin unearthed documents showing it was providing propaganda support through the railway company to the Chinese Communists' struggle with Nanking. The Soviets claimed the documents were forgeries, but it was doubtful anyone in China could create that authenticity. After Chang said he wanted no intemperate response, Donald and the USSR's Boris Oustrounoff recommended an expert enquiry into CER's operation, but it got no support. Trying to eliminate squeeze and inefficiency, and impatient with the inertia of older civil officials and with bright young men who weren't very bright, the warlord was becoming isolated in his government.

Mukden officials hatched a plan for the senior Chinese in the company, its vice-president, Lu Jung-huan, to take over. Dashing back to Harbin, he dissolved the railway labour union and closed down associated Soviet offices. The Russian manager and assistant manager, along with 60 labour leaders, were expelled from Manchuria. Lu was himself under investigation, but having become a patriot in the eyes of the public he was difficult to remove from the railway he had rescued for China.

On 13 July, the Soviet government protested the precipitate action and gave Mukden three days to rectify it. With no response, the USSR severed all diplomatic ties with China and created the Special Far Eastern Army under General Blyuker. Blyuker had trained the Nationalist Army in Canton in association with Borodin, but the Chinese didn't know about his new army, and in guessing that Russia would prefer to resolve the issue by negotiation rather than risk escalating into a confrontation with Japan and its ambitions for the region, they guessed wrong. Japan was quite happy for the Soviets to soften up the Manchurians and let Russia know that.

After a few months of skirmishes between Soviet and Manchurian troops along the northern border, the Special Far Eastern Army launched a full-scale attack with air support, occupying the border city of Hailar, then numerous cities along the railway line. The Manchurian army, superior in numbers but lacking the skill and the tank and air support of the Red Army, was routed with huge casualties among both soldiers and civilians.

Donald started discussions with Russia's foreign affairs, but Nanking was opposed to direct Soviet negotiation with Manchuria. On 22 November, Russia offered peace for a return to the status quo, reinstatement of its managers, and release of all arrested Soviet citizens. With Mukden breaking with Nanking four days later and agreeing, the Russians were back where they started and the Red Army withdrew. Japan watched from the sidelines, satisfied with the way things had gone.

This was all new territory for Donald, struggling to decipher the interests pulling in different directions. Still coming to terms with the decisiveness with which the two disloyal generals had been dispatched, he found he was advising a strange and mercurial young man, at times disarmingly frank with a capacity for self-criticism, but also given to frustrated outbursts of abuse at officials in his government. The mood swings driven by his addiction were becoming a liability. In the midst of trying to get Moscow to agree to a commission of enquiry, the Young Marshal had lost all interest and gone to a demonstration of newsreels with sound by agents for the American company, Fox. Needle-pricks covering his back, he didn't go anywhere without an aide carrying a briefcase with morphine and syringes.

Mentally and physically unable to conduct state affairs, the Young Marshal had been obliged to go along with policy decisions of the old

WH Donald in his late twenties

WH Donald in his sixties

Editorial office, *China Mail*, Hong Kong

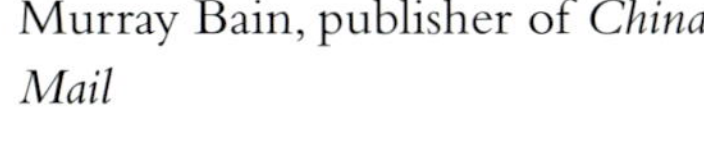

Murray Bain, publisher of *China Mail*

Mary Donald on honeymoon, Macao, December 1905

Mary Donald in a sedan chair, Hong Kong, with her husband in front and brother James Wall at the back

Scuttled Russian warships in Port Arthur, 1904

Revolutionary flags hung out over Nanking Road, Shanghai, 1911

Yuan Shih-k'ai

Chang Hsun, Imperial commander at Nanking

Sun Yat-sen, 1912

Charlie Soong

Roy Anderson in a sedan chair

Review of workers' militia in Chapei, Shanghai, March 1927

Tuan Ch'i-jui

Feng Kuo-chang

Wu Pe'i-fu

Feng Yu-hsiang

Chiang Kai-shek (with Madame Chiang) inspects his front line in the battle against warlords, 1928

Pockmarked Huang

Big-eared Tu

Chang Tso-lin ('the Old Marshal')

Chang Hsueh-liang ('the Young Marshal')

Assassination of Chang Tso-lin ('the Old Marshal'), near Mukden, Manchuria, 4 June 1928

Bustling street scene, Mukden

Japanese troops march into a Manchurian town, 1931

Edda Ciano, Chang Hsueh-liang, Donald, Madame Chang, 1931

Chiang Kai-shek (centre) touring northwest China (Donald is third from right)

Chang Hsueh-liang ('the Young Marshal') conferring with Donald

Donald and Madame Chiang in Shanghai, September 1937

Nanking Road during Japanese air raid on Shanghai, 1937

HH Kung and Hitler

TV Soong

Donald chats with Jimmy McHugh

Chiang party in western China mountains

Picnic stop during a tour of western China: (left to right) Madame and Generalissimo Chiang Kai-shek, Donald, Captain Walther Stennes

Donald & his yacht, *Mei Hwa*, April 1940

Shanty where Donald lived with other internees, Santo Tomas University

(left) Mourners at Donald's funeral: HH Kung and Madame Chiang at front, journalist Randall Gould at left behind Kung, Mayor KC Wu at right behind Madame

(below) Donald lies in state at funeral parlour; around him, HH Kung, Madame Chiang and JL Huang

Muriel Donald, aged 43 (passport photo)

Muriel Donald in her teens (left)

Mary Donald, aged 23

Mary Donald, aged 45 (passport photo)

guard, decisions which had failed to eliminate corruption from within CER or give China a more equitable hand in its running. This was a man beset by demons, a sensitive man with no ambition and resentful of the expectations of him, both during his father's lifetime and after. Donald had to do something about it or his role in Manchuria would come to nothing. He told his charge he couldn't help him unless he weaned himself off the pavemal and suggested rehabilitation at the Peking Union Medical College (PUMC).

'I know, I know,' said Chang, 'but I can't just go there and lock myself up for a month or two. The rumour-mongers would have a field day.'

'If we can't throw this stuff off somehow, you'd better resign and go through a proper course of treatment,' was the reply.

So the Young Marshal took up physical exercise and a regimented diet to get fit enough to combat the effects of morphine withdrawal. He and Donald went for long horse rides and played golf most days, getting Chang so tired he could go to sleep without the drug. But shaking off the addiction, even under medical supervision, sometimes generated such agony he would beg to start taking his doses again, saying, 'If I ever get hold of Dr Ma, I'll court-martial and shoot him.'

Dr Ma was the army doctor who prescribed pavemal as an opium cure. After the speedy despatch of the two generals, Donald couldn't be quite sure if Chang was being serious or just colourful.

•

With the Nationalists strengthened in Nanking after the rival Peking government's collapse, Chiang Kai-shek allowed the warlords who had nominally supported his Northern Expedition—Feng Yu-hsiang in the north-western provinces and Yen Hsi-shan in Shansi—to operate semi-independently in return for recognition of Nanking as the central government of China. It was a temporary respite. By 1930, Feng and Yen were moving to depose Chiang. Crucial to the outcome would be which side the Young Marshal would support with his army.

Lobbied in Mukden by representatives from both sides, Chang escaped to the coastal town of Hulutao to find he'd been followed by the people he was trying to avoid. For a month he was duchessed, gambling and drinking through the night, lapsing badly into old habits and unable to make coherent decisions. Donald threatened to abandon him unless he resumed his exercise regime. Persuaded to go further down the coast, Chang took the train to Peitaiho with his adviser going on ahead.

Donald pointed out that if the Young Marshal sided with Nanking the challenge would collapse, while if he sided with the Peking rebels the civil war and China's woes would continue. With a delegate from Nanking expected that evening, it was time to make a decision; Chiang was following the right course for unification of China and Feng was really the only warlord to overcome. Yen's Shansi Army had just suffered a crippling setback at the hands of Chiang's force.

Donald advised Chang to tell the delegate that he would side with Chiang if the Nationalist Party allowed non-members to hold office and other parties had a right to seats in parliament.

The Nanking emissary came to the house where Chang was staying with his entourage. Meeting in private while Donald waited in the reception area downstairs, the two eventually came back down. The Young Marshal was buoyant. After seeing his visitor out, he said excitedly, 'Come on up. They have agreed to everything.'

Next day, the Peking coalition announced a new government headed by Wang Ching-wei. Named on its State Council, Chang immediately contacted the Peking man who had lobbied him earlier, and assured him whatever inference he might have drawn from their conversation was wrong. He did not offer his support to the Peking group, he said, and he would not be doing so, sending the envoy scuttling back in panic to the old northern capital.

Returning with Donald to Mukden, Chang convened Manchuria's Political Council in his mansion's upstairs conference room to get backing to side with Nanking. The adviser arrived at 9 p.m., the time Chang thought the meeting would finish and, finding it still in session, settled down with a book and a pot of tea. It was a long wait. At one in the morning, Chang came down with a telegram the meeting had decided to send to Chiang. The warlord had prevailed over an old guard cautious with the memory that a similar move by his father had backfired badly.

When Donald had read the telegram, Chang asked what he thought of it.

'Not much,' said the blunt Australian. 'You haven't called on the J'issimo to do anything and you have considerations that have to be met.' 'J'issimo' was his new nickname for Generalissimo Chiang.

'It's just the first telegram,' replied Chang. 'I had to tie up the people upstairs first.'

A few days later, he ordered his troops south through Shanhaikwan Pass, where the Great Wall of China meets the sea, to occupy Hopeh province. He now had control of the northern end of the railways to Wuhan and Nanking and access to customs revenue coming through Tientsin. The Feng–Yen coalition collapsed, with Yen fleeing to Dairen and Feng stripped of his army, his troops taken over by the Manchurian.

Back in Mukden after taking Tientsin, Chang told Donald a letter had come from Bertram Lenox-Simpson offering him two million Chinese dollars and a monthly retainer if he could keep his customs post. Donald was horrified

'That's bribery,' he said, stating the obvious. 'He must have a low opinion of you.'

Donald himself had a low opinion of Lenox-Simpson. They had clashed in the past. An Englishman who had lived in China for more than 30 years, he had written extensively about the country under the nom-de-plume of Putnam Weale. With a reputation as an opportunist, Lenox-Simpson had been appointed Customs Commissioner at Tientsin by Yen at the height of his campaign against Chiang, pushing out the Nanking-appointed commissioner and his staff. With the Shansi warlord now on the run, the Englishman was in a desperate position, looking to buy his way out of trouble and, if he was lucky, retain the lucrative customs revenue.

When the Young Marshal announced that he was meeting with Lenox-Simpson one evening, his adviser cautioned, 'Watch yourself'.

The next day, Chang related what had taken place, with Lenox-Simpson arriving in his usual overbearing manner, full of bluster.

'Marshal, I'm glad you agree with my proposal!'

'Where did you get that idea?' the young warlord had asked.

'You sent for me after I laid out my plan for customs, didn't you?'

'I sent for you to hand over customs,' said Chang.

It was dawning on Lenox-Simpson that this wasn't going as well as he expected, that the Manchurian wasn't greatly swayed by his money. He was in serious strife, possibly aware of the fate of the two generals in this same room. Cornered, the Englishman asked what he should do.

'Ask Yen Hsi-shan.' But the Shansi warlord was long gone.

'Will you give me two weeks to straighten out my affairs?' asked Lenox-Simpson.

'Two weeks to rob customs?' said the Young Marshal. 'I give the order now to hand over customs to the people you and General Yen pushed out.'

Donald studied the morphine-ravaged figure of his young charge with a mixture of pride and admiration. Here was a Chinese who had turned down a substantial bribe despite the prevailing culture of squeeze. The Australian felt a surge of hope in his heart. This young man had integrity and courage. Was the sleeping giant waking at last?

'Young Marshal,' he said, 'why did you invite Lenox-Simpson here if you knew what he was proposing?'

'Don,' the Manchurian replied, 'I wanted to see how an Englishman looks when he loses face.'

In October, three Chinese claiming to be agents of the failed rebel coalition called at Lenox-Simpson's house in Tientsin and shot him. He died six weeks later without the assassins ever being identified. Disgruntled employees of Tientsin customs were suspected, but the killers might have been sent from Nanking or Mukden or they might have heard that Lenox-Simpson had a considerable amount of money stashed away. Putnam Weale had run out of sponsors and no-one seemed interested.

Chang went to Nanking in November to finalise the political marriage. With Japan already antagonistic to any deal that brought Nanking and Mukden closer, he didn't take any of the Japanese advisers imposed on him, but Donald came on the pretext he was a 'newspaper man'.

At a plenary session in Nanking, the provincial leader who had ensured Nanking's grip on the north got a warm reception. With various elements of the military consolidated into an army for national defence,

Chiang Kai-shek accepted the Manchurian's extended base, made him his deputy commander-in-chief and gave him command of the Northeastern Army of 400 000 troops. Most of Chang's own army moved from Manchuria into the region around Peking as part of the new arrangement, leaving only a token and inexperienced force behind.

In the new political structure, the Young Marshal had to spend a third of his time in Peking, supervising the absorption of Shansi troops and Feng's former army, with all their resentments and rumours, into the new Northeastern Army. The rest of his time was back in Mukden as chairman of the Northeastern Political Council where, re-energised, he was able to prevail over the concerns of the old guard. However, he would soon find more difficult opposition than his father's old cronies.

A mission had come from Tokyo to warn that flying the Nationalist flag in Manchuria or joining the Nanking government would be regarded as an 'unfriendly act'. At a meeting with the Japanese, Chang had jumped to his feet, saying. 'Manchuria is a Chinese province and I am a Chinese subject. I don't take orders from Japan.'

He stormed out of the room, returned to his headquarters and ordered the Nationalist flag be flown. The Japanese were finding the Young Marshal anything but the pushover they had expected. In fact, Chang was biding his time. He had not forgotten who murdered his father.

Chiang and Chang were political yin and yang. With unlimited ambition, the generalissimo was prepared to use all military and political means to achieve it. The Young Marshal, on the other hand, had no political or military ambition and would 'give up his job tomorrow if he could', according to one observer. He was intensely loyal, however, and Chiang was like an older brother to him. The Japanese, already concerned at the close cooperation between the two, found themselves further aggravated by China's refusal to negotiate new railway deals and its development of a new port at Hulutao in competition with Japanese-controlled Port Arthur.

Japan's economic presence and political interest in Manchuria had been growing since the Russo-Japanese War nearly 30 years before. The Russian-built South Manchurian Railway, connecting Harbin to Port Arthur, had been transferred to Japanese control after the war. Railway guards, stationed along the line to provide security for the trains and tracks, were actually regular Japanese soldiers of the Kwantung Army. From time to time, they carried out manoeuvres outside the railway zone and raids on local villages. All complaints from the Chinese government were ignored, but by 1931 a new Japanese momentum was building in Manchuria.

Captain Nakamura, a Japanese army officer on leave, was reported by the Tokyo press in July to have been murdered in Manchuria three weeks before, along with three companions. The bodies were not found and one story had it that Nakamura had been executed as a spy. Travelling in civilian clothes and claiming to be an 'agricultural representative', the military man had stopped at towns along the Chinese Eastern Railway, taking notes. Arrested near the militarily sensitive Mongolian border by Manchurian soldiers, the four were summarily executed, then cremated to hide the evidence.

The report inflamed public opinion in Japan, adding to its existing anti-Chinese sentiment which the military was quick to capitalise on and demand a stronger foreign policy against China. The Chinese foreign minister, CT Wang, undertook to investigate the allegations, but before anyone could take their cause further, another 'incident' occurred.

Colonel Itagaki and Lieutenant-Colonel Ishiwara, the ideological leaders of the Kwantung force, wielded more effective power than its commander, General Honjo. Under their influence, mid-level officers devised a plan to invade Manchuria from the leased zone. It was approved in Tokyo, but only as a response to Chinese aggression. However, when the minister of war sent an envoy to curb the Kwantung Army's adventurism, the power group realised it didn't have the luxury of waiting for a Chinese response to provocation. They would have to manufacture it.

Weakened by morphine, the Young Marshal came down with typhoid fever in Peking, checking into the PUMC's Rockefeller Clinic. A heavily guarded wing of the hospital was taken over, but after several weeks Chang had recovered enough to move back to his Peking residence. On 18 September, he dined with Donald at the British Legation and afterwards decided to see the famous female impersonator Mei Lan-fang at the Peking Opera. While Donald went home—he hadn't sold the house on Tsung-pu Hutung—Chang saw his show. Handed a radiogram from Mukden when he got back to his house, he read it in dismay. At midnight, he phoned his adviser.

'Come over,' the panic-stricken voice said. 'The Japanese are in Mukden.'

Thinking he was joking, Donald said, 'Go to bed.'

An hour later, Jimmy Elder arrived at Donald's house and confirmed that the Japanese were indeed invading Mukden. They joined Chang who, at three in the morning, tried to contact officers in the Mukden barracks and found a switchboard operator in a high state of anxiety.

'I can't talk any more,' he said. 'The Japanese have entered my office.'

The Japanese had found some excuse, unclear in Peking, to invade Manchuria beyond their leased zone. It came to be called the Mukden Incident, in keeping with the Japanese propensity for labelling acts of war that weren't outright war as 'incidents' (*jihen*). On the northern outskirts of the city, a junior officer of the Kwantung Army had placed a small quantity of dynamite near a section of railway track owned by Japan's South Manchuria Railway. The explosive was detonated at 10.20 p.m., but so minor was the damage, affecting only a short section on one side of the line, that ten minutes later a train passed over it without stopping.

The site was chosen because it was close to a garrison of Chinese troops. With the bombing blamed on Chinese dissidents, skirmishes broke out between Chinese and Japanese soldiers, giving the latter the excuse they needed to attack the garrison and the walled city of Mukden.

This was not a welcome turn of events for Chiang Kai-shek, already caught up in conflict in the south of China. Earlier in the year, Hu Han-min was arrested in a dispute over the constitution, but Chiang was forced by party pressure to release him. Hu's supporters set up a rival government in Canton, intended to be a model of probity in contrast to Nanking. At the time the Japanese invaded Manchuria, the generalissimo was steaming up the Yangtze to deal with the southern dissidents. He didn't want a second conflict and, in any case, the Soviets had already shown how ill-equipped the Manchurian army was to repel a formidable opponent.

The Young Marshal was under instruction not to risk his troops in battle in the event of Japanese aggression. Consequently, when overnight shelling of Mukden's arsenal began, the guard commander passed on Chang's order not to resist if the attackers tried to enter. Returning from reassuring workers in their homes, the commander found 50 Japanese soldiers had broken into the compound and was summarily shot. The Japanese then forced their way with grenades into workers' quarters. More than 30 were killed or wounded, mostly with bayonets. Next, the raiders went to the main office building, throwing grenades and killing civilians and a few soldiers, none of them resisting the attack.

Two artillery pieces had been secretly hidden a week before in a 'well' dug at the Japanese officers' club in Mukden. On the morning of the 19th, they were brought out, one firing on the main garrison in the city, the other on Mukden airfield. Chang's fledgling airforce was destroyed and soldiers, mostly irregulars and conscripts, fled the barracks and Mukden.

Arriving on the day of the Mukden Incident, the Tokyo envoy, Major-General Tatekawa, had willingly allowed himself to be distracted, taken to a restaurant with geisha entertainment while the plot was carried out. However, not all Japanese officials in Manchuria were happy with the turn of events. The Japanese consul, protesting the aggressive overreaction when he became aware of it, was silenced by a Kwantung officer's gesture of drawing his sword, and the Kwantung commander in Dairen, General Honjo, outraged to be told the invasion was taking place without his permission, had to be persuaded it was in his interest to authorise it retrospectively.

By evening, the fighting was over with 500 Chinese and two Japanese killed. General Honjo moved his headquarters to Mukden, the Japanese commander in Korea sent reinforcements over the border and the Kwantung Army pressed on to other parts of Manchuria. Japanese planes flew over Harbin to the north and dropped leaflets in Chinese and Russian, urging residents to be peaceful and carry on their businesses. All was quiet in Mukden, although shops remained closed and people stayed off the streets.

Returning to Nanking, Chiang Kai-shek met with government leaders to review the Manchurian situation. Donald was flown in Chang's Ford

Trimotor plane to join the discussion. Having determined not to resist the invasion, there was little either the Young Marshal or the generalissimo could do, but feeling was strong and students marched in protest with black armbands and banners proclaiming 'Death before Surrender'. Chang's Peking house was besieged by students demanding he declare war on Japan. At a press conference, he denounced Japan's actions: 'The Japanese claim for the cause of their action, sabotage by Chinese dissidents, sits uncomfortably with their history of manufacturing war.'

Donald advocated petitioning the League of Nations rather than a futile military response. The Chinese foreign ministry protested to the Japanese government, calling for an immediate stop to its military operations in Manchuria, and appealed to the league in Geneva. The former did nothing—the venture was largely outside its control—and the latter went through the motions very slowly. Meanwhile, Mukden adjusted to its new reality with Chinese police maintaining order under Kwantung supervision and civil organisations restoring trade and commerce with Japanese army support. Within two weeks, half of Mukden's businesses had re-opened.

In early October, the Japanese military severed all relations with Chang Hsueh-liang 'in view of the insincere attitude he still maintains towards Japan'. All Japanese advisers attached to his staff were ordered to vacate their posts. His military adviser, his job now done, was to leave Peking for Mukden that weekend. Chang's personal effects from his Mukden residence were packed into 417 cases and shipped to Peking with a note lamenting his 'forced absence'.

The League of Nations eventually passed a resolution later that month calling for Japanese troops to withdraw within three weeks. Japan wasn't interested in the league's resolutions and insisted on direct negotiations with the Chinese government. These continued spasmodically with little outcome. Major cities were occupied against minimal opposition and, within five months of the Mukden Incident, the Imperial Japanese Army had overrun Manchuria.

Chinese public opinion condemned the Young Marshal for not resisting the Japanese invasion, unaware that it had been ordained by Nanking and despite the Northeastern Army being inadequate to the task. Marshal

Chang insisted publicly the decision had been his, not the generalissimo's, but Chiang didn't fare much better anyway. The Canton faction of the Nationalist Party forced Chiang to take responsibility at a government conference in November and he resigned as premier soon after.

•

The Japanese had been complaining for some months about anti-Japanese boycotts in Shanghai. It came to a head—or, more correctly, was brought to a head—early in 1932 when Japan's military attaché, Major Ryukichi Tanaka, secretly paid Chinese thugs to attack five Japanese Buddhist monks near the San Yu towel factory. Two of the monks were badly injured and one died later, spurring retaliatory arson on the towel mill by young Japanese. 'Insults' didn't always need to be manufactured, however. The editorial of *Min-kuo jih-pao* (*Republic Daily*), published in several treaty ports, referred to a Korean assassination attempt on Emperor Hirohito as having 'unfortunately' failed.

The vigorous Tanaka, a protégé of the Kwantung Army's Colonel Itagaki, issued press releases exaggerating the Chinese threat and claiming a bomb had been set off at the ambassador's residence, although no damage was reported. Japan demanded an apology and compensation for the monks that were attacked, punishment of the unknown assailants and closure of all anti-Japanese associations. Japanese marines threatened to march through the International Settlement and burn down the *Min-kuo* offices.

In setting up barricades of sandbags and barbed wire around the strategic North Railway Station, the Cantonese 19th Route Army moved closer to the Japanese quarter of Hongkew, provoking a claim they were about to attack Japanese civilians. Wearing bamboo peasants' hats and shivering in summer uniforms, they had not been paid by the bankrupt Nanking government. Their continuing presence in Shanghai was already a cause of alarm in the International Settlement. Nanking, still under southern factional control with no Shanghai financier contacts, sent a representative to plead with Chiang to return. To clear the way, Wu T'ieh-ch'eng, a military man and loyal Chiang supporter, was installed as the new mayor of Shanghai.

Donald was at a weekend meeting in Nanking of the Chinese Indemnity Committee, of which he was a trustee appointed by the Nationalist government, when Mayor Wu came to the capital to consult about his city's predicament. Without Chiang's leadership, the government was rudderless and of little help to him. Late on Sunday night, the mayor rang Donald in his hotel and urged him to come back to Shanghai with him and help deal with the Japanese problem. The two had known each other since Cantonese days. Instead of flying back to Peking to join the Young Marshal, Donald caught the early morning train with Wu to Shanghai.

They spent the train journey deep in discussion. Donald's advice was to bow to the Japanese demands if they would otherwise resort to force, the same rationale as non-resistance in Manchuria. The boycotters had overreached themselves and had few friends—better to sacrifice them than the city.

Next morning, Donald joined Wu at a meeting with the International Settlement's municipal council and some of Shanghai's consuls. All believed Japan would use force if its demands weren't met, that they were looking for a pretext to do so. Mayor Wu undertook to advise the boycott associations to close down or be closed by either Chinese officials or Japanese naval forces.

Admiral Shiozawa, with the Japanese fleet on the river, had instructions from Tokyo to take prompt action at his discretion, should the need arise. A need had arisen, although it had nothing to do with boycotts or other Shanghai 'insults'. The Kwantung Army, working through Tanaka, needed to divert international attention from Manchuria. Interservice rivalry spurred the Imperial Japanese Navy to grab an opportunity to match the army success in the north.

On the evening of 27 January, Japan's Shanghai consul Kuramatsu Murai demanded Wu disband all anti-Japanese groups and return all confiscated goods by 6 p.m. the following evening. Anti-Japanese headquarters were closed and boycotted warehouses opened; an apology was issued and compensation and arrest of the monks' assailants promised. Murai publicly accepted the Chinese assurances and advised other consulates accordingly. In the late afternoon, a mass meeting of 5000 students and workers protesting Wu's acceptance of Japanese demands was dispersed by military police just arrived from Nanking. Chiang was starting to reassert control over the capital.

Donald had been at the meetings with Murai. At dinner that evening with his old friend from *The Times*, David Fraser, he told how the acceptance of Japanese terms had relieved a dangerous predicament for Shanghai. It was the outcome everyone was seeking—except the Communists and, as it turned out, Admiral Shiozawa who intended to press on with his plans regardless.

At cocktails onboard his flagship that evening, the admiral told Hallett Abend of the *New York Times* that his marines would go ashore at 11 p.m. 'to protect nationals and preserve order', claiming 6000 Japanese residents of Shanghai had pleaded for protection against hostile Chinese troops. At eleven, Shiozawa announced this intention to the municipal council, but said the action would not commence until 7.30 in the morning. At the same time, trucks were dropping squads of marines under cover of dark at the International Settlement's boundary. They crossed into Chapei, the Chinese quarter, preceded by Japanese civilian vigilantes who fired at Chinese military police to attract return fire that would justify the marines joining the fray.

Back in his room in the Astor House Hotel, Donald was relaxing after the day's successful deliberations. Hearing gunfire close by, he went to the window and was alarmed to see Japanese marines prowling along the street. This shouldn't be happening, he thought, and phoned the mayor.

'They can't be,' said Wu. 'The Japanese consul has agreed. He advised the other consulates.'

'You listen and tell me what this is then, if it's not shooting.'

He opened his window, letting in cold winter night air, and held the telephone handset outside so his friend could hear the crossfire for himself.

'He lied!' said the mayor, hanging up and immediately notifying Western consulates of the attack taking place despite the consul's acceptance of his assurances.

Japanese marines on motorcycles roamed the streets with machine guns. By 11.30 gunfire echoed through the International Settlement and Westerners in evening clothes parked near Chapei to experience the excitement. Evacuating soldiers from 19th Route Army turned back and rushed into the dense residential areas more familiar to them than to Japanese marines. Enfiladed fire was effective down alleyways at passing patrols.

Overnight, the marines attacked North Station, but they were spread thin and targeted by Chinese snipers. Buildings along the settlement border were set on fire to prevent their use by the riflemen. Street lights were shot out, and in the pre-dawn, bombs were dropped by planes from the Japanese carrier *Notoro* on the Whangpoo River. Japanese warships lobbed shells into Chapei and at the fort at Woosung, where the river flows into the Yangtze.

North Station was gutted by fire and bombing, but reinforced Chinese defenders still occupied it and forced the attackers back to the settlement where they put up barbed-wire and armoured car defences to block any Chinese counterattack. Vigilantes, calling themselves *ronin* after the bandit samurai of Japan's shogunate era, were seen grabbing Chinese in the streets and executing them as snipers. Women, children and the elderly poured into the International Settlement in vehicles loaded with what possessions they could grab.

In Nanking, Chiang called for negotiation with Japan, and in the beleaguered city the British and American consuls mediated between the Chinese and Japanese military with Mayor Wu and his ad hoc adviser present, but increasingly sidelined by the rapidity of events. The 19th Route Army had no intention of following the widely criticised non-resistance of Mukden, but nonetheless the two sides agreed that night to a ceasefire, with Murai to request Tokyo to pull back Japanese troops to the settlement. By dawn both sides were firing at each other again, having used the ceasefire to bring in reinforcements.

On 29 January, Japanese warships further up the Yangtze shelled Nanking's wharves preparatory to marines landing at the Nisshin Steamship Company's wharf, ostensibly to protect evacuating Japanese. The next day, Chiang met with his advisers in Nanking and decided to temporarily move the capital inland to Loyang, avoiding the intimidation of naval bombardment. Nanking was too close to Shanghai for comfort.

For the whole of February, the two sides struggled to prevail in Chapei without breaking the stalemate. The battered wreck of North Station remained steadfastly and symbolically in Chinese hands. The outnumbered Japanese naval force was reinforced from 14 February with army units brought down from Manchuria, gradually bringing the force up to 100 000 men with aerial and naval bombardment support. At the same time, Chiang sent his German-trained 5th Army into Shanghai, although Chinese numbers were still only half those of the increased enemy force.

At the end of the month, Japanese soldiers were able to get behind Chinese lines and the defenders couldn't dislodge them. Shortage of supplies and manpower had become decisive. A few days later, both the Cantonese and Nanking armies withdrew from Shanghai and the League of Nations passed a resolution demanding a ceasefire. The Chinese agreed to stop fighting while Japan refused. A week later representatives from the league arrived in Shanghai to force a Japanese surrender while sporadic fighting continued mostly outside the city. It wasn't until May that China and Japan signed a ceasefire agreement which forbade China to garrison troops around or in Shanghai, but allowed some Japanese troops within the city. The agreement was widely regarded by the Chinese as yet another humiliation, accusing the Western powers of appeasing Japanese aggression.

By early February there was little either Wu or Donald could do for Shanghai. It had become purely military, no longer a diplomatic exercise, so Donald rejoined the Young Marshal in Peking. International repercussions were developing over Manchuria and Chang wanted Donald on the case.

In December 1931, the League of Nations had finally made a move and commissioned an enquiry to determine the causes of the Mukden Incident and assess the Japanese claims it had acted in self-defence and in pursuit of the legitimate interests of Manchurians. The commission of five was headed by the English Lord Lytton and it was to spend six fact-finding weeks in Manchuria after meeting government leaders in China and Japan. At the outset, Lytton stated that they were not arbitrating between Japan and China, but trying to find a durable settlement.

In a move calculated to give substance to the claim of self-determination, what had been Manchuria was proclaimed on 18 February as the

'Manchu state' of Manchukuo, although Manchus were a minority there, more than 95 per cent of the population being Han Chinese. Pu-i, the Manchu emperor who had abdicated in favour of Yuan Shih-k'ai twenty years before, was installed as regent, but he was a figurehead with no real authority. That remained in the hands of the Japanese military.

Having met Japanese leaders, the Lytton Commission moved in mid-March to China, where Wellington Koo was attached as a Chinese assessor. Donald was brought into the Chinese team as an adviser and his attractive Russian secretary went with him. By late April, the commission and its entourage prepared to move on to 'Manchukuo'.

Officials of the puppet state tried to prevent Koo accompanying the commission, citing a fear he might be assassinated by hot-headed supporters of the new regime. The real reason was his friendship with the former Manchurian warlord. The inclusion of Chang's most trusted adviser, Donald, would hardly have pleased them either, some of them opportunists who had been bureaucrats in past warlord administrations. Only after the commission made clear that if Koo was not allowed to enter Manchukuo, it would not be going there either, was Koo eventually allowed to come with his team.

Given Japan's recent history of government by assassination, execution by outraged Manchurians seemed less likely than by Japanese. There was no incident, but the hosts lost no opportunity to make the delegation as uncomfortable as possible, providing poor accommodation on trains and in hotels. While it was mildly amusing to the Chinese delegation, a commission made up of Westerners was singularly unimpressed.

Bronson Rea was hired by the Manchukuo government to accompany the Lytton Commission in Manchuria and plead Manchukuo's case. Donald's path would cross Rea's, sometimes at a distance, sometimes nearer. They would exchange a few words, acknowledging they knew each other, but nothing to indicate their once close relationship. Working with an allowance of US$60 000 for 'expenses for engaging Americans and Europeans' and another of US$25 000 for 'intelligence', Rea's transfer of allegiance had been complete. In conversation when he referred to 'us', he sometimes meant Americans, but mostly referred to Manchukuo or Japan.

Members of the Lytton Commission, and the Chinese delegation with it, were constantly under surveillance so ham-fisted that commissioners resented the Japanese assumption they weren't smart enough to work it out. They became alert to concocted evidence and the blocking of access to information. Chinese were being arrested for trying to see members of Koo's staff and detained until the commission left Manchuria.

While he was working there, Donald flew back and forth for consultation, particularly between Peking and Shanghai, making the six-hour flight—it would have been 40 hours by train—six times in late June. Mostly he flew in the luxurious twelve-seater Trimotor with couch, wireless telephone and 'all the comforts of home, excepting the bath', as he described in a letter to his sister, Florence. Since the break-up of his marriage, Will Donald was corresponding more with his family back in Australia, particularly with Florence and his brother, Herbert.

The Young Marshal had a fleet of light planes at Donald's disposal. Although not permitted to take off or land, he often took the controls during flights. A two-seater, trying to fly through a storm near Newchwang on the Manchurian coast, came down on one occasion, landing on its nose and damaging wing, propeller and undercarriage. The pilot and Donald were badly shaken, but otherwise unhurt. Another time, the Trimotor got bogged at Shanghai taxiing across a field, the undercarriage sinking to its hubs in the mire. It took six hours for workers to dig the plane out.

Koo's delegation didn't go on to Tokyo with the commission after hints it was not welcome there. It didn't matter much; its work was already done. Commission members were coming to the view that Japan had long planned the occupation of south Manchuria and the Manchukuo government had been foisted on Manchurians, some officials holding posts out of fear. They were not certain the railway line explosion had actually happened.

Lytton had already been commenting privately that the Japanese were not looking good in Manchuria and that Japan might be thankful for a way out without loss of face from the mess it had created. Japan's financial position was strong, but the invasion of Manchuria and Shanghai had been costly and would continue to be if there was no resolution.

The Lytton Report was made public in October 1932. It didn't comment on the cause of the Mukden Incident, simply stating the Japanese allegation that Chinese were responsible. The commissioners were in no doubt that the claim was false, but the French delegate insisted Japan not be portrayed as aggressor. The report did state, however, that the invasion following the incident was not legitimate self-defence and the new state of Manchukuo did not arise from a genuine independence movement. It wouldn't exist without the Japanese military.

When the findings were finally announced in Geneva the following February, the Japanese delegation walked out and Japan withdrew from the League of Nations, but by then Japan was firmly in control of Manchuria. All the Lytton Report had demonstrated was the weakness of the League of Nations and its inability to enforce its decisions.

Japan's thirst for expansion had not abated. In January 1933, it claimed two bombs had been found concealed in the Japanese border post at the strategic coastal town of Shanhaikwan. In retaliation, the town was shelled by artillery and destroyers anchored opposite Port Arthur. Japanese troops swarmed through the city gate to be driven back twice by riflemen. A hole was blasted in the city wall, allowing the attackers through for bayonet-to-bayonet fighting among low mud huts in narrow winding streets.

The defenders held on for three days against superior firepower before eventually capitulating. Chang was criticised by warlords and generals for not sending more troops. Proclaiming their own eagerness to fight, they never actually did so. The occupation of Shanhaikwan, wedged between the end of the Great Wall and the sea, meant Japan held the key route for China to protect the province of Jehol, on the southern side of Manchuria.

Short, stout and walrus-moustached, the governor of Jehol, General Tang Yu-lin, had an opium factory in his palace grounds and traded in plundered Manchu treasures, a typically corrupt warlord. The Japanese appointed him Vice-Chairman of the Privy Council of Manchukuo, but he hadn't taken up the bribe or the position. In response, a convoy of troop trains came from Mukden to clear out the Jehol 'bandits' who had 'invaded' Manchukuo, claiming the province as part of Manchuria. The bandits were actually Tang's North Chinese soldiers and they came down to strategic mountain passes on shaggy Mongolian ponies to hinder Japanese and Manchukuoan troops (called for the occasion the Jehol Pacification Expeditionary Force) gathering at the rail-head in the province's north and facing a difficult task advancing in winter's snow and frequent blizzards over mountains defended by 150 000 Chinese.

TV Soong, now Nanking's minister of finance, had gone to Peking to arrange for imperial treasures Tang held to be moved to Nanking for their protection, ostensibly from the Japanese advancing towards Chengteh, Jehol's capital. Soong and the Young Marshal decided they would go to Chengteh to survey the military position there. Donald went with them, driven through the same blizzards the Kwantung Army was enduring in the northern mountains.

Arriving after an uncomfortable journey, they entered Chengteh through Tang's triumphal arch. An accomplished bureaucrat with his Harvard training, Soong was developing a taste for politicking. He harangued a meeting of soldiers and civilians with the assurance that Jehol was Chinese territory which the national government would never give up. In truth, the civilians probably considered the Japanese no worse a prospect than their own corrupt governor.

Chang and Donald investigated the capital's defences. The only troops to be seen were guarding the governor's opium factory. Tang's main force had fled north to the apparent safety of the mountains. The general was urged to set up defences to resist the Japanese when they got to the capital, but the fashionably dressed Manchurian and the plain-spoken foreigner were of no consequence to him. Their fruitless mission over, the visitors left for the chilly drive back.

Jehol's steep mountains were ideal terrain to defend, but with no shelter in the narrow valleys the defenders were vulnerable to air and artillery attack. The Japanese advanced through snowstorms and biting gales, shin-deep in snow, blizzards sometimes reducing visibility to zero and temperatures so low that machine guns jammed. The defenders vanished, their commanders either deserting their troops or changing sides. Chinese soldiers on the ground often waited until Japanese planes had flown past before firing so they would not be attacked.

By 3 March, with the Japanese approaching, General Tang wandered around Chengteh in a daze. A fortnight before, he'd performed for journalists as a one-man Chinese rodeo in his *yamen*, then addressed them from an antique Manchu throne. Now he seemed confused, almost oblivious.

'I'm in a difficult position,' he told reporters. 'I don't even know where my troops are!'

He fled from Chengteh on horseback that night with 200 bodyguards. From Peking, the Young Marshal denounced Tang as a 'traitor to China' and ordered his arrest, but he was long gone.

The next morning, 3000 defenders with rifles and machine guns stood by without firing a shot as the Kwantung Army marched into the city. The governor had commandeered lorries to carry his purloined property to safety, trucks that might have transported his troops. Chinese soldiers and refugees streamed south, many of them on foot in the freezing conditions. The pass was mayhem, jammed with wheelbarrows, carts, camels and motorcars. Chang ordered the gates of the Great Wall shut by the Peking garrison, trapping Jehol's defenders outside China. Tang's truckloads of treasures arrived at the Great Wall, without the governor, and promptly disappeared.

Chinese newspapers had been calling Chiang Kai-shek a traitor and a coward for not sending enough troops to help the 19th Route Army in Shanghai and for his non-declaration of war on Japan, trusting instead the toothless League of Nations. Wang's troublesome southern faction of the Nationalist Party was now making loud noises about the capitulation in Jehol, demanding the removal of the Young Marshal from command of the Northeastern Army.

Chiang arranged a meeting on 9 March with his northern commander, bringing an army train up from Nanking to the railway station at Paoting, 150 kilometres out of Peking. He had attended the imperial military academy there many years before. Chang and Donald took a special train down from Peking, pulling in on the other side of the platform where the army train was already standing. Soldiers stood about, some alert and on guard. Although there was no sign of the generalissimo, it was clear which carriage was his.

'You stay here, Don,' said the Young Marshal.

Chang walked across the platform while Donald returned to their coach's luxury to watch proceedings through its window. The Manchurian boarded the headquarters coach and disappeared from sight.

With all interior drapes drawn—Chiang wasn't going to assist assassins—the Australian couldn't see what was going on behind them, but his wait was a short one. Ten minutes later, the Young Marshal stepped back on the platform, his face and manner revealing nothing apart from the ravages of addiction.

Back in their carriage, Chang described the meeting to his adviser. It had been short, cordial and formal with no antipathy in the older man's demeanour, more like a problem they had to solve together. It started with a homily.

'China is like an unstable ship,' Chiang had said, 'best righted by jettison of something onboard,' without suggesting where to apply this figure of speech.

'I should resign my commission,' Chang said.

'You should do what you sincerely believe to be best for China.'

No undertaking was made and none was asked, but both understood what the political situation required. Donald, too, understood without having to be told. His mind was already moving to an opportunity this turn of events was creating.

The two returned to the old capital where the Young Marshal announced his resignation from command of the Northeastern Army and the handing over of it and his airforce to a new commander to be appointed by Generalissimo Chiang Kai-shek.

Chiang went through a ritual of refusing to accept his commander's resignation, then two days later accepting it with reluctance. The charade of refusal completed, Chang Hsueh-liang addressed his gathered troops in a passion of patriotism and duty.

'We came into China proper to effect national unification,' he said, 'but the result is that we are now homeless. Although our sacrifice is great, it is worthwhile. After my departure, you must obey Generalissimo Chiang's orders and support the government unanimously. You must all be aware of the fact that in permitting me to resign the generalissimo wishes me well.'

Chiang meanwhile handed command of the Northeastern Army to the pro-Japanese general, Ho Ying-chin, who advocated no direct confrontation and later signed a ceasefire with Japan.

Chapter 10

The cure

'Young Marshal,' said Donald, 'you have nothing to do now except twiddle your thumbs. It's too good an opportunity to let slip by.'

While they waited for Chiang Kai-shek's protocol of refusal prior to accepting the resignation of his commander of the Northeastern Army, Donald proposed Chang Hsueh-liang take the opium cure developed by an American, Dr Harry Miller. On 14 March, when his resignation was accepted, Chang addressed his troops. The next morning, he flew in the Trimotor to Shanghai with his two addicted wives, accompanied by Bill Donald and Jimmy Elder.

Donald and Elder had gone to Shanghai a few days earlier, while Chang's resignation was up in the air, and met Dr Miller in his office in the Shanghai Sanitarium. The doctor was told the time had come to do something about the 'young fella's addiction'. At official meetings, he was getting injections every fifteen or twenty minutes and couldn't sleep or even rest without them. It was the generalissimo's view that this couldn't go on, and Chang himself was anxious to find a cure. He had tried at Mukden years before, without success, and at the Rockefeller Clinic in Peking while recovering from typhoid fever. Madame Chang, now very frail, was also addicted, as was Chang's concubine, the younger and sturdier Chao Yi-ti, described to the righteous doctor as a household guest. Asked if he could reduce the cravings for pavemal so that Chang would be able to go to Europe in April, Harry Miller replied simply, 'Yes, I can.'

'Tell me about the cure. Will he suffer?' asked Donald.

'He will know nothing. They'll be unconscious.'

Miller had two stipulations: Chang and his family had to come to Shanghai—the demands as medical director of the Seventh-Day Adventist sanatorium precluded his going to Peking—and both Madame Chang and Miss Chao had to take the cure as well. A cured addict living in a house with two people still dependent was a recipe for failure.

When Donald and Elder returned to Shanghai with the Chang family and entourage, TV Soong took charge and put them up in a large house in the French Concession that had once belonged to the Green Gang's notorious Big-eared Tu. Soong's father, Charlie Soong, had been a close friend of Miller. Chang's retinue included a bodyguard and his own doctors, there to administer his drugs until the cure started. Antagonistic to something that would put them out of work, they were sowing seeds of doubt in the young man's mind. Donald told them Miller was coming the next day to start the cure.

'Shouldn't you get his consent?' asked one of the doctors.

'It will be done with or without consent.'

When Donald told Chang what had been organised, his already sallow face clouded with indecision.

'Let's wait,' he pleaded. 'Let's wait.'

'There's no turning back now, and no delays,' said his adviser sternly. 'You're often saying you want to be cured. The time's come to do it.'

Arriving in the morning with his nurses, Dr Miller was invited by a footman to wait in the reception area. They were left unattended for some time, wondering whether anyone had been told of their presence, until a Chinese doctor came down the stairs.

'Could I do something for you?' he asked in a distant tone.

'I'm here to see the marshal,' the American replied, 'to undertake his cure.'

'How exactly do you plan to treat him?'

'We have a plan,' said Miller defensively. 'No need to go into detail here. It's the marshal we're treating.'

Miller's detoxification method was controversial, with at least one person known to have died while undergoing it. It wasn't something he wanted to discuss or worse, debate, with someone wanting to block him from his patient. He hadn't spoken to Chang this time round, but was confident the warlord believed in him. Their paths had crossed several times over the years and in the past Chang had made generous donations to his work.

'Who do you plan to treat first?' the house doctor asked.

'We'll start with the marshal and, when we have him well underway, we'll treat the ladies.'

'Very well, but we think you should attend to the women first, and if they get along all right, then try the marshal.'

Miller was getting impatient, sensing no-one was going to take him to his patient, that the doctor was going to continue talking for as long as it took for the visitor to give up.

'We'll begin with the marshal, as I said,' he answered firmly. With that, he turned and left, indicating to his nurses to come with him.

A couple of hours later, Chang called Miller back to the house where he was met by the same doctor with the same outcome. Soon after that, Donald was surprised to see the Young Marshal still up and about and Dr Miller and his nurses nowhere to be seen. On making enquiries, he found they had gone back to the sanatorium and went there to find out why the treatment had not begun.

Miller explained what happened and said, 'When you get those doctors out of my way so I can get past the entry hall, we will start.'

Without further delay, Donald cleared the way. Miller returned again and this time was taken straight to his patient. The American saw immediately the enormity of his task when he came face to emaciated face with a pallid ghost in dandy's clothes. Madame Chang looked even more wasted, weighing only 38 kilograms.

'Marshal, I have taken others through this cure,' Dr Miller said. 'I will do the best I know how and will stay with you right through. There is no reason why we can't succeed.' He paused to ensure his next point was unequivocal. 'But it must be clearly understood that I have complete authority over this place, including over your bodyguard, your staff and your physicians. You must understand that they are to take orders from no-one but me; not from you or anyone else. No matter what you say under any circumstances, I am to have complete authority. If you agree to that, we will succeed. If you don't, there is no point in going ahead.'

The Young Marshal didn't need time to consider this proposition. He immediately called his chief of staff.

'General T'an,' he said, 'you're to listen only to Dr Miller. He has complete control and authority over this household and will be given anything he wants. Listen to him and only him, follow his orders and instructions to the letter.'

Turning to the American, Chang said, 'I'm completely in your hands.'

After a day of delays, it wasn't until eight that evening that the treatment could begin. An enema was followed by a rectal anaesthetic, putting the patient quickly into a deep sleep. The mansion's spacious entry hall was rearranged as a medical ward with Chang moved to a hospital bed brought from the sanatorium. This proved a good move for a second reason, not unexpected: his own bed was found to have tablets hidden under the sheets and pillows and even in the mattress by Chang's personal physicians.

When the patient was sound asleep, cantharidin was applied to his skin. Obtained from the blister beetle, Spanish fly, the powerful irritant's medical use dated back to ancient Greece. Serum was drawn from the blister that developed and injected into Chang's bloodstream.

With Chang asleep, Dr Miller began the same procedure with his concubine. He had decided that Madame Chang's heart was not strong enough and the cure involved too great a risk for her—and for him. Miss Chao was younger and stronger, although not enthusiastic about taking the cure, doing it mostly because Chang had told her to. She remained awake all night, lying on her back so a large blister could be raised on her stomach, and having to be restrained some of the time by a male nurse on each limb.

Next morning, Madame Chang accused the doctor of leaving her out of the cure because Donald wanted to save only her husband and his concubine, leaving her as the only addict in the family.

'Soon he'll be well and I'll be left in enslavement,' she whined.

'We thought it wise to treat the marshal first, to see how things go,' Miller said, ignoring the fact that Miss Chao was already undergoing the treatment.

'But I want to start now,' the woman insisted. 'Today!'

The American discussed the issue with Donald, pointing out the risks, and was persuaded to disregard her heart condition and start her on the cure. It was a risk worth taking. She had little to lose. As it turned out, she held up remarkably well.

The patients were kept under sedation for three days with less habit-forming sedatives than the opium that consumed them. The two women's beds were put either side of Chang's in the house's grand entrance to facilitate monitoring of their progress. Intravenous medications kept up their body fluids. The three white-sheeted hospital beds made a bizarre tableau, huddled with their occupants in the centre of a vast opulent vestibule with dark drapes, artworks and ornate curios decorating the perimeter.

After the third day, the sedation was reduced, introducing the potential horrors of diarrhoea, vomiting and severe cramps over several days. Hot compresses were used to ease the symptoms of withdrawal, but as the tranquillisers were eased further, the result was increasing pain and discomfort.

One time, with the opiate's influence wearing off, the Young Marshall got out of bed and grappled with Miller's male nurses. Coming into the room, Donald shouted at him to get back in his bed. Compliance was short-lived, Chang lashing out with his fist and kicking as his adviser put a blanket over him. For a while, refusing to take anything by mouth, he was fed by a tube and complained in a loud voice that echoed through the building that the Americans were abusing him.

Miller became aware that the Chinese doctors were talking at length with Chang's guards and, concerned they were about to sabotage the treatment, sought out the chief of staff.

'General T'an, please get the marshal's doctors out of this house,' he said. 'I don't care how you do it, but get them out!'

He left, returning later in the day to Miller's temporary office.

'They are gone,' T'an reported simply.

Using the very Chinese strategy of disingenuousness, he had told the doctors that the cure had been ordered by the minister of finance and if something went wrong he would be looking for a scapegoat—or scapegoats—to blame, probably to have shot. Although he knew the doctors wouldn't interfere, he said, it would be most unfortunate if the minister jumped to a wrong conclusion and ordered an unjust execution. The doctors needed no further hint and returned that day to Peking.

It was just as well the physicians had gone. Going through the extreme torture of withdrawal, Chang became increasingly vocal and violent, biting Miller's finger while he was manhandled by the nurses under the doctor's direction. Sometimes his craving would be so strong he would hit himself, but Miller was determined not to give him the comfort of sedation and prolong the cure. Then, just as the medical team was wondering if they were making any real progress, the patient's demeanour turned about. The Young Marshal began to wilt dramatically, sobbing in boundless misery.

He told a story that had been locked inside his mental fortress for half his life, how his father had demanded his elder son follow in his military footsteps when he wanted a professional education, his distress at going into battle and seeing his soldiers killing people, people who were not guilty of any crime and had as much right to live as he had, how duty would occasionally require him to condemn men to death, how it haunted his soul to such a degree that his only road out was the way of the poppy, and how, soon after he started, his wife fell into the habit and opium took over their house, picking up Miss Chao as a spoil of war.

Chang Hsueh-liang was rounding a corner. Still thin, he had developed a healthier complexion. His discomfort was easing rapidly, his behaviour no longer belligerent or irrational. He was able to build up his strength through exercise and a healthy diet. Madame Chang and the concubine were likewise making remarkable headway and after only three weeks all three had recovered sufficiently to prepare for the intended voyage.

•

On 11 April 1933 the extended family of Chang Hsueh-liang set out for Europe on the Italian steamship, *Conte Rosso*. Chang's party included his wife and their four children, his concubine, and two of his advisers, Bill Donald and Jimmy Elder. Irina went with them as Madame Chang's secretary as well as for her linguistic skills. The party was accompanied by Dr Read Calvert, a colleague of Dr Miller, and a nurse from Shanghai Sanitarium.

Also onboard were Count Galeazzo Ciano, returning home from three years as Italian consul-general in Shanghai, and his wife, Edda, Mussolini's eldest daughter and an admirer of Hitler. Elegant and flirtatious, Edda Ciano had sat opposite the Young Marshal at a dinner in Peking for the Lytton delegation. At the end of the evening he passed a note to her inviting her to join him on a tour of the Imperial Summer Palace the next day. They met several times as a group of five—the Cianos and Chang and his two 'wives'—and Edda and Chang later exchanged letters, although there's no evidence the relationship went beyond flirtation . . . and no certainty it didn't. While her husband had lovers, Edda indulged in poker and gin. She also worked hard, with her husband's encouragement, to promote trade between China and Italy, persuading the Young Marshal to buy three Fiat planes for the Chinese airforce.

The *Conte Rosso* was a plush liner, its interior in fifteenth-century style finished in oak with embossed leather panels. The forward section of the main promenade was set up as an open-air restaurant to take advantage of the tropical climate of much of the voyage. In the music and dancing salon, the stage sat on Ionic columns. In these plush surrounds, the flirtation between the warlord and the diplomat's wife continued, but there was another objective—unless it had been the objective all along. Ciano wanted to sell more Italian weapons and aircraft to the Chinese government through Chang. To further this, he'd offered resort accommodation and a motorboat in Italy to Chang's party and had arranged for the Young Marshal to meet his father-in-law, Benito Mussolini, *Il Duce*.

Disembarking in Rome on 4 May with his entourage, the Young Marshal was immediately struck by Italy's 'national revival' under Mussolini, and went on to meet Adolph Hitler and Hermann Goering. Arriving in Britain in July, he was less impressed with the increasingly ineffective Labour prime minister, Ramsay MacDonald. The party stayed in a rented house in Brighton where his children went to a local school. Chang played golf, went horse-riding, renewed an interest in some old hobbies and hosted all-night black-tie poker parties. He put on weight, colour returned to his face. Increasingly anti-Japanese, he became critical of Chiang's withholding of a military response in Manchuria.

Chang took a suite in London's Dorchester Hotel and, coached by Donald in the politics of Europe, met various luminaries. TV Soong was in London at the time for the World Economic Conference and met with Chang and his political adviser. Donald was proposing the Young Marshal disband half his army when he got back to China, take the other half to Sinkiang and restructure it on more modern lines. Chang asked the finance minister to mention this plan to Chiang, but he was vehemently opposed to it.

'You can't go to Sinkiang,' said the brusque Soong. 'I need your army in China.'

'You're as selfish as all the other politicians,' snapped the Young Marshal.

The group took a motor tour of Europe, starting in Paris and getting to Copenhagen by November, having visited Leningrad. Its progress and who made contact with it was routinely noted by Japanese legations and consulates across the continent and sent back to Tokyo. Japan's fear was that the Manchurian might stir up Chinese students in Europe against it, and was particularly concerned at the role Donald might be playing. Intercepting cables from China, the Japanese were aware the Young Marshal had been approached to return to China to direct a military campaign against them.

In Copenhagen, Chang got a telegram from the officers of his Manchurian army: 'REVOLT HAS BROKEN OUT IN FUKIEN STOP THERE IS MOVEMENT UNDER WAY TO GET US TO JOIN FACTIONS AGAINST CHIANG KAI-SHEK STOP COME BACK AT ONCE'.

Leaders of the 19th Route Army, highly regarded for defending Shanghai against the Japanese and sent to South China to suppress the Communists, had instead negotiated peace and, with Nationalist Party leftists, broken with Chiang and set up a Fukien People's Government. Among their anxieties was the generalissimo's appeasement towards Japan. Chang wanted to return immediately, but Donald suggested he go on ahead instead and report the lie of the land. Next day they all went to

Sweden, where Chang stayed while Donald made his way to Venice and embarked for Shanghai.

Soong had returned to China from Europe and the US to find Chiang had built a debt with the Shanghai banks of $60 million while fighting the Communists. The leader accused his minister of causing a recent defeat by not providing sufficient funds. Soong resigned in October and the far more compliant HH Kung was appointed instead. The shuffle changed nothing. Power remained in the hands of the extended Soong family.

Donald met with the former finance minister in Shanghai.

'Being minister of finance is no different from being Chiang Kai-shek's dog,' he told Donald.

Soong, still smarting from the meeting in London, tried to persuade Donald to get Chang to stay in the Philippines and not come back to China.

'Neither of us can persuade the young fella against his wishes,' observed the equally curt Australian.

Although the Fukien rebellion wasn't faring well, with promised aid from the Chinese Communist Party not materialising, and would collapse by January, Nanking was in disarray. The climate was right for the absent Manchurian to recover his position in the political framework of his country. Donald cabled the Young Marshal in Europe, saying that he should return to China to mend his relationship with Chiang and repair his reputation.

Chang and most of his entourage, but without Jimmy Elder and a son who stayed at school in England, returned to China on the *Conte Verde*, sister ship of the *Conte Rosso*, arriving early in the new year of 1934. Donald joined the ship at Manila to bring Chang up to date with political moves in his homeland and plan a strategy to resume a role in its government.

Donald had formed a friendship with the American, Langhorne Bond, operations manager for the CNAC (China National Aviation Corporation) airline in Shanghai, playing golf with him regularly. The two were lunching with Madame Chiang, as the west called Soong May-ling, and the conversation turned to Chang Hsueh-liang.

She asked Donald, 'What does the Young Marshal want?'

'Madame, as strange as it may seem to you, the Young Marshal wants only to serve China the best way he can.'

Chiang had successfully suppressed the Fukien revolt, noted no involvement of Manchurian troops in it, and saw value in renewing his alliance with the Young Marshal, inviting him to a meeting in Nanking. Donald went, too, and suggested to Chang his best strategy might be candour about the image of China overseas.

At the meeting, Chiang said, 'I suppose you're anxious to know what job I'm giving you.'

'I'm not looking for a job,' answered Chang, 'and when I've finished, you may not want to give me one.'

He said how impressed he was with Hitler and Mussolini, how they had transformed their nations, and tried to persuade Chiang of fascism's advantages. Then he moved on to the image of China.

'Europe doesn't think much of you or China,' he said.

The pair launched into a litany of the things they had picked up on their European sojourn; the Young Marshal with smooth candour, his adviser characteristically blunt.

Chiang didn't react, taking it all in. At the end he said, 'We're going to Hangchow tomorrow. You should join us there and we'll talk some more.'

Chang and Donald went to Hangchow the next day and joined the generalissimo and Madame Chiang for dinner in the private room of a restaurant by the city's serene West Lake with its temples, pagodas and gardens. In his relentlessly forthright manner, Donald launched into a confronting denunciation of China's woes, tempered by his obvious genuine concern, with May-ling translating.

'You are ignorant of what's going on because no-one dares correct you,' he said. 'You might lose face and someone might lose his head. China is plagued with graft, full of swindlers who will steal anything.'

'Opium is flooding the country,' he went on. 'It flows up and down the Yangtze right past your front door. Thousands die of it every month. Millions die because you can't stop killing yourselves in civil war. There is the obesity of wealth on one hand, the hog wallow of poverty on the other. The rickshaw man and the wharf coolie are worse off than the horse and camel in many other lands.'

And so on, in a tirade of some hours, all the while translated in a sing-song voice by the bubbly May-ling, and all the while received in stoic, dignified silence. It may not have been news to Chiang, but he hadn't been confronted with it before. Nothing was disputed. Outside, the night water sparkled from scattered lanterns at the lake's edge and from slowly-moving glow-worm sampans.

When the adviser had finished, the Young Marshal continued, berating the generalissimo for his apathy in the face of corruption and the inefficiency of his government. This time, May-ling translated in American-accented English for the benefit of the Australian. By the time the two guests had finished voicing their concerns, it was nearly midnight. In the silence Chiang paused, looking thoughtful, then thanked them as if they had brought him up to date on some minor but useful matter.

As the party left the restaurant, Madame Chiang said to Donald, 'You were wonderful. We needed that!'

'We', not 'he'. She saw herself as part of the leadership of China with a burning desire to change it for the better, and sensed the same passion in the Australian. Walking through the lobby, she said, 'Why don't you come and work for us? Working together, the two of us could do much for China.'

Donald said he didn't work for women because they 'can't take it', meaning the rough-and-tumble of public life.

May-ling responded, 'If I couldn't take it, I wouldn't have dared to translate everything you said tonight.'

Chang, eavesdropping on the conversation, said, 'That's right. She even kept in your goddamns!'

Donald laughed. He was about to travel up the Yangtze to investigate conditions, part of a plan he and Chang had to re-immerse themselves in China's political machine. 'I'll write you some letters while I'm up there,' he said to Madame Chiang. 'If you can get the generalissimo to act on them, then someday I just might be working with you.'

A few days later, Chang Hsueh-liang was restored as second-in-command of Nationalist forces and put in charge of 'bandit suppression' (that is, an anti-Communist campaign) in Central China with headquarters in Hankow. He was re-energised by his return. Jimmy McHugh, risen to naval intelligence officer in Shanghai, caught up with Donald and met the Young Marshal a few times, noting his good health and how he bubbled with chat—and how much his ideas sounded like Donald's ideas. At his adviser's urging, he campaigned for social reform and a drive against corruption, even badgering Chiang to take a more resolute stand against the Japanese, but Chiang remained obstinately focused on the Communist insurgency. Chang mended fences with TV Soong and they talked together about establishing a 'fascist party', but nothing came of it.

Langhorne Bond was in Hankow on business and took time off for a round of golf with Donald. After the game, he was asked if he would 'like to meet the young fella'. Chang's Hankow headquarters were surrounded by guards, but the two walked straight past saluting soldiers. As the American tells it, his companion told a private secretary they'd like to see the marshal and they waited in the reception area. After a while a young man came in, sat down with them and chatted convivially with Donald for a while, then politely excused himself and left. Donald got up and the two visitors went outside.

'What happened to the Young Marshal?' asked Bond. 'Was he busy?'

'That was the Young Marshal we were talking to.'

Chang set up the Central China Economic Investigation Bureau in Hankow—its director, WH Donald—to boost trade in the interior and develop China's natural resources. The new director called for the manufacture in China of goods that were being imported from Japan, often made with Chinese raw materials exported duty-free. HH Kung, the new vice-premier, was urged to increase customs police and crack down on smuggled goods coming into China under Japanese protection. While 'smugglers swagger about with pistols in their belts', Chinese customs officers at frontier posts were unarmed at the insistence of the Japanese government to avoid clashes with Japanese soldiers.

Pursuing the opium menace, Donald wrote to Madame Chiang that he had seen free lottery tickets offered with opium purchases in a window opposite a statue of Sun Yat-sen in Hankow. Detailing how opium money was paid to police, he suggested the military also had a share in proceeds. Next day, Chiang issued a decree making dealing in opium a capital offence.

Opium was seen being stacked into postal vans off steamers from upriver, suggesting foreigners in China's administration could be involved in the trade or, at least, turning a blind eye to it. In an unattributed article in the Hankow *Herald*, Donald noted caustically, 'Yesterday I expected to see on the Bund the decapitated heads of a number of persons, including the British commissioner of customs and the French chief of the post office. But there were no heads there at all.'

Donald sent a copy of the article to Madame Chiang before it was published. It was one of several press contributions drumming up action on the opium issue, one he had taken to heart as central to the problems China faced. The Young Marshal brought similar pressure to bear in public statements and discussions within government circles.

In time, Donald received a telegram from Madame Chiang: 'PLEASE FLY TO NANKING TOMORROW'. He met her with her sister, Madame Kung, at the latter's house.

'You, of course, are free to express whatever opinion you choose and we can't do much about it,' said the leader's wife, 'but Chang Hsueh-liang is a military officer and the generalissimo will not tolerate an officer under his command criticising him in speeches.'

'Madame, I don't know what you're talking about,' said Donald cautiously.

'Chang said in a speech that Chiang Kai-shek had shortcomings.'

'No,' replied Donald. 'He said that people said he had shortcomings, but the Young Marshal said that even if he did, their duty and the duty of the country was to stand by him.'

She didn't take issue with this disingenuous argument, possibly because the meeting, ostensibly to object to Chang's speech, was actually to re-establish contact with the Australian. May-ling chewed over what she'd seen and heard before making her next move.

In October, the generalissimo and his wife arrived in Hankow on their way to Loyang to open a new branch of Nanking's Central Military Academy. Chiang met with the Young Marshal to confer about the anti-Communist drive in the upper Yangtze, after which Donald was invited to join the three of them on the trip to Loyang.

'I'm much too busy to go gallivanting around the countryside on a sightseeing trip,' he objected, but they were insistent and he relented.

It would be the beginning of the next phase of Donald's adventure in China.

Chapter 11

Madame and the generalissimo

Bill Donald was sitting in an eerily familiar salon car watching rural China pass by. Generalissimo Chiang Kai-shek and Madame Chiang had left Hankow railway station for Loyang in the old empress dowager's train that Sun Yat-sen had used to tour China more than twenty years before. On their way with Chang Hsueh-liang to open a new military academy in October 1934, they had invited his principal adviser to join them. The line wound its way to the low pass at Wushengkwan through the Haiyang Mountains of north China. While Chiang and the Young Marshal conferred in another carriage, Madame Chiang was busy at the other end of the salon with paperwork. She came down and sat with Donald, throwing a handful of documents on the table.

'I can't do this work anymore,' she said.

If there was a hint there, the Australian didn't take it. He said he'd amuse her with stories if she couldn't focus, telling her of his early days in China and of the uprisings while she was at school in America, moving on to various problems Chiang and his government faced and were not attending to.

In the afternoon, Madame joined Donald again, still overwhelmed by her paperwork.

'Why won't you help me?' she whined.

'I can't. I'm in another camp. I imagine these documents are confidential, but if you request it, I'll be glad to help.'

'Well, I'm asking you,' she replied. 'There's nothing in China that's closed to you.'

'Nothing?' asked Donald breezily as documents were pushed to his side of the table, a mass of reports and appeals to the generalissimo.

'Does your husband know what he wants to do with all these requests?'

'Yes,' she said.

Donald went through the documents one by one, making shorthand notes on some, asking what specific reply was wanted for others. It took a couple of days to write replies to letters and make notes for action by Chiang. By the next afternoon, he gave the stack back to Madame, who looked through it with a mix of relief and admiration.

'This is easy!' she said.

'Yes,' said Donald. 'Apparently.'

After the generalissimo opened Loyang's new academy, the party was quietly drinking tea in the salon, waiting for the clang and shudder of the engine coupling for their journey back. Donald pointed out they were not far from Si'an, the cradle of Chinese civilisation, and if they put the locomotive at the other end they could go there instead and have a plane stand by to fly them back to Hankow. In Hangchow, Donald had put to Chiang that, with officials never knowing what reforms were needed and provincial chiefs reluctant to report the truth, no leader ever knew enough to govern China effectively. Here was a chance to rectify that.

Following the Yellow River west by rail, they arrived at the ancient capital in bright autumn sunshine. The eastern end of the Silk Road and home to the Terracotta Army, Si'an is the product of 3000 years of Chinese history. Met by troops goosestepping to 'John Brown's Body', the Chiangs visited temples, ancient graves and the Huach'ing thermal springs just outside the city, but instead of the few hours planned, they spent three days in Si'an attending meetings and making speeches.

In a local hall, Chiang thanked mission workers for their efforts and urged them to cooperate with his New Life Movement. The audience responded with an appreciative murmur, and May-ling followed with a short, earnest speech asking them to be frank about what reforms were needed. Not expecting the initiative to be thrown back to them and unready for the candour requested, the foreigners were silent, rigid in their discomfort and unsure how to respond.

'What Generalissimo Chiang and Madame Chiang are asking,' Donald interjected, 'is for you to say to their faces what you say behind their backs.'

Jolted into response, they took this as licence to speak their minds, telling of the people's misery and particularly of the destructive impact of opium on their lives. Once a profiteer from China's opium trade, Chiang listened patiently. At the end, a local committee was formed with missionaries and Chinese members of Chiang's own New Life Movement.

Looking for an ideology to counteract Mao's Marxism, Chiang had launched the New Life Movement early in 1934. Based on the four Confucian virtues of propriety (*li*), justice (*yi*), integrity (*lian*) and conscientiousness (*chi*), to which was added the military virtues of austerity, discipline and patriotism, the movement rooted in traditional Chinese values was already being hijacked by the sensibilities of middle America.

US-educated May-ling was passionate about hygiene, obsessed with the filth of city streets and the dirtiness of Chinese kitchens. She carried clean sheets with her to put on chairs and floors. Under her influence, New Life was morphing into the promotion of healthy living, cleanliness and slogans like 'be prompt', 'avoid wine, women and gambling' and 'don't spit', described by *Time* magazine as 'a big dose of the Castor oil of Puritanism'. In the cities, Boy Scout and Girl Guide units were encouraged and the Chiangs attended their parades, but it was a message lost on most rural Chinese, more concerned with survival than clean living.

May-ling met with officials' wives, urging their involvement with the people. After undertaking to set up a clinic for the treatment of opium addicts, she was taken to visit the Shensi Provincial Orphanage where she ordered a feast for the children. Pleased with their reception in Si'an, Chiang agreed to his wife's suggestion, prompted by Donald, that they continue north where no national leader had ever ventured, to the semi-arid provinces of Kansu and Ninghsia, home of the Muslim Hui people.

In Lanchow, where the Yellow River rushes out from the mountains, they visited woollen mills and walked the streets talking to locals, accompanied by only a few soldiers despite warnings about assassination attempts. Launching a local New Life chapter attacking opium use and footbinding, the previously stand-offish Chiang was relaxing and becoming more animated.

Next, they flew to the remote border town of Ninghsia over kilometres of sharp-peaked, light-brown loess hills. Barren and inhospitable, their wind-worn gulches and gullies resembled a petrified tidal rip. Occasionally, looking down, they would see oarsmen on sheepskin rafts taking hides and wool down fast-flowing streams. After some time, the landscape opened to the red sand ridges of the Little Gobi Desert.

'What a sand trap,' commented Chang, a keen golfer.

Farms appeared alongside waterholes as the plane approached Ninghsia with its old Ch'ing garrison of crumbling walls and its mud-coloured pagoda. Beside the airfield were lines of soldiers and cavalry on ponies. Bugles played, people cheered. The party was greeted by two brothers, both called General Ma, and driven past lines of soldiers and citizens to the city where the band played 'When Johnny Comes Marching Home'.

The energised party travelled by plane. Madame suffered air-sickness, often lying on the floor with smelling salts to her nose and using an oxygen tank to cope with high altitudes. From Ninghsia they went to Kaifeng in central China and Chang returned to Hankow. His adviser stayed with the others who flew on to Tsinan (in Shantung), then Peking. Spurred perhaps by fellow health-faddist Donald, the hygiene-obsessed Madame Chiang insisted they all have medical check-ups at the Rockefeller Clinic in Peking.

Chiang had suffered mild indigestion for years but the doctors showed little interest in it. Slight, wiry and with delicate features, he carried himself stiffly. His very dark, grey eyes, piercing and luminous, were never at rest. Rising at dawn, he would work till dusk, but he had no hobbies and no relaxation except reading. The tour of the northwest had been a tonic for him, forging a new pride in his country and a new confidence in himself. Growing in him was a sense of responsibility for China's future, unlike his countrymen's usual drift with power into vanity and venality. People in remote regions had seen their generalissimo and felt a few moments of personal contact with him, so now in their minds only one person stood as their leader. China was unified as much by Donald's casual suggestion of a journey through the northwest as by any strategic campaign.

The Chiangs were invited to Mongolia by two princes and, wanting to build on the gains already made, took their entourage, including Donald, by rail to Inner Mongolia, sending a goodwill envoy on to Mongolia. The goodwill was not universal. After a bomb was tossed into their bodyguard's carriage, killing two, it was decided to travel only by plane, hopping from airfield to airfield, giving speeches to huge crowds gathered there.

At the north China provincial capital of Taiyuan, its streets cleaned and houses painted for the visit, Chiang got a tumultuous response to a speech about the virtues of clean living in this centre of flourishing opium and cocaine trade. They were joined in Taiyuan by the Chiangs' brother-in-law, HH Kung, up from Peking. While Chiang went back to Nanking, Madame, Donald and Kung went on to Peking, Tientsin, Tsingtao and Shanghai.

Donald's presence on the trip had had limited impact on Chiang, but he'd continued to help Madame with her papers. She came to rely on him for help and advice, particularly in dealing with Westerners for her husband.

Donald told her, 'You think like a man!'

In fact, May-ling thought like a Westerner, refined by his coaching, and spoke English with a noticeable Southern accent, but her manner was feminine, tempered Chinese. On returning to Nanking, she asked Donald to become her adviser.

'What? Adviser to a woman?' Donald blustered to others later. 'To the most capricious animal heaven ever created? Not on your life.' But to Madame Chiang he didn't say 'Yes' and he didn't say 'No'. To her, that was a 'Yes'.

Donald had limited understanding of women. Sometimes naive, sometimes misogynist, he was more a man's man by now, with whatever youthful good looks he might once have had lost in the depredations of time. Ruddy-faced, white-haired and getting stout as he approached 60, he had worn heavy glasses since his ocular problems. He was, however, never uninteresting. Cheery, loquaciously convivial and kind, he was full of vitality and laughter, a constant source of anecdotes, sufficiently dominating of the conversation that once he started a story, nothing and no-one would stop him.

Paying little attention to Chinese sensitivities or protocols, he pronounced everyone's name in an exaggeratedly foreign way—Chiang as a nasal 'Chee-ang' rather than the more authentic clipped 'Jong'—and not just Chinese names. He claimed once to not understand a reference to Cardinal Richelieu, pronounced in good French, until it was clarified it was the person he called 'Ritch-liew'.

Madame Chiang's proposal to Donald got tepid support from the generalissimo, but she wouldn't give up easily, arranging a lunch with the two men so her husband might see him as more than a foreigner hanging around. Foreign food was served with Donald reluctant to eat Chinese food and refusing to use chopsticks. Chiang ate in silence, having no language in common with the Australian and nothing to say to his wife. Over dessert, he finally turned to their guest and asked through his wife how he would reconstruct China if he had the power.

'First I would shoot everybody who spoke about "saving face",' said Donald. 'Then I'd shoot everybody who said "it cannot be done". Then I'd shoot every damn fool in the administration.'

Chiang thought for a while before his face spread into a wide grin. 'Unfortunately, I don't have that much ammunition!'

With the ice broken, Chiang agreed to his wife's wish and Donald moved into a bungalow outside Nanking's East Gate, near the Chiang residence where he worked during the day. Sitting at a large desk across from Madame, he started with a pile of correspondence that had accumulated while the Chiangs were away, writing replies, making margin notes in shorthand. Leaving home first thing in the morning and having breakfast with Madame, he would not return till evening. He often ate with the Chiangs—never Chinese food and never with chopsticks—taking the opportunity to feed his ideas to the generalissimo through the fluently bilingual May-ling. Continuing to refer to Chiang as the 'J'issimo', he started calling Madame the 'M'issimo'.

Sometime later, the Young Marshal came from Hankow and phoned Donald, complaining that he never saw him anymore. The Australian invited him to tea at his workplace that afternoon.

'You'll see why you never see me.'

In the afternoon, Chang was ushered into the office used by Donald and Madame to find them at opposite ends of the large desk, each working intently at a typewriter. They all had tea together, during which Madame and the Young Marshal had an animated discussion in Chinese. Donald heard his name mentioned several times, but he couldn't follow the conversation, so he returned to reading letters and scribbling notes while sipping his tea. After a while, Chang came over and slapped his erstwhile adviser on the back.

'It looks like I've lost you,' he said.

'Yes,' answered the older man. 'I damn well think you might have.'

'I'll miss you.'

'Tommyrot,' said Donald.

•

While the generalissimo was touring the northwest, the Communist forces in the south, led by Mao Tse-tung, were secretly moving west from Kiangsi where they had retreated after Shanghai's bloody purge of 1927. It was the beginning of the Red Army's famed Long March. When their move was spotted, Chiang ordered fifteen divisions to encircle them as they crossed the river into Kwangsi, but half the Red force had got through before the government's Kwangsi troops arrived with air support and inflicted the Communists' biggest defeat of the Long March. With the Red Army appearing to head towards the southern plains, Chiang ordered them cleared of people, and their crops destroyed, but the Reds changed direction and turned north into the wild interior of Kweichow. So began a game of cat and mouse where the retreating force stayed constantly on the move, zigzagging out of the grasp of the well-equipped army of the central government.

The generalissimo directed the campaign from Peking where his teeth were being fixed. After spending New Year in his home village of Sikou, the Chiangs set out in January to join the pursuit of the 'bandits', the term he used for China's Communists. Donald was recovering from pneumonia in Shanghai's Country Hospital, but he joined them in Hankow six weeks later.

The party went up the Yangtze by gunboat, the wide river at that time of the year overflowing its banks onto the fields alongside, carrying yellow earth back and out to sea. At Ichang, they transferred to an Italian steamer that took them to Chungking, up rapids rushing through the river's gorges. In the cool of early spring, Chiang wore a trilby and Madame a long coat and fur wrap. Travelling by daylight only, they would anchor in the early afternoon, go ashore by sampan and, if it was a rural area, hike a few kilometres before returning to the boat for dinner. Where they visited towns along the way, their opium dens temporarily closed, the party would be carried from and to the river in sedan chairs.

The entourage included Chiang's security adviser, a German, Captain Walther Stennes, and Madame's new nurse-companion, the American, Marion Satterlee. A Storm Trooper before Hitler came to power, Stennes had spent time in prison for his part in a revolt against Goebbels before coming to China. Donald struck up a friendship with the newly wed Mrs Satterlee, a new audience for his reminiscences. He told her he'd come to China when he was sixteen and lied about his age to get a job, which wasn't true, and that his wife refused to live in China and was now in San Francisco with their daughter, which was.

They came to Chungking, sitting on a high hill in Szechwan at the junction of the Yangtze and Kialing rivers. Wide stone steps were climbed in the rain to get from the river to the roadway where motorcars and rickshaws waited. Setting up headquarters in a local militarist's villa, Chiang met with missionaries and local officials, persuading them to shut down opium shops. Madame organised local women against the drug.

Chiang's personal Ford Trimotor had been brought to Chungking by its American pilot to fly the party over cone-shaped hills to Kweichow's provincial capital, Kweiyang, where they stayed through April. Cleaned and festooned with flags by troops sent two weeks earlier, the frontier city had meagre food supplies, and power for only five hours in the evening. The visitors stayed in a former warlord's house with ill-fitting windows and sliding doors jammed open. With spring not yet warming, they slept in tents pitched inside the building, a fire with local coal filling the room with smoke.

Donald and Stennes had looked at the China Inland Mission there as possible accommodation, but found it unsuitable. When they were leaving the compound, the small son of a Chinese servant opened the gate for them.

'You're a very nice little gatekeeper,' said Donald in quite passable Mandarin.

Showing the visitors around, a surprised Reverend Butler exclaimed, 'I thought you didn't speak Chinese!'

Donald explained that he let it be known he didn't so he wouldn't be constantly approached to use his contacts. When people came to him, he always called for an interpreter. After 30 years listening to interpreters, however, he understood quite a lot of Chinese and caught the drift of what was said, but he didn't go into important meetings without someone to interpret.

After the Nationalist Army inflicted heavy casualties in a battle north of Kweiyang, Chiang reported to Nanking that the Communist backbone was broken. The Red Army was depleted, but it had not in fact been eliminated and, constantly on the move, it continued its withdrawal towards Yunnan, further west.

The generalissimo flew with his party to Kunming in the far west to oversee a trap he was setting, but the Communists avoided the city and headed instead for the upper Yangtze, crossing into Szechwan. Chiang ordered boats at the crossing be secured, but the Reds moved at night, crossing at a different point and turned north, arriving at the Tatu River, swollen by the spring thaw, when only a small Szechwan detachment was there to oppose them.

It took three days for Chiang's force to close in on the Communists, who immediately marched 160 kilometres upstream to an old chain bridge with planks removed. When the bridge was repaired, the rearguard of the Red Army crossed the river and marched on to the Great Snowy Mountains, connecting with another Communist force migrating from above the Yangtze under Chang Kuo-t'ao. Mao's force marched on to Shansi in northern China, arriving in October 1935, while Chiang concentrated on Chang's larger army and drove it further west.

In a remote village in the upper Yangtze, Chiang and his party, following the fleeing army, came across a butcher with the national flag tied around his waist like an apron. Asked for an explanation by the outraged visitors, he said that blood showed up less on the flag's red background. A fuming Chiang wanted the man hanged on the spot for his disrespect, but Donald, the new adviser, counselled differently.

'Hanging one butcher isn't enough,' he said. 'It'll have no impact beyond here and the government's to blame for his ignorance anyway. Something more has to be done to rehabilitate the national flag.' What he proposed was obligatory flag-raising ceremonies across the breadth of their wide country.

'People are loyal to their families, to their village, to their province even, but they don't know the meaning of a national emblem, of patriotism. Here's an opportunity to change that.'

Chiang issued the order that day: every morning and night, school children, students, soldiers, officials and organisations were to rally around flagpoles to salute the national symbol of China. The butcher's neck was spared.

•

Back in Nanking, Donald coached May-ling in handling Westerners who had or might have a useful interest in China, in the press or in business or the diplomatic corps. Often the three were intertwined. When the Chiangs entertained foreign visitors, Madame would receive the guests. After a brief chat, the generalissimo would enter and tea would be served. Usually he'd stay about half an hour with Madame interpreting, despite probably having a reasonable command of English, before leaving his wife to chat further with the visitors.

Another part of Donald's job was to feed the foreign press. In 1936 David Fraser was still in China with *The Times* and his Australian friend provided him with titbits as he moved around the country with the Chiangs. Writing to new supervisors in London, Fraser assured them Donald was deep in the confidence of the Chinese.

'His political judgment is not always good,' he wrote, 'and he's furiously anti-Japanese, but he persists in the urge for reform for China.'

Foreign correspondents had long complained that their dispatches were so heavily censored they were sometimes received with only punctuation marks left. The *New York Times* was said to have received a cable from its China correspondent, 'TIMES NEW YORK STOP STOP STOP STOP STOP STOP STOP SIGNED JAMES WOOD'.

Donald had known Hollington Tong for twenty years, having exchanged news items when the Australian was acting correspondent on *The Times*. He wired the former editor of *China Press*, recovering from illness, and offered Tong the position of chief censor of all outgoing foreign press telegrams. In the quite possible event of being attacked by Japan, it was felt China needed a sympathetic foreign press. Slender, soft-spoken and well-groomed, Tong disliked censorship like any newspaperman, but was persuaded by his friend of the patriotic purpose of building foreign goodwill through the press.

Characteristically haphazard in managing his personal finances, Donald had no formal position with the Chiangs and therefore no contract or salary, although all his expenses were covered. Madame became aware that the finance ministry in the time of the warlord Hsu Shih-ch'ang had dishonoured its undertaking to cover half the running costs of the Bureau of Economic Information which Donald had headed. As the money had come instead from Donald's personal funds, she instructed the Ministry of Finance—her brother-in-law was the current minister—to make good the debt.

Handed a cheque for US$36 000, Donald reacted with the delight of a small boy and gave it to Jimmy McHugh to deposit in his Hong Kong account with National City Bank. Some of it met ongoing living expenses, but a substantial amount was used to commission a yacht to be built for him in the British colony. Called *Mei Hwa* (beautiful flower) it reflected Donald's growing restlessness, his belief he needed a break from China and its seemingly unsolvable problems, but that conflicted with his equally fervent belief that China still needed his guidance to emerge from its dormant state. It would be a conflict to play out in his emotions for some years yet.

In the backblocks again with Chiang, Donald picked up a chill on Omei Shan, a sacred Buddhist mountain in Szechwan. After a night of uncontrolled shivering and aches in every muscle, he was flown to Shanghai to enter its Country Hospital. The fever persisted, and with doctors having no idea what caused it, Donald decided to go to Hong Kong. If his yacht was ready, he would take it on a trial voyage to recuperate from the unidentified fever.

Mei Hwa was still under construction, so he went instead by regular steamer to Java, where his health recovered as he basked in the sun. Returning to Hong Kong, he spent seventeen days in a hotel after the fever revived, then took a steamer to Saigon for the warmer weather. Symptoms persisted in the highland air of Dalat and subsided again on returning to Saigon. Back in Hong Kong, Donald spent the next two months in a nursing home, the nature of his illness still undiagnosed.

Early in 1936, a letter came from Madame Chiang telling him he had to get well as she'd been nagging the generalissimo to reorganise his aviation corps and his response had been to summarily appoint her the secretary-general of the overarching Aeronautics Commission, controlling China's airforce.

'If you'll help with the work,' she wrote, 'I'll take the job.'

Donald wrote back that he would, took a steamer to Shanghai and checked into the Seventh-Day Adventist sanatorium for a further series of inconclusive tests. One evening a doctor brought to his room a colleague with past success treating tropical disease in Panama. The 60-year-old was given a shot of salvarsan, an arsenic-derived antibacterial compound initially developed to treat syphilis. The Panama doctor's theory was that it would 'knock out' both patient and fever, but only the patient would recover.

For a week, Donald could barely lift his head. As he was reviving, the M'issimo was visiting Shanghai briefly and came to see him before returning to Nanking the next afternoon from nearby Hunjao Field. Donald packed his belongings in the morning without consulting the doctors, paid his hospital bill and headed for the airfield. He was already in the plane when a surprised Madame arrived to board it.

'I'm fed up with hospitals,' he said.

While Donald was sidelined with his Szechwan fever, the Kwantung Army demanded the removal of the 'unfriendly' governor of Chahar in the north. Many of the soldiers near the Great Wall were the Young Marshal's dispossessed Manchurians, taking pot shots from time to time at the occupiers of their homeland.

Japan attacked across the wall in January, and a week later announced a treaty had been signed. Judging China's military not yet capable of taking on the Japanese, Chiang played for time and the secret deal also handed much of Hopeh province to Japanese control. Many of the Chinese troops withdrawn from Chahar were sent to Si'an where the Young Marshal had been transferred to finish off the Communists, but anger was building against the generalissimo for not letting Chang lead them back to Manchuria.

A revolt in the south demanded Chiang formally resist Japanese aggression. Local armies advanced northwards, financed ironically by Japan, its interests served by disunity in China, whatever the pretext. The move, however, was widely condemned throughout China and, when the Kwangtung airforce defected to Chiang, the southern revolt collapsed.

Consolidation of China's unity drew new Japanese aggression with increasing 'incidents', taking issue with 'anti-Japanese' sentiment in the Chinese press. Investigated by the national government, there were arrests, some textbooks were censored, some editors jailed. With public disquiet growing louder, asking when the Japanese would be put in their place, Chiang stated that China would respond when the limits of its endurance were reached. At a conference with the foreign press soon after, Madame Chiang was quizzed on what exactly her husband meant with that statement. An American journalist beat around the bush, conscious of the indirect manner of handling these things in China.

'Do you suppose an eventuality is likely to take place soon . . . that is, in what spirit do you think the nation would take any more aggressive action on the part of Japan?' he asked. 'When the generalissimo says "limits of our patience" does he . . . will he . . . '

At that moment, Donald came into the room and Madame cut across the fumbling question with her Western directness.

'Don, Morris is asking me how much longer we're going to stand for this Japanese flimflam.'

There was no reply and the journalist let the matter drop as another question was asked amid the sniggers.

After the Young Marshal was moved to Si'an, Mao sent an emissary from the Communist refuge in Shansi urging a united front against the invader, Japan. To Chang, the Red Army was resourceful and dogged with widespread public sympathy. People questioned a crusade against the Communists, who treated them well. Some of Chang's soldiers, captured and handled with decency, had been impressed with their captors' commitment to their cause. He was disposed to take a 'passive' role in the civil war, although not prepared to oppose Chiang Kai-shek openly or attack the Nanking government.

Secret talks with Chou En-lai in a Catholic church lasted all night and led to an Agreement to Resist Japan and Save the Nation, calling for a united government and army. The Young Marshal shared some arms, ammunition, radio equipment and medicine with the Communists, and exchanged liaison officers. His colleague, the commander of the local Shensi Army, General Yang Hu-cheng, signed a non-aggression pact with them and agreed to stage fake battles.

Later in the year, Chang came to Nanking and stayed at Donald's bungalow, where they got talking about the difficulties he was having with his troops and their officers. His army had suffered funding cuts and many of his best troops had been transferred to the central forces.

'China is no place for an honest man,' he complained. 'I've learnt my lesson the hard way. You know how we talked about reorganising my troops. I tried to do that but I've been blocked and blocked and blocked.'

'By your own officers?'

'They have more ways of passive resistance than you could imagine. And worse, the attitude of the Communists has changed, but when I try to discuss this with the J'issimo, he refuses to listen. Flies into a rage and says, "You have my order to exterminate the Communists. Carry out this order." He won't discuss anything with me.'

'Why don't you resign?' asked Donald.

'I can't resign while my father's body is still in my house in Mukden and the Japs are in Manchuria.'

Donald told his friend he should write down his concerns and give it to the generalissimo, offering to find out if Chiang was prepared to have a round-table talk with the Young Marshal and General Yang. He asked

Madame to suggest to the generalissimo that he discuss with his field commanders changes they'd seen in the Communists.

'I have given my orders and they must be carried out,' said Chiang in mid-translation and Donald said no more.

To get away from the oppressive seasonal heat of the Yangtze valley and the pressure to deal assertively with Japan, the Chiangs moved with Donald and their staff to the summer resort of Kuling on Lushan mountain. Relations between the Chiangs had been frosty since the generalissimo's previous wife, Jennie, had returned in March from America and come to Nanking, but Chiang could not afford a break-up of his marriage. Nicknamed Miss Mou (Miss So-and-so) by others, Jennie stayed discreetly in the background.

Returning to Nanking in October, Chiang left his wife and her adviser to organise the airforce while he flew to Si'an. Intent on finishing off the Communists, having driven them into the remote north, he planned to deal with the Japanese after that. Chang's troops resented the order to fight fellow-Chinese and not Japanese, believing Chiang was not using his own troops in the anti-Red campaign. Marshal Chang and General Yang tried to persuade him to come to terms with the Communists, but he still wouldn't discuss it and scolded them for easing their attacks.

The generalissimo flew back to Loyang for a celebratory lunch with his wife to mark his 50th birthday. He blew out candles on two large cakes and watched an hour-long parade in his honour. Donald had flown up with Madame Chiang, and Chang had come from Si'an for his commander's celebrations. In gloomy conversation with his former adviser, Chang said he was making no progress. His 'bandit suppression' troops, mostly dislocated Manchurians, would not fight the Communists and Chiang was threatening to return to Si'an and order them into the field.

'They will mutiny if he does that,' said their commander.

'Why won't the troops fight?' asked Donald.

'They're not afraid of bullets,' explained Chang, 'but the Communists say, "Why are you fighting us? We're Chinese. We should both be fighting the Japanese. You're fighting so generals can get money for high living. Motorcars, concubines, silk gowns, rich houses. They don't even pay you wages!" That's all true, but I can't get the J'issimo to understand.'

Chiang's strategy continued to be to pacify the nation by defeating the Chinese Communist Party, then attend to the Japanese. Taking control of a vast nation like China was proving to be a difficult task for a Chinese leader. The generalissimo believed it would ultimately prove too great a challenge for the Japanese, so he had the luxury of time with them, less so with the Communists who were now on the defensive. If his commanders in the northwest wouldn't pursue the final stage of his campaign to eliminate the Communists from China, he would find a commander who would.

Chapter 12

The Si'an Incident

On 4 December 1936, Chiang Kai-shek flew to Si'an to coordinate a major assault on the Red Army, holed up in the neighbouring province of Shansi. The city laid out a festive welcome of cleaned streets, rickshaw men in new suits and a gigantic sign on its northern gate: 'Long live Chiang Kai-shek, the revolutionary leader'. Donald's northwest tour had paid off. Arriving with a bodyguard of 45 men and 50 soldiers of the Loyang Regiment to patrol his compound, Chiang wanted to take a closer look at the rapprochement between the dislocated Manchurians and the Communists, and at the growing relationship between Marshal Chang and General Yang reported by Shensi's governor, Shao Li-tzu.

The generalissimo established headquarters at the hot springs resort near Lintung. His generals, including Chen Cheng, brought to replace Chang, stayed at the China Travel Service's guesthouse in Si'an. If no progress was evident in the main campaign, he would move the armies of Chang and Yang to Fukien and replace them from the central Nationalist Army.

With a decisive strike to start on 12 December, he met with the Young Marshal earlier in the week. Still resentful at being dubbed 'the non-resistant general' after the loss of Manchuria, Chang told his commander-in-chief that his troops were so enraged at the Japanese that they were considering joining the Communists to fight them. The response was a demand he carry out his duty and obey orders.

'I can't follow those orders without troops,' said Chang.

'Then you resign your post or I take it from you.'

'I cannot give up my army as long as my father lies under the feet of the Japanese!'

Chiang grew hysterical, shouting that he was going ahead with the campaign with a new commander, if necessary, and Chang, Yang and their troops would be transferred to south China in disgrace. Slamming the door, he left with his bodyguard for Lintung, 25 kilometres out of Si'an along a road freshly sealed for his visit.

Two days later, students carried banners through the streets of Si'an calling for an end to the civil war against the Communists and a more aggressive policy towards Japan. Mostly from Manchuria's Dongbei University, relocated to Si'an, they intended to march to Chiang's temporary headquarters in the afternoon, but were blocked by police at the city gate. Aware of the rally and its intent, Chiang had instructed the Shensi governor to break it up. When protesters started streaming through the gate, police fired on them, wounding two schoolboys and causing the demonstration to waver and scatter. In the confusion, a group of students broke through to the road to Lintung. Sensing further trouble, Chang drove out and urged them to turn back. After some discussion, with a promise that their concerns would be raised with Chiang Kai-shek, they returned.

That evening the Young Marshal went out to Lintung with General Yang to report on the day's events, mentioning that he had told the students he represented the generalissimo and would pass on their demands.

Chiang said, 'You have no authority to say you represent me.'

'I did it to get the students to return to the city.'

'You can't even command the students!'

One of the officers who came with the local commanders butted in, 'Could you?'

'Yes,' said Chiang, 'I could. I'd machine-gun them.'

'Oh, you'd machine-gun them but you won't machine-gun the Japs,' retorted Yang and the matter dropped.

Chiang should have sensed he had a problem with the Shensi warlord, but when his bodyguard commander warned him the next day that Si'an was unstable, he took no precautions.

The visitors left and, on their way back to Si'an, Yang said, 'Now's the time to act. The only way to make him listen is to bring him into the city.'

Yang was proposing his troops surround Chiang's headquarters and compel him to come into Si'an by car. Troubled by the rough-house reputation of Yang's men and their commander's own ruthlessness, Chang suggested he send his Manchurian guard to carry out the task. If Yang agreed and the plan worked, he argued, Yang could take the credit; but if it failed, Chang was prepared to take the blame. He didn't want soldiers getting carried away with the task and the nation's leader ending up harmed—or worse.

After some discussion, Yang agreed, the Young Marshal sending a small unit from within his own bodyguard to the hot springs with specific instructions not to maltreat the generalissimo. They were to surround the guesthouse at night and tell his guards at dawn they were taking him to the city for a conference.

Chang was a guest at a Friday reception in Si'an where the generalissimo referred to his anti-Communist campaign and announced some minor appointments. While Chiang was driven back to Lintung in light snow, Chang attended another reception. After it broke up at ten, he and Yang conferred on the coming action. Finally at midnight, he returned to his headquarters to talk with his senior officers in the second-floor conference room. Under a brass chandelier and large wall maps, they checked everything was in place to bring Chiang safely to the provincial capital and make him see reason.

'Unless absolutely necessary, no shot should be fired,' their commander instructed. 'The generalissimo must be taken alive and unharmed at all costs. If he gets hurt, I will shoot you.'

At 5.30 on Saturday morning, Chiang Kai-shek was in a long white nightshirt staring out the back window of his room into the dark. While he was gathering his thoughts, four trucks with 120 armed soldiers, led by 25-year-old Colonel Sun Ming-jui, arrived at the guesthouse gates and demanded they be opened. In the hiatus following refusal, someone fired a rifle—or someone thought he heard a gunshot and retaliated. A confused exchange of fire resulted, no-one knowing how it started, no-one sure why they were shooting.

Chiang heard shots, then excited shouting and the commotion of forced entry. An aide burst into his room with one of his guards, shouting almost incoherently that there was a mutiny of some sort and urging him to flee. Leaving his dentures on the bedside table, the generalissimo tried to get out the side door, only to find it locked. Pulling a robe over his nightshirt, he climbed out the back window and scrambled over a 3-metre garden wall unaware of the 10-metre drop into a moat on the other side. He fell heavily and further than he expected into a few centimetres of icy water, twisting his back and spraining his ankle in the process. Hobbling up the rocky hillside behind the villa, his feet were bleeding from the fall. Snow covered the thorny scrub underfoot.

After the opening exchange of gunfire, Chang's men rushed across the terraces of the old Imperial springs. Guards were overpowered or killed, and the intruders stormed into the guesthouse. By the time they got to Chiang's room he was gone. His bed was still warm, his dentures, a diary and some documents left on the bedside table. Bags and a coat and hat hung on the coat-rack, his car stood in the drive outside, but he was nowhere to be seen. The raiders began to search the surrounds and particularly Mt Lishan at the back. The commander of the generalissimo's bodyguard, his nephew Colonel Chiang Hsiao-hsien, was captured and shot, suspected of being the leader of secret groups that had been kidnapping student radicals.

In the city the morning bustle of rickshaws and people continued as if nothing was happening, while Yang's troops entered the China Travel Service's guesthouse where Nanking officers were staying, and locked them in its rooms. Local public figures loyal to Chiang were arrested, including Shensi's governor.

In Si'an, the Young Marshal was kept abreast by phone of progress at Lintung. Even with an understated report, he was aghast. This was not going the way he wanted. His own men were there, not Yang's, to prevent an outbreak of cold-blooded stupidity. Now people were being killed and the mission's quarry had disappeared.

'If we don't find him safe,' he moaned histrionically, 'I'll have to offer my head to Nanking on a plate!'

With feet bleeding and wrenched back, Chiang limped in pain up the darkened slope to the top of a hill. He could see the distant, darting lights of Chang's soldiers combing the mountainside. The sound of fighting in the guesthouse had ceased. After resting for a while, alone in the chill emptiness, he decided to return to the compound, descending in the pitch black. Halfway down, he stumbled and fell into a shallow cave with prickly shrubbery covering its opening. Spikes pressed sharply into his skin, but he couldn't get to his feet. Waiting in the darkness, exhausted, freezing and in pain, he had no idea where he was on the side of Mt Lishan.

As dawn's thin glow lit softly falling snow, Chiang took stock. He could move gingerly now, but with the sound of soldiers resuming their search, saw no reason to leave his shallow hole. He lay where he was, flat against the rockface in the space behind a large boulder known locally as Tiger Rock.

The searchers noticed a shadow moving next to the rockface. When they threatened to open fire, their generalissimo appeared, bent and moving with difficulty, a pale figure in a torn robe. Shaking from exhaustion and cold, he remained in his shelter, staring at his captors. Colonel Sun came over and saluted him, urging him to come back to the guesthouse.

'You call me "Generalissimo",' said Chiang. 'Why do you do that?'

'Because you are the generalissimo.'

Slowly gathering the ascendancy, Chiang stared at him with a steely gaze, wincing from a darting pain. Fury was building inside him and it fortified him.

'I shall not leave here. You can shoot me where you are.'

'We don't want to shoot you,' pleaded the boyish-looking colonel. 'We merely beg you to come back to the house.'

Sun got on his knees and tearfully begged his commander-in-chief to come out of the hole. Chiang said he was too cold and in pain with his bleeding feet, too lame to walk any further. He wanted a horse.

'We don't have a horse here, but I'll carry you down,' said Sun, already kneeling in the snow.

Chiang hesitated over the decision, then shuffled from the cave. Bending over the colonel's muscular back, his head bumped against close-cropped hair as the young officer got to his feet. Sun carried his leader on his back with difficulty, sometimes nearly buckling under the weight, until he reached the bottom of the hill where a car was waiting.

When they got to the resort, bodies were lying on the ground where they'd fallen in the pre-dawn raid. Continuing to Si'an in the car, the colonel grabbed the opportunity to stress the urgency of going to war against Japan.

'I am the leader of the Chinese people,' the generalissimo responded firmly. 'I represent them and I believe my policy is correct. No arrest or pressure will change my course.'

Chiang was surprised to find himself brought to a wing of General Yang's headquarters. He had assumed the Shensi commander was still loyal, since the attackers at the springs had all been Manchurians. As he arrived, a military band played 'Frère Jacques', the Nationalist Party's theme song, and Yang's officers saluted the hobbling captive.

'Don't salute me!' he shouted at them.

A pale, respectful and somewhat relieved Chang, his hands rigidly at his side, came forward and helped Chiang, incandescent with rage and pain, from the car and inside to a room with a bed. A doctor was on hand to tend his injuries as Chang assisted him into the bed, all the time cursed by his commander. The room was small, with a single wooden bed against a wall and grubby drapes. A bucket stood in one corner, brooms in another. The musty smell of disuse hung in the room.

When the doctor left, the Young Marshal returned, bowed and apologised for the discomfort caused. Sitting on the bed, seething, Chiang made no response.

'I wish to lay my views before Your Excellency, the generalissimo.'

'Do you still call me the generalissimo?' demanded Chiang, launching into a tirade of fury. 'If you still recognise me as your superior, you should send me to Loyang; otherwise you're a rebel. Since I'm in the hands of a rebel you had better shoot me. There's nothing else to say. Which are you, my subordinate or my enemy? If you're my subordinate, you should obey my orders. If you're my enemy, you should kill me without delay.

You should choose either of these, but say nothing more because I won't listen to you.'

'I believe I haven't disobeyed your orders in any way. Please don't get angry. Consider this carefully.' The Young Marshal's intonation was respectful.

Before he could continue, the generalissimo lay back on the bed, pulled the blanket over his head and turned his face to the wall. His captor spent the day trying to speak to him, trying to reason, but his reward was a volley of abuse, to be told there would be no place for his bones to lie quietly. He tried to persuade Chiang to come to his house with the comforts of central heating and a modern water supply. More to the point, he needed to keep Yang's officers away from their prisoner. He couldn't risk one of them losing his temper and harming him. Enough damage had been done already.

'You can shoot me here,' said Chiang petulantly. 'I won't come.'

He refused to move to more comfortable and safer quarters, refused to eat anything, refused tea. A guard offered him a fur-lined coat, but it was waved away. In time, however, his rage eased and he said his duty to the Chinese race prevented him from obeying the demands of rebels, just to save his own life.

Chang made broadcasts during the afternoon on Si'an radio, explaining his efforts to persuade the generalissimo to fight the Japanese, but the transmitter's power was weak and its existence was not widely known. In any case, Nanking did all it could to jam the transmission.

A telegram was sent to Madame Chiang, a close friend of the Young Marshal for some years, explaining his reasons for detaining her husband 'temporarily', saying there was no intent to ill-treat him.

'My conscience is clear,' he wrote, 'and I can show it in broad daylight. Madame, you may feel calm, and if you wish to come to Si'an you are welcome to do so.'

A similar message was sent to HH Kung, the acting leader of the central government.

A *Telegraph to the Nation*, addressed to the Nanking government, was also prepared and sent to the provinces, the press and schools. China's sovereignty had been impaired since losing Manchuria five years before, it explained, and humiliated by coerced agreements. The nation's leader should establish a front for national defence, not surround himself with unworthy advisers. His long-term colleagues could no longer sit still and witness it, but were offering Chiang advice while guaranteeing his safety. The document listed eight demands and was signed by Chang, Yang and several senior officers of their two armies. The demands included admitting all parties into the Nanking government in a reorganisation to save the nation, stopping the civil war, releasing anti-Japanese patriots arrested in Shanghai, and calling a National Salvation Conference. Curiously, there was no direct call to declare war on Japan.

•

On the day her husband was detained in Si'an, Madame Chiang had arranged a noon meeting in Shanghai of the National Aviation Commission which she headed. Feeling off-colour, she postponed the meeting till five and lunched with her Australian mentor, who afterwards went back to the Park Hotel where he was staying, then to the cinema next door. Donald got back to his hotel room in time to get to the postponed meeting to find his table covered with phone messages, most of them from Madame. Ringing her Shanghai home, he was told she'd gone to the Kung house.

Her brother-in-law had come earlier in the afternoon to tell her there had been a mutiny in Si'an with no news of the generalissimo. She had left in an extremely agitated state and was still distraught when Donald phoned her shortly after, wanting to know where he'd been and asking him to come over as fast as possible. She didn't explain.

When the Australian arrived, the Soong sisters were deep in intimate discussion. May-ling jumped up.

'Don, the Young Marshal has mutinied!'

Donald smiled at this unexpected development.

'What are you smiling at?' Madame demanded. 'The generalissimo is missing. We don't know what's happened! We don't even know if he's alive!'

Donald explained that he was smiling at the thought of the Young Marshal mutinying. Then he quickly reassured her that if Chang was there, the generalissimo would be unharmed and in no danger.

May-ling said it was reported he was already killed.

'I don't believe that,' said Donald, 'and we should keep calm until we find out.'

The Australian's presence had a settling effect on those gathered in the Kung house. The only foreigner there, indeed the only person not a member of the Soong family, the trust he'd built over the years was now paying a dividend for all. It was decided the best move was for Donald, as a friend and former adviser of Chang, to fly to Si'an and determine the state of play there and the generalissimo's health. He would take whatever first steps presented themselves for resolving the crisis.

After dinner, Donald left by train with Madame and the Kungs, reaching Nanking in the early morning. From the moment they got to the Kung residence there, a procession of government leaders and advisers began arriving. In the hubbub, the debate was about whether to retaliate decisively by bombing Si'an, or take the rebel leaders at their word that Chiang was alive and wait for more definite news. Madame Chiang pondered in passing whether the kidnappers might have a reasonable grievance.

Donald wired the Young Marshal that he was flying to Si'an and to make sure gunners did not shoot at the plane. Returning to the reception room, he found everyone deep in discussion, despondent, anxious and tense. They ignored Donald's presence, as if he wasn't supposed to be there.

He remarked to May-ling, 'They don't seem to like me. They still regard me as the Young Marshal's man.'

General Ho Ying-ching, the pro-Japanese minister of war, led the discussion, talking as if Chiang was already dead and that the only option available to them was retribution. Thickset and round-faced, he dismissed Madame's plea not to attack as a woman's emotional response, then tempered his certainty,

'Even if the generalissimo is still alive, what is the fate of one person compared with the fate and future of an entire nation?'

Advised that the Australian would be flying to Si'an to try to negotiate Chiang's release, Ho went back on the offence.

'Nobody is going to Si'an!' he declared. 'We're attacking Si'an.'

Donald pointed out he was an independent citizen, not subject to the regulation that applied to government workers and entitled to assess his own risk. In any case, he didn't believe the generalissimo had been killed. He was going and General Ho wasn't going to stop him.

After lunching with Colonel Huang Jen-lin, a Chiang aide Madame insisted go with him as interpreter, Donald still had no reply to his Si'an cable. Nonetheless, he decided to fly to Loyang in Chiang's Ford Trimotor, bringing with him letters from May-ling for her husband and his captor, and one of Chiang's diaries. Arriving just before sunset, Donald and Huang went to the Nationalist Army's Loyang headquarters to be told Si'an was in flames from planes sent that morning, that red flags were flying and soldiers were digging trenches along the city wall.

In the 'burning' city, Chiang had refused to eat or get out of bed. During the day, he wrote two wills. One, to his wife, said he was prepared to sacrifice his life for the sake of the people and, if that was what fate determined, she was to look after his two sons. The other was to those sons telling them they must regard May-ling as his only wife and look after her, although she was thc mother of neither.

For much of the day the Young Marshal tried to reason with his prisoner with little success, communication made difficult by their different dialects—Chiang's of Chekiang, Chang's of northern Manchuria—with different pronunciations and colloquial idioms. Ordinarily their conversation was modified to accommodate the difference, but now the generalissimo just ranted and stormed, making no effort to ensure he was understood by someone from another part of China.

The next morning, Monday 14 December, Donald and Huang flew over the mountains, warned they wouldn't be able to land in the burning city. Approaching above the thermal springs where Chiang had been staying, they could see no activity. Traffic on the road to Si'an looked normal with no military vehicles about. The walled city's gates were open. No fires were to be seen, no red flags, no trenches. The airfield had about twenty planes tied down, but not a soul moving about them. Circling over the Young Marshal's house several times, the procedure to notify that unexpected arrivals need transport, they saw three cars leave the yard and head for the airfield. So far, nothing seemed out of place in the burning city.

Descending, they saw the bald head of Jimmy Elder on the edge of the landing strip, waving his hat. Greeted at the bottom of the Trimotor's steps, Donald asked if his telegram to Chang had got through.

'No, Don. Haven't seen it, didn't get it,' said Elder. He explained that Chang had sent a telegram to Donald on Saturday. 'Did you get that, asking you to come to Si'an?'

'No. Nothing.'

The visitors were driven to the marshal's residence; Huang waited while Chang took his one-time adviser to meet General Yang. With Elder translating, Donald paraphrased the message of May-ling's letter to Chang.

'This is a poor show when China has just got a taste of unity,' he said. 'It can't afford to sacrifice that. The Japs would come out winners and China a serious loser. For this country's sake, stop all this tommyrot. You should announce the leader's release as soon as possible.'

It was a point Elder had been making in an argument with Chang when Donald's plane came into earshot, but it was not a point Yang was willing to contemplate. Like his accomplice, he was already in too deep.

Next, the Manchurian and the Australian went to see the detained man, lying on his camp bed in the cold, bare room, his face to the wall.

'I knew you would come,' he said to Donald with tears in his eyes as he was given the letter from his wife.

After Chiang had digested the letter's content and shed a few more private tears, Donald told him he was there to make arrangements. Madame was waiting in Nanking to come to Si'an, a prospect so alarming to Chiang that he erupted in fury again, fearful for her safety in the hands of his captors even if he thought he had the Young Marshal's measure.

'I don't want her to come,' he screamed. 'You have no right to bring her here!'

He turned his face back to the wall. Donald stepped over to the window in dignified wounded silence, gazing out at nothing in particular.

Chang came over to him, whispering, 'Go on. Say something.'

Matching the detainee for petulance, the Australian said, 'I've got nothing to say. I resent someone—even him—jumping down my throat like that.'

'He's been jumping down my throat for weeks.'

The Young Marshal pleaded with Donald to talk to Chiang. Finally Donald said, 'I think it will be better if you come with me to a house near the Young Marshal's place. There's central heating, hot and cold bath water . . . you can be there peacefully by yourself.'

Chiang weighed up this proposition. 'I'll go with you,' he said.

'I'll leave while you get dressed.'

Huang later told Donald he overheard Chang telling his men, 'If we can't move him today, I'm worried they'll change guards tonight.' Yang's guards were expected to soon replace his own.

The generalissimo came out in uniform, limping but with the air of a burden lifted, tense but relieved at the same time. The sentry saluted; guards outside the building sprang to attention and saluted also. At the bottom of the entrance's stone steps, a car waited. Chiang gestured towards its back door.

'Han-ching, you get in,' he said, using the Young Marshal's pet name.

'I'll sit with the driver,' Chang replied.

Chiang pressed him on the matter, but he was adamant and eventually Donald and the generalissimo got in the back seat, the Young Marshal in the front. As they pushed through eerily normal traffic taking no notice of them, Chiang seized Donald's hand and clung to it all the way to the grassy courtyard of a dwelling opposite Chang's headquarters.

Standing to attention while Chiang was shown into his new room, the Young Marshal was asked to sit down. The gesture appeared not to register. He remained at attention, swaying slightly. Donald sat in a chair, worried about Chang's zombie-like state. He hadn't slept since Friday. Chiang sat on the edge of the room's wooden bed, berating the lurching young man. Any mumbled protest simply fuelled the tirade. The situation deteriorating, Donald pulled at Chang's coat and told him to go over the road. They could talk over dinner. The Young Marshal bowed, saluted his commander and left, a sleepwalker withdrawing.

As the door closed, Chiang's bold front vaporised. He turned to the Australian with a look of helplessness, waving his hand despairingly, and said in his own language, 'See, it is finished!'

'What is finished?' asked Donald in his rudimentary Chinese.

'It is finished.'

Ah-wang, Donald's former house-boy and now Chang's valet, came to attend to the generalissimo's needs. Donald talked for a while before turning on a bath tap.

'Have a hot bath and go to sleep,' he said gently with Ah-wang translating. 'Dinner will come later and I'll see you after that.'

When he heard that Donald had come with Huang, sent by Madame, Chiang wanted to see the colonel, but Chang refused to allow it. Eventually he relented a little and let Huang observe through a patch rubbed clear in the door's whitewashed glass. With a gun jabbed in his back and a guard on either side, a hunched Huang saw his leader propped up in bed, talking to Donald through the house-boy interpreter. The generalissimo looked thin and pale, but he was clearly alive.

Donald had his dinner across the road with the Young Marshal and was told he should leave in the morning for his own safety.

'If they bomb the city, you and the generalissimo will be killed.'

Chang must save the J'issimo at all costs, was Donald's response. He was already accused of assassinating him and if he was killed later by the bombing, it would appear to confirm that.

Later, General Yang and several officers called by to discuss the fate of the city. Planes had dropped pamphlets during the day warning that it would be bombed if Chiang was not released. The officers were indignant that their prisoner wouldn't talk to them or sign the documents that would ensure their safety.

'It's curious that people who live in Shensi know the mule is the most obstinate of beasts, but don't recognise the same quality in a human,' mused Donald aloud. He was referring to Shensi being the home of the best mules in China. The officers laughed at the idea of Chiang's mulishness, but Donald hadn't finished the point he was making.

'Don't do anything to make your position worse,' he continued, 'but frustrate your enemies' wish to involve you in Chiang's death. They say he's been killed already. You must protect his life so they can be proved wrong.'

As the evening drew to a close, Donald sent telegrams to Madame Chiang, Reuters and the *New York Times*, assuring them that Chiang Kai-shek was safe and staying in a house with him.

'I'll fly to Loyang tomorrow,' he told his host, 'and contact Madame to persuade Dr Kung to come here and secure the J'issimo's release.'

'If the bombing starts, I'll put the generalissimo on a plane out of Si'an,' promised the Young Marshal.

On Tuesday morning, Chiang's emotional seesaw continued with a visit by Donald and Chang. Given a list of the rebels' eight points to be considered, the topics already cabled to Nanking, the generalissimo exploded, refusing to discuss them any further. Told that Donald was flying to Loyang, Chiang forbade him to go even though he would phone Madame, report on her husband's welfare and get HH Kung to come to Si'an.

'I'm an independent person with my own ideas and values,' said the exasperated go-between, 'and I'm leaving in a few minutes.'

Donald said to Chang, 'Tell the J'issimo I don't understand why he doesn't open his eyes and his ears to what's happening and open his mouth less.'

The younger man refused and, when Donald asked why, said Chiang would think he was disguising his thoughts as translation.

'You think he doesn't know I have my own opinions?'

'I'll get Jimmy Elder to translate.'

While the Young Marshal was gone, Chiang said, 'You know about the eight points?'

'Yes,' said Donald.

'They are impossible.'

'I don't think so,' was the reply in halting Mandarin. 'You should look at them carefully.'

At that moment, Elder arrived and was surprised that Donald and Chiang seemed to have been conversing—in which language, he wondered—but before he could pursue it, Chiang waved a paper about, saying, 'How can I agree to these?'

Elder translated and a discussion took place about the eight points.

'If I agree to this,' said Chiang, pointing to the demand that he obey the will of Sun Yat-sen, 'I agree to all of them.'

'But you do obey the will of Sun Yat-sen, don't you?' asked Donald.

'Yes, I do.'

'Then you agree to these eight points.'

Chiang listened to the translation and said nothing. Donald was leaving for Loyang and said he would be back in the afternoon.

While the generalissimo and his adviser discussed the eight points, Chang told the sidelined aide he would be allowed to enter the guarded room to get a letter for Madame Chiang. Huang was not to discuss any matters concerning the detention or he would not be allowed to leave Si'an.

Asked about May-ling's health, the aide then stood by while Chiang wrote his letter. When finished, it was read aloud three times: how he would sacrifice his life for his country if needs be and not bring shame on his wife, how she was to return his body to his parents and regard his two sons as her own children, and that she was not to come to Shensi. Aghast, Huang knew he would not be leaving Si'an.

Outside the room, Chang was furious and took the letter. Guards arrived and told the aide they would move him to a better room. He assured them he was quite comfortable, but they insisted and took him to his new room—a cell.

With bad weather closing in, Donald flew with Elder down the Yellow River to Loyang. Snow was falling on the hills and the cloud ceiling was low. He phoned May-ling from the Nationalist Army's Loyang headquarters to let her know her husband was safe, warm and resting, urging her to get Kung to Si'an next morning so they could secure Chiang's release.

'Did you send telegrams?' asked Madame.

'Yes. Three of them.'

'They brought them and said you were a traitor working for Chang against China.'

'They' were Nanking's pro-Japan clique allied to General Ho, and Donald was a traitor for saying Chiang was alive when they said he was dead.

'I told them that if you signed the telegram it was the truth,' said the unhappy voice. 'I'm having a terrible time. You must send no more telegrams. You must come to Nanking and not go back to Si'an. They'll kill you if you do.'

Donald insisted he was going back to Si'an in the morning. The weather was getting worse, but he was not afraid. The city was quiet with no fires, no red flags, no sign of warfare, but the generals there were getting jumpy with Nanking's threat to bomb.

'I'll phone before leaving,' he added, 'so arrange for Kung to come.'

'You tell the J'issimo these people are trying to kill him.'

'I've already done that.'

'Tell him again from me.'

Elder was flying on to Nanking. As he was in the room when Chiang read out his letter, he was able to pass on its content to Madame. It gave him a welcome opportunity to get out of Si'an, unconvinced of the wisdom of his friend's alliance with the violent and unscrupulous Yang. Telling Madame Chiang that the generalissimo's only hope for freedom was by accepting his captor's demands, he added that if the government attacked Si'an, Yang's troops' first move would be to murder him.

Donald spoke to Madame in the morning before leaving Loyang. The Nanking government had refused to allow Kung, or anyone else, to go to Si'an and the war minister was refusing to cancel his order to attack the city. She pleaded with her friend and adviser not to go back, but he'd already failed to keep his promise to return the afternoon before. The weather was looking bad. Snow was falling and would probably do so for several days, so he might not be able to come back to Loyang for a while.

'Keep up the fight, M'issimo,' he said. 'You'll win in the end.'

Before he left, Donald gave the Loyang commander a plan showing the position of the house where Chiang was held. If the house was bombed, he told the general, he would advise Madame Chiang who had ordered it. At the airfield, he noticed munitions being loaded on Douglas bombers which took off at the same time as his Trimotor. Some of the bombers circled him in the air, either as a threat or out of curiosity, he couldn't be sure. Bombs were dropped on railway stations and one on an open field with no-one in sight. With snow falling heavily, the bombers wouldn't risk flying over mountains in poor visibility, but Donald's smaller plane with its American pilot followed the Yellow River west between the steep cliffs of the Sanmen Gorge and through to the flood plain of Kwanchung where Si'an nestled between the Wei River and the Ch'inling Mountains.

Back with the kidnapped leader, the Australian passed on Madame's message and that Nanking had refused to allow Kung to come.

Chiang asked, 'Why don't they bomb the city?'

'God sent heavy snow to stop the bombers getting to Si'an,' explained Donald. 'They had to turn back.'

In the far north, the Communist Mao Tse-tung heard the news of Chiang's incarceration with excitement. Here was an opportunity to avenge the 1927 Shanghai massacre, he told a gathering of followers in a large cave. The Nationalist leader must be put on trial. Chou En-lai was to go to Si'an representing the Chinese Communist Party, but Mao's glee was short-lived. Instructions came from Moscow overruling him and insisting on a united front to oppose the Japanese. Stalin's priority was containing Japan on his eastern frontier and he believed Chiang Kai-shek the only Chinese commander capable of bringing that about. Whatever their political differences might be, a way had to be found to free him.

Travelling by mule to a makeshift airfield built by Standard Oil years before, Chou met a plane sent by the Young Marshal hoping the Communists could help dig him out of the mess he found himself in. When he got to Si'an, Chou met with Chang, telling him, 'If Chiang Kai-shek promises to turn on the Japanese, he should be released to head the national struggle. If he refuses, he should be executed.'

Si'an's heavy snowfall was showing no sign of easing, and no bombers crossed the mountains from Loyang. Chiang was in such an erratic state, he was irritated they didn't come.

'It's their duty to do so!' he complained.

A worried Chang commented it seemed the prisoner wanted to be a martyr, while Donald tried to convince Chiang it was a poor strategy.

'A live Blackie [Madame's pet dog] is worth an acre of dead lions,' he observed. 'Your duty is to keep alive for the good of the country, not die for it. I don't want this ceiling scattered all over me even if you do.'

The snow continued, with captors, captives and observers cooped up in Si'an, dealing with whatever developed. Chang and Yang and their officers had read the diary Donald had brought from Nanking and now accepted that, contrary to their earlier belief, Chiang's long-term strategy included opposing Japan's incursions into China. His plan was to defeat China's Communists—bandits, he called them—while building the Nationalist Army to the strength necessary to oppose the Kwantung Army. Chiang's current diary, picked up during the Lintung raid a week before, was consistent with that.

The rebels were also coming to the realisation they didn't have the wide support they expected. Telegrams and reports, critical of the action they had taken, were coming from all over China. While this was in part because Nanking controlled—and sometimes altered or fabricated—news from Si'an, it was nonetheless what people in China and overseas were hearing and believing. Public support for Chiang had grown, even with his fate uncertain, not the outcome General Ho's coterie sought. The Young Marshal came to Donald waving a sheet of paper, shouting that a broadcast from Nanking blamed him solely for the leader's detention and didn't mention he was still alive.

Bill Donald was not completely cut off from the outside world, however, nor was the integrity of his reports at Nanking's mercy. A Congregational missionary in China, the American-educated New Zealander Reverend George Shepherd had become closely involved with the New Life Movement and was, as a result, a confidant of the Chiangs. He and Donald were the two foreigners they most trusted. During the Si'an Incident, as it came to be known, Shepherd in Nanking and Donald in Si'an exchanged messages in private code between Chiang and May-ling.

On Saturday 19 December, the snow ceased falling. A coded message arrived from Madame that TV Soong was coming to Si'an and Donald was to return in his plane.

'What does he want to come here for?' grumbled Chiang.

'The family expect him to be overjoyed to be freed,' remarked Donald to Chang. 'They don't realise he wants to be a martyr!'

Later in the day, the generalissimo asked when the Nanking delegation would come and Donald said, 'Maybe today.'

Pointing to a patch of sunlight on the wall, he added, 'Do you see the sun shining there. God kept it snowing for his own reasons and now he's making way for a plane to come through the clouds.'

Soon after, another telegram came from Madame via Shepherd that Nanking had refused to allow Soong to leave, then a further cable that he was going as a private citizen. The government might be able to block the use of government planes, but they could do little to stop the wealthy Soong travelling in his own plane.

Before Donald could reply to this last cable, a plane could be heard in the distance, almost certainly Soong's. The Australian got his bags and, as he was leaving the compound, three cars arrived; in one car was the former minister of finance, now chairman of the Bank of China. Soong told Donald not to go to the airport, but come with him to see Chiang.

'I need to have a long talk with you,' he said.

Chiang was so overwhelmed at seeing his wife's brother enter his bare room, he couldn't speak. Soong gave him a letter from May-ling that said, in part, 'If at the end of three days TV does not return to Nanking, I will come to Si'an to live or die with you.'

When the generalissimo burst into tears, Soong gestured to Chang and Donald to leave and the brothers-in-law talked privately for half an hour. Chiang told Soong his captors had changed their view on reading his diaries and now knew he intended to defend China against Japan eventually. The main threat, he concluded, was from Nanking's pro-Japan clique preparing to attack Si'an. Soong, however, had arranged a three-day truce with the Nanking clique before leaving.

By the next day, after several rounds of discussion, the generalissimo grudgingly agreed in principle to lead a united front against Japan and put the civil war on hold, but stipulated he must be released first. He was sympathetic with some of the eight-point plan, he said, but would promise nothing under restraint.

On 21 December, Donald returned with TV Soong to Nanking to report to May-ling and decide their next moves. The Young Marshal was no longer a threat. Indeed, said Donald, he would fly out with Chiang if they were attacked—if that became possible. The situation was more precarious with Yang, especially if the war minister resumed his planned Si'an assault. The three of them decided they should fly to Si'an the next day, along with Chiang's chief of secret police, Tai Li. Madame had no appetite for austerity and would bring a handful of staff, including her *amah*.

In the morning, she decreed an emissary sent down earlier from Si'an, the unrelated General Chiang Tung-wen of her husband's bodyguard, should also return with them. He was not enthusiastic, apparently frightened of something apart from the peril he thought he'd escaped.

'I'm no use to you there,' General Chiang pleaded futilely. 'Please don't ask me to go.'

In the corrugated metal Fokker Trimotor, Madame stretched out while Donald observed the guard commander's growing fear. Approaching Loyang about lunchtime, Donald suggested a stopover for lunch and Madame ordered the pilot to land. As they finished their meal, she suddenly got up and left the room. A few minutes later, Donald looked out the front window and saw her with the police chief and the Loyang commander hurrying out the gate. He couldn't see General Chiang anywhere, but as TV Soong was still in the next room, he sat down and read while he waited.

Half an hour later, Soong came into the room and said they had to rush. May-ling had rung to say they should come into the city, giving no reason. On the road, they saw cars coming towards them and stopped. In one, Madame was holding a struggling General Chiang by the arm.

'No wonder the generalissimo can't fight the Communists, with a general like you,' she said loudly for all to hear.

May-ling told her mentor what had taken place. Because he didn't want to go to Si'an for some reason, the general had fled to a house in the city. Getting word where he had gone, she knocked on the door with her two military companions. Told he was not there, she noticed his hat on a rack near the door and said, 'Bring me the owner of that hat.'

A sheepish General Chiang came to the door and protested that not only would he be of no use in Si'an, but he would make matters worse.

'I just came to ask you to join me at lunch,' said the generalissimo's wife sweetly.

Unconvinced, he said he didn't realise and got doubtfully into the car under the watchful gaze of the two senior officers.

'Now we go to the airfield,' instructed Madame.

Driving down the highway to meet Donald and Soong, the reluctant man had struggled to break away from his captor's grip, explaining his terror of Si'an. While in Nanking and not expecting to return, he had made broadcasts blaming the Young Marshal as the prime instigator of the incident in Si'an. Knowing the fate of Generals Yang and Ch'ang in Mukden eight years before, he was now in panic that Chang would have him shot as soon as he returned.

With the plane circling Si'an and General Chiang looking pale and worried, Madame turned to her adviser, pressed a small revolver into his hand and said quietly, 'Don, you must promise to shoot me if any soldiers lay their hands on me.'

Donald said calmly, 'No-one will trouble you.'

'I know these half-bandit soldiers and you must promise to shoot me if they try to grab me. I would sooner die than fall into their hands.'

'You'll be okay,' Donald reassured her.

'You must promise. You take this gun.'

Donald promised and put the gun in his pocket, although he had no intention of using it. By then the plane was losing altitude, coming down on the airfield near a group of cars.

'There's Han-ching,' said the Australian.

'How shall I speak to him?' Madame asked.

Donald said to talk as if nothing had happened. It shouldn't be difficult as the Young Marshal had protected the generalissimo's life.

Landing in failing light, the Fokker came to a halt on the muddy grass strip and the passengers alighted into a circle of torches held high in the biting evening cold by Manchurian soldiers in sheepskin caps. When the petrified general got cautiously out of the plane, he found himself face to drawn face with the object of his fear stepping from behind the torchlight in his neatly pressed uniform.

'Oh, you've come back,' said Chang, smiling malevolently, but the exhausted and contrite rebel had more pressing matters on his mind.

Met by Donald at the door, the warlord was advised, 'You talk quietly to Madame.'

The Young Marshal went over to May-ling, bowed and was greeted cordially. They conversed politely without mentioning her husband. She shook a tense General Yang's hand, but as they spoke he calmed down. Madame asked that customs not go through her luggage, not because she had anything to hide but because she disliked having her things messed up.

Driving to the Young Marshal's headquarters with Donald and her brother, Madame was asked if she wanted to see her husband immediately or rest briefly.

'Let's go to your place first and have tea,' she said. 'There's no rush. I need to talk with you.' She wanted to appear calm, but asked that Chiang not be told of her arrival before she saw him.

Over tea, Chang was at great pains to explain his actions to his visitor. She didn't enter into a discussion and, soon after, they all crossed the road in the dark to the bungalow in which Chiang was held, walking to the detention room past armed soldiers. The detainee had noticed there was no sound of gunfire or heavy planes that day, but failed to make the connection. The appearance of May-ling in the evening was both unexpected and ecstatic, difficult to deal with in his heightened emotional state.

Tears trickling down his cheek, he said, 'Why have you come here? You've walked into the lion's mouth.'

'I've come to see you,' his soulmate replied.

Chiang gabbled in excitement. 'Although I begged you not to come, I knew I couldn't prevent you,' he said, showing her a passage in the Bible he had been reading that afternoon. '"Jehovah will now do a new thing, and that is, He will make a woman protect a man." And now you are here!'

May-ling passed him a spare denture brought from Nanking. He put his hand to his face, twisted to make an adjustment, and turned back with a wry smile. Donald and TV Soong left the reunited couple to private conversation and took a walk in the snow-covered courtyard under the watchful but unconcerned eyes of sentries around the wall.

Imploring his wife not to ask him to compromise and not mentioning concessions he'd already made, Chiang said he was determined not to agree to anything under duress. He was ready to die for the good of China. 'If I make a pledge to gain my own release,' he said with passion, 'I would be a contemptible coward and deserve to be killed.'

'We must be cautious and patient,' said May-ling, adding gently that the rebels realised they had made a grave mistake and that a solution could be found.

He looked wan and ill, legs and feet cut by brambles and bruised by rocks. She opened the book to Psalms and read to him until he drifted into deep sleep.

Madame came out to the ghostly courtyard and she, Donald and TV Soong walked about discussing options, then met with Chang and talked long into the evening. May-ling warned him that his actions could have disastrous consequences and the important question now was how to get out of it. She reproached him for thinking he could get her husband to respond to force.

'Had you been here,' the Young Marshal said, 'events would not have gone as they did.' He asked Madame to try to persuade her husband to curb his anger. 'We don't want him to sign any documents. We're not seeking any money, nor control of any territory. All we ask is to be able to explain our ideas to him.'

Donald suggested the generalissimo be liberated before Christmas Day as a gift to the nation. Chang was willing to argue for the prisoner's release with his accomplice Yang and the recently arrived Chou En-lai. Leaving to do that, he returned after 2 a.m. to report that the Shensi commander and his senior officers would not agree.

'They say my head is safe since TV and Madame are friendly towards me,' he said, 'but what about theirs? They say they'd be worse off if they now released the generalissimo.' General Yang wanted the written undertaking to protect himself.

Two days of intense and continuing discussions and negotiations followed among the players in the Si'an drama. TV Soong had several rounds of talks with the Shensi commander and the Communist emissary, the banker explaining, arguing, suggesting. He suggested to his brother-in-law that he give some ground so his captors could withdraw some demands while saving face. It was all very Chinese. Admitting there was some worth in Chang's arguments, Chiang promised to consider them more fully with the Central Government in Nanking, but he was not prepared to sign any document to that effect.

Worried about the volatility of his accomplice, the Young Marshal proposed getting Chiang hurriedly out of Si'an in disguise to where he would have the assured protection of Manchurian troops, and thence to Loyang, but was assured by Donald that neither the prisoner nor his wife would agree to that. The journey could be damaging to Chiang's fragile health and, in any case, it was undignified for a leader to escape in disguise.

Chang's argument for release had split the rebel camp, however, putting Chou in a key position to leverage the outcome favoured by the Communists. The Nanking group was prepared to consider resistance against Japan and heard that the Reds were not interested in detaining Chiang. A window was opening in the fortress.

There were signs of the protagonists softening their positions. The police chief agreed to release some political prisoners and provide guarantees of safety for Yang and his officers. The banker Soong offered sweeteners to the Shensi commanders of money, brandy and cigarettes. A new cabinet was agreed with Soong at the head, no pro-Japanese cliques and General Ho replaced. The fly in the ointment was Chiang's agreement in principle to the eight rebel demands being limited to a verbal promise in the presence of his wife and brother-in-law and Yang's insistence on a written assurance.

On the afternoon of Christmas Eve, the Young Marshal tried a different tack, telling Madame the visiting Communist had considerable influence over Yang and might be able to persuade him to relent. She agreed to meet him after dinner. With Chou commenting that her husband was the only man able to lead the country, they talked until eleven, after which he went to talk to Yang.

Persuading the Shensi commander to be satisfied with Chiang's verbal assurances of unity, to take Soong's money and go into exile, Chou next met with the obstinate national commander. Lying on his bed, looking old for 50, tired and pale, Chiang invited his former academy colleague to sit beside him.

'We haven't met for ten years,' said black-bearded Chou. 'You might look like an old man now, but you're my commander from Whampoa. If you take action against the Japanese, everyone will obey you.'

The generalissimo thanked him profusely, insisting his strength and prestige as the nation's leader had to be maintained. At a later meeting, Madame told Chou that China's internal problems should be solved by political means, not military force.

'We are all Chinese,' she said, echoing the Communist argument of the last year.

•

Christmas Day, 1936. Bill Donald left presents by the fireplace of the hotel where the Soong entourage was staying—a portable typewriter for May-ling, a travel rug for her husband—but the most important gift was going to be Donald's suggested present to the nation.

In the morning, the Young Marshal brought over a suitcase and discreetly left it next to Donald's already-packed bag, with instructions to tell no-one whose it was. Chang was nervous about Yang, worried he might turn around and arrest the Nanking group. Donald told him the plane for Loyang must leave before four in the afternoon anyway. There were no lights at its airfield.

An apparent calm belied the tension permeating the Manchurian headquarters. The cage was not to be rattled at any cost. Chang's pilot, the American Roy Leonard, was told to get the plane ready at the airfield for prompt use, but was given no further information. He went out to the aircraft to find it guarded by Chang's men.

The forgotten Colonel JL Huang, detained since Chiang's reading of the letter to his wife, was playing chess with his jailer when a messenger arrived to talk to the guard. Told simply he could go, without further discussion, Huang walked out of the building and over to Chiang's bungalow. The first person he saw was an ebullient Donald.

'Merry Christmas, JL,' said the Australian.

'What's merry about it?'

'Why, we're going back to Nanking. Haven't you heard?'

Donald, always in a hurry, dashed off. The aide next ran into the Soongs, May-ling and TV, who wished him a Merry Christmas, confirmed they were all going and told him he would follow on Boxing Day with her *amah* and secretaries.

After lunch, with bags ready and everyone waiting anxiously, General Yang arrived to confirm he'd release the detained leader, and took Chang to pass on the good news. The generalissimo ordered his field commander to stay in Si'an with his Manchurian army, but was told by Chang, 'I've been accused of mutiny and other things without justice. If you order me to stay here, I must refuse and will at least be guilty of mutiny. I undertook to go to Nanking if this failed and take whatever punishment was coming.'

Two cars came up to the bungalow where Chiang had been held and stopped with their engines idling. The gates opened and the generalissimo came out, thin and walking with difficulty in a plain long gown. Leaning on his wife, he was followed by her brother, Donald and the Young Marshal. As the Chiangs got into the back of the first car, Chang hesitated momentarily, then climbed into the front seat, having cleared his mind of any lingering doubts he might have. The first car drove off, with Donald, Soong and the police chief following in the second.

Nervous, and tense from delays during the day, Chiang repeatedly assured Chang alongside the driver he would live up to the agreed conditions.

'If I don't,' he said, 'you are free to no longer regard me as your leader!'

Si'an's airfield was decorated as if for a VIP arrival, people gathering with banners and a brass band standing by. The pilot already had the engines of Chang's Boeing turning over. The two cars skidded around a corner and hastily up to the plane. Chang was first out of the front car, ordering his troops to push back the encroaching crowd. He climbed into the cabin and sat in the co-pilot's seat. Generalissimo and Madame Chiang went up the gangway, followed by Donald and Soong, and the door closed immediately behind them.

Madame sat in the front seat of the cabin and said to Leonard, 'Are you ready to go?'

Wheel blocks were pulled away and the throttle pushed forward without further ceremony. The band didn't play a note. General Yang had no time to change his mind. The Boeing took off, heading to Loyang while Chiang Kai-shek, eyes shut and face haggard, slept on the single lounge. When they were airborne, the Young Marshal took control, banked over an encampment of his troops and rocked the plane to acknowledge them. They had retained a steadfast loyalty to the young warlord through all their trials and tribulations, but unknown to any of them an era had come to a close.

Landing at Loyang in fading light on a narrow, sand-swept field, soldiers rushed towards the plane as it taxied to a halt. When Madame Chiang emerged first, they stopped and saluted. Marshal Chang came next and a couple of soldiers pointed rifles at him.

'No!' said Madame. 'Let him alone.'

She put her arm around him and he put his around her. As the rescued leader was carried out, hats were thrown in the air. Cheers rang out as his feet hit the ground. They were driven to Chiang's house in Loyang for dinner and, for the generalissimo, his first real sleep in two weeks.

Overnight, the government's Junkers arrived bringing Huang and Madame's staff. The aide had decided to risk landing at night rather than stay in Si'an where Yang might change his mind. The Chiangs flew with Donald to Nanking next day, Chang and Soong following in the former's Boeing with an escort of pursuit aircraft. A heavy dust storm blew in from Mongolia and the pursuit planes disappeared in the swirling clouds.

Roy Leonard said, 'Maybe we'd better not go to Nanking.'

'It doesn't matter,' said Chang. 'If someone kills me, I don't care.'

The planes arrived at Nanking's military airport, which was teeming with excitement. Looking out as they circled, they could see thousands of people gathering around the airfield and nearby streets.

Donald said to the generalissimo, 'You should pay the Young Marshal two million dollars. He's helped to make you great.'

The government Junkers landed first and Chiang stepped down its gangway, alert and confident, his health sufficiently restored for the purpose. The enormous crowd that had gathered in expectation cheered, crying out, '*Wan-tsai*' (a thousand years).

After Chiang was driven away and with the crowd dispersing, the second plane landed. Marshal Chang emerged and walked slowly and with obvious emotion down a human tunnel of soldiers, his head erect under a black pillbox hat. Placed under close guard, he was arrested and taken to the house of TV Soong.

In towns along the Yangtze, the Christian holiday was celebrated with joyful cries and exploding firecrackers, expressing not the birth of Jesus but a nation's relief that the crisis was over. Having played a significant role in the leader's liberation, Donald shared his adopted country's joy, but he was apprehensive about his protégé's fate in a move as simultaneously rash and idealistic as the original act of kidnap had been.

Chapter 13

Disillusioned

Chang Hsueh-liang accepted blame for the Si'an Incident, allowing Chiang Kai-shek to recover loss of face from being captured, but the generalissimo never forgave him for the humiliation he felt he'd suffered and for halting his crusade to destroy the Communists. As the Young Marshal had expressed regret for his actions and had come voluntarily to Nanking, there were grounds for Chiang to forgive and release him, but he didn't.

During his court martial for mutiny, Chang denounced the court as 'crooks and hypocrites' and, at one point, shouted that Chiang was the only member of the government 'worth a damn'.

'None of the rest of you,' he exclaimed, 'would be any loss to China.'

While he admired the leader, Chang said, parts of the homeland had been lost to Japan, and he had acted on his own initiative in wanting to rectify that. That evening, Donald was with the Chiangs, both angry at the outburst.

'Why did the Young Marshal talk like that?' Madame asked.

'Because he has the courage to say what he thinks,' said Donald.

'How does the young fool expect us to help him if he won't keep his mouth shut?' complained Chiang. 'Now I can do nothing for him.'

What Chiang had intended to do is not clear. When the hearing was over, the judge sent court minutes to him for approval, but instead of reading them, he sent back a pre-written document to be read to the court. It pronounced a prison sentence of ten years. The same day, he wrote to government members requesting an immediate pardon, which was duly granted on 4 January.

The Young Marshal's prison term was cancelled, but he was not released, remaining in detention with no restoration of his civil rights. After two weeks with TV Soong, he was moved to a guarded three-room bungalow in the Hsuehtou Mountain Hostel overlooking Sikou, Chiang's hometown. Chang's new residence had a temple next door, peach blossom in the garden and tea plantations stretching below. Several days later, his wife joined him. The Changs couldn't have hoped for a more picturesque setting for their incarceration.

The Nanking clique that had seen Chiang's detention as an opportunity to be rid of him worked hard to sanitise the Si'an story. When an article in *The North China Herald* contradicted the version they were promoting, they suspected the hand of the former journalist. There were rumblings in the Nationalist Party about Donald, a whisper that the foreigner was a traitor to China. Captain Stennes, Chiang's security adviser, came to Donald's house in his well-cut riding breeches and high yellow leather boots with a Tommy gun under his arm, proposing to stay the night. He thought someone might try to assassinate the outspoken Australian and felt duty-bound to provide protection.

'There's no need to stay,' said Donald. 'I'm not afraid of them. They don't have the guts to do it.'

The next day an editorial in the Nationalist *Central China Daily News* demanded he be expelled from China and escorted to his own country. Donald wrote to Chiang, 'As your underlings feel so free as to attack me, I feel my usefulness to you has now ended.'

It was attached to a note to Madame asking her to pass it on. She phoned next day from Sikou to say her husband was furious. He had dismissed the paper's editor, demanded two others be relieved, and ordered the paper to withdraw its editorial and apologise. This was the first of several attempts by Donald to sever the relationship, some half-hearted, but evidence of a growing disenchantment.

With May-ling's support, Donald argued that Chiang now knew who his real enemies were and should take a hard line against them but, having gone to his hometown to lick his wounds and recover his health, the generalissimo hesitated to act on the warning. Attempts to further intimidate the Australian ceased when he threatened to give details of their actions and inactions to the European press, including texts of actual messages sent from Si'an during the crisis, so they could be compared with those published in Nanking.

Chang wrote to Donald from his guesthouse prison inviting him to come and marvel at the beauty of the azalea-covered mountain. The Australian regularly travelled up the hill and played cards with him. Although he slowly withdrew from active interest in politics and took up study of the Ming dynasty, Chang initially wanted to return to Manchuria with his army. Donald lobbied Chiang on his behalf, but was constantly stonewalled.

'When do you think the Young Marshal will be released?' Donald asked.

'It's not a matter of when will they release him,' was Chiang's response, 'it's when will they kill him?'

Chiang's back injury from the fall in Si'an gave him continuing pain, but he ignored his doctors' advice and wife's pleas to rest. In February, he consulted a Shanghai specialist who diagnosed a compression fracture of the vertebra and told him his injury might have healed already but for his workload. Chiang would not allow a plaster cast be put on him, so a brace was made instead to support the injured section of his spine. Adding to his woes, the recuperating leader had four teeth extracted, resulting in an even worse temper than usual. Chiang had become a lonely figure with few confidants outside his family and the two foreigners, Donald and Reverend Shepherd.

In the absence of the leader, a long statement about the events in Si'an was read out at the February plenary session of the Executive Committee, purporting to come from him. It claimed he was forced to accept the rebel's eight points and said he would submit them on Chang's behalf but oppose them as not in China's interests. The session congratulated Chiang on his courage and refused to consider the eight points because they were submitted through rebellion. No changes in cabinet were made despite Soong's promises in Si'an. Whatever undertakings had been made there had been swept to one side by the committee.

On the other hand, the Chinese public was united in its hostility to Japan's incursions. With Donald's tutoring, Madame Chiang identified the generalissimo publicly with China's destiny and promoted him as its indispensible leader. Public clamour had demanded his release in Si'an and was now directed against Japan. He had no choice but to go along with it.

By April, Chiang was back at the helm, his confidence and authority regained and showing the hallmarks of a dictator. He appointed a team of German military advisers led by General Alexander von Falkenhausen, to whom orders were to be referred by the minister of war, still General Ho, before they could be issued. Von Falkenhausen was telling those who should be persuaded—diplomats, the foreign press—that 'the Chinese army now had little reason to fear Japan', but privately admitted the Chinese army was not capable of fighting a modern war.

Donald had established a daily routine in Nanking with May-ling. Starting about eight in the morning at his desk or, depending on the weather, on the bungalow porch, he dictated replies on her behalf. At ten, he went to Chiang headquarters to work with her until two. Lunching with the Chiangs at some stage, he still ate only foreign food and never with chopsticks. He would return to his bungalow for a catnap in an armchair, then read the papers and listen to an old iron radio with a powerful shortwave receiver he had in his office. Surrounded by his accumulated clutter, Donald jotted down highlights of international news, speeches and anything else that might be relevant, auditing them for the Chiangs through May-ling. At four in the afternoon, he returned to work with her until she was too tired, then back to his own desk for more dictating and typing, after dining either with the Chiangs or elsewhere. Even in his 60s, he was still prodigiously energetic, but he was developing an inflexibility of routine built on the certainty of his own opinions.

The adviser had become gatekeeper for foreigner access to the Chiangs. None, other than key military advisers like General von Falkenhausen, could see either except through him. He had taken on the role of the British consul he had resented so many years before in trying to meet with the viceroy of Canton.

Through Madame Chiang, Donald effectively controlled the foreign office, aviation, publicity and the New Life Movement. She was prepared to speak on any subject with apparent authority, as long as it was off the record, but anything on the record was written for her by Donald or a ghostwriter under his supervision. He built up her public persona with an array of human virtues and all-embracing knowledge. At first sight, she embodied the construct: full of energy and ideas, slim, charming and exquisitely dressed, utterly American in her speech and business-like manner; but in reality, according to Ilona Sues who had joined the office as a typist, she was 'selfish, petty, and capricious as a prima donna'.

In early June, a new foreign adviser joined the military hierarchy. After a series of disputes with his superiors in the US Air Corps, Captain Claire Chennault had retired through 'ill health'. He was then hired through contacts by Madame Chiang to investigate China's airforce. Taken to meet his new employer in Shanghai's French Concession, Chennault was waiting in a dim, cool reception area when a vivacious young woman in modish Paris frock came in, bubbling with energy and speaking English in a Southern drawl. Accompanied by her ruddy-faced Australian adviser, she wanted the hard facts about her airforce and how to rectify them. Chennault promised a full report within three months.

The energetic and opinionated American was unimpressed with China's airforce. Less than 100 of its 500 craft were airworthy and corruption was rife, but he would come to find the older Australian an indispensible ally. An implacable foe of Chinese graft and inefficiency, Donald, too, saw the need for a strong airforce and introduced Chennault to the inner circles of Chinese government, relaying problems directly to Chiang when needed and mediating between the American and Madame when tempers flared between these two volatile personalities.

In Europe in 1934, Foreign Minister Kung had been wined and dined by Mussolini who offered a mission of 40 military pilots, headed by General Scaroni, and engineers and mechanics to assemble Italian planes in China. The American trainers they replaced had graduated only the best students, but cadets had been drawn from the upper social echelons, and influential families had protested to Chiang. The Italian flying school at Loyang graduated every Chinese cadet as a full-fledged pilot regardless of ability.

Claire Chennault got to Nanking to find Italian pilots swaggering about in full uniform, and Scaroni, decked out in medals and gold braid, driving around in a big black limousine. The Chinese loved their elaborate ceremony and flowery courtesy, but the Italians, unlike Chiang's German advisers, were aiding Japan by sabotaging China's preparation, either intentionally or through incompetence. The assembly plant at Nanchang made Fiat fighters that became firetraps in combat and Savoia-Marchetti bombers so obsolete they were used only as transports.

But the American never produced his promised report. The Japanese made sure of that.

•

Under a long-standing agreement, countries with a legation in China maintained a small force to protect the rail connection between Peking and the port of Tientsin. Japan's detachment was significantly larger than others and, without notice, carried out a training exercise on the night of 7 July 1937 close to Lukou bridge. Known as Marco Polo Bridge to Westerners because the explorer had described its predecessor, it was near the walled town of Wanping on the outskirts of Peking. A few shots were exchanged with startled Chinese troops guarding the bridge, but there were no casualties. When the Japanese found one of their men missing, their demand to be allowed to search Wanping was refused. Although the Chinese offered to conduct the search with one of their officers, Japanese soldiers tried to force their way into the town. They were driven back.

Both sides sent reinforcements to the area and in the morning Japanese machine-gunners shelled the town. Infantry and armoured vehicles overran the stone bridge only to be forced off under cover of mist. The antagonists reached an amicable settlement and troops withdrew to their original positions with Chinese soldiers guarding Lukou bridge as before.

Tensions simmered for over a week with troop build-up and cease-fire violations by both sides. The Japanese issued an ultimatum for the expanded Chinese presence to withdraw by noon the next day and shelled Wanping again. The Chinese retaliation was bloody and bitter, but they were forced to retreat. The enemy moved into the area around Peking and were negotiating with the Nationalist government when events, this time in Shanghai, overtook them.

China had been losing territory to Japan piece by piece through the series of 'incidents' so that Manchuria and North China had come under Japanese control. Chiang and his military strategists believed the Japanese intended to seize sections of territory along railways to Wuhan and central and East China, easily reinforced from Manchukuo. Inferior in training and equipment, the Chinese army was incapable of resisting them.

Chiang decided to establish a second front in Shanghai rather than wait for his army to be trapped there by a relentless thrust south, then east. Weighing up its political advantage—the patriotic pursuit of the invader—against his limited military strength, he wanted time to move the Yangtze valley's vital industry to the west, away from Japanese incursion, and intensify the war to draw international condemnation. The Western powers had considerable investment and assets in Shanghai.

With war in the wind, China's factional leaders met at the Nanking Military Academy, pledging troops and loyalty for the duration of a war against Japan under Chiang's leadership. Donald and Chennault were the only foreigners present. On 6 August, with the conference over, Chiang announced China had reached the limits of its tolerance. The airforce was moved north to Kaifeng on the Yellow River. Having formed the United Front, the time seemed right to escalate to full-scale war with Japan.

Three days later, Lieutenant Oyama of the Japanese Marines was shot dead by Chinese police near Shanghai's military airport of Hunjao, supposedly because he had tried to enter the facility. In fact, the incident was instigated by Chiang to heighten the tension between the two adversaries. Japan demanded police be withdrawn from Shanghai and fortifications surrounding the city be dismantled. Both sides started deploying troops into Shanghai despite the 1932 treaty banning Chinese troops from the city.

A war council meeting at the Nanking Academy a week later was confident, on the basis of the 1931 stalemate, that the Japanese threat to Shanghai could be contained. Donald and Chennault were again at the meeting, on one side with Madame translating proceedings. A message came to Chiang who read it, then handed it to his wife while he addressed the council.

'They are shelling the Shanghai Civic Centre,' gasped a tearful May-ling. 'They are killing our people! They are killing our people!' They had been killing her people for some time, but it wasn't the moment to make that point.

'What will you do now?' asked Chennault.

'We will fight!' was Madame's answer.

The battle for Shanghai had actually begun that morning. After a few days of failed negotiation, Shanghai police exchanged rifle fire with Japanese troops. Later in the day, Japan's army attacked Chapei and its navy fired on Chinese positions in the city. China's airforce began bombing various Japanese targets next morning and Nanking issued a Proclamation of Self-Defence and War of Resistance. The Sino-Japanese War had begun in earnest.

Under Chennault's direction, the airforce launched bombing raids against the dilapidated Japanese cruiser *Izumo*, moored off the Bund. Two of the bombs fell short because bombsights had not been adjusted for flying below thick cloud over the International Settlement. One was a dud but the other fell on Nanking Road, killing nearly a thousand shoppers and passers-by gazing up at the planes. Japanese fighters responded over the next few days. Unlike the Chinese, Japan was able to replace aircraft lost in combat. It was impossible for China to compete in the long term in an air war.

The Chinese plan was a surprise attack to push the enemy back to the Whangpoo, then blockade the coast, but Japanese concrete fortifications were resistant to howitzers, the heaviest weapons the Chinese carried. Unable to destroy the bunkers, their commander decided to encircle them instead, setting up sandbag blockades around each stronghold until Japan brought tanks into the fray, repelling the attacks. When fighting in the city centre ground to a stalemate, the Japanese staged amphibious landings on the northeast coastal arm 50 kilometres away.

While the Chinese might have relished an opportunity to have a go at the invader, foreigners caught up in it were far from enthusiastic. The airline CNAC (China National Aviation Corporation), 55 per cent owned by the Chinese government in partnership with Pan American, had replaced its civilian managing director with an airforce colonel. When the war started, it was made a transport division of the airforce and its American pilots were pressured to make military reconnaissance flights and transport supplies. They refused to continue flying, the US maintaining strict neutrality at the time, and decamped to Hong Kong. Donald's erstwhile golfing mate and now CNAC vice-president, Langhorne Bond, was sent to sort it out, convinced CNAC couldn't operate without its American pilots.

In Nanking, Bond wrote to Madame Chiang, arguing the importance to China of maintaining a connection to the US through Pan Am. He was contacted by his Australian friend that night to say they had discussed his memo and agreed with him.

Meeting at his house outside the city wall, Donald said in his usual blunt manner, 'I'm busy, Bondy. What do you want from us?'

'I'm busy, too,' said the American. 'We need to remove the military director of CNAC and appoint a capable civilian in his place.' Bond spelt out his problem and said Pan Am was insisting it adhere to US policy.

He waited with his pilots in Hong Kong and a week later a telegram from Donald asked him to recommend three Chinese he thought capable of doing the job. Bond did so. One was promptly appointed managing director and the American pilots returned to CNAC to resume commuter flights only.

Donald was the go-to man and the fixer, hiring a team of assistants to present Madame Chiang to the international press and raise Western awareness of China's predicament. *Life* and *Time* magazines were gushingly reverential, with an August feature in the latter headlined 'Mei-ling Helps Her Husband Rule China'. Publisher Henry Luce and his wife had become enamoured of May-ling. *Time* proclaimed the Chiangs 'Man and Wife of the Year' for 1937.

Other American magazines and newspapers joined the Madame Chiang fan club. Taking *Liberty* editor, Fulton Oursler, to interview her in Nanking, Donald told him he was lucky to have tea with her as she was 'on the verge of a nervous collapse'. 'Madame sees almost no-one,' Donald added. 'But she defies her doctors!'

By September, regular Japanese missions over the capital were bombing largely non-military targets: refugee camps, power plants, waterworks, radio stations and densely populated southern Nanking. Central Hospital, with a large red cross painted on its roof, was another devastated target. The Japanese warned foreign legations and ships to leave the city and the charmingly ineffectual US ambassador, Nelson Johnson, left with his staff, but the British and the French held firm. China's government refused to move its capital from Nanking.

Donald wrote about dogfights with China's inexperienced pilots, the steady drone of engines punctuated by anti-aircraft gunfire, and the volcanic puffs from bombs with flames leaping high and the ground shaking. When air-raid warnings wailed, Donald would rush from his house outside Nanking's East Gate up a wooded hill at the foot of Purple Mountain with whomever was with him at the time—sometimes Ilona Sues, later Jimmy McHugh—and either work from a briefcase he brought with him or lie back in the sunshine and recollect his bygone adventures in China. Increasingly, he was preoccupied with his own past and sought out new listeners for his reminiscences.

He would take Little Jimmie, the sixteen-year-old spotter who could see planes before anyone else would hear them. There might be an hour or more between the first and second alarms, time usefully filled with anecdotes. When the second siren rang out, Jimmie would jump to his feet, scan the skies and give a high-pitched shout, 'Master, can see four . . . nine . . . many.'

Donald would follow the boy's pointing finger and fix on the planes with his field glasses, providing commentary on flying direction, bombs released, explosions sighted, colour of smoke, targets hit, for his companion to jot down until the raiders completed their mission and flew away. He'd go back to his Hermes typewriter in the office and churn out more news stories from what he'd just seen, circulating them to the international press under the letterhead, 'Headquarters of the Generalissimo'. Japan, he wrote, believes it is able to bring China quickly to ruin, 'since the Powers seem not to be interested so long as their property and nationals are not injured'.

The typist, Ilona Sues, a Polish woman in her 30s, was hired by Madame Chiang at Donald's suggestion to conduct a study of the ministry of propaganda and recommend how it might be reorganised. Her unofficial role had no executive power and only the dubious security of being told that Madame and Donald would back her if things got difficult. Donald's plan was to kick the minister out of office and set up a new publicity board under the softly spoken Hollington Tong.

Tong and Sues were to prepare a report on minister Cheng Kung-po for Chiang, but Tong begged off as Cheng and his staff were his friends. Sues was given the task as she was a foreigner and she produced two reports on the activities of the propaganda department and its expenditure. Furious at its content, Chiang ordered the department abolished and in its stead a small up-to-date board set up under Tong for foreign publicity. The minister was sent on a 'study tour' of Italy. A delegation pressured Chiang to not sack Nationalist Party members or relatives of highly placed members. Instead of dismissing excess staff, Chiang transferred them to other ministries.

Everything was done in the context of Japan's continuing aggression. Madame wanted to see her dentist in Shanghai before the city finally fell and decided to combine that with an inspection of emergency hospitals at the front line. The Nanking–Shanghai road was pitted with shell craters and under frequent Japanese air surveillance. The British ambassador, Sir Hughe Knatchbull-Hugessen, had been wounded in the spine two months before when a Japanese fighter machine-gunned his Armstrong-Siddeley on the road. On the same road on a late October evening, Madame in blue woollen slacks and shirt was chatting to Donald in the back seat of their open tourer when a Japanese bomber appeared overhead, a short distance from their destination. Speeding up in alarm, the driver hit a bump and the car slid off the road, throwing the passengers out of the car. Donald saw May-ling's body hurtling over his head before he landed unharmed but shaken beside the overturned vehicle. The plane flew on and Madame's body lay crumpled and unmoving in a mud puddle. Donald hurried over to her. Her face was pale and streaked with mud, her limbs limp but nothing seemed broken. Pulling her from the ooze, he listened to her breathing and realised she was still alive.

'Madame! Madame?' said the anxious adviser as onlookers gathered around. He shook her limp form gently

'Come on, wake up. You'd better wake up.'

Covering his concerns as he always did with a joke, he began singing a popular song: 'She flew through the air with the greatest of ease. The dashing young girl on the flying trapeze.' Then, his bravado faltering, he said, 'Come on, Madame, wake up! I wish you could see yourself now, you sure are a beauty!'

There was no reply from the comatose May-ling.

Panic was setting in but Donald continued: 'You're covered with mud! Your face and your clothing and . . . '

Suddenly, May-ling stirred and began a low moaning. Donald stood and, with his hands tucked under her armpits, pulled her carefully to her feet.

'There you are,' he said loudly as if he'd never had any doubt about her recovery. 'You're all right. You can walk. Come on, let's go and find a house.'

May-ling stood and looked around, bewildered and swaying.

'I don't think I can walk.'

Donald would hear none of it, making her go with him to the nearest farmhouse, where she changed into spare clothes she carried in her handbag. Back in the car, which had been righted by locals, a pale and shaken May-ling tried to plan ahead. With a map in his hand, Donald said she could choose between going back to Nanking or comforting the wounded before going on to Shanghai.

'We'll go to Shanghai,' said Madame.

As the car moved tentatively forward, she tried to assess her wellbeing.

'I can't breathe,' she said. 'It hurts me to breathe.'

'Then don't breathe,' responded Donald.

'But I can't live if I don't breathe . . . '

She inspected the soldiers that night and was driven on to the city, to her house in the French Concession. In the morning, a doctor found a broken rib and told her to rest in bed until it mended. Donald visited, full of sympathy now the crisis was over.

'Why were you so cruel out at the wreck?' May-ling asked skittishly.

'Because once you let a women lie down and think she's hurt, she never gets up.'

Madame Chiang was back at work in Nanking six days later, accompanied by her Australian adviser.

•

Through September and October 1937, Japanese had landed in waves on the coast northeast of Shanghai under cover of naval and aerial bombardment. Bitter battles were fought in coastal towns, but Chinese small-calibre arms were no match for Japanese firepower and hastily built defences offered little protection, many collapsing in the rain. Orders were to defend towns to the last man, with reinforcements brought in for overnight counterattacks. With Japanese troop strength increased to 200 000 by October, the seesawing battle of attrition continued in its favour, although its army only advanced 5 kilometres over six weeks until the key town of Dachang fell on 25 October.

Chinese troops started withdrawing the next night from positions they had held in the city since mid-August. Because the Nine-Power Treaty Conference had began in Brussels, with possible Western intervention in the conflict, Chiang kept some troops in downtown Shanghai, but Japanese reinforcements were landing south of Shanghai and threatening to encircle them. China's central command ordered completion of the withdrawal from Shanghai to protect Nanking. In defending the city, China had suffered 250 000 casualties, including 60 per cent of its small cohort of German-trained elite soldiers. Japan's casualties were 40 000.

In September, China had brought a case against Japan to the League of Nations which was unable to raise any sanctions against the invader. With a speech in October by President Roosevelt calling on the United States to help nations fight aggressors, Britain convened the Nine-Power Treaty Conference. Unlike the League of Nations, the US was a member. The Conference dragged on, Japan declining to attend and the Western powers desperate to appease. It adjourned indefinitely on 24 November, having achieved nothing.

In November, the Japanese army started advancing towards Nanking. Two lines of fortifications, known as the 'Chinese Hindenburg Line', had been built with German assistance to protect the road to the capital if Shanghai should fall, but the defenders were still untrained and the defences uncoordinated. Many retreating units lost contact with their commanders and making their way to defensive towers found civilian officials had locked them and fled.

Chinese troops were carrying out a scorched earth strategy in the area surrounding Nanking, setting fire to towns and villages on the outskirts. Donald told staff of the new publicity unit to move inside Nanking's walls as all the buildings they had been using at the foot of Purple Mountain, as well as the houses of the Chiangs and the Kungs and his bungalow, would be dynamited so the enemy couldn't use them as cover.

A former Hunan warlord, Tang Sheng-chih, was named commander of the Nanking Garrison of 100 000 mostly untrained conscripts to put up token resistance to the enemy advance. As civilians fled the city in droves, the defenders were overrun by Nationalist troops retreating from Shanghai. Some garrison officers were shot for refusing to move out of their path. Many of the fleeing troops killed and robbed civilians of their clothing to escape detection. Chiang ordered Tang to continue the futile defence to save face with the public by asserting Nanking was defended before its capture.

Chiang's plan, on General von Falkenhausen's advice, was to draw the Japanese deep into China using its vastness as a defensive tactic, and wear down the enemy in a protracted war of attrition in the hinterland. Military headquarters was moved to the temporary capital of Hankow, and the generalissimo announced the capital would eventually be transferred to Chungking.

Donald visited the US Embassy on the morning of 6 December, looking tired and dispirited, despondent about the foreign powers' treatment of China. Purchased planes were in Hong Kong, Manila and Indochina, but they were not permitted to be shipped to China for fear of aggravating Japan. Germany was offering to mediate peace negotiations as Japan expressed a desire for a 'pro-Japanese' government led by Wang Ching-wei, Chiang's long-time political rival, with General Ho to head its army. Donald suggested for the first time that Chiang might be thinking of giving up the fight.

By evening Chiang had decided to join the exodus out of Nanking and, at daybreak the next morning, the Chiangs left with Donald in their Sikorski seaplane, heading south for Poyang Lake. The unnerved generalissimo recited poetry to himself during the flight. From the lake they were carried up to the mountain resort of Kuling for a week of walking and mental recuperation, while McHugh, now US Naval Attaché, took Madame's Buick limousine to Hankow. Donald had given his Locomobile key to an American missionary who was staying in the safety zone set up for Nanking's foreign community. He would never see his car again.

That same day, the commander of the approaching Japanese army issued an order of restraint as the occupying force of a foreign capital, under threat of unspecified 'severe punishment'. The advancing force arrived outside the walled city on 9 December and dropped leaflets into Nanking urging surrender. General Tang expressed public outrage while privately negotiating a truce. The Nanking Safety Zone committee recommended a three-day ceasefire to Tang so the Chinese could withdraw their troops without fighting. The proposed agreement had to be accepted by Chiang and was sent to him in the mountains by radio from the American gunboat *Panay* on the Yangtze. The generalissimo rejected it. He was not prepared to accommodate the enemy publicly. At 1 p.m. the next day, the order was issued by the Japanese commander to occupy Nanking by force.

Three days of mountain guns and heavy casualties were required for the Japanese to penetrate the high solid walls, iron doors and strategically placed machine-gunners defending Nanking. Civilians crowded into the safety zone to escape the air bombardment. By the time Chiang ordered a retreat across the Yangtze, his troops were fighting in isolated pockets and couldn't stage a coordinated withdrawal. The retreat became chaotic panic, with fleeing soldiers looting shops, shedding their uniforms and often robbing civilians of their clothing. The Nanking Massacre followed for six weeks, beginning under the pretext of eliminating Chinese soldiers in civilian dress, but escalating as innocent men were executed and women and children raped and killed.

Chiang had become obsessively introspective and puritanical, regarding salvation as rising from discipline and hard work. He moved with his wife and his adviser down to Hankow and announced he'd focus his attention on military affairs, handing leadership of the government to his wife's brother-in-law, HH Kung. However, China's government was effectively replaced by its military headquarters anyway and unoccupied China was divided into five war zones.

Jimmy McHugh, Donald's golfing friend from his Peking days, had moved to Nanking shortly before he drove to Hankow in Madame's Buick. When Donald came to the temporary capital, he and McHugh regularly played nine holes on dewy grass soon after sunrise. The Australian would talk incessantly about the Chiangs, but the attaché found this was a different Donald from the perpetually cheery person he had known. He had become irritable, dogmatic and self-centred, expecting the younger man to accept his version of events without discussion and often rebuking McHugh for questioning him.

Living as a recluse in a large ramshackle flat by the river, more fixated on health than ever, Donald once asked McHugh when he was going to Hong Kong to get him a bottle of Stearn's Bi-Colates, two bottles of quinine hydrochlorate ('the kind that doesn't cause buzzing in the ears') and three packets of Aspros. The only non-medicinal requested was a basket of mangoes. He had become Madame Chiang's constant companion, claiming she wouldn't let him leave her and went nowhere without him. Each morning after golf, they would try to resume the pattern of work established in Nanking, but the energy of that earlier time was dissipating in an air of desperation.

Before dinner, the Chiangs took a regular evening stroll and were often joined by Donald, discussing the war with May-ling while her husband recited poetry aloud to himself. If he wanted to attract the generalissimo's attention he clapped his hands and Chiang would turn to his wife and ask slowly what the adviser wanted. When Donald asked May-ling if she knew what her husband was thinking, he got a helpless look in return. 'Days with him were like the silence of a lonely Arctic night,' Donald wrote to a friend.

Donald was pre-occupied with Madame's crusade to eliminate corruption from Chinese aviation, with overpriced sales and 'squeeze' (bribes) paid to Chinese officials. With May-ling's younger brother, TV, and older sister, Ai-ling (Madame Kung) generally considered major grafters, it was going to be an uphill battle for the increasingly disgruntled Australian. The Kung family had particularly feathered its own nest, although HH Kung may not have been knowingly complicit. Vain, affable and of little judgment, he was dominated by his calculating wife. Their 21-year-old son David had been installed as head of Central Trust, which handled purchases of war supplies, and 'special secretary' to the minister of finance, his father. When HH Kung was overseas, all financial documents were sent to the Kung residence for approval by David.

Central to the issue were competing American aircraft sales agents, William Pawley and AL Patterson. Patterson doubled and sometimes trebled the price of American aircraft sold to China to provide larger squeeze for officials handling the orders, his 'US catalogues' specially printed in China with inflated prices. The squeeze on plane purchases was collected by an agent of Madame Kung and the sale was processed through Central Trust.

Pawley, a former president of CNAC airline, did most of the aviation sales in China through HH Kung. Embroiled in a squabble with Chennault about deficiencies with Curtiss Hawk fighters, he insisted he'd never paid a cent of squeeze despite his millions of dollars of business and asked his country's naval attaché to request a hearing through Donald. McHugh argued that the Americans were only playing the game by the rules as they found them, but all he got in reply from his friend was a snort and to be told the British refused to sell planes under those conditions.

When Madame Chiang and Donald flew to Hong Kong to investigate an American aircraft salesman's complaint he'd been unable to sell planes for two years because everyone demanded squeeze, they invited McHugh to join them. In Hong Kong, McHugh dined with Cyril Rogers who had been in the colony since 1935 on behalf of the Bank of England, pursuing banking and currency reforms in China. Rogers told McHugh that Finance Minister Kung had little credit in London banking—his son was driving around Hong Kong in a Cadillac at that time and still head of Central Trust—and that China was on the brink of economic ruin, spending its reserves. China's credit abroad had been seriously misrepresented to Chiang by Kung.

The urbane Rogers wanted to brief Chiang Kai-shek, but thought he should talk to Madame Chiang first, perhaps through WH Donald who he hadn't met. Late that night, McHugh rang Donald at his hotel to suggest a meeting with Rogers. The Australian had just returned after an exhausting evening at the Kung's Hong Kong residence in which TV Soong, who was also visiting the colony, had been subjected to a three-hour tirade by his sister, May-ling.

Donald attacked McHugh over a local newspaper report of their visit, which he'd wanted kept from the public. It took a while for the American to get a word in about the English banker.

'Jimmy, you let every Tom, Dick and Harry who wants something get to me through you,' the older man complained. McHugh had been hearing this sort of rebuke for two months and was getting sick of it.

'This bloke's of no importance,' Donald continued. 'I know he's after Kung's head and wants to talk finance with the M'issimo. She knows nothing on that subject. I put through the reforms Rogers is working on.'

At this point it occurred to Donald that McHugh might be calling from Rogers' hotel room. That was confirmed, and Donald quietened down, ticking off McHugh for not telling him, and agreeing to speak to Rogers.

Donald met Rogers in the morning, regaling him so much with his own achievements in currency reform that the banker decided not to talk to Madame Chiang. Knowing London was about to refuse Kung's request for further credit, Rogers had already avoided a meeting with him in Hankow, pleading illness. The minister had responded by telegraphing flowers, followed by a bellboy with more flowers from David Kung.

By the time McHugh rang to find how the meeting with Donald had gone, the Englishman had decided to fly to Hankow for a private meeting with Chiang and, if he didn't get a favourable response, to return to England. The attaché then rang his Australian friend expecting another hostile outburst, but found him surprisingly affable. Donald was blowing hot and cold, wavering between hope and disillusionment.

Madame and her adviser talked at length with the sales agent for the North American Aircraft Co, the principal reason for their trip to Hong Kong. A former CNAC pilot, Jim Norris doubted if honest business could be done in China, detailing the demands on him for squeeze. He offered to return to China and stage a corrupt contract, but nothing would ever come of that proposal. It was getting too close to home.

After five weeks in Hong Kong, the party flew back to Hankow to find Chiang had called off the investigation of the Aeronautics Commission, either because of its impact on his airforce during a war or because Ai-ling had confronted him about rumours of her corruption and demanded he take action against them or her husband would resign. Kung was an easy source of funds for Chiang's military campaigns, whereas TV Soong had always fought with him, so he may have dropped the investigation to appease her.

On Donald's advice, May-ling resigned from the Aeronautics Commission in February 1938, citing injuries suffered in the car accident near Shanghai. The post was offered to TV Soong who repeatedly refused, but Chiang was insistent and gave a dinner to announce it. In the end, Soong accepted the post and did little more in it than propose the removal of General Chow, head of China's airforce and a Chiang crony. It didn't happen.

•

Fortunes in the war between Japan and China were slowly turning. The invaders moved on Soochow in wintery conditions to encircle the temporary capital of Hankow. Flying to Soochow, Madame visited wounded soldiers in a hospital, while her husband and his generals set up a trap devised by his German advisers. Chinese troops were to retreat into the walled town of Tai'erhchwang where trenches had been built and artillery positioned around its narrow streets running between stone houses. The Japanese fought for three days to get to the town and force their way into it, only to find themselves cut off from the rear in confined spaces under fire. Air-dropped supplies fell behind Chinese lines. They eventually fought their way out of the town, but left 8000 dead comrades behind.

Elsewhere, the Japanese struggled to maintain the upper hand in Shansi against Chinese Communist forces. Japan's invasion was still slowly moving forward and the Japanese public knew nothing of these setbacks, but the soldiers did and their sense of invincibility was faltering while Chinese confidence was growing.

To frustrate the northern advance on Hankow, Chiang ordered breaches in dykes on the Yellow River and the Grand Canal. Millions of litres of river water flooded into the valley, in some places 3 metres deep and 30 kilometres wide. Japanese soldiers trying to repair the breaches were fired on from Chinese pillboxes.

The enemy had penetrated various parts of the country, but the occupation was confined to the immediate vicinity of its army. Chinese guerrillas operated throughout Manchuria and China, waging a new kind of war that the invaders had difficulty comprehending. Donald observed in a letter to an associate in England that the Japanese were no longer fighting old provincial armies but the youth of China, better trained and with a high patriotism previously absent.

'The spirit they show is remarkable,' he wrote. 'The country is alive with youngsters in uniform. If this generation does not defeat the Japanese, then the next one will.'

China had all the time in the world. Japan, looking for a way out without sacrificing its gains, had channelled feelers for peace negotiations through Germany's ambassador late in 1937. The terms were unacceptable, but Chiang resisted Donald's urging to publish them. Soon after, a revised proposal was read by the same diplomat to Madame Chiang, Kung and Donald since the generalissimo had refused to receive it.

'I'm instructed to hand you this without comment,' the ambassador said.

Madame replied, 'I should think so! How are your son and your daughter?'

The envoy answered the question, 'bowed like an automaton, and retreated', Donald wrote later.

At the same time, the German government was pressuring Chiang's German advisers to persuade China to take up Japan's offer. They ignored the instruction and Germany's ambassador told fellow diplomats the advisers were becoming an embarrassment, but when Japan's staunchly anti-Communist envoy raised the issue, he tartly responded, 'Would you prefer the Chinese army had Russian advisers?'

In Hong Kong, TV Soong was approached by Italy's Ambassador Cora with 'very lenient' peace terms with Japan: recognition of Manchukuo, military garrisons and economic privileges in North China, a neutral zone around Shanghai and indemnity.

'Indemnity for whom?' asked Soong. 'For China in recompense for the bombing of Shanghai and the destruction of Nanking?'

'There always has to be an indemnity after every war and Japan naturally expects something,' replied the ambassador.

Soong told him no terms were acceptable that didn't restore occupied territory.

A changed German leadership formally recognised Manchukuo and ordered its advisers home from China. General von Falkenhausen attempted to stay on, but when veiled threats were made to his family in Germany, he complied. Chiang held a farewell dinner on 27 June for his long-time advisers, now more Chinese than German, and made a special train available to take them to Hong Kong where the Japanese consul held another reception for them.

The Japanese had another problem on their northern front. Fighting had broken out in late July at Changkufeng in the first of a series of border skirmishes between the Soviets and the Kwantung Army. With the Chinese trying to monitor developments, Donald arrived at the Ministry of Information, filling the room with his personality.

'Where's Holly? Tell him Don has come to see him.'

Telephone wires lay around the floor of the former Japanese Club taken over as the ministry's Hankow headquarters. The Japanese advance was about 160 kilometres from the temporary capital.

'What's all this about, Holly? Are you putting in a direct line to Emperor Hirohito?'

Hollington Tong had appeared from an office to the side, smiling diffidently.

'If the Russkies start hammering the Japs,' Donald continued, 'your fat generals will just lie back, fan their fat bellies and let the Russkies do all the fighting. Better beat them yourselves without the Russians.'

As it turned out, the Japanese were driven out of the disputed territory and the Russians satisfied themselves with that. It was Donald back to his vintage best, talking straight and burying the harsh truth in a joke, but it didn't last.

By August, Bill Donald was ill again with 'fever' and was flown in Madame's plane to Kunming in the mountains of Yunnan to recuperate. Suffering dizziness from high blood pressure, exacerbated by stress from overwork and disenchantment, he rented a lakeside cottage from a Chinese doctor at the nearby missionary hospital. Jimmy McHugh was given the task of bringing heavy luggage by train to Hong Kong, steamship to Haiphong and train to Kunming via Hanoi. The American spent two weeks with his convalescing friend before returning to Hankow.

The lake was peaceful and the surrounding country wild and beautiful, but it wasn't in Donald's nature to relax and enjoy scenery. Tiring of reliance on the hospital for supplies, he moved to the newly built—but not officially opened—Lake Hotel, returning to the cottage five days later because there was 'no service' at the hotel. His giddiness continued, ascribed to altitude with his system under strain. Moving to a hospital in Dalat in the Indochinese highlands, the impact of altitude unsurprisingly didn't abate, and it wasn't until he moved down to sea level at Nhatrang and then Saigon that he started to show any recovery.

May-ling wired, urging her mentor to come back to Hankow if he felt strong enough. Donald booked himself on a small steamer from Haiphong but then he heard the Japanese were landing on the coast near Canton, so he flew instead to Kunming on 20 October, leaving two days later for Hankow. He planned to arrive at dusk when any enemy aircraft that were about should have returned to base, but a radio call warned that several Japanese were in the air around Wuhan. They were still about at sunset and his plane diverted for the night to Ichang, further up the Yangtze.

Taking off again at dawn, they arrived at Hankow with a blue fog hanging close to the ground. No people, planes or cars stood by the airfield. As they taxied off the runway and a man came out waving on a bicycle, it occurred to Donald that the fog smelt like exploded munitions—and that's what it was. They had landed in the middle of a Japanese air attack.

Baggage was grabbed as passengers alighted hurriedly and dashed for cover. Soon after the plane took off for the relative safety of Chungking, the bombers reappeared to drop more explosives. They had gone upriver after their first raid, but the mist over the Yangtze had hidden Donald's plane coming down from Ichang.

The Australian had arrived as Hankow prepared for the marauding Japanese. Thousands had crowded into the foreign concessions, refugees camping in the streets. Daily bombing had left belongings strewn about. Donald joined a crowd watching a US-funded ambulance loading up a high government official's wealth from a bank.

In an open car the next day, the generalissimo and his wife reviewed troops on the Bund. Dining with Hollington Tong and Donald that night, the sound of Japanese gunfire on Hankow's doorstep, Madame proposed moving on again. Having decided to cease the city's defence so it wouldn't be destroyed by bombing, Chiang wrote a statement for Tong to deliver to the press. Defenders were already melting away with the capital transferred to Chungking in western China.

Much of the Yangtze valley's industry had been relocated to the mountainous upper Yangtze. Machinery from Shanghai's factories was packed in rowboats, covered with branches and leaves and taken up the river, hidden among reeds when Japanese bombers were heard. Munitions factories were being set up in caves in Szechwan.

Donald went with the Chiangs to the airfield with only a few bags of personal possessions. Their plane left Hankow after dark, and workmen immediately began disabling the airstrip. The plane's radio wouldn't operate, making it unsafe to land in the dark at their destination. On returning they were lucky to find enough undamaged field to land. Another plane, with a functional radio, was provided and the party flew south to Hunan to set up on the sacred mountain of Hengshan near Changsha.

From these new headquarters, the Chiangs toured the front with Donald and Captain Stennes, witnessing destruction wherever they went. Often they looked more like they were on a camping holiday, with the party sitting in the sunshine by a stream or waterfall, cooking meals on an open fire. The generalissimo might do his one dish of rice-cooked egg, chopped ham and greens in an iron pot, Donald could muddle through browning sweet potatoes, but otherwise Madame did most of the cooking. The idyll served as a distraction, but they couldn't ignore China's reality.

Refugees crammed the highways, their belongings carried on their shoulders, their children in baskets. Much of the city of Kweilin was already levelled by bombing and its people were living in large caves as air-raid shelters. Enemy planes continued to attack the city, although they were starting to lose significant numbers of planes in the cloud-covered mountains. The Chinese capacity to endure suffering made eventual Japanese conquest of the country doubtful.

The relocated government in Chungking had taken over the city's hotels, office buildings and schools. An airstrip had been created by paving a sandbar in the Yangtze with stone, the river rushing by on both sides. Airport buildings were made of straw matting on bamboo poles. Terraced rice paddies sat either side of the river.

The Chiang party landed on a chilly December day and was carried in sedan chairs up the steep, zigzagging stone steps to the city on its rocky plateau 200 metres above. In 1935, they had climbed these same steps in pursuit of the Communists. Now, four years later, they were on the run from the Japanese. They were driven in a procession of black cars, splashing muddy water from potholes in the road, to their new residence, a two-story, ten-room house behind a well-guarded stone wall. Entering under a huge rubber tree, they climbed steps interwoven with roots into a beautiful garden, terraced with azaleas and bamboo.

Now with pure white hair and tending to repeat himself, Donald moved into a solid foreign-styled house next to the Chiang's residence. In Peking, he had been famous for his dinner parties and picnics, in Nanking for entertaining visiting journalists, but by Chungking he was more reclusive, often lunching with the Chiangs—sometimes along with McHugh—but seldom taking evening meals with them. Dinners were never sumptuous anyway, with guests sometimes offered a New Life dinner at 40 Chinese cents (2.4 US cents) and no alcohol. Toasts were made with tea. This was wartime and austerity reigned.

Jimmy McHugh had brought his recently acquired Ford to Chungking via Changsha with the new British ambassador, Sir Archibald Clark Kerr, as company over the last leg. The US attaché stayed in a house across the Yangtze with his own ambassador, the cheerfully overweight Nelson Johnson. McHugh was his ambassador's contact with the Chiangs. Every day, he had to cross the river in a sampan, pushing crabwise through the strong current, then climb the long stone steps to the city.

The Chiangs and their retinue were entertained on Christmas Day by leaders of the New Life Movement, with carols in Chinese and the pudgy aide, JL Huang, as Santa Claus. Christmas dinner was ham, turkey and a flaming plum pudding with a single Chinese 10-cent coin. Donald got the serve of pudding with the coin, Chiang telling him he could give it back when they returned to Peking. Later, sharing leftovers with the Kungs, Donald and Reverend George Shepherd were the only foreigners remaining in the group. Like at a Victorian soiree, the blindfolded missionary played blind man's buff with the women. Under the shadow of war, such simple pleasures were to be treasured, no matter how fleeting or paradoxical.

Chungking had been the target of bombing raids for the previous year, one Sunday leaving over 200 dead, but the Japanese, unable to consolidate the occupied part of China and drawn into the interior where the lines of communication were stretched and constantly broken, were becoming demoralised. It was a year and a half since Japan broadened its war against China in Shanghai. No-one, including the Japanese, imagined the Chinese would still be fighting in 1939.

Donald railed in his letters overseas about Western nations looking for profits from financing Japan's exploitation of conquered China. The past history of foreign exploitation of China, he wrote, was of 'the arrival of big men with bigger ideas and still bigger brass bands who were going to make millions out of the natural resources of this country; how they festooned the lobbies of the old Wagon-Lits Hotel, and later the Hotel de Pekin at Peking; how they overflowed the corridors and the reception rooms of Legations, Embassies, and Chinese Yamens, and how they swelled with hopes one day and flattened with disappointment the next, till, at last, they collapsed like busted bladders, and crept off as quietly as possible to the railway station homeward bound, baffled and bewildered that their importance and their standing in their own countries meant nothing, or so little in China.'

If that was the experience in peacetime, Donald wondered, how could Japan exploit this country of hostile people?

Japan continued to look for a path out of its predicament, mired as others would be later in the century in an unwinnable Asian war. Chiang's long-time rival, Wang Ching-wei, formerly on the left wing of the Nationalist Party but suspected now of Japanese sympathies, had told Chiang in December he was flying to Kunming to make a speech. His wife, family and furniture already out of China, he flew instead to Hanoi and publicly proposed settlement with Japan, attracting the unwelcome interest of the party's agents. The press labelled him a traitor and 'a piece of rotten meat'. Following a failed assassination attempt, the wounded Wang was flown to Shanghai where he started talks with the Japanese to set up a rival government of China.

Everything was in a state of flux. The American writer Emily Hahn approached the Soong sisters to write a book about them. May-ling, already horrified by a book by John Gunther, asked Donald what to do. Should she be writing her own story?

'Yes, but you won't get around to it for years,' he advised. 'Somebody's bound to write this book sooner or later and you can't stop them. This woman's willing to cooperate. Why not let her try it? Better than someone digging around, looking for dirt.'

Donald sent a note that a car would come to Hahn's hostel in the afternoon. Duly arriving with Jimmy McHugh in his Ford, they drove to look at Donald's new house, under construction on the side of a hill overlooking Chialing River, then to his current house next to the Chiang residence for tea and talk in a study full of old books, maps and papers. She passed the test and would meet with Madame Chiang next morning.

But by 1939, cracks were appearing in the Chiang Kai-shek team. Tensions and irritations pulled at the three of them, strains in the political marriage and Chiang looking less to the highly opinionated Australian for advice. Britain's ambassador, Clark Kerr, an Australian-born Scot with an initial high regard for Donald, now saw him as 'restricted to carrying private messages to Chiang Kai-shek and to getting small jobs done . . . no more than a garrulous old man full of prejudices'.

May-ling's older, dominant sister, Ai-ling, through her marriage to the head of the Executive Committee and president of the Central Bank, had access to financial plans and upcoming policy changes with government bonds. An acquaintance got into Donald's ear about her financial manipulations and ostentatious display of wealth while the nation's suffering mounted. When he raised it discreetly with May-ling, she turned on him.

'Don,' she responded, 'you may criticise the government or anything in China, but there are some persons even you cannot criticise!'

Donald's frustrations were boiling over, as he swung between self-mockery and despair. Sent to Chiang headquarters to get a statement from Madame Chiang, a young man from the ministry of information was directed to Donald's house next door. Giving his visitor a piece of chocolate cake, Donald said, 'Madame keeps me in cake.' He sent a note to McHugh that he was 'at the end of my nervous strength', and had booked a flight to Hong Kong, from where he would take a steamer across the Indian Ocean to Madagascar.

'This will keep me out of the way of people who may bother me to tell them about China,' he wrote. 'Talking on China is more exhausting than anything else.'

He left in June on the Dutch liner SS *Ruys* for Batavia (now Jakarta) and across the Indian Ocean via Mauritius and Reunion to Madagascar, where he stayed for two weeks until the *Ruys* returned from Africa. Coming back via Zanzibar, Mombasa and the Seychelles, Donald changed ships at Sumatra and reached Hong Kong in mid-September. It hadn't been the restorative voyage he had hoped, giving him no relief from the catarrh that had dogged him for years. He complained there had been 'nothing to see and Madagascar had nothing to show'.

Donald underwent surgery in Hong Kong for his catarrh and recuperated by sailing his custom-built yacht around the colony's islands as he had in the smaller *Waratah* a lifetime before. Designed for single-handed sailing in the open sea, *Mei Hwa* was built of teak with a copper bottom and stainless steel rigging. He'd ordered the 39-foot cutter in 1935, but it had been in the care of its builder in the three years since it was completed.

After its Hong Kong trial, *Mei Hwa* was loaded onto a freighter bound for New Zealand, from where he planned to sail to Surabaya and decide where to go from there. On finding the ship's only available berth was in a three-berth cabin and being unprepared to share, he cancelled his ticket, had the yacht unloaded and returned to Chungking instead, still torn between the mission that had consumed more than half his life—to wake the sleeping giant—and giving up.

With major ports in Japanese hands, alternative ways were sought to get supplies from overseas into unoccupied China. Largely at Donald's urging, a 1150-kilometre road had been built connecting the railhead at Lashio, Burma, with Kunming in Yunnan, to transport goods unloaded at Rangoon, Burma's capital. The British socialist politician, Sir Stafford Cripps, was coming up the Burma Road in January 1940 to Chungking where he wanted to arrange a side trip to the Soviet Union. Donald advised Chiang it would be in China's interests to talk with Cripps and travelled with a Chinese delegation to meet him in Rangoon.

After sorting out problems with the travel arrangements, Donald returned to China while Cripps was escorted through the magnificent scenery east of the Himalayas, stopping along the Burma Road at the Curtiss-Wright aircraft factory at Loiwing. The outcome of a deal between TV Soong and William Pawley, the aviation salesman Madame and Donald had been investigating, was that the factory had been moved from Hangchow as the Japanese pushed into the Yangtze valley.

Cripps was met by Donald at Kunming, staying at the lakeside hotel and giving Chiang's adviser time to fully brief the visitor. It was an opportunity for Bill Donald to give full voice to his preoccupation as raconteur to another new listener who found him 'full of charm and modern Chinese history', a man with a strong sense of what was right and wrong for China. Five days later, they flew to Chungking in Chiang's private four-seater Beechcraft.

After a few meetings with Chiang—'impressive in his modesty and sincerity'—Cripps was asked to stay for a few months and help plan industry or return to chair a council of foreign advisers. The visitor was interested in the offer, meeting with Donald and Madame Chiang in Hong Kong on his way out of China. She said of her husband, 'You must never forget he has a truly oriental mind.' She had in mind his preparedness to agree out of politeness with proposals he had no intention of carrying out and his refusal to get rid of old associates who were loyal. The long way round often seemed to him the shortest way home.

When Cripps got back to England, he was somewhat surprised to receive a letter from Donald and Madame Chiang advising against taking up the position. All his efforts, they warned, would be defeated by the Chinese people who had to work out their destiny in their own way. It was a change of tune for a man who had been advising Chiang his country's future lay in securing the right foreign advisers, but this was a man whose tune was changing in many ways.

Donald's enthusiasm was waning, his health faltering. He silently seethed at the treatment of his prodigy, the Young Marshal, still under house detention. A barrier had grown between him and Madame. Her prodigious energy was deserting her, requiring escape to Hong Kong to recover from bouts of nervous exhaustion, skin rashes and migraine headaches. On the other hand, Chiang, reborn as an ascetic, was faring well, less dependent on his wife's understanding of the West. He was going it alone with little expectation of Western intervention to rescue China and less need for his dogmatic foreign adviser.

A speech Donald wrote for May-ling in April contained derogatory references to Germany, by then at war with Britain. The generalissimo advised removing them.

'I'm not at war with Germany,' he commented.

'I am!' said Donald, insisting they stay.

Chiang was concerned the speech might provoke Germany's recognition of a Wang Ching-wei puppet government and called Donald a traitor, more devoted to Britain than China.

The Australian was at the end of his tether. He left Chunking on 2 May 1940, with only a brief goodbye to May-ling and without a word to her husband, flying to Hong Kong. Within a few days he had left the colony. Any opportunity Madame Chiang might have wished to find to rescue the situation had already vanished.

Chapter 14

Escape and capture

When WH Donald left Chungking and the Chiangs in high dudgeon for Hong Kong, he didn't leave alone. With him was twenty-year-old Ansie Lee, the daughter of a wealthy Hong Kong realtor. Seconded by Madame Chiang from the Chungking secretariat, she had been working with the Bureau of National Economic Research, co-headed by Donald. The Australian planned to occupy his escape writing memoirs and work on that scale needed secretarial assistance. A highly competent typist, Ansie agreed to join him. Having left the colony for Chungking, she was clearly an adventurous young woman, even if she described herself dismissively as 'a spoilt, rich Hong Kong girl'.

In later years, the bureau had been a means of generating a salary for the Chiangs' adviser who had no formal position with them. Donald arranged for the regular payments to his account to cease, but despite his passionate campaign against corruption he arranged for Miss Lee's salary payments to continue after she left with him for Hong Kong.

Donald had *Mei Hwa* loaded once again, this time on a cargo ship bound for New Britain; he and Ansie following on a British steamer via Borneo and New Guinea. He could sail the yacht in Hong Kong single-handed, but to cruise around the Pacific Ocean he needed additional crew. While on the lookout for deckhands, he gave a talk to the local

Nationalist Party, stressing China's will to win its conflict with Japan, telling of Chiang Kai-shek's dislike of pomp and love of poetry, and of Madame Chiang's concern for the homeless. He had severed his bond with China's leading couple, but it wasn't easy letting go.

Failing to find suitable crew in Rabaul, they took the freighter *Yunnan* to Tulagi in the British Solomon Islands with *Mei Hwa* onboard. On arrival, Donald went ashore with the *Yunnan* captain who introduced him to Tulagi's collector of customs as a passenger disembarking.

Asked what he was here for, Donald said, 'Because this is the last port of call for the ship.'

'I meant, what are you going to do here?' the customs officer clarified.

'Just stick around a bit.'

The irritated official told Donald that he had to pay a bond of £50 in cash to disembark. 'We don't want deadbeats here,' he said.

Donald took a book of American travellers' cheques from his pocket.

'We don't take foreign money here,' chipped in a clerk standing nearby.

The *Yunnan* captain put up the £100 bond for Donald and Ansie and they were allowed to disembark, but it was a sign of what was to come. Local 'blackbirding' regulations in the British protectorate made signing a crew in Tulagi difficult, and eventually the man who helped negotiate the generalissimo's release in Si'an gave up, defeated by colonial intransigence. His yacht was shipped back to Hong Kong as deck cargo and Donald and Ansie took a ship to New Zealand.

The cruise through the islands writing his memoirs had become a pipedream. In six months since leaving China, he was still fiddling with the preparation, using the excuse that many of his documents were still in Nanking even though he'd brought his collection of diaries with him. This was a man who prided himself on his prodigious memory for people and places. If Ansie Lee was supposed to spur him on, she was having little success.

From Chungking, May-ling had moved temporarily to Hong Kong for an operation on her sinuses amid chronic concern about her health. Britain's ambassador Clark Kerr was shown recent correspondence between her and Donald, but she didn't elaborate, talking as if he was just holidaying. Meanwhile, Chiang's closest advisers were working hard to undermine any reputation Donald still had in Chungking. There were long-standing resentments over the influence he and Madame had on the leader.

In Auckland, cables were waiting for Donald from relatives and others asking him to come to Australia, but he was adamant he wouldn't return to his homeland while its government 'traded with the enemy' with scrap metal and other strategic materials. In January 1941, they sailed to Fiji where Donald met up with some of his family, then left on the sugar boat *Limerick* for Papeete.

Unsettled and aimless, Donald found Tahiti a dreary paradise. Some of his fading health was recovered swimming in the crystal Pacific water and cycling around the island. It was quiet and restful, but he couldn't make any inroads into his book. A letter from Madame asked him to fly back, and he replied that he needed four to six months to book a steamship. While Ansie stayed in Papeete, he took a month-long cruise to the Marquesas and returned to a cable from Chungking suggesting he 'GO TO SOME MORE ACCESSIBLE PLACE OR GO BACK TO HONG KONG', adding solicitously, 'WE DO NOT WISH TO INTERFERE WITH YOUR REST'.

The more May-ling persisted with the fiction that this was a holiday, the more the fiction became fact. Donald was listening with increasing interest to shortwave radio, keeping in touch with the war in Europe and the stand-off between Japan and the United States. The Japanese might achieve for the generalissimo what he had been unable to achieve himself, drawing the West into conflict with them. With the distractions and his motivation waning, Donald abandoned the book, explaining to a friend, 'I would have to do too much debunking and hurt too many people.'

Another letter came from Madame. She was planning a goodwill tour of America later in 1941 and wanted Donald on hand for the guidance she knew she needed. He cabled back: 'I AM RETURNING'.

With no direct route from Papeete to Chungking, logic said get to Hong Kong. The best way to do that was through Honolulu. Donald and Ansie scoured Papeete in vain for any kind of shipping to Hawaii, finally taking a freighter to New Zealand and connecting to the liner *Mariposa* back up to Honolulu. They arrived in November.

A cable to his old friend WL Bond asked to arrange two seats on a Pan American Clipper from Honolulu to Hong Kong. Donald wanted to return urgently but couldn't book a flight in Hawaii because of the number of US military personnel and engineers going out to American island bases. War was in the air.

A few days later, Pan Am wired Bond that a reservation had been approved, but Donald couldn't be located in Honolulu. He and Ansie were already at sea. Impatient, the Australian had continued to look for a ship going to Hong Kong and found the freighter SS *Robert Dollar*, carrying arms for Canadian troops stationed in the colony after Britain, wanting to avoid antagonising Japan, rejected Chiang's offer of Chinese troops.

On the morning of 8 December, with the *Robert Dollar* south of the island of Ambon, its captain was told that Pearl Harbor had been bombed and America was at war with Japan. With attacks reported on Malaya and Hong Kong, the ship diverted to Manila, arriving shortly before General MacArthur withdrew his troops to the Bataan Peninsula and declared Manila an open city.

The Japanese captured Manila three weeks after Donald and Ansie arrived. Detained by the occupation force along with other Europeans at their hotel, they were taken to Sulphur Springs where Donald befriended the registrar, a German veteran of the World War I. When the Australian was transferred in February to the large internment camp for foreign non-combatants on the grounds of Manila's University of Santo Tomas, he left the diaries and preliminary notes for his memoirs with the old German to be locked away in his shed.

After days of chaos and hope, it became clear that MacArthur was not about to drive the Japanese out of the Philippines. A routine developed for the 2500 civilians held at Santo Tomas, a camp governed by a committee of prisoners, under Japanese supervision, and a multitude of sub-committees. Two university buildings and a gymnasium had been converted to living quarters, although detainees were allowed to build shanties as long as they were open enough for guards to see what was going on inside. Teachers organised classes for children. Doctors and nurses continued their professions, as did prostitutes. The younger working men all wore shorts, becoming tanned and fit.

People met in the endless queues, lining up for coffee, meals, showers, toilets, the clinic—little went unqueued. Meals were a mush of pulverised wheat, corn, rice or cassava, or else a vegetable stew, and occasionally, meat. The succulent tropical vegetable, talinum, was always available, but bread disappeared from the dining table, then milk. Soap, toilet paper and sugar were rationed in turn. Internees mostly maintained a cheerful outlook despite the hardships, but some cracked under the strain, others became listless and jittery.

Donald kept busy and out of sight with Ansie in a secluded corner of the library, repairing books, but their lives were moving in different directions, their new associations reflecting their disparity. The 68-year-old built himself a shanty out of bits of wood and branches. Ansie, housed in a large women's dormitory, revealed an artistic side with sketches of camp life. Conscious of talk about her relationship with the much older Australian, she attached to Hank Sperry, an American whose British wife had hooked onto another American.

For Donald, some faces were already familiar, among them Corwin 'Chappie' Chapman, a casual acquaintance from Nanking days, and Jack Percival, another Australian. A *Sydney Morning Herald* journalist, Percival had seats for his wife and himself on the 'last' plane from Manila in December, but his chief, visiting Manila at the time, commandeered one. Mrs Percival had refused to leave her husband behind and both were in Santo Tomas as a result.

The Japanese authorities would have been extremely interested to know they had Chiang Kai-shek's foreign adviser in custody, his advice never to their benefit. In all likelihood, they would have executed Donald, but his captors were not aware he had left China. Guards had been brought down from Japan, not across from the battle zone. A few of the detainees knew who Donald was, but it wasn't someone at Santo Tomas who let the cat out of the bag.

With speculation in China about what had become of her adviser, Madame Chiang asked Langhorne Bond at a Chungking dinner if he knew where his friend was. She had heard nothing since the cable that he was returning. On a request from Generalissimo Chiang, US Secretary of State Cordell Hull wired his high commissioner in Manila about the whereabouts of WH Donald, to be advised he had been in Manila in December. Muriel Donald, living in California with her mother, picked up that her father might be interned in Santo Tomas and wrote to American authorities asking to be notified if he was brought to the US, but his whereabouts continued to be uncertain.

On a visit to London in August 1943, TV Soong changed all that, telling the British press that Donald was a prisoner of the Japanese in Manila, an act either of vindictiveness—he and the increasingly cranky Australian had fallen out before Donald left China—or stupidity. A few months later, the *kempeitai* (military police) came to Santo Tomas and inspected the camp register while Donald, unaware of the closeness of the threat, busily bound books in the nearby library. Donald was registered as 'William Donald. A. Scot', which confused the Japanese police—was this WDA Scot or was it William Donald, a Scot?—and expecting a much younger man than this person's 68 years, they left without asking to see him.

For nearly a year, volunteers had been called to transfer to a subsidiary camp in the College of Agriculture at Los Baños, 60 kilometres inland from Manila on the huge lake, Laguna de Bay. Some had taken up the offer, others had been forced to go. When told of the *kempeitai* visit, Donald and Ansie got themselves on the next batch of transfers, arriving by truck in April 1944.

Los Baños was tropical and wet. The camp's 2000 detainees were accommodated in 21 college buildings converted to barracks. Thatched palm-leaf roofs leaked, woven matting walls rotted and wall-supports were ant-infested. Sanitation was crude but adequate. Males between eighteen and 40 logged the nearby forest although Donald, always willing to do things about the camp, was too old for such punishing work. Meals served twice a day were a breakfast of corn meal and rice mush, and dinner of meat—local water buffalo or pig—with vegetables, mostly grown in the college gardens, and rice. Nonetheless, deficiency diseases were rampant, both Donald and Ansie suffering beriberi.

Donald was looking old with signs of deteriorating health. He had lost 25 kilograms and his voice had become husky. He began to fret about the memoirs on which he had failed to make serious inroads with Ansie, becoming obsessed that all he had done for China—in recent years, his centrality to the maelstrom of Chinese politics had consolidated in his mind—would be lost in the mists of time, unrecorded for posterity. In October, he was moved into a six-man cubicle in a barracks a kilometre away to allow expanded Japanese occupation of the college buildings. His new room-mates included his old Nanking friend, Chappie, two Americans working in Manila for Coca Cola when the city was captured, and a Jardine Matheson engineer from Shanghai who continually sat, sometimes reading, sometimes sleeping, but often just sitting.

Chapman kept a diary, a chronicle of the camp's rejuvenated expectations with formations of planes seen in the distance and bombs heard somewhere in the vicinity. Faith and hope said an Allied advance must be approaching. His friend's diary prompted Donald to again pursue a journal of his life with the Manchus, the warlords and the generalissimo. He asked Chappie to take down his impromptu dictation and they began assembling the story of WH Donald in daily sessions. A month later, their narrative well advanced, 30 big bombers flew directly over the camp, their US insignias clear for all to see. The end was nigh on many fronts.

In the new year of 1945, the dull routine of camp life was disrupted by an astonishing and inexplicable incident. Just before midnight on 6 January, the secretary of the detainees' administrative committee was woken by a Japanese guard and told that every shovel in the camp had to be brought immediately to Commandant Iwanaka. As he went about this task, the committeeman noticed the commandant's car, the garrison's International and the college's Oldsmobile truck all standing in front of Iwanaka's office.

Called to a 3.30 a.m. meeting in the office, where they found staff packing, the administrative committee was told by the commandant he had been ordered to release the internees to the committee's care. They would be left with two weeks provisions and the recommendation that they stay within the camp. Iwanaka wanted a list of people then in the camp signed in duplicate. Money and items confiscated from prisoners were returned, and they were told the Oldsmobile would be brought back in ten days. Failing that, ten sacks of rice would be sent as the estimated value of the truck. By 5 a.m., the Japanese were gone.

Its unexpectedness was disorienting. Patrols were set up to protect supplies in the kitchen and prevent looting of the guards' barracks and the office. At a sunrise meeting of residents, the chairman explained events as best he could, pointing out there had been no news of actual Allied landings on Luzon and that the camp presumably remained surrounded by Japanese. Two sentries were still at the camp gate, although whether they were to stop people getting in or out was unclear.

A radio transmitter was activated to contact US forces, and the American and British flags were raised with anthems playing on loudspeakers. For most of the residents, including the ailing Bill Donald, it was all too surreal and sudden to make much sense. 'Released' internees raced around the compound embracing, kissing and congratulating each other. By late afternoon, they were listening to the Voice of Freedom, KGEX San Francisco, and whatever foreign shortwave stations they could pick up. They were free, in that they were no longer detained by the Japanese, but they had nowhere to go. One form of detention had been replaced with another. Too bizarre to last, it couldn't and didn't.

At 9.30 that night, a truck with Japanese soldiers arrived at the gate. Surprised to find the camp abandoned, they shut down the radio equipment and left men behind while they went away to find more guards. A week later, Iwanaka and his staff returned, resuming duty as if nothing had happened, offering no explanation of their departure.

Donald returned to recording his recollections with Chapman, but the mood had changed, both sides unsettled for their own reasons by the anticipated arrival of the Allies. The Japanese wouldn't admit to themselves or their charges what they knew in their heart, that the dream of a powerful Japanese empire would soon sink in ignominious defeat. The internees worried that they would be slaughtered before they could be rescued. The commandant insisted the committee post a notice that internees were not to congregate in the open when 'planes are heard or seen in the vicinity of the Camp', by which was meant American planes. Several internees had been slapped and threatened by guards for watching planes pass overhead.

Rations in Los Baños were running low with further supplies sporadic and often little more than raw rice. Hospital patients were dying daily.

Donald kept his head down, continuing to work on his memoir. In mid-February, two internees stole out of the camp one night to meet with a local Filipino guerrilla commander named Colonel Ingles. On their return, one of them, committee secretary George Gray, briefed the administrative committee about a planned guerrilla raid to liberate the camp. Apprehensive about Japanese reprisals, the committee decided to have no further contact, but Gray met with Colonel Ingles again a few days later.

The regional commander of Japan's forces inspected the camp, expressing doubt that more food would be available. Any internee caught outside the camp would be shot on sight, he said, unaware that three of them had left camp two nights before to join Ingles's band and provide intelligence for the US Army's support of the coming raid. Itching to liberate Allied internees, the guerrillas met American scouts and were told the US would drop paratroopers and bring amphibian transports across Laguna de Bay to back up a guerrilla assault on the camp. For the next two days, American planes strafed and bombed Japanese garrisons nearby to draw their attention away from Los Baños.

Overnight on 22 February, Filipino guerrillas surrounded the internment camp, launching an attack as the sun rose, while the guards did morning calisthenics. Nine American transport planes flew in from the east and released a confetti of paratroopers into the adjacent countryside. Los Baños was still behind enemy lines.

A volley of gunfire from the guardhouses was the first sign something was afoot, Japanese sentries racing through the camp to take cover where they could, trying to get to useful defensive positions. Barefoot guerrillas in ragged clothes prowled about the compound, firing in all directions, grinning like kids on an outing. Figures darted through the early morning gloom. In the pandemonium, internees huddled silent on barrack floors, bullets whistling about and hand grenades exploding outside. In their cottage, Donald and his housemates ducked for cover while the raid took its course. Nobody cheered. That would draw unwanted attention and they weren't sure how this would play out.

A rumble of heavy machines approaching from the nearby lake, then heavily-kitted paratroopers exploded through the main gate in full fire. The battle escalated, but the defenders were no match for a second assault force. Firing died down, intermittent shots as guards were driven out of concealed positions, those who could find a way out escaping to the surrounding forest. The paratroopers were a Texan unit and its husky soldiers rushed through the barracks, shouting in Southern accents at cowering occupants to pick up minimum belongings and head quickly to the lake shore.

A convoy of twenty amphibian tractors brought up from the lake stood at the main gate revving their engines. People rushed in all directions with packages and bundles. Hospital cases and those who couldn't stride briskly were put on the amphibians. Anyone fit enough walked the 2 kilometres to the lake's edge where more amphibians waited. Donald was picked up by a couple of burly paratroopers, carried to the gate and put on a vehicle with little time to think of possessions, but Chapman had picked up the scribbled memoir along with his own things.

The garrison barracks were set on fire by the Americans as the last internees were leaving. As intense heat and sparks from the burning palm-leaf huts carried the inferno across camp, Donald was taken past gaping Filipinos to the lake's edge. From there a two-hour journey across Laguna de Bay got the convoy to Mamatid beach, from where it had set out before dawn that morning. Reminding them they were still in a war zone, an enemy machine-gun nest fired as they left the shore, but it was soon silenced by US artillery.

Trucks and ambulances took 2000 liberated civilians to the town of Muntinlupa, 30 kilometres away, joyful Filipinos shouting '*Mabuhay!*' (long life) along the way. At New Bilibid Prison, refashioned as a refugee way station, the evacuees were given chocolate and a stretcher slotted into an iron double-bunk with two scratchy blankets. Donald sat among them on hard ground, hot and dusty despite a water truck's spray. Drinking water was on offer and small amounts of bread and butter, coffee and meat. Gum was handed out to chew. This part of the Philippines was in American hands.

Detainees liberated from Los Baños were sent to Santo Tomas where Donald and Chapman set up a shanty with three others. The unfinished war—Hiroshima was still six months away—made repatriation slow, especially for an Australian who wanted to be taken to the United States, not his homeland. With visions of reviving his career, Donald thought his American contacts might help. In any case, as he wrote to his sister, 'When I think of all that has happened in the face of the years of warnings which I gave I am filled with bitterness against the appeasers. That is why I would not go to Australia before the war involved them. That is why I hesitate now.' Donald was not letting go of his hostility for Japan.

Listless days followed as evacuees waited for word of onward arrangements. One day in April, while Donald was sitting aimlessly with friends on Santo Tomas's main steps, the camp's scratchy PA system ordered him to report to the office 'on the double'. Returning with a telegram and an amused look on his face, he said Roosevelt had arranged for a plane to take him to the US, assuming, probably correctly, it had been set up by Madame Chiang.

Donald was tickled at the thought of calling on the US president in his internee's clothes, the ragged shorts and worn-out shirt he had on the day of his rescue, but his friend, Charles Moat, offered instead a suit he had recovered from storage in Manila.

'I'll tell the president I'm dressed by the House of Moat,' Donald said.

An army lieutenant, Robert Tierney, was assigned to accompany Donald to the US, along with the wife of an American general. Mrs Margaret Seales was a pain in the backside. Repeatedly vowing to never set foot in the Philippines again, she refused to be air-lifted. Others, including Ansie Lee and Hank Sperry, her fiancée when he could divorce his current wife, had been shipped by freighter to various destinations throughout March, but Mrs Seales insisted on going first-class on a passenger liner and, as the wife of a high-ranking officer, with the services of an aide-de-camp. That was Lieutenant Tierney and meant Donald was at the mercy of this demanding woman's whims.

It took some time to find a ship that met with her satisfaction, the US-Dutch liner *Noordam*. Also transporting the seriously wounded from the battle for Manila to American hospitals, but not registered as a hospital ship, it was going to head south and rely on its speed for protection from attack. When the *Noordam* stopped over at Leyte, Tierney and Donald urged Mrs Seales to relent and fly the rest of the journey but she was adamant and they continued unescorted, eventually arriving at San Francisco without further incident.

Robert Tierney would subsequently acknowledge his homosexuality and claimed to historian Winston Lewis 30 years later that he and Donald had a sexual relationship onboard the *Noordam*, the Australian wanting them to travel together while he once again attempted to write his autobiography. No evidence supports this claim and Donald's subsequent letters to Tierney are cordial but no more. The two never met again.

On arriving at San Francisco, Margaret Seales was taken to hospital where she later died, but Donald's arrival seemed more auspicious. Met at San Francisco by a large group of Chinese, he saw it as a sign that he would be welcomed back as an influential policy figure in China's political machinery. He would be sadly disappointed. Already yesterday's man with nothing to offer the geopolitics of the post-war world, in the United States he would be seen as a problem to be kept out of the way.

Chapter 15

Yesterday's man

By the time Donald got to California, the San Francisco Conference was already underway, a gathering of representatives from 50 countries which would establish the United Nations. The former adviser to the Chinese government attended several sessions eager to re-establish his credentials in Far East policy-making, but it didn't turn out that way. In the chit-chat between sessions, he ran into various people from China or whose past had taken them through China. He sought out the Australian and New Zealand delegations, to whom he was a legendary figure, and basked in their glib adulation, writing to Corwin Chapman in Shanghai of both countries pressing him to become their Far East adviser.

Neither side pursued that social exchange further, and Donald found getting even a semblance of traction with Americans at the conference a difficult task. He wrote a press release outlining what was owed by the Allies to China—financial and technical assistance, regret for its betrayal between 1937 and 1941—but it was censored at MacArthur's headquarters and returned with the comment, 'We cannot pass such controversial statements by Mr WH Donald.'

Argumentative and increasingly erratic, Donald was swimming against the current. He blew the dust off his old propaganda campaign about the Rape of Nanking, but that was ancient history. He found the conviction widespread that the Communists had fought on alone in China against the Japanese and insisted they were 'idlers' and 'murderers'. No-one was interested and by the end of May he was telling Chappie, 'I don't know what's happening at the Conference and I don't care.'

Although he had put on weight since Los Baños and gained strength, Donald's health was deteriorating and there were long delays getting appointments with doctors and dentists. Constantly tired, he cut his workload back to mornings only. An abscessed lower tooth was removed along with the last of his upper teeth. A temporary plate was fitted, but his gums became infected. Unable to chew, he dined on soup and scrambled egg, and couldn't laugh for fear his 'clappers might fly out'. After several days of the problem, another dentist reluctantly agreed to finish the job.

Now he was in America, away from the foreign-ness of China and the privation of Los Baños. He had often written nostalgically to his old friends the Rathvons about their New Rochelle life he had shared briefly on a visit to the US: green lawns, their son's upturned bike, the corner drug store, going to the movies with the family. He speculated gleefully about the two Rathvon kids growing up and offering his flippant services as nanny. One time he had commented, 'Perhaps I'm lonely!'

On his liberation from Los Baños, Donald had found a letter from his daughter waiting for him. She had written on spec a month before. A week later, he wrote from New Bilibid Prison describing life in the camp and the raid that freed him, signing off 'With all affection—Dad.' It was the beginning of a constant flow of letters between the two over the next few months, giving him a taste of the domestic life he had sometimes hankered after.

Muriel lived in modest circumstances with her mother in Paradise City, northern California. They had emigrated in 1927 and Muriel had built a career as a radio journalist after first working as a grocery checker. Mary got occasional home-nursing work and although her father was a wealthy Sydney widower with a successful construction company, there were no signs of her family helping out. In a histrionic letter to a friend late in her life, Mary claimed without explanation that her father disinherited her when she married Donald. Sometimes bitter about her husband, she also believed he was used by people.

The daughter managed to meet with her father a few times while he was in San Francisco—whether it was with her mother's approval or even knowledge is unknown. The resulting frequent letters between them opened a window for both onto what might have been, poignant and beyond reach.

Donald would write about the weather and what the dentist was doing to him. Muriel wrote about her cold, for which he suggested smelling salts, her love of birds and her dream of setting up a ranch. Her father told of his frustrated efforts to find money to cover his living expenses, hoping his house in Peking was still standing. His advice, as always, was in the form of a homily.

'Be of good cheer,' he wrote, 'and trust mostly to yourself. If you are self-reliant and independent you can get along well. Never depend on anyone. I never did, but I never got on well, for I never did have any money sense. I was always content to get enough to eat, and perhaps that is not wise . . . Lots of love, as ever, Dad.'

By June, having lost interest in the San Francisco Conference, he was heading to New York by train with a line of credit from the bank and a typewriter given to him by a friend. He stayed in the Adirondacks with Harold Hochschild and on Long Island with KC Li, an expatriate Chinese metallurgist and adviser to the Chinese Embassy in Washington. Dr Li was in frequent contact with Madame Chiang who, while she was in New York, met her erstwhile adviser in a Manhattan hotel. He told friends she said he must return to China although he was equivocal about this himself. The accuracy of that is open to doubt. Donald was having difficulty distinguishing between what was and what he wished it would be.

He was weak and tried to recover his strength with horse-riding, walking, rowing and sailing. Eventually it got to be too strenuous. To escape the approaching winter chill, he took a train back to San Francisco to catch a steamer to Tahiti, with a view to going on to New Zealand or Australia. After a struggle with post-war red tape, he got permission to go to Tahiti on SS *Permanent*, leaving 25 October. He wrote to Muriel that he was slowly getting over his aches and pains, but was still weak. He'd been told it was just aging, but he had his doubts.

In his cottage by the Tahitian sea, Donald was surrounded by palms, mangoes and breadfruit trees. Surf thundered on the reef nearby. With a kerosene lamp for light and nothing much to do, he went to bed at eight and rose at five, the routine of the internment camp. He cycled and swam daily. His muscular contractions were easing, but he was still constantly short of breath.

Christmas approached. Scarcely able to breathe, a fluoroscope of his lungs revealed something was wrong, but the hospital in Papeete was ill-equipped to do anything for it. Donald telegraphed May-ling and was put on a US Navy plane to Honolulu, diverted from Samoa. He was taken to the naval hospital at Aiea Heights overlooking Pearl Harbor.

In January 1946, Admiral MD Willcutts, the US Pacific Command's chief medical adviser, told medical officer Clayton Ethridge that the Australian being brought from Tahiti was to be treated as a VIP because of his connection with Chiang Kai-shek and the need for President Truman's envoy to China, General George Marshall, to broker a rapprochement between the Chinese Communist Party and the Nationalist Party. By coincidence, Dr Morton Willcutts, then a medical officer with the US Marine Detachment in Peking, had treated Donald at the Rockefeller Clinic in 1934.

Dr Ethridge conducted a range of diagnostic tests on Donald's respiratory system. The resulting x-ray evidence, backed up by pathology, showed 'extensive lung disease, possibly malignant'—in other words, lung cancer. With his right lung collapsed and its tissues disintegrating, he was told he was a year too late coming to them.

Donald took news of the diagnosis with characteristic dry humour. 'In Los Baños, many died from starvation and I had the comfort of failing to die,' he said. 'Looks like the Good Lord was only putting me to one side to attend to me later.'

Having digested this reality, Donald was determined to return to China, to see Madame again and to try to patch up his differences with the generalissimo. He contacted May-ling, and in late January Hollington Tong arrived in Honolulu, an emissary from Chiang and the Nationalist Chinese government.

'Holly, as always you arrive like the cavalry when the battle is almost lost,' the husky-voiced patient said. 'Or are you a messenger from the gods?'

Tong's brief was to expedite Donald's affairs so he could make the trip to China. He and Ethridge spent two months battling with the US state department's concern that the return of the highly opinionated Australian might impede Marshall's efforts to forge a coalition government there.

•

One night soon after Donald arrived in Hawaii, the night editor of Honolulu's *Advertiser* rang one of his reporters, Earl Selle, and assigned him to a story on WH Donald. Selle had lived in China at one stage, working for the *Shanghai Evening Post*, and had a useful background familiarity with his subject, but his future in journalism was in serious doubt. During the war, his eyesight had deteriorated and by 1946 he was nearly blind.

Walking down a gloomy hospital corridor to Donald's private room, Selle knocked on the door.

'Come in,' called a cheery expectant voice, nasal and croaky.

Entering, the reporter was greeted by a beaming 70-year-old, hand held out, buoyant at someone actually wanting to hear what he had to say.

'Hello,' said the American. 'What are you here for?' He had been told of Donald's diagnosis, but wasn't sure he should reveal that.

'Oh, I'm sitting here looking at the green hills. I've been watching the sun and then the rain against my window. And I'm waiting to die.'

A discomforted Selle fumbled a courteous protesting response. The long leaves of a banana plant outside brushed across the window. Other sounds came in dribs and drabs and bursts. Footsteps in the corridor. Voices. Occasionally, running and excited shouting. Then silence again.

'I never argue with people,' said Donald with a sly knowing smile.

They talked for some time—or, more correctly, Donald talked. He was not going to pass up an opportunity to expound his view on where China was going and what it needed to get there: American support for Chiang Kai-shek's government rather than the Communists. He acknowledged that the government needed to clean its house, sweep out the venality and corruption that infested it, but predicted that would happen, given time, and China could pick up scientific developments and Western improvements without the delays of trial and error.

'She can buy experience,' claimed Donald. 'She won't have to wallow in it.'

Selle asked where the Young Marshal, still under house detention in China, would fit into this vision of the future.

'I think he is the strongest personality in China today,' said the former adviser proudly. 'You will hear more of him.'

Selle was back at the naval hospital the next day. Donald railed against China's Communists and the Western appeasers they had gulled. He'd lost interest in the Japanese, defeated and devastated as they were by the two atomic bombs.

At the end of the session, his visitor said, 'I'd like to write your memoirs.'

It was manna from heaven for the dying man. He felt a surge of hope that this abandoned dream might yet come to fruition, forgetting the reasons it had fallen through in the past. The response was so enthusiastically positive that Selle decided to up the ante, saying he would need money to cover his expenses and talking the patient into advancing him $5000 against future royalties from the book.

Donald had made desultory attempts to find a press agent in New York, but his argumentativeness and bombast had driven everyone away. There were no overtures from publishers when his story, well-known and romantically exotic enough, should have attracted a significant advance. Instead, he found himself in the hands of a third-rate newspaperman to whom he paid an advance instead of receiving one.

By the next morning, Donald was having doubts about the wisdom of agreeing to this project, but he didn't voice them.

'On this day fourteen years ago,' he said, 'I was leaning out of a window at Astor House holding a phone so Mayor Wu could hear the gunfire.'

'I was walking past Astor House, Don, as the firing started,' replied Selle.

Two days before, Selle was calling him 'Mr Donald'; the next day, 'WH'. Now it was 'Don' as if he'd known him for years. Selle's escalating familiarity and obsequiousness was beginning to irritate the Australian, but once he gathered momentum with his story—some recalled, some patched from snippets of memory—his qualms fell by the wayside. He had so much to say and so little time to say it, he certainly didn't have time to worry about the vehicle for his memories or even their accuracy.

Selle was with Donald most mornings for the next month or so, arriving and setting up his dictaphone on a metal hospital trolley. Some days the dying man rambled on for an hour. He needed only a couple of questions to get started, like switching on a small machine, and his story would come pouring down the sluiceway, often more rhetoric than substance, but that was for Selle to sort out.

Sometimes Donald struggled visibly, the pressure on his one working lung too great for sustained talking. Out of breath and fighting his body to continue, he would have to stop. Doctors came in with long needles, tapped a litre of fluid from his lung—a process called aspiration—and Selle would not be able to see him for a day or two. Steadily Donald weakened. He became morose and an antagonism grew towards his biographer.

Donald had recovered some records and memorabilia from the old German in Manila and passed them to Selle, although they were mostly sentimental souvenirs, little of much biographical use. Selle began to pressure the sick man for more intimate personal detail, saying publishers would not be interested in a book without it. In the argument that developed, Donald said he was calling off the project and wanted $4000 of the advance back. Having already used most of the money to feed his family, Selle back-pedalled furiously, insisting he'd been misunderstood. The ad-libbed memory flowed again, but Donald never mentioned his wife and daughter and his biographer was unaware of their existence until much later.

Hollington Tong had meanwhile been working assiduously to clear the way for the Australian to get back to China. Through Dr Ethridge, medical permission was obtained to fly him to Shanghai and be transferred to the Country Hospital there. Official clearance for the flight was slow to come and at first refused. Tong flew to Washington and lobbied the appropriate people on behalf of the Chinese government. Two weeks later, he returned with approval for the flight.

Donald was flown to China in a US Navy VIP DC-4, set up with galley, dining room and bunks. Worried that he was planning to abandon the book, Selle and his wife visited him in hospital before he left, with Mrs Selle draping a lei around his neck, the Hawaiian custom to ensure the departee's return.

'Do I have to wear this?' asked Donald.

Taken to the airfield by ambulance and lifted onboard, he waved his Panama hat at a handful of well-wishers, mostly Chinese. A few, including Admiral Willcutts, came onboard to wish him luck while the plane's engines were warming up. Tong and Ethridge were to accompany the patient to Shanghai. At 10.30 in the evening the plane left Pearl Harbor, flying into uncertain weather for what would prove to be Bill Donald's last tactical move.

Island-hopping across the Pacific to China, the plane brought the dying man to Shanghai on a foggy, drizzly, mid-March morning. Within a few minutes of landing, General Chennault, the American who'd found Donald so useful in setting up an effective airforce in China, came aboard and embraced him warmly. They talked about old times while Ethridge arranged the transfer by stretcher and ambulance to the hospital, 5 kilometres down Nanking Road from the Bund.

The Country Hospital had re-opened after the Japanese occupation, its corridors bleak and empty, the building cold and inhospitable, but it was a quiet haven from the bustle of Shanghai. Donald's room was blank and antiseptic until May-ling arrived the next morning, as well-dressed and charming as ever despite the war, and transformed the room with Chinese prints, colourful drapes and a quilt, comfortable chairs and knick-knacks. Warm sunshine flooded into the room from a change in the weather. Wit and good humour flowed between Donald and Madame, striking Ethridge that this was a couple with a genuine fondness for each other.

After ten days, Dr Ethridge returned to Hawaii, leaving his patient in the care of Dr James Cheng, who Donald had known for 25 years, and Miss Fawcett, a quaint old British nurse. Madame Chiang came to see him every day for a while, but eventually flew back to join her husband in Chungking. Donald's days were spent reading and meeting guests and every couple of weeks being aspirated with a long needle through his back. He was frail but joked about how solemnly the American doctors had told him he had lung cancer and, desperate to see Madame, mooned over her to his visitors like an abandoned lover.

Earl Selle wrote asking Donald to send more material before a planned visit to China, but instead he got a letter asking him to stop writing the memoir. Donald said he didn't want to offend people or expose too much. May-ling had pressed him to get it stopped, having been told about it by Hollington Tong. Donald wrote to Reverend George Shepherd, explaining, 'I do not want my last breath to be criticism or condemnation, for who am I to condemn?'

The Chiangs were concerned about what Selle's book might reveal from Donald's remembrance that they didn't want in the public arena. In American eyes, Chiang's government had a serious problem with corruption and China's graft had long been a hobby-horse with their former adviser. Selle resisted Donald's request and was visited by an emissary from Madame Chiang, sent to prevail politely upon him to give up the book. Failing that, the emissary offered a large sum to submit the finished manuscript to her. Selle refused, saying he couldn't see anything to prompt her concern.

As 1946 dragged wearily on, Bill Donald read and wrote letters, the doctors hoping aspiration would dry out the water in his lung, but it didn't and he got weaker. When his sister, Florence, wrote from Australia proposing to visit him, he replied that China, with civil war, famine and skyrocketing prices, was no place for someone unfamiliar with it.

'You couldn't stay in my room because I'm not supposed to talk,' he wrote. 'It exhausts my lung power.'

On one occasion, the generalissimo visited Donald in hospital while he was in Shanghai, holding the dying man's hand and making a speech. It would be the last time he saw his former adviser.

By August, Donald couldn't use pen or typewriter and only wrote when someone took his dictation. He told Muriel he'd tried to calculate her age but couldn't as his brain didn't work for mathematics, the brain that had once provided economic advice to China's government. In October he wrote he'd sent $16 000 from the sale of his Peking house.

She was to keep $10 000 and deposit the balance in his account with the National City Bank of New York.

Early in November, Donald's condition deteriorated rapidly. Notified, Madame Chiang arrived by air from Nanking and went to her mentor's bedside with JL Huang, who had travelled with Donald to Si'an when the generalissimo was held there. Huang, the former colonel, was now a major-general. Donald conversed feebly and seemed to know the end was near. May-ling returned at eight that evening to read the Bible to him and he said he'd like to see Dean Trivett.

The dean at Shanghai's Trinity Cathedral, Trivett used to look in and chat with Donald while doing his rounds at the hospital, even though the Australian was not a believer. He had just returned to the deanery, some distance from the hospital, when the phone rang to say Donald was dying and wished to see him. Rushing back to the room, he found Madame Chiang at the bedside, reading Psalm 91 to the dying man.

Huang, standing by in military uniform, said, 'The dean is here.'

Madame jumped up, shook Trivett's hand and said, 'May I leave him to you now?'

Told Donald's pulse was stable, Madame and Huang left and Trivett talked to the patient who, utterly drained, was barely able to respond.

'You'd like to rest, wouldn't you?' asked Trivett.

He nodded weakly and the dean left him with his physician, Dr Cheng, watching discreetly from the side of the room. Donald's eyes closed and the doctor left the room. A nurse looked in from time to time during the night. Shortly after midnight he lost consciousness, his breathing became laboured and the weakened beat of his pulse grew feebler. Death came gently after 71 years of well-lived life.

•

A few days later, Dean ACS Trivett officiated at the funeral service for William Henry Donald, arrangements handled by JL Huang. The body lay in state at a funeral parlour before it was taken to the Soong family plot in the Chinese cemetery in Hunjao Road, just outside the city. Laid out in a blue-grey patterned jacket, white shirt and tie in a European-style coffin, Donald was covered with the flag of Nationalist China. Around him were placed Chinese and Australian flags, numerous floral wreaths, and a cross of yellow chrysanthemums from Madame Chiang's garden. The cross was inscribed, 'In memory of an old and valued friend—Generalissimo and Madame Chiang.'

Chiang was not at the funeral. Aside from the pallbearers—'Chappie' Chapman, Claire Chennault, JL Huang, Hank Sperry, James Cheng and Hal Timperley—the only other graveside mourners were Madame and her brother-in-law, HH Kung.

EPILOGUE

The adventures of WH Donald in China had fascinated the Western press between the wars and particularly the Australian press, but after the war interest was in creation of a new world order. By then, Donald was a grumpy old curmudgeon, dying. After the obituaries had run their course, he rapidly became a forgotten figure. Today, he is better known in China than Australia.

Selle completed his biography, relying extensively on what Donald had told him. He did little independent research beyond writing to his subject's friends, but before he died Donald had asked most of them to ignore Selle's requests. Published in 1948, *Donald of China* did not sell well.

Mary Donald wrote to Selle, after receiving legal advice that a claim of damages for unauthorised use of material would be unlikely to succeed, claiming her husband as its co-author.

'Selle's book was a travesty full of discrepancies,' she would write to Winston Lewis, 'and the foreword [noting the late discovery of the marriage] was an utter lie.' She'd received a 'vituperative' letter from Selle's wife saying he was blind and had used US$5000 of his own money on the book.

The executor of Donald's will was his friend, Martell Hall, who had been with the National City Bank of New York in Hankow. The estate was made up of houses in several Chinese cities (all destroyed by the Japanese except the already-sold Peking house), a case of silverware held in a Shanghai bank, shares of little value in rubber plantations, disparate bank accounts and a Sydney life insurance policy. It didn't amount to a great deal. All was bequeathed to his daughter, Muriel, except the life insurance payout of £220 which went to his brother, Herbert.

There were two payments of $10 000 to be made to Madame Chiang, still very wealthy although power was sliding out of her grasp in China's revived civil war. The first bequest had already been used to establish a scholarship in Donald's name, and the second cheque was sent with a letter from Hall advising her of Mary and Muriel Donald's grim financial state.

Hall had told Muriel she should have no qualms about him pursuing the money on her behalf. He wrote to her: 'In view of conditions in China, the almost certain misuse of any funds which you could remit to any charity there, and the vast wealth of the Soongs and Kungs, my own personal view would be that you should retain what little legacy your father left you without dissipating among some 400 million Chinese.' Martell Hall was an old China hand.

Hollington Tong wrote to Muriel with an offer from Madame to write the second cheque across to her. Accepting the offer, she wrote back that her mother had not asked for or got financial support from her husband since she left China and had been ill for some time without medical care.

Selle also wrote to Muriel, acknowledging his agreement with her father to give her a percentage of royalties from the book, but they were meagre and he was unemployed with no savings.

Muriel wasn't much better off herself. She and her mother eked out an unhappy shared existence in California, Mary Donald (no-one called her Polly any more) never divorcing and Muriel never marrying. Working in radio as a news editor, Muriel was the principal breadwinner, paying off their home from her salary, the trickle from her father's estate and the sale of the Peking house. Mary told her daughter she was more like her father than her mother, but what they did share was declining health. Muriel suffered from an ulcerated leg and both had drastic surgery in 1969, the mother for cancer, the daughter a thyroidectomy. Mary Donald died on 14 June 1972, aged 90; Muriel ten months later.

In the aftermath of the Pacific War, China was engulfed in the civil war between the Nationalists and the Communists, whose eradication had been prevented by the Si'an Incident. The Reds were eventually victorious and the generalissimo and his government retreated to Taipei in Taiwan as the alternative Republic of China to the Communists' People's Republic of China in Peking (now Beijing).

With the evacuation of the Nationalists from mainland China, Chang Hsueh-liang, the Young Marshal, was transferred to Taiwan where he remained under house arrest until 1990, the world's longest-serving political prisoner. His first wife and children were allowed to settle in the United States and Madame Chang released him from his vows, enabling him to marry his former concubine, Miss Chao, in 1964. Emigrating to Hawaii, the Young Marshal, the former opium addict, now Peter Chang, died in 2001, aged 100.

A curious incident took place at the Chiang Kai-shek house in Taipei in 1955, where the Australian journalist, Denis Warner, was at a private dinner with Sir Wilfred Kent-Hughes and his wife. The reactionary Kent-Hughes was a minister in Robert Menzies' conservative Australian government.

Warner had met Donald in Honolulu after the war. Aware of Donald's reputation and believing him to be close to the Chiangs, he raised Donald's name in conversation and was surprised to hear Madame Chiang dismiss him as 'a funny little man' who had worked for her husband in some minor capacity for a while. She didn't appear to Warner to be dissembling and it didn't seem a taboo subject. He concluded his understanding must have been wrong and Donald was in fact someone of no consequence to the Chiangs.

Clearly that is not true, so for whose ears was the disingenuous response made? There was no reason to mislead the journalist and Kent-Hughes was a politician of no importance, in fact regarded as something of a joke in his own country. That leaves only the generalissimo, driven in defeat to Taiwan, his dream of unchallenged leadership of post-war China in tatters. The Si'an Incident had prevented him from disposing of his Communist rivals when he was in a position to do so and Donald had been instrumental in that. That or the Australian's temerity in withdrawing from his patronage in 1940 must have been unforgiveable to the self-absorbed Chiang.

If Madame Chiang found it convenient to forget her friend and adviser, Muriel Donald's emotions worked in the reverse direction. Her few meetings with her father after the war had a profound and lingering impact on her. They may have had a similar effect on Donald whose sentimental letters to the Rathvons so long before had seemed at odds with a man prepared to sacrifice family for the importance of his mission.

Will Donald's male pride would never have let him express a longing for what he had personally lost through his own actions, if indeed that was what he felt, but his daughter had no such compunction. In her letter to Hollington Tong about her father's estate, she commented on the years she and her father put behind them in the short, precious time they had spent together in San Francisco.

'We found how very much alike we were,' she wrote, 'and in that bond of "likeness" in looks and actions we drew quite close. I like to believe anyway, that after that there was a warmth for me he had not felt before as there was a warmth for him that I felt.'

The man who had it all—adventure, fame, influence and the journalist's ability to not let the truth get in the way of a good story—perhaps missed out on the warm heart of a fulfilled family life. 'Tommyrot!' he would have said defensively.

AUTHOR'S NOTE

Biographies, as with history generally, rely heavily on eyewitness accounts of their subjects' activities throughout their life, including accounts by the subjects themselves. But what should the biographer do when these accounts contradict each other or are in dispute with other available information? And what should he do with those parts of his subject's story where no-one provides a first-hand account?

It may be counter-intuitive, but an eyewitness account might not be an accurate description of the event witnessed. Often it's written some time after the event and is not actually a memory of what happened but a reconstruction, drawing on what memory would be expected to recall if it were working better. It becomes a description of what should have happened rather than what did happen.

Wishful thinking enters into the picture as well. We all think of what we *should* have done in a situation if we'd been more on the ball, and often retell the story as if we had done that. Why would we imagine no-one else is prey to rewriting history to make themselves look cleverer?

People can have other reasons to massage events. They may have a particular political or ethical view which they want the event to reflect, or they may want themselves to appear less culpable, or they may turn a second- or third-hand account, with its potential inaccuracies, into a first-hand account to appear closer to a famous person.

The biographer has to weigh up conflicting or doubtful accounts and make a judgment about what actually happened. The story of William Henry Donald is sourced from a number of mostly unpublished recollections of varying reliability. The only published biography, to date, drew from interviews with Donald as an old man dying of lung cancer in an

Hawaiian hospital. Written by Earl Selle and released in 1948, it sold poorly. Donald was concerned his achievements would disappear into anonymity and exaggerated them. Selle appears to have made little effort to check the information he was given.

Two other accounts of WH Donald's life were never published. Corwin Chapman wrote down a dictated memoir while he and Donald were held in a Japanese internment camp in the Philippines during World War II. More reliable than Selle's book, it still has many of its failings and never progressed beyond transcription. James McHugh's draft biography drew on stories he was told in over a decade of friendship with the loquacious Australian, but it was written over twenty years after Donald's death and relies heavily in some parts on Selle's account.

Elsewhere, the details of Donald's life can be found in what little of his published writing and personal letters have survived, and in Winston Lewis's extensive correspondence from the 1960s and 1970s. Some of the letters are in archives of the people to whom Donald wrote, but what the Japanese didn't destroy of Donald's own collected papers was burnt after his death at his instruction.

When the biographer has made a judgment about which versions of each event in his subject's life he can rely on, he moves on to the next problem: gaps in the record of his subject's activities. What should he do with them?

The academic historian might have an obligation to stick to demonstrable facts—although I know some would debate this—and not wander into conjecture, so that where there is no evidence, gaps are left as gaps, no matter how relevant the missing detail should be. The biographer's obligation, however, is to engage his reader with the spirit of his subject's life, while keeping it as accurate as he can. Skating over fascinating episodes for lack of hard evidence doesn't serve the reader well. Instead of ignoring an incident, my preference is informed conjecture about the detail, consistent with what is known about its participants. I call it speculative non-fiction and it is probably more widespread than writers will generally acknowledge.

This book resorts to speculative non-fiction where detail of important events in Donald's life is limited. My speculation is as informed as

I can make it and I haven't deliberately altered the facts that are reliably 'known', just to enhance the story. I have tried to stay true to the spirit of his story, using the No-More-Gaps of speculation to fill the cracks and crumbling plaster in the wall of Donald's life. The Chapter Notes indicate where this approach has been used.

ACKNOWLEDGEMENTS

First, I'd like to thank my friend Jian Wu for drawing my attention to the possibility of Donald as a subject. We were having a bite to eat after I finished my first book and I said I was looking for a suitable subject for another book. He said, 'What about WH Donald?' I'd never heard of Donald, but Google surprised me with what it turned up. Now, Jian's suggestion is a reality.

Second, my heartfelt thanks to historian Winston Lewis for his relentless research on Donald, and to his widow, Dorothy. Winston dug up information and wrote to people over some twenty years or more, but unfortunately died before he was able to convert his research into a book. Dorothy gathered and filed her late husband's documents—all eleven boxes of them—and gave them to Sydney's Mitchell Library. It was a goldmine for me, including letters from countless people no longer alive by the time I started work on the book. Winston wanted to provide a more realistic account of Donald's life and career than the only previously existing, rather hagiographic one by Earl Selle. I hope my book fulfils at least some of the ambitions Winston had for his.

Many have provided assistance in one form or another in the realisation of this book. They include—and I hope I've got all of them here—Professors David Zhang Wei, Xing Jianrong and Gao Cunxiao in China; Jian Wu for translation and other advice; Zhizhen Qu, Tenei Nakahara, the Carl A Kroch Library (Cornell University) and Carol Leadenham and the Hoover Institution Archives (Stanford University) for material from US archives; the staff at Mitchell Library, Sydney; Peter Wall, James Wall and Janice Wood for tracking down details about Mary Donald and her family; Geoff Barnes and Denise Hunter for items from their home libraries; and the Sydney Record Centre for its shipping passenger manifests. I'm grateful to all these folk for their contributions, be they great or small, to getting this story into print.

What I write starts bumpily with wooden expression and slowly gets pared back to something that might be able to do justice to the extraordinary tale it tries to tell. My gratitude goes to my wife, Jan Stretton, as the first filter of the drafted manuscript, drawing my attention to clumsy or ambiguous expression and suggesting changes that might bring the story even more to life. Richard Walsh did a critique of the first six chapters to ensure the narrative was building the right momentum. After those word police, the copy editor, Susin Chow, went through the delivered manuscript with the professional scrutiny I would expect. These people have produced a far more readable work than the one I wrote.

Finally my thanks to Allen & Unwin who have taken a third punt on me as an author and especially to Richard Walsh and Rebecca Kaiser for their confidence in the project and feedback and constructive suggestions on the result, and to Ann Lennox for shepherding (if that's the word) the manuscript through to the bookshop. The result is what you, the reader, have in your hand.

BIBLIOGRAPHY

Books

Abend, Hallett—*My Life in China 1926–1941* (1943) Harcourt Brace, New York

Armamento, Vidal Brigoli—*The Indomitable* (1972) Viking, Pasay City, Philippines

Bergère, Marie-Claire—*Sun Yat-sen* (1998) (transl. Janet Lloyd) Stanford University Press, Stanford CA

Berkov, Robert—*Strong Man of China: The Story of Chiang Kai-shek* (1938) Houghton Miflin, Boston

Bertram, James M—*Crisis in China: the Story of the Sian Mutiny* (1937) Macmillan, London

Bickers, Robert—*The Scramble for China: Foreign Devils in the Qing Empire, 1832–1914* (2011) Allen Lane, London

Booker, Edna Lee—*News is my Job: A Correspondent in War-torn China* (1940) Edna Lee Booker, Shanghai

Boorman, Howard L (ed.)—*Biographical Dictionary of Republican China* (1967) Columbia University Press, New York

Burgess, Pat—*Warco: Australian Reporters at War* (1986) William Heinemann Australia, Melbourne

Cameron, Nigel—*Hong Kong: The Cultured Pearl* (1978) Oxford University Press, Hong Kong

——*An Illustrated History of Hong Kong* (1991) Oxford University Press, Hong Kong

Chennault, Claire Lee—*Way of a Fighter: the Memoirs of Claire Lee Chennault* (1949) (ed. Robert Hotz) GP Putnam's Sons, New York

Chiang Kai-shek—*A Fortnight in Sian: Extracts from a Diary* (1937) China Publishing Company, Shanghai

Chiang, May-ling Soong (Madame Chiang Kai-shek)—*Sian: A Coup D'Etat* (1937) China Publishing Company, Shanghai

Ciano, Edda Mussolini (as told to Albert Zarça)—*My Truth* (1976) (transl. Eileen Finletter) Weidenfeld & Nicholson, London

Clune, Frank—*Sky High to Shanghai* (1947) Angus & Robertson, Sydney

Connaughton, Richard—*The War of the Rising Sun and Tumbling Bear* (1991) Routledge, London

Cooke, Colin—*The Life of Richard Stafford Cripps* (1957) Hodder & Stoughton, London

Courtauld, Caroline & May Holdsworth—*The Hong Kong Story* (1997) (with additional text by Simon Vickers) Oxford University Press, Hong Kong

Crow, Carl—*China Takes Her Place* (1944) Harper & Brothers, New York

Crozier, Brian—*The Man Who Lost China* (1976) Angus & Robertson, London

Denby, Jay—*Letters from China and some Eastern Sketches* (1911) Murray and Evenden, London

Dikötter, Frank, Lars Laamann and Zhou Xun—*Narcotic Culture: A History of Drugs in China* (2004) University of Chicago Press, Chicago

Dong, Stella—*Shanghai: The Rise and Fall of a Decadent City* (2001) Perennial, New York

Elder, Chris (ed.)—*Old Peking: City of the Ruler of the World* (1997) Oxford University Press, Hong Kong

Elleman, Bruce A—*Modern Chinese Warfare, 1795–1989* (2001) Routledge, London

——*Wilson and China: A Revised History of the Shandong Question* (2002) ME Sharp, New York

Esherick, Joseph W—'Founding a Republic, Electing a President: How Sun Yat-sen Became *Guofu*' in *China's Republican Revolution* (eds Eto Shinkichi and Harold Z Schiffrin) (1994) University of Tokyo Press, Tokyo

Estorick, Eric—*Stafford Cripps: A Biography* (1949) William Heinemann, London

Farmer, Rhodes—*Shanghai Harvest* (1945) Museum Press, London

Faure, David (ed.)—*Society: A Documentary History of Hong Kong* (1997) Hong Kong University Press, Hong Kong

Fenby, Jonathan—*Generalissimo: Chiang Kai-shek and the China He Lost* (2004) Free Press, London

——*The Penguin History of Modern China: The Fall and Rise of a Great Power, 1850–2008* (2008) Allen Lane, London

French, Paul—*A Tough Old China Hand: The Life, Times, and Adventures of an American in Shanghai* (2006) Hong Kong University Press, Hong Kong

——*Through the Looking Glass: China's Foreign Journalists from Opium Wars to Mao* (2009) Hong Kong University Press, Hong Kong

Geil, William Edgar—*Eighteen Capitals of China* (1911) JB Lippincott, Philadelphia

Gould, Randall—*China in the Sun* (1946) Doubleday, Garden City NY

Gunther, John—*Inside Asia* (1939) Hamish Hamilton, London

Guo Cunxiao—*Fragments of History (Li Shi De Sui Pian)* (2004) Baihua Literature & Art Publishing House, Tianjin PRC

Hahn, Emily—*China to Me* (1944) Doubleday Doran, Garden City NY

——*Chiang Kai-shek: An Unauthorized Biography* (1955) Doubleday, Garden City NY

——*The Soong Sisters* (1942) Hale, London

Haverstock, Nathan A—*Fifty Years at the Front: The Life of War Correspondent Frederick Palmer* (1996) Brassey's, Washington

Hsu, Immanuel CY—*The Rise of Modern China* (1990) Oxford University Press, New York

Jin Chongli—'Two Issues Concerning the Wuchang Uprising' in *China's Republican Revolution* (eds Eto Shinkichi and Harold Z Schiffrin) (1994) University of Tokyo Press, Tokyo

Jordan, Donald A—*China's Trial by Fire: The Shanghai War of 1932* (2001) University of Michigan Press, Ann Arbor MI

Jowett, Philip and Stephen Andrew—*Chinese Civil War Armies 1911–49* (1997) Osprey Publishing, Oxford

Kasanin, Marc—*China in the Twenties* (1973) (transl. Hilda Kasanina) Central Department of Oriental Literature, Moscow

Kawamura Noriko—*Turbulence in the Pacific: Japanese–U.S. Relations During World War I* (2000) Praeger Publishers, Westport CT

Kershaw, Alex—*Jack London: A Life* (1997) Harper Collins, London

Kimura, Yukiko—*Issei: Japanese Immigrants in Hawaii* (1988) University of Hawaii Press, Honolulu

King, Paul—*In the Chinese Customs Service: A Personal Record of Forty-Seven Years* (1924) T Fisher Unwin, London

Leonard, Captain Royal—*I Flew for China* (1942) Doubleday Doran, Garden City NY

Li, Lillian M, Alison J Dray-Novey and Haili Kong—*Beijing: From Imperial Capital to Olympic City* (2007) Palgrave Macmillan, New York

Lo Hui-min (ed.)—*The Correspondence of G.E. Morrison,* II. 1912-1920 (1978) Cambridge University Press, Cambridge UK

Lubow, Arthur—*The Reporter Who Would Be King* (1992) Charles Scribner's Sons, New York

Lucas, Celia—*Prisoners of Santo Tomas* (1975) Leo Cooper, London

Martin, Brian G—*The Shanghai Green Gang: Politics and Organized Crime, 1919–1937* (1996) University of California Press, Berkeley CA

McCormick, Frederick—*The Flowery Republic* (1913) John Murray, London

Mellor, Bernard—*Lugard in Hong Kong: Empires, Education and a Governor at Work, 1907–1912* (1992) Hong Kong University Press, Hong Kong

Mitter, Rana—*The Manchurian Myth: Nationalism, Resistance and Collaboration in Modern China* (2000) University of California Press, Berkeley CA

Moore, Raymond S—*China Doctor: The Life Story of Harry Willis Miller* (1969) Pacific Press, Mountain View CA

Nathan, Andrew J—*Peking Politics 1918–1923: Factionalism and the Failure of Constitutionalism* (1976) University of California Press, Berkeley CA

Nozinski, Michael J—*Outrage at Lincheng: China Enters the Twentieth Century* (1990) Glenbridge, Macomb IL

Pakula, Hannah—*The Last Empress: Madame Chiang Kai-shek and the Birth of Modern China* (2010) Phoenix, London

Palmer, Frederick—*With Kuroki in Manchuria* (1904) Charles Scribner's Sons, New York

Pao Ming-ch'ien—*The Foreign Relations of China: A History and a Survey* (1922) Nisbet, London

Patrikeeff, Felix—*Russian Politics in Exile: The Northeast Asian Balance of Power, 1924–1931* (2002) Palgrave Macmillan, London

Pearl, Cyril—*Morrison of Peking* (1967) Angus & Robertson, Sydney

Pleshakov, Constantine—*The Tsar's Last Armada: The Epic Journey to the Battle of Tsushima* (2002) Basic Books, New York

Pomerantz-Zhang, Linda—*Wu Tingfang (1842–1922): Reform and Modernization in Modern Chinese History* (1992) Hong Kong University Press, Hong Kong

Pott, FL Hawks—*A Short History of Shanghai* (1928) Kelly & Walsh, Shanghai, www.earnshaw.com/shanghai-ed-india/tales/library/pott

Powell, John B—*My Twenty-five Years in China* (1945) Macmillan, New York

Rea, George Bronson—*The Breakdown of American Diplomacy in the Far East* (1919) self-published, New York

Reinsch, Paul S—*An American Diplomat in China* (1922) Doubleday Page, Garden City NY

Rhoads, Edward JM—*China's Republican Revolution: The Case of Kwangtung, 1895–1913* (1975) Harvard University Press, Cambridge MA

Roberts, JAG—*Modern China: An Illustrated History* (1998) Sutton, Stroud, Gloucestershire

Roth, Mitchel P—*Historical Dictionary of War Journalism* (1997) Greenwood Press, Westport CT

Schiffrin, Harold Z—*Sun Yat-sen: Reluctant Revolutionary* (1980) Little Brown & Co, Boston

Seagrave, Sterling—*The Soong Dynasty* (1985) Sidgwick & Jackson, London

Selle, Earl Albert—*Donald of China* (1948) Invincible Press, Sydney

Semenoff, Commander Vladimir—*Rasplata (The Reckoning)* (1909) (transl. LAB—Prince Louis Alexander of Battenberg) John Murray, London

Shai, Aron—*Zhang Xueliang: The General Who Never Fought* (2012) Palgrave Macmillan, London

Shavit, David—*The United States in Asia: A Historical Dictionary* (1990) Greenwood Press, Westport CT

Snow, Edgar—*Far Eastern Front* (1933) Harrison Smith & Robert Hass, New York

Spence, Jonathan D—*The Search for Modern China* (1990) WW Norton & Co, New York

Strand, David—*Rickshaw Beijing: City People and Politics in the 1920s* (1989) University of California Press, Berkeley CA

Sues, Ilona Ralf—*Shark's Fins and Millet* (1944) Little, Brown & Co, Boston

Taylor, Jay—*The Generalissimo: Chiang Kai-shek and the Struggle for Modern China* (2009) Belknap Press, Cambridge MA

Thompson, Peter—*Shanghai Fury: Australian Heroes of Revolutionary China* (2011) William Heinemann, Sydney

——and Robert Macklin—*The Man Who Died Twice: The Life and Adventures of Morrison of Peking* (2004) Allen & Unwin, Sydney

Thomson, John Stuart—*China Revolutionized* (1913) Bobbs-Merrill, Indianapolis

Tikowara Hesibo—*Before Port Arthur in a Destroyer: The Personal Diary of a Japanese Naval Officer* (1907) (transl. Capt Robert Grant) EP Dutton & Co, New York

Tipping, EW—'Australians in the Near North' in *Near North: Australia and a Thousand Million Neighbours* (eds, Robert J Gilmore and Denis Warner) (1948) Angus & Robertson, Sydney

Tong, Hollington K—*Dateline: China* (1950) Rockport Press, New York

Wakeman, Frederic Jr—*Policing Shanghai, 1927–1937* (1995) University of California Press, Berkeley CA

Warner, Denis and Peggy Warner—*The Tide at Sunrise: A History of the Russo-Japanese War, 1904–1905* (1974) Charterhouse, New York

Waters, Thorold—*Much Besides Music* (1951) Georgian House, Melbourne

Watson, W Petrie—*The Future of Japan* (1907) EP Dutton, New York

Weale, BL Putnam—*The Fight for the Republic in China* (1917) Dodd Mead & Co, New York

Welsh, Frank—*A Borrowed Place: The History of Hong Kong* (1993) Kodansha International, New York

Westwood, JN—*The Illustrated History of the Russo–Japanese War* (1973) Sidgwick & Jackson, London

White, Barbara-Sue (ed.)—*Hong Kong: Somewhere Between Heaven and Earth* (1996) Oxford University Press, Hong Kong

Wiltshire, Trea—*Old Hong Kong* (1997) FormAsia, Hong Kong

Wood, Frances—*No Dogs and Not Many Chinese: Treaty Port Life in China, 1843–1943* (1998) John Murray, London

Woodhead, HGW—*A Journalist in China* (1934) Hurst & Blackett, London

Wright, Arnold (ed.)—*Twentieth Century Impressions of Hong Kong, Shanghai, and Other Treaty Ports of China: Their History, People, Commerce, Industries and Resources* (1908) Lloyd's Greater Britain Publishing, London

Zhang Kaiyuan—'The 1911 Revolution and "Seize the Hour, Seize the Day"' (transl. Li Yadan) in *China's Republican Revolution* (eds Eto Shinkichi and Harold Z Schiffrin) (1994) University of Tokyo Press, Tokyo

Papers, articles, letters, websites, diaries.

American Society of International Law—'International law involved in the seizure of the *Tatsu Maru*'—*The American Journal of International Law*, 2, 2, April 1908, pp. 391–7

Barrett, David—letter to Winston Lewis, 24 July 1969 (Lewis, Box 1)

Bertram, James—'"Chinese Donald": Salute to an Honest Man', *NZ Listener*, December 1946

Bickers, Robert A and Jeffrey N Wasserstrom—'Shanghai's "Dogs and Chinese Not Admitted" Sign: Legend, History and Contemporary Symbol' (1995) *The China Quarterly* 142, pp. 444–66

Blanton, Sybil—'Guide to the papers of George Ernest Morrison' (1977) The Library Council of New South Wales, Sydney

——and JB Capper (eds)—Papers of George Ernest Morrison (Correspondence 1850–1923), Mitchell Library, Sydney MLMSS 312

Bond, WL—letter to Winston Lewis, 3 September 1969 (Lewis, Box 1)

——letter to Winston Lewis, 2 July 1971 (Lewis, Box 1)

Branson, Roy—'Harry Miller: Adventist Hero of Social Reform' (2000) *Adventist Review*, 10 February 2000, pp 13-20, www.adventistreview.org/2000-06/story2.htm

Bren, Frank—'Don' (2001) www.donaldofchina.com

Brown, Joe A—'Manchurian Notes', US Department of State, 16 May 1932 (Lewis, Box 5)

Butler, Rev. Rowland—letter to Winston Lewis, 27 February 1969 (Lewis, Box 1)

Butt, Rudi—'Newsies in the Nineteenth Century' (2010) in *Hong Kong's First*, www.hongkongfirst.blogspot.com

Carey, WF—letter to Dr Paul Reinsch, 25 March 1920 (Lewis, Box 4)

Chan, Pearl—letter to James McHugh, 8 July 1939 (Lewis, Box 4)

Chao, Thomas Ming-heng—*The Foreign Press in China* (1931) China Institute of Pacific Relations, Shanghai

Chapman, Corwin C—'Chang Hsueh-liang' (1945) memoirs dictated by WH Donald at Los Banos Internment Camp, Philippines, unpublished (Lewis, Box 9)

——'The Revolution in China' (1945) memoirs dictated by WH Donald at Los Banos Internment Camp, Philippines, unpublished (Lewis, Box 9)

——logs kept of internment camps at Santo Tomas and Los Baños, January 1943 to April 1945 (Lewis, Box 9)

——letter to Winston Lewis, 24 April 1970 (Lewis, Box 2)

Chiu Ming-wah—'Resistance, peace and war: the *Central China Daily News*, the *South China Daily News* and the Wang Jingwei Clique during the Sino-Japanese War, 1937–1945' (2005) PhD thesis, University of Hong Kong

Clark Kerr, Sir Archibald—memo to Foreign Office (GB), Chungking, 13 May 1940 (Lewis, Box 8)

——memo to Foreign Office (GB), Chungking, 6 November 1940 (Lewis, Box 8)

——telegram to Foreign Office (GB), Chungking, 13 February 1941 (Lewis, Box 8)

Cranford, Lieutenant Thomas Jr—letter to US Department of State, Tokyo, 13 July 1932 (Lewis, Box 5)

CNN International—'Arsenic killed Chinese emperor, reports say', 4 November 2008, www.edition.cnn.com/2008/WORLD/asiapcf/11/04/china.emperor

Cripps, Sir Stafford—'Report on the position in China', HM Government Foreign Office, 29 April 1940 (Lewis, Box 8)

Cunningham, Edwin—letter to Charles Tenney, 16 March 1920 (Lewis, Box 5)

Donald, Mary—letter to Noel Croucher, undated 1967 (Lewis, Box 2)

——letter to Winston Lewis, 9 March 1971 (Lewis, Box 2)

Donald, Muriel—letter to Silas Strawn, 20 September 1940 (Lewis, Box 5)

——letter to Hollington Tong, 27 July 1948 (Lewis, Box 11)

Donald, WH—'Still at anchor: now sheltering in Honcohe Bay', *China Mail*, 10 May 1905

——'At anchor in Vanfong Bay', *China Mail*, 16 May 1905

——'The neutrality of Indo-China: how the Russian fleet is assisted', *China Mail*, 17 May 1905

——letter to Dr GE Morrison, Shanghai, 4 July 1912 (Blanton and Capper, Vol. 66, No. 25-33)

——letter to Dr GE Morrison, Shanghai, 4 August 1912 (Blanton and Capper, Vol. 66, No. 329-339)

——letter to Dr GE Morrison, Shanghai, 30 November 1912 (Blanton and Capper, Vol. 71, No. 119-121)

——letter to Mrs Morrison, 1 June 1913 (Blanton and Capper, Vol. 109, No. 319-322)

——letter to Dr Paul Reinsch, Peking, 12 March 1914 (Lewis, Box 4)

——letter to Mrs Morrison, Shanghai, 23 June 1915 (Blanton and Capper, Vol. 84, No. 551-552)

——letter to Dr GE Morrison, Yokohama, 5 May 1918 (Blanton and Capper, Vol. 99, No. 241-243)

——letter to Dr Paul Reinsch, Peitaiho, 16 July 1918 (Lewis, Box 4)

——letter to Mrs Morrison, Peking, 10 October 1920 (Blanton and Capper, Vol. 114, No. 11-13)

——letter to Mrs Morrison, Peking, 26 October 1920 (Blanton and Capper, Vol. 114, No. 57-59)

——'Letters 1923-1945 from William H Donald' in 'Nathanial Peter Rathvon letters received, 1923–1947.' Hoover Institute Archives, Stanford University, Stanford CA

——letter to Stanley K Hornbeck, Peking, 18 February 1932 (Lewis, Box 5)
——letter to Florence Orr, Peking, 7 July 1932 (Lewis, Box 5)
——letter to Berkeley Gage, Hankow, 14 March 1938 (Lewis, Box 8)
——letter to Berkeley Gage, Hankow, 23 March 1938 (Lewis, Box 8)
——letter to James McHugh, Hankow, 19 April 1938 (Lewis, Box 4)
——letter to Kenneth Cantlie, Wuchang, 3 May 1938 (Lewis, Box 5)
——letter to Harold Timperley, Chungking, 30 December 1938 (Lewis, Box 8)
——letter to James McHugh, 25 May 1939 (Lewis, Box 4)
——letter to Kenneth Cantlie, Wuchang, 2 July 1938 (Lewis, Box 8)
——will, 2 August 1938 (Lewis, Box 11)
——letter to Berkeley Gage, Chungking, 15 January 1939 (Lewis, Box 8)
——letter to Stanley K Hornbeck, Chungking, 21 January 1939 (Lewis, Box 5)
——letter to Stanley K Hornbeck, Chungking, 23 January 1939 (Lewis, Box 5)
——'From Chiang's Headquarters', *Asia*, April 1939
——letter to James McHugh, Hong Kong, 9 September 1939 (Lewis, Box 4)
——letter to Sir Archibald Clark Kerr, Hong Kong, 4 October 1939 (Lewis, Box 8)
——letter DK (Liu Da-jun), Chungking, 1 May 1940 (Lewis, Box 2)
——letter to Berkeley Gage, Solomon Islands, 30 October 1940 (Lewis, Box 8)
——letter to Muriel Donald, Manila, 4 March 1945 (Lewis, Box 11)
——letter to Florence Orr, Manila, 12 March 1945 (Lewis, Box 5)
——letter to Corwin Chapman, Berkeley, 25 May 1945 (Lewis, Box 9)
——letter to Muriel Donald, Berkeley, 18 June 1945 (Lewis, Box 11)
——letter to Muriel Donald, Berkeley, 19 June 1945 (Lewis, Box 11)
——letter to Corwin Chapman, San Francisco, 20 June 1945 (Lewis, Box 9)
——letter to Muriel Donald, Berkeley, 20 June 1945 (Lewis, Box 11)
——letter to Corwin Chapman, New York, 23 August 1945 (Lewis, Box 9)
——letter to Muriel Donald, New York, 15 September 1945 (Lewis, Box 11)
——letter to Muriel Donald, Berkeley, 16 October 1945 (Lewis, Box 11)
——letter to Corwin Chapman, Berkeley, 21 October 1945 (Lewis, Box 9)
——letter to Florence Orr, Papeete, 1 November 1945 (Lewis, Box 5)
——letter to Corwin Chapman, Papeete, 7 December 1945 (Lewis, Box 9)
——letter to Corwin Chapman, Honolulu, 10 March 1946 (Lewis, Box 9)
——letter to Martell Hall, Shanghai, 1 April 1946 (Lewis, Box 11)
——letter to Rev. George Shepherd, Shanghai, 18 April 1946 (Lewis, Box 4)
——letter to Florence Orr, Shanghai, 15 May 1946 (Lewis, Box 5)
——letter to Corwin Chapman, Shanghai, 2 July 1946 (Lewis, Box 9)

——letter to Muriel Donald, Shanghai, 12 August 1946 (Lewis, Box 11)

——letter to Florence Orr, Shanghai, 27 September 1946 (Lewis, Box 5)

——letter to Muriel Donald, Shanghai, 12 October 1946 (Lewis, Box 11)

Duffy, Michael—'Primary Documents: 21 Demands' Made by Japan to China, 18 January 1915' in *firstworldwar.com* (2009) www.firstworldwar.com/source/21demands.htm

Dunn, Richard L—'Uncertain Wings: Curtiss Hawk 75 in China' (2008) in *The Warbird's Forum: Annals of the Chinese Air Force* (ed. Daniel Ford) www.warbirdforum.com/uncert.html

Earnshaw, Graham—*Tales of Old Shanghai* (2001) www.earnshaw.com/shanghai-ed-india/tales/tales.htm

Elliston, HB—'China's No. 1 White Boy', *The Saturday Evening Post*, 19 March 1938

Etheridge, Clayton B—letter to Winston Lewis, 12 March 1970 (Lewis, Box 1)

Ferlanti, Federica—'The New Life Movement in Jiangxi Province, 1934–1938', *Modern Asian Studies* 44,5 (2010), pp. 961–1000

Ferrell, Robert H—'The Mukden Incident: September 18–19, 1931', *Journal of Modern History*, 27, 1 (March 1955), pp. 66–72

Fleischer, BW—letter to Dr Paul Reinsch, New York, 3 April 1918 (Lewis, Box 4)

Foster, Queene Hooper—'James Gordon Bennett, Jr' (1998) Heritage Series Lecture, www.nyyc.org/gui/nyyc1/uploadfiles/Model.pdf/JGB.pdf

Fraser, David—letter to Dudley Braham, 27 January 1914 (Lewis, Box 3)

——cable to *The Times*, Peking, 11 March 1915 (Lewis, Box 3)

——letter to Wickham Steed, 6 April 1915 (Lewis, Box 3)

——letter to Harold Williams, 6 February 1924 (Lewis, Box 3)

——letter to Dawson, Harbin, 26 May 1932 (Lewis, Box 2)

Fukushima Teruhiko—translation of miscellaneous Japanese intelligence reports: 'Research Material 1979' (Lewis, Box 3)

Gauss, CE—letter to Nelson Johnson, Shanghai, 11 January 1937 (Lewis, Box 5)

——letter to Nelson Johnson, Shanghai, 1 February 1937 (Lewis, Box 5)

——letter to Nelson Johnson, Shanghai, 1 May 1937 (Lewis, Box 5)

Gilbert, Alvin—letter to WJ Calhoun, Nanking, 1 December 1911 (Lewis, Box 9)

——letter to WJ Calhoun, Nanking, 2 December 1911 (Lewis, Box 9)

Gilbert, Rodney—'Semi-Foreign', *The Living Age*, 10 February 1923, pp. 351–2.

Goodman, Bryna—'Semi-Colonialism, Transnational Networks and News Flows in Early Republican Shanghai', *The China Review* 4, 1 (2004)

Gould, Randall—letter to Winston Lewis, 9 January 1976 (Lewis, Box 1)

Gracey, William—letter to ET Williams, Nanking, 28 October 1911 (Lewis, Box 9)

——letter to ET Williams, Nanking, 16 November 1911 (Lewis, Box 9)

——letter to WJ Calhoun, 28 November 1911 (Lewis, Box 9)

——letter to WJ Calhoun, 30 November 1911 (Lewis, Box 9)

——letter to WJ Calhoun, 5 December 1911 (Lewis, Box 9)

Greene, Sir Conyngham—telegram to British Foreign Office, Tokyo, 24 October 1917, with attached handwritten notes (Lewis, Box 8)

Guo Cunxiao—'New version of Donald's story: The man who laid the foundation for the friendly relationship between China and Australia (Duan na zhuan xin pian: zhong ao you hao guan xi de dian ji ren)', *Singtao Daily*, July 2002

——'1938, Letter from Donald to Timperley about Japanese war crimes in China (1938, Duan na zhi han tian bo lie tong chi ri ben qin hua zui xing)' in *The Years of Memorable Friendship Between China and Australia* (2010) China International Culture Press

Gwulo— Old Hong Kong, www.gwulo.com

Hall, Martell—letter to Muriel Donald, Bombay, 29 November 1947 (Lewis, Box 11)

——letter to Muriel Donald, Bombay, 7 July 1948 (Lewis, Box 11)

——letter to Muriel Donald, Bombay, 16 April 1949 (Lewis, Box 11)

Hall-Patch, EL—'Political situation arising out of the Sian Incident', note on conversation with Donald, Shanghai, 12 January 1937 (Lewis, Box 8)

Heichert, MB—'Record of Events of January 7, 1945 Affecting Los Banõs Internment Camp' (Lewis, Box 3)

——and George Grey—'Summary of the Events Leading to the Rescue of the Los Banõs Internment Camp on February 25, 1945' (Lewis, Box 3)

Hickman, Kennedy—'Russo-Japanese War: Battle of Tsushima' (2011) in *About.com—Military History*, www.militaryhistory.about.com/od/naval battles1900 today/p/tsushima.htm

Ho Tung, Sir Robert—'The Chinese in Hong Kong' in *Present Day Impressions of the Far East and Prominent and Progressive Chinese at Home and Abroad* (ed. W Feldwick) (1917) Globe Encyclopedia, London

Hochschild, Harold—letter to Winston Lewis, 18 August 1969 (Lewis, Box 2)

——letter to Winston Lewis, 17 July 1975 (Lewis, Box 2)

Howe, RG—letter to Sir Hughe Knatchbull-Hugessen, British Consulate in Nanking, 28 December 1936 (Lewis, Box 8)

——memo, Shanghai, 7 November 1936 (Lewis, Box 8)

Hoyt, Frederick B—'Apologist for Japan: the case of George Bronson Rea' (1975) 1975 Convention of the Organisation of American Historians, Boston MA, 18 April 1975

Hui, Samuel—'Fly Boys of the Generalissimo' (2008) in *The Warbird's Forum: Annals of the Chinese Air Force* (ed. Daniel Ford) www.warbirdforum.com/cafhist.htm

Johnson, Nelson T—memo of conversation with WH Donald, 9 April 1931 (Lewis, Box 4)

——letter to 'colleagues', 19 March 1936 (Lewis, Box 5)

——memo to US Secretary of State, 12 January 1937 (Lewis, Box 5)

——memo of conversation with Royal Leonard, 15 Januray 1937 (Lewis, Box 5)

——'Chiang Kai-shek's serious condition and its possible consequences', report to US Secretary of State, Nanking, 11 May 1937 (Lewis, Box 5)

Knatchbull-Hugessen, Sir Hughe—letter to Anthony Eden, British Embassy in China, 2 March 1937 (Lewis, Box 8)

Laamann, Lars—'drugs and drug consumption' in *Encyclopoedia of Contemporary Chinese Culture* (ed. Edward L Davis) (2005) Routledge, Oxford

Lamont, Thomas W—'The Chinese Consortium and American trade relations with China and the Far East' (1921) *Annals of the American Academy of Political and Social Science*, 94, pp. 87–93

Leser, Jeff (ed.)—'The Russo-Japanese War Research Society' (2002), www.russojapanesewar.com

Lewis, Winston—notes from interview with Robert Tierney, 1 December 1974 (Lewis, Box 4)

——letter to Mrs Maxine Leonard, 23 May 1975 (Lewis, Box 1)

——letter to Carl Mydans, 10 November 1977 (Lewis, Box 1)

——'The Quest for William Henry Donald (1875–1946) That Other Australian in China' (1988) *Review* (Asian Studies Association of Australia) 12, 1, July 1988, pp. 23–9

Lewis, Winston (ed.)—Papers, 1887-1996, re WH Donald with papers of the Donald family, ca 1872–1978. Mitchell Library, Sydney MLMSS 7594 (11 boxes)

Lewisohn, W—letter to Winston Lewis, 12 February 1970 (Lewis, Box 1)

MacMurray, JVA—letter to his mother, Peking, 8 February 1914 (Lewis, Box 4)

——letter to his mother, Peking, 4 March 1915 (Lewis, Box 4)

——letter to President Wilson, Peking, 5 April 1915 (Lewis, Box 4)

Magruder, Major John—'Developments in Connection With the C.E.R.' Report no. 7577, US Legation, Peking, 26 August 1929 (Lewis, Box 5)

——'Developments in Connection With the C.E.R.' Report no. 7586, US Legation, Peking, 6 September 1929 (Lewis, Box 5)

——'Probable Developments in the Sino-Russian Dispute.' Report no. 7613a, US Legation, Peking, 4 November 1929 (Lewis, Box 5)

Manning, JL—'Report of Approximate Conditions of Los Banõs Internment Camp #2', 13 December 1944 (Lewis, Box 3)

Margetts, Lieutenant-Colonel NE—memo of conversation with WH Donald, 10 and 11 December 1930 (Lewis, Box 4)

Mattingly, Major Robert E—'A Pungent Collection . . .' in *Herringbone Cloak—GI Dagger: Marines of the OSS* (1979) Marine Corps Command and Staff College, Woodridge VA, www.ibiblio.org/hyperwar/USMC/USMC-OSS/USMC-OSS-4

Mayer, Fred—letter to JVA MacMurray, Peking, 10 July 1924 (Lewis, Box 4)

McHugh, James—*The Unknown Era*, rough draft of unpublished manuscript (Lewis, Box 3)

——'Diary fragments, 1938, Jan.' in 'James M McHugh papers, 1930–1965' (Box 11, folder 13) Division of Rare and Manuscript Collections, Cornell University, Ithaca NY

——'Present political situation in China', 20 January 1938 (Lewis, Box 3)

——letter to Commander HE Overesch, 16 February 1938 (Lewis, Box 3)

——'Memorandum of conversation with Mr TV Soong', US Embassy, Hankow, 26 February 1938 (Lewis, Box 3)

——memo to Nelson Johnson, Kunming, 28 August 1938 (Lewis, Box 4)

——memo to Nelson Johnson, Kunming, 29 August 1938 (Lewis, Box 4)

——notes re Harold Timperley, US Embassy, Chungking, 8 March 1939 (Lewis, Box 3)

——memo to Nelson Johnson, 23 May 1940 (Lewis, Box 5)

Millard, Thomas F—*The ABC's of the Twenty-One Demands* (1921) Chinese Students' Committee on Washington Conference, New York

Mitter, Rana—'The Last Warlord', *History Today* 54, 2 (February 2004)

Moat, Charles—letter to Winston Lewis, 21 February 1970 (Lewis, Box 1)

——letter to Winston Lewis, 7 April 1970 (Lewis, Box 1)

Morrison, Dr GE—letter to Wickham Steed, 17 February 1915 (Lewis, Box 3)

——letter to WH Donald, 26 November 1917 (Blanton and Capper, Vol. 96, No. 101–107)

Nassau, Benjamin—letter to Martell Hall, 30 June 1948 (Lewis, Box 11)

——letter to Muriel Donald, 3 February 1949 (Lewis, Box 11)

New York Times—'Wireless workers back from the scene of war', *NY Times*, 31 August 1904.

North-China Daily News—'The Twenty-one Demands: how details of an historic document were divulged to the world', *North China Daily News*, 1 September 1932

——'Funeral of the late Mr W.H. Donald', *North China Daily News*, 11 November 1946

North China Herald—'Inside story of Sian coup disclosed: Generalissimo's dramatic fortnight in captivity', *North China Herald*, 30 December 1936, p. 528

——'Vivid account of mutiny: picked troops under "Young Marshal" participate', *North China Herald*, 30 December 1936, p. 528

——'Nanking clique's selfish motives: used Sian coup to grip power', *North China Herald*, 13 February 1937, p. 46

Nunneley, Mrs Vivian—letter to Noel Croucher, Paradise City CA, 10 May 1975 (Lewis, Box 2)

Peck, Willys—'Foreign military advisers and the Sino-German barter agreement', report to US Secretary of State, Nanking, 28 May 1937 (Lewis, Box 5)

——telegram to US Secretary of State, Nanking, 12 July 1937 (Lewis, Box 5)

Perkins, Arthur—diary of Santo Tomas Internment Camp (Lewis, Box 3)

Perkins, E Ralph (supervising ed.)—'Foreign Relations of the United States: Diplomatic Papers, 1945. Vol VII. The Far East, China.' (1969) United States Government Printing Office, Washington DC

Powell, Halsey—report to US Minister in China, Harbin, 27 July 1929 (Lewis, Box 4)

Pratt, Lionel—letter to BW Fleischer, 5 February 1918 (Lewis, Box 4)

Qi Ya Zhong—'Tatsu Maru II' (1908) Qi Ya Zhong Publishing, Hong Kong, www.multiculturalcanada.ca/node/405167

Radetzky, Ross (ed.)—'The Tragic Battle of Chemulpo, February 9, 1904' in *The Japan-Russia War*, www.cityofart.net/bship/ru_chemulpo

Rea, George Bronson—'Memorandum concerning the organisation of an international construction corporation for the financing, construction and equipment of railways in the Republic of China', 26 May 1914 (Lewis, Box 4)

——letter to WH Donald, Washington DC, 21 October 1917 (Lewis, Box 5)

——letter to Brigadier-General Nolan, 1 February 1921 (Lewis, Box 5)

Reinsch, Paul—Report #538, 10 February 1915 (Lewis, Box 4)

——Report #540, 15 February 1915 (Lewis, Box 4)

——Report #597, 5 April 1915 (Lewis, Box 4)

——Report #747, 7 September 1915 (Lewis, Box 4)

——letter to ET Williams, 28 November 1916 (Lewis, Box 5)

——letter to WF Carey (Siems-Carey Railway & Canal Co, New York), Washington DC, 10 April 1920 (Lewis, Box 4)

Roosevelt, Kermit—letter to Winston Lewis, 2 March 1970 (Lewis, Box 1)

Roosevelt, Mrs Theodore Jr—'Escape From Shanghai', *The Saturday Evening Post*, 30 October 1937

Satterlee, Mrs WC—letter to Winston Lewis, 5 March 1977 (Lewis, Box 1)

Selle, Earl—letter to Mary Donald, 1 September 1949 (Lewis, Box 11)

——letter to Muriel Donald, 8 January 1957 (Lewis, Box 11)

——letter to Winston Lewis, 8 March 1969 (Lewis, Box 1)

Siegelbaum, Lewis—'1929: Chinese Railway Incident' in *Seventeen Moments in Soviet History* (2012) www.soviethistory.org

Sit, Tony—'The Life of Empress Cixi' (2001) *China in Focus*, 10, 18, www.sacu.org/cixi

Soong, May-ling (Madame Chiang)—letter to James McHugh, Chungking, 16 June 1939 (Lewis, Box 3)

Stahl, Alfred J—*How we Took It* (1945) privately published monograph (Lewis, Box 3)

Steed, Wickham—letter to David Fraser, London, 12 March 1915 (Lewis, Box 3)

Strawn, Silas H—'American Policy in China' (1928) *The Annals of the American Academy of Political and Social Science*, 138, 1, pp. 38–45

Thomas, WA—'An Intra-Empire Capital Transfer: The Shanghai Rubber Company Boom 1909–1912' (1998) *Modern Asian Studies*, 32, 3, pp. 739–60

Tours, BG—report to Sir Miles Lampson, Mukden, 2 August 1929 (Lewis, Box 8)

Trivett, Dean ACS—'Treatise', undated, Shanghai (Lewis, Box 1)

——letter to Winston Lewis, 24 April 1970 (Lewis, Box 1)

Uichanco, LB—'Annual Report of University of Philippines, College of Agriculture', 19 August 1946 (Lewis, Box 3)

US Department of Navy—letter to Winston Lewis, 6 May 1969 (Lewis, Box 2)

US State Department—'Political implications of the New Life Movement in China', Nanking #473, 21 May 1937 (Lewis, Box 4)

Van Rossum, Helene—'MacMurray's films of China, 1925–1929' in *The Reel Mudd* (2010), John Van Antwerp MacMurray papers (MC094), Seeley G Mudd Manuscript Library, Princeton University, www.blogs.princeton.edu/reelmudd/2010/07/macmurrays-films-of-china-1925-1929

Votaw, Maurice—letter to Winston Lewis, 27 March 1974 (Lewis, Box 1)

Walker, Dale L—'Jack London's War', www.jacklondons.net/journalism/jacklondonswar.html

Warner, Denis—letter to Winston Lewis, 17 June 1970 (Lewis, Box 2)

Wilson, Murray—letter to Winston Lewis, Robina QLD, 26 April 1992 (Lewis, Box 1)

Witham, PE—letter to Sir Archibald Clark Kerr, Hong Kong, 4 October 1939 (Lewis, Box 8)

Woo, Philip—'The Chinese Revolution of 1911' (1980) (adapted by TK Chung) in *TheCorner* [sic] *of the World*, www.funfront.net/hist/china/chin-revo.htm

——'The Early Republic and the Warlord Period, 1912–1928' (1990) (adapted by TK Chung) in *TheCorner* [sic] *of the World*, www.funfront.net/hist/china/warlords

Xiang Ah—'First World War & China—Japan's Twenty-one Demands', www.republicanchina.org/Japan_Twenty-one_Demands.pdf

CHAPTER NOTES

Chapter I A different world

Detail of Donald's travel is in shipping passenger manifests in the Sydney Record Centre, recording him on *Changsha* to Hong Kong from Melbourne via Sydney.

The only source of the journey from Kowloon to Victoria is Selle, *Donald of China.* It's doubtful Donald bothered describing the journey when he had so many more important things to get across to Selle. I included the episode as part of the story despite the lack of reliable detail because it sets up the exotic world Donald is entering. Selle's details must be speculation. I offer what I hope is more informed speculation.

Donald's background is given in Klam, *William Donald, Journalist,* as well as disparate other sources.

The story of Petrie Watson's visit is told in Selle, and McHugh's unpublished work, *The Unknown Era.* The latter seems to have relied heavily on the former. McHugh may have heard the story from Donald and used Selle as an *aide memoire* or he may have used Selle's version as his source (as I have). Selle would not have been aware of Watson's existence except through Donald.

Donald's experiences on *China Mail* draw from Wright, *Twentieth-Century Impressions of Hong Kong*, especially Donald's contribution, 'The Press', and from McHugh's unpublished notes.

'Intercepted Letters' was extracted in White, *Hong Kong.*

The yachting altercation is described by Selle, naming David Wood, a senior official of the Public Works Department, as the belligerent yachtsman. Selle later incorrectly describes Wood as chairman of *China Mail*, by then privately owned by the Bain family. Wood was not in a strong position to carry out the reprisals, but Henry May, the Colonial Secretary, was. Donald had a run-in with

May over a story in *China Mail* so there was a history of antagonism between them, and May was commodore of the Royal Hong Kong and Corinthian Yacht Club with a penchant for standing on the dignity of his position. If the incident happened, as Donald claimed it did, May seems more likely the antagonist than Wood.

The 1895 Canton uprising is sourced from Seagrave, *The Soong Dynasty*.

Chapter 2 Hide-and-seek

The Japanese attacks on Port Arthur and Chemulpo, and subsequent episodes in the blockade that followed are drawn from Semenoff, *Rasplata* and Tikowara, *Before Port Arthur in a Destroyer*, the authors being officers in the participant navies, from Connaughton, *The War of the Rising Sun and Tumbling Bear*, and the website of the Russo-Japanese War Research Society.

Life for journalists in Tokyo waiting to get to the front is described by Haverstock, *Fifty Years at the Front*, Lubow, *The Reporter Who Would be King*, and Palmer, *With Kuroki in Manchuria*. Donald's observations of Japan and his fellow journalists are in his articles in *China Mail* (12/2/04 and 11/3/04) and *The Advertiser*, 6/7/04.

Jack London's part is told by Kershaw, *Jack London*, and Walker, *Jack London's War*.

The episode with 'Smiler' Hales comes from Selle, *Donald of China*, and Thompson, *Shanghai Fury*.

Mr Yokohama accompanying journalists in Korea and the Japanese crossing of the Yalu River are primarily from Haverstock.

Donald's romance and marriage to Mary Wall has been pieced together from various records. The marriage certificate is in the Mitchell Library's 'Donald papers', one of its witnesses appearing with a Wall family member on shipping passenger manifests in the Sydney Record Centre and arrivals and hotel guests listed in the *South China Morning Post*. Janice Wood, a grand-niece of Mary Donald, identified the guests and the close connection between Wall and Turtle families, as well as her grandfather James Wall's frequent visits to China.

Thompson deduced Mary met Donald in Sydney from a letter written late in her life, where she said she met him on a visit to Australia. As she migrated to Australia at the age of five—unlikely to be described as a visit—and the letter was hand-written in apparent haste, I suspect she meant to say she met him on a visit to Hong Kong where her older brother had already visited on a few occasions. There is nothing otherwise to suggest they met in Australia before Donald went to Hong Kong.

The journey of the Baltic Fleet across the Indian Ocean is drawn from Semenoff, Warner & Warner, *The Tide at Sunrise*, Westwood, *The Illustrated History of the Russo–Japanese War*, and Pleshakov, *The Tsar's Last Armada* (with different dates from a different calendar system).

The *Daily Express* commission of Donald is in Selle, and also in McHugh, *The Unknown Era*, probably sourced from Selle.

Many newspaper sources report the Baltic Fleet passing by Singapore, including *China Mail*, 10/4/05. *China Mail* also reported the fleet leaving Madagascar on 11/3/05 and sighting of the fleet in Cam Ranh Bay on 17/4/05.

Donald's editorial about the *South China Morning Post* claim of exclusivity is in *China Mail* on 12/4/05, and his 'McLiar' article on 2/5/05.

The movement of the Baltic Fleet around the coast of French Indochina and the arrival of Nebogatov's fleet are from Semenoff, Warner, Westwood and Pleshakov, along with various news reports of the time. The detail of Donald's exploits in Indochina relies on his evocative reporting in *China Mail* from 10/5 to 18/5/05. It is considerably at odds with the version in Selle and McHugh, where he is claimed to have seen the fleet in its original shelter in Cam Ranh Bay. The fleet is known to have been moved out of Cam Ranh before shipping records show Donald on *Armand Behic*. Donald's memory in Hawaii, going back forty years, is unreliable and this is a constant difficulty with Selle.

The Battle of Tsushima is reported by Donald (albeit second-hand) in *China Mail* on 9 and 10/6/05 and in Brisbane's *Courier* on 22/6/05.

Chapter 3 The viceroy

The Bain family's privatisation of *China Mail* is described in Wright, *Twentieth Century Impressions of Hong Kong*.

The meeting with King, the vigil at the viceroy's *yamen* and meeting with the viceroy and his advisers is drawn from Selle, *Donald of China*, and McHugh, *The Unknown Era*, probably from Selle. Both place the episode in 1904 although neither King nor the viceroy were appointed to their positions until September 1907. The meeting must have taken place after that, but before the *Tatsu Maru* incident in February 1908. Much of the detail otherwise is consistent with other sources. The viceroy's advisers are named in Mellor, *Lugard in Hong Kong*, and King, *In the Chinese Customs Service*. However, Wen Shih-tseng is described by Selle as a tutor for the viceroy's son, surprising for a man in his seventies and unusual to be an adviser as well. Mellor and *China Mail* (9/2/08) both call Wen a *taotai* (administrative head) which seems more likely. Most probably Selle misheard Donald and McHugh copied it, although both should have been familiar with the word.

The offer to Donald of the role of adviser to the viceroy is told in Selle.

The prime sources of the *Tatsu Maru* seizure are *North China Herald*, 28/2/08, *China Mail* 9/2/08, Rhoads, *China's Republican Revolution*, and King.

Donald's advice to the viceroy and follow-up action is from Selle and McHugh. Boycotts and other public protest following the seizure, described in *North China Herald* and Rhoads, is consistent with that, without naming Donald as involved. The Hawaiian fish market action is from Kimura, *Issei*.

Bennett's offer of a position to Donald and his visit to Hong Kong is sourced from Selle.

The visit of Li Sum-ling to the US comes from a US vice-consul report of 24/8/08 and *South China Morning Post*, 21/8/08.

Chapter 4 Fall of the Manchus

The events of China's Republican revolution are drawn from a wide range of sources, both books and the internet, and told as relevant to Donald at the time. The principle sources relied on are Hsu, *The Rise of Modern China*, Fenby, *The Penguin History of Modern China*, and the websites *Xinhai Revolution* in Wikipedia and 'The Chinese Revolution of 1911' in *TheCorner of the World*.

Sun's presentation to Li Hung-chan is in Chapman, 'The Revolution in China', and Boothe's attempted financing of his revolution is in Schiffrin, *Sun Yat-sen*.

Forensic work on Kwang-tsu's death is reported in CNN International, 'Arsenic killed Chinese emperor'.

Bain's death is noted in Ho Tung, 'The Chinese in Hong Kong'. Selle, *Donald of China*, asserts Donald's departure followed a dispute with the chairman of the *China Mail* board, a government department head. This is unlikely for a number of reasons but I have not found a record of the board at that time. I have left it as uncertain. Donald's subsequent enterprise is told in Selle and Thompson, *Shanghai Fury*.

Donald's home life is from Thompson, and a Lewis letter to Hochschild, 26/7/76. All letters and memorandums referred to in these Chapter Notes are in the Lewis papers (the Mitchell Library's 'Donald papers') unless stated otherwise.

The involvement with Tonkin Pulp & Paper is from Selle and Lewis's letter to Bertram & Sons, 13/5/74, with the meeting with Waters told by Waters, *Much Besides Music.*

The Donalds' arrival in Shanghai draws on Thompson and Chapman, as well as a number of sources describing Shanghai at that time. Wikipedia's 'History of the Astor House Hotel (Shanghai) 1900–1922' was a source of much of the description of that hotel.

Donald's friendship with Charlie Soong comes from Chapman, Selle and Thompson, as does his involvement with the revolutionists and his suggestion of Wu as a figurehead of the movement, along with Seagrave, *The Soong Dynasty*. Donald is quoted as saying he knew Soong May-ling (later, Madame Chiang) as a young girl, but she was already in the US at school when he met Soong and didn't return to China until she was 20.

Donald's visit to the Nanking floods and meeting with the former viceroy of Canton is described in Selle and Thompson.

Donald's understanding of the issue of railway companies is found in Chapman.

Donald's meeting with Everard Fraser comes from Chapman, Selle and Thompson. The first two are first-hand from Donald and describe him as reminding Fraser that they had already met when he was British consul in Canton. Although Donald had a run-in with the British consul when he made contact with the viceroy there, it wasn't with Fraser who was never the Canton consul.

Chapter 5 How we took Purple Mountain by stealth

Crow's comment about Donald is in Crow, *China Takes Her Place*, along with his influence on Millard.

Donald's letter to Fraser is reported in *New York Herald*, 4/11/11.

Shanghai before and during its uprising is described by Dong, *Shanghai*. The taking of the city by rebels and of Hangchow subsequently is also sourced from Fenby, *The Penguin History of Modern China*, Seagrave, *The Soong Dynasty*, and *The Times*, 4/11/11. The role of the Green Gang in the rebellion is from Martin, *The Shanghai Green Gang.*

Yuan's mission to Li and Huang are outlined in Hsu, *The Rise of Modern China.*

Events in Nanking prior to attack are from Gracey letters, 15/10–16/11/11 and *North China Herald*, 25/11/11.

The concern expressed by Standard-Vacuum Oil in Chinkiang is in Gilbert's letter to Williams, 18/10/11.

The New Army's demand for return of its breaches and its move outside the city is in Gracey's letter, 10/11/11.

Donald's adventures with Anderson in Chinkiang, on the railway line, and on and around Purple Mountain are drawn primarily from Chapman, 'The Revolution in China'. Selle, *Donald of China*, tells of the same general series of events, but with significant differences in detail, much of which stems from the assertion of Donald leading the attack on Nanking from Purple Mountain. This is highly unlikely and there is no evidence to support it. The revolutionary armies' movements towards Nanking and up Purple Mountain are covered by *North China Herald*, 2 and 9/12/11, without any mention of Donald as a leader. Thompson, *Shanghai Fury*, covers the events also, drawing from the same sources, but assigns Chapman's more modest role to Donald.

Chapman's account ends abruptly with the cannons set up to fire on T'aip'ing Gate. Donald's dictation had reached this point the day before American troops rescued them from Los Baños and the memoir was never resumed. Selle's account continues with Donald and Anderson leading the attack and Donald helping the viceroy escape from Nanking disguised as a woman, too fanciful and recycled to be very convincing. I have preferred to rely on the Gilbert and Gracey letters of 1/12–5/12/11 and *New York Herald*, 3/12/11 for this part of the story.

Donald watching Tang's arrival and his contact with Wu and Morrison is from Thompson. His spotting of the newspaper report of Sun's return is in Selle.

Chapter 6 The unshining Sun

Sun forgetting his codebook is noted in Fenby, *The Penguin History of Modern China*, and Thompson, *Shanghai Fury*. Sun reading of the Wuchang uprising and subsequently attempting to meet leaders in the US, Britain and France is sourced primarily from Seagrave, *The Soong Dynasty*.

His arrival in Shanghai is described by Bergére, *Sun Yat-sen*, and Taylor, *The Generalissimo*. The meeting that day with Lea comes from Selle, *Donald of China*, Fenby, *Generalissimo*, and McHugh, *The Unknown Era*. Morrison's view of Lea is quoted in Pearl, *Morrison of Peking*.

The description of Sun's inauguration is drawn primarily from the *New York Herald*, 3/1/12.

Sun's choice of Wang over Wu, and Wang's communiqué after the manifesto are from Pomerantz-Zhang, *Wu Tingfang*.

The session in which Sun's manifesto is drawn up is described in Selle and McHugh. Several sources confirm Donald as its principal author.

Donald's letter to Morrison about the squatters in Nanking is quoted in Bergére.

Sun's dismissal of finance is described in Donald's letter of 4/7/12.

The empress dowager's edict on relinquishing power is quoted in the *New York Herald*, 13/2/12.

Sun's statement about the importance of transportation is sourced from Fenby, *The Penguin History of Modern China*.

Donald's visit to Peking to meet Morrison and the offer of a position to Morrison by Yuan are from Pearl.

Sun's grand inspection tour of the railways of China is drawn primarily from Seagrave, cross-referenced to Selle. Sun's crackpot ideas expressed during the journey are in Selle and McHugh. Sun wanting Donald to sit next to him is from Selle, his response to the socialist question from Elliston, 'China's No. 1 White Boy'. The story of Sun's map and Donald's move to keep reporters from viewing it is drawn from Selle, Seagrave, both Fenby books, Schiffrin, *Sun Yat-sen*, and Donald's letter, 4/7/12.

Donald's complaints to Morrison about Sun are in his letters of 4/7 and 4/8/12 in the Morrison papers in Mitchell Library, Sydney. He also tells of advising Wen against joining T'ung-meng Hui and of Sun reactivating his political ambitions in the 4/8/12 letter.

Sun's nickname of 'dabao' is in Bergére.

Sun's reputation as a womaniser and Donald's comment are drawn from Hahn, *Chiang Kai-shek*. His infatuation with Soong Ai-ling and approach to her father regarding it are from Selle, McHugh and Seagrave.

Chapter 7 21 Demands

Rea's move from Manila to Shanghai and his view on the importance of railways is sourced from Hoyt, 'Apologist for Japan'.

The involvement of Reiss and Spielman in Sun's scheme is from Rea's 1/2/21 letter.

Donald's comment about 'wire-pullers' and purchase of *China Gazette* is from his 4/8/12 letter.

Bennett's offer of the Peking position is in Donald's 30/11/12 letter.

Rathvon wrote to Lewis on 19/1/70 that Donald was given the house by the Chinese government, but a search of Peking records by Professor Zhang Wei revealed he bought it through his government connections. Donald's letter of 15/9/45 is consistent with this, noting a Chinese was used as a front for his purchase. As the Rathvons were close friends of Donald over many years, they might be considered a well-informed source, but the house was bought before they met the Donalds and their version is not completely at odds with the researched version anyway. Mary Donald claimed in a bitter letter many years later that it was bought with her family's money although she claimed in the same letter that her father had disinherited her when she married.

Mrs Anderson was described as 'vapid and pretty-pretty' by MacMurray in his 4/3/15 letter.

Sung's assassination and its aftermath is drawn from Fenby, *Generalissimo*, and Hsu, *The Rise of Modern China*.

Morrison's grumbles about China and Yuan are from Pearl, *Morrison of Peking*.

Donald's letter to a Sydney friend about Morrison is quoted in Pearl. His attempts to placate Morrison after the *Bulletin* article are in letters on 4/10 and 7/10/13.

Donald's rescue of Wang from Yuan's henchmen is sourced from Fenby, *The Penguin History of Modern China*.

Chiang's military magazine is noted in Fenby, *Generalissimo*.

Donald's congratulations to Mrs Morrison are in his letter of 1/6/13.

Fraser's recommendation of Donald to *The Times* is in his letter to Braham, 6/1/14.

The attempts by Rea and Donald to set up a railway consortium are culled from Hoyt, Fraser's 27/1/14 letter, Donald's letters to Reinsch,12/3/14, and Pauling & Co Ltd, 16/4/14, and Rea's memorandum of 26/5/14. The concerns of participants and China's Ministry of Communications are drawn from extensive correspondence between a variety of people in the Lewis papers.

An article on 1/9/32 in *North China Daily News*, possibly written by Donald, is a source of much of the story of Japan's 21 Demands, particularly of the Chow dinner with Funatsu, Donald's later visit to Chow, Donald passing his information to other reporters, the *Times*' response and Donald's visit to Morrison to obtain a copy of the Demands

Hioki's meeting with Yuan is sourced from Pearl, and MacMurray's letters of 4/3/15 and 5/4/15.

The Japanese reporter's approach to Reinsch is in the ambassador's report of 10/2/15. Yuan's meeting with Morrison at that time is in Pearl.

The *Times*' editing of Donald's report and reactions to it are culled from Steed's 12/3/15 letter, Fraser's response of 16/3/15 and sarcastic follow-up of 6/4/15, and Morrison's letters to Steed, 17/2 and 24/2/15.

The 21 Demands are set out in Duffy, 'Primary Documents'.

The Japanese attempt to devolve the 21 Demands into 'demands' and 'requests' is drawn from a Reinsch report of 5/4/15, Fraser's cable to *The Times*, 11/3/15, and cables between Hioki and Kato, 12/1–10/2/15, (Fukushima translations) discussing strategy to conceal detail of the Demands.

The Foreign Office approach to Donald to advise is from Fenby, *The Penguin History of Modern China*, McHugh, and an undated clipping in Smith's Weekly, 'Chinese Donald'.

Chapter 8 The day of the warlord

Mary's illness is discussed in Donald's letter of 23/6/15.

Soong Ching-ling's elopement and her father's pursuit to Yokahama are sourced from Seagrave, *The Soong Dynasty*.

Donald's meeting with the dying Yuan is described in Selle, *Donald of China*, and used in Fenby, *The Penguin History of Modern China* and *Generalissimo*, and Thompson, *Shanghai Fury*. Hsu's assessment of Yuan after his death is in *The Rise of Modern China*, p. 482.

The Pacific Press experience with Fleischer is drawn from Pratt's letter of 5/2/18 and a Fleischer letter to Reinsch, 3/4/18.

Rea's dispute with Reinsch is from the Reinsch letter of 28/11/16 and letters between Reinsch and Carey of 25/3 and 10/4/20.

The campaign of Reinsch, Donald and Anderson to support the US position against Germany is sourced from Reinsch, *An American Diplomat in China*, Pearl, *Morrison of Peking*, and McHugh, *The Unknown Era*.

The restoration of Imperial China by Chang Hsun is from Hsu, *The Rise of Modern China*, Fenby, *The Penguin History of Modern China*, and Pearl.

Notification of Morrison and Wu of the restoration is in Donald's cable to Morrison, 1/7/17, in the Lewis papers. The circumstances are described in Pearl.

Rea's move into US Intelligence is sourced from a Rea letter to Donald, 21/10/17, and Hoyt, 'Apologist for Japan'.

Donald's visit to Tokyo to investigate the arms deal is drawn from a Greene telegram of 2/11/17.

Morrison's attempted meeting with Pratt is described in his letter of 26/11/17.

The Donalds' visit to Japan is drawn from Donald's letter, 5/5/18.

The Consortium of Banks in China and its objectives are outlined in memorandums of 8/18 and 24/9/18, and in a Donald letter to Reinsch, 16/7/18.

Chiang's dissolute life in Shanghai is drawn from Fenby, *Generalissimo*, and Dong, *Shanghai*. His marriage to Jennie is in Hsu and his meeting of May-ling is in Seagrave. Rea's transition to pro-Japanese is sourced from Hoyt and a number of letters and memorandums, among them MacMurray to Coxe, 24/7/20, Rea to Lansing, 9/9/19, Drysdale to Nolan, 7/2/21, and memorandums by Burnett, 17/1/23 and Hodges, 18/12/19, all in the Lewis papers. His meeting with Odagiri is in the *Peking and Tientsin Times*, 16/3/20.

Rea's return to the *Far Eastern Review* and Donald's subsequent resignation is in an ONI secret report of 16/2/20. His published statement is in a Rogers undated letter to MacMurray

The events leading to Mary's departure from China are drawn from her undated letter to Croucher, and from Thompson.

The *Times* reprimand of Donald is in a memorandum from its Foreign Department of 29/10/18.

The setting up of the Bureau of Economic Information is from Thompson. Thompson has also outlined Donald's social life of that time.

Donald's interaction with the Far Eastern Republic's mission and with Kasanin is sourced from Kasanin, *China in the Twenties*.

Donald's attempts to find a buyer for the Morrison house are sourced from correspondence between Donald and Mrs Morrison, Oct–Dec 1920, in the Morrison papers.

The Backhouse swindle is from Chapman's dictated Donald memoir.

Hochschild's purpose in China is outlined in his letter to Lewis, 18/8/69. The anecdote about Donald following him to the woman's home is in his 17/7/75 letter to Lewis.

Donald's meeting with Northcliffe is drawn primarily from Woodhead, *A Journalist in China*, and Thompson.

Sun's bombardment and escape in Canton is sourced from Fenby, *Generalissimo*, and Hsu.

Chiang's visit to the USSR is drawn from Fenby, *Generalissimo*. Borodin is quoted as calling Sun an 'enlightened little satrap' in both Fenby books.

Donald in his Western Hills lodge and with his domestic staff is described from Booker, *News is my Job*, McHugh, and Donald's letter to the Rathvons, 21/11/23 in the Hoover Archive. Donald's visit to the US and Britain is drawn from a Roosevelt letter to Lewis, 2/3/70 and referred to in several of Donald's letters to the Rathvons. Fraser's letter of 6/2/24 announces his intention to visit *The Times*.

Sun's illness and death is covered primarily in Hsu and built on from sundry other sources. Chow's illness is told in McHugh, his bedside visit by Donald in Selle. Anderson's illness and death comes from Selle. A copy of his death certificate is in the Lewis papers.

Mary Donald's visit to Shanghai is from Donald's letter to Helen Rathvon, 15/5/25 in the Hoover Archive.

Donald's golf with McHugh and Strawn is from McHugh.

The *Chungshan* incident is drawn from Seagrave.

Chiang's meeting with Huang and, later, Tu are sourced from Hsu, Seagrave and Martin, *The Shanghai Green Gang*. His meeting with Soong Ai-ling is from Fenby, *Generalissimo*. Chiang's persuasion of Jennie to make a sacrifice is sourced from Fenby, *Generalissimo*, and Hsu

The purge of China's Communists in Shanghai relies primarily on Dong and Hsu. Chou's escape is in Powell, *My Twenty-five Years in China*, Fenby, *The Penguin History of Modern China,* and Hsu.

Jennie's misadventures in New York are from Fenby, *Generalissimo*.

Chiang's wooing of and marriage to May-ling is sourced from Fenby, *Generalissimo*, and Seagrave.

Chapter 9 The Young Marshal

Chang Tso-lin's revenge of his father's murder is told in Chapman's memoir in the Lewis papers.

The Young Marshal's dissolute Peking life draws from Mitter, *Manchurian Myth*, and Shai, *Zhang Xueliang*, as does the story of his father's threat to have him executed.

Donald's complaint to the Old Marshal about the damage to his home is from Thompson, *Shanghai Fury*.

Chang's problems with opium and pavemal and their origins are from a number of sources, including Chapman, 'Chang Hseuh-liang', Fenby, *The Penguin History of Modern China*, and Boorman, *Biographical Dictionary of Republican China*. The replacement drug is sometimes called pavinol. Morphine pills under different names were widely used in China at the time to wean addicts off opium. Pavemal and pavinol may have been the same product. The assassination of Chang Tso-lin draws principally from Chapman and Fenby, *Generalissimo*.

The pressure on Donald in the bureau is from Thompson.

Donald's letter to Elliston of his fleeing is told in Elliston's article, 'China's No. 1 White Boy'.

Donald's offer of a position by Chang is sourced from McHugh, *The Unknown Era*. The journey to Mukden and meeting with the Young Marshal is re-constructed from Abend, *My Life in China*, and Thompson.

The visit by the emissary of Yang and Ch'ang, the journey to Tsitsihar and the meeting with Ch'ang are from Chapman.

The execution of Yang and Ch'ang is sourced from two unsourced interpreter's reports of 12/1 and 15/1/29 in the Lewis papers, and Mitter. Other sources give varied accounts with different reasons for Chang to be absent and different officials carrying out the killing. Most (but not all) have the two being shot in Chang's mansion and at his instigation. Donald's drive with Chang the following day is from Chapman.

Elder's background is culled from letters from Barrett (24/7/69), Bond (3/9/69) and Gould (9/1/70) to Lewis and Lewis's letter of 23/5/75.

Chang's marriages and concubine are outlined in Shai, notably his marriage to his second wife. Irina's background is drawn from Wilson's letter of 26/4/92, and a *Sydney Morning Herald* article, 22/10/36.

Donald's advice regarding CER and negotiations with Russia are sourced from the Powell report of 27/7/29, the Magruder reports of 26/8, 6/9 and 4/11/29 and from Spence, *The Search for Modern China*.

Chang's distractions and Donald's ultimatum to him are drawn from Chapman and the Tours report of 2/8/29.

Chang's escape to Hulutao, then Peitaiho is outlined by Chapman and the Margetts memos of 10 and 11/12/30. Chang's meetings with the Nationalist Party emissary and then his Political Council are from Chapman.

Chang's meeting with Lenox-Simpson is in Chapman, with support from Chao, *The Foreign Press in China*.

Japan's warning about flying the Nationalist flag is from Chapman.

The Nakamura murder is sourced from the *North China Herald* (15/9/31), Ferrell, 'The Mukden Incident', and Shai.

Chang's admission to PUMC for treatment of typhoid is sourced from Chapman and Boorman. A variety of other sources agree he was there for typhoid, others (e.g. Fenby, *Penguin History*) claim he was being treated for his opium addiction. Abend acknowledges the public explanation was typhoid but speculates it was a cover for drug treatment. Donald, from whom Chapman gets his version, would have known which it was and would have no reason to maintain the fiction by then if that was what it had been.

The details of the evening in Peking spent by Donald, Chang and Elder when the Japanese attacked Mukden draws primarily from Chapman. The events in Mukden, and collaboration of Chapman's story, are sourced from the *North China Herald* (22/9, 29/9 and 6/10/31), Hsu, *The Rise of Modern China*, Fenby, *Penguin History*, Spence, Shai and Ferrell.

The Japanese military's severing of relations with Chang is reported in the *North China Herald*, 6/10/31.

Events leading to Japan's attack on Shanghai are drawn principally from Jordan, *China's Trial by Fire,* and Fenby, *Generalissimo*.

Donald's accompanying of Wu to Shanghai is told from Donald's letter of 18/2/32, Jordan, Fenby, *Generalissimo*, and Thompson.

The Chinese delegation with the Lytton Commission in Manchuria is described in Cranford's report to the US State Department (13/7/32), Donald's letter of 7/7/32, and the *Sydney Morning Herald*, 1/8/32. Lytton's comment about the Japanese is from Fraser's letter of 26/5/32. Rea's involvement with the commission is drawn from an Office of Naval Intelligence (US) Note of 16/10/33.

Donald's air crash at Newchwang and the plane bogged at Shanghai are in his letter, 7/7/32.

The visit of Chang, Donald and Soong to Chengteh is sourced from Fenby, *Generalissimo*. The Japanese invasion of Jehol was covered by *Time* between January and March 1933 and is drawn also from Fenby's *Penguin History*. Tang's rodeo and press conference are described in *Time*, 6/3 and 13/3/33.

Chang's meeting with Chiang and his resignation are from Chapman, and Fenby, *Penguin History*.

Chapter 10 The cure

Donald and Elder's visit to Miller, and Miller's arrival and treatment in Shanghai are drawn primarily from Moore, *China Doctor*, Chapman, 'Chang Hsueh-liang', and Selle, *Donald of China*.

Chang's relationship with Edda Ciano is sourced from Shai, *Zhang Xueliang*.

The *Conte Rosso* is described in the *New York Times*, 19/2/22. The Chang party's journey in Europe is sourced from Shai, Thompson, *Shanghai Fury*, and Fenby, *The Penguin History of Modern China*. Detail of destinations and dates are found in a series of cables from Japan's diplomatic missions to Uchida, then Hirota (Japanese foreign ministers) reporting the party's presence, 11/3/33–5/1/34. They are in the Fukushima translations. The meeting with Soong in London is in Chapman.

Background to the Fukien rebellion is in *The Times*, 24/11/33. The telegram advising Chang is quoted in Selle and Thompson.

Donald's meeting in Shanghai with Soong is sourced from Chapman, Selle and Thompson. His subsequent lunch with Madame and Bond is from Thompson.

The meetings of Donald and Chang with the Chiangs are drawn from Chapman, Fenby's *Generalissimo* and Thompson, as well as a report from Shimizu (Japan's Hankow consul) to Hirota, 8/3/34 in Fukushima.

Donald taking Bond to meet the Young Marshal is from the Bond letter of 3/9/69.

The problems with customs and opium smuggling that worried Donald at the time are from Chapman.

Donald's meeting with Madame Chiang is culled from Chapman, Pakula, *The Last Empress,* and Sues, *Shark's Fins and Millet.*

Chapter 11 Madame and the generalissimo

Donald's journey with Madame Chiang to Loyang, and the tour of Si'an and beyond draws largely from Chapman, 'Chang Hsueh-liang' and also from Hahn, *Chiang Kai-shek* and *The Soong Sisters*, Fenby, *Generalissimo*, and Pakula, *The Last Empress*. Madame's obsession with hygiene is from Taylor, *The Generalissimo*, and Hahn, *Chiang Kai-shek*. The assassination attempt on the train is from Berkov, *Strong Man of China*.

Details of the New Life Movement are sourced from Fenby (including the quote from *Time*), Taylor, Seagrave, *The Soong Dynasty*, and the *North China Herald*, 2/5 and 20/6/34.

Madame's offer of a job to Donald is drawn from Sues, *Shark's Fins and Millet.*

Donald's mispronunciation of Chinese and other languages is from Sues and Gunther, *Inside Asia.*

Donald's lunch with the Chiangs draws from Gunther, Sues and Fenby.

The Chiang party following the Communist withdrawal is sourced from Hahn, *The Soong Sisters*, Fenby, and Pakula. The visit to Kweichow is in the *North China Herald*, 10/4/35. Background to Stennes is from Gunther and Mrs Satterlee's experience is told in her letter of 5/3/77. The incident with Donald talking in Mandarin is from the Butler letter, 27/2/69. The story of the butcher and the bloodied flag is in Sues.

The Chiang's entertainment of Westerners is drawn from Gunther.

The appointment of Tong as chief censor of foreign press, including the censored cable, is sourced from Tong, *Dateline: China.*

Madame's payment to Donald for his arrears from the Bureau of Economic Information is told by McHugh in *The Unknown Era.*

Donald's illness and eventual escape from Shanghai is primarily from Chapman, with further detail from Donald's letter to Peter Rathvon of 13/7/36 (Hoover Archive).

The press conference with Madame Chiang is from Hahn, *The Soong Sisters.*

Chang's visit to Donald for advice is drawn from Chapman.

Chiang's birthday celebration in Loyang is from Fenby.

Chapter 12 The Si'an Incident

Chiang's arrival in Si'an and meeting with Chang is drawn from Shai, *Zhang Xueliang*, Berkov, *Strong Man of China*, Seagrave, *The Soong Dynasty*, Fenby, *Generalissimo,* Chapman, 'Chang Hsueh-liang' and the Howe letter of 28/12/36.

The student protest is from Shai, Berkov, Chapman and the *North China Herald*, 30/12/36.

The aftermath of the Chang and Yang meeting with Chiang is sourced from Chapman, Fenby and Shai.

The attack at the Lintung guesthouse and Chiang's escape and subsequent discovery and return to Si'an is re-written from a wide range of sources that contradict each other on a number of key points. They are Fenby, Chiang, *A Fortnight in Sian*, Leonard, *I Flew for China*, Shai, Berkov, Chapman and Seagrave. Much of the material in this chapter is drawn from the above sources.

A particular inconsistency is whether Chiang escaped alone or accompanied. Berkov, for instance, has him escaping with a bodyguard, dismisses the accounts that have the bodyguard informing on him, but his bodyguard has disappeared anyway by the time Chiang is discovered in the cave. Other accounts have him escaping with two servants or aides who either go no further than the guest-house wall with him or simply disappear from the account somewhere on the mountain. All accounts have him alone by the time he's found in the cave. It seems to me the most likely scenario is that he made a solitary dash for safety when he realised he was under serious threat. Chiang's own version has two staff leave his room with him, but they have disappeared by the time he's scaled the wall. He links up with some guards at a temple at the base of the mountain and climbs the mountain with them, but they are attacked by rebels and some guards are killed. When Chiang goes down the mountain side and falls in the cave, he is alone—no bodyguard, no rebels. Like others before me, who also had access to Chiang's version, I have doubts about the credibility of this detail.

Chang's response to reports of Chiang's disappearance is sourced from Shai.

Chiang's reception on being brought to Si'an is drawn from the above sources. His demand that Chang decides if he is his enemy or his subordinate is sourced from Crow, *China Takes Her Place*.

The telegrams sent by Chang are sourced from Berkov and Shai.

The message in Shanghai for Donald to come to the Kung residence and the subsequent meeting with government officials in Nanking is drawn primarily from Chapman, Chiang, *Sian*, and Abend, *My Life in China*.

The account of Chiang's wills is sourced from Shai.

The difference in dialects between the two protagonists and the effect of that is sourced from Shai.

Donald and Huang's flight to Si'an and being met by Elder is drawn from Chapman.

Donald's meeting with Chiang and Chiang's move to the new house is from Chapman, Berkov and Fenby. Donald's meeting with Yang and his officers is from Chapman.

Huang's observation of Chiang through the door glass and Chiang reading out his letter for Madame is sourced from Hahn, *Chiang Kai-shek*.

Donald's flight to Loyang and phone call to May-ling is from Chapman.

The arrival of TV Soong in Si'an is drawn from Chapman, Berkov, Fenby and Seagrave.

Chou's journey to Si'an is described by Shai.

Donald and Shepherd's use of coded phone messages is sourced from US State Department report, 21/5/37, and Berkov.

Chiang's bodyguard commander's attempts to avoid returning to Si'an are sourced from Chapman.

Madame handing Donald her revolver is sourced from Hahn and Chapman. Her arrival with Donald at Si'an's airfield is drawn from the same two sources as well as Shai. The meeting of Madame and the generalissimo is drawn from Chiang, *Sian*, Chiang, *A Fortnight in Sian*, Fenby, Hahn, Seagrave and Shai.

Chou's meeting with Madame Chiang, Yang and her husband is told from Shai, Fenby and Seagrave.

Chang's secret preparation to leave is sourced from Chapman, Huang's release from Hahn.

The journey to Si'an airfield and the flights to Loyang and then Nanking are drawn from Chapman and Shai. The flights also draw from Leonard, *I Flew for China*, and Fenby.

Chapter 13 Disillusioned

Chang's trial and the repercussions with the Chiangs are drawn from Chapman, 'Chang Hsueh-liang' and Shai, *Zhang Xueliang*. Donald's question of Chiang about Chang's future is in Chapman.

Stennes' offer of protection to Donald is sourced from Chapman.

Donald's response to the Nationalist editorial is quoted in Chapman and the general reaction is described in a British Foreign Office intelligence report, 25/1/37, and Hall-Patch note, 12/1/37.

Chiang's injuries from Si'an and reluctance to get medical help are drawn from Berkov, *Strong Man of China* and a Johnson report, 11/5/37.

Von Falkenhausen's confidence that China's army could defeat Japan is noted in Fenby, *Generalissimo*, a Knatchbull-Hugessen memo of 18/7/37 and the Gauss letter, 1/5/37. His private view that they were not yet fit for battle is sourced from Fenby, *The Penguin History of Modern China*.

Donald's daily routine is drawn from Sues, *Shark's Fins and Millet*. This is also the source of Sues' assessment of Madame Chiang.

The engagement and involvement of Chennault in China's air force is culled from Chennault, *Way of a Fighter*, and Seagrave, *The Soong Dynasty*. The previous history of American and Italian air advisers and trainers is primarily from Chennault.

The story of the Marco Polo Bridge Incident is told principally from the two Fenby books, with additional material from the Peck telegram, 12/7/1937.

The military planning meetings before and after the Oyama shooting are drawn from Chennault and McHugh's memorandum for *The Unknown Era*.

China's attack on *Izumo* and accidental bombing of Nanking Road is drawn from Chennault and Fenby, *Generalissimo*.

The solution of the CNAC pilot issue by Bond through Donald is told in Bond's letter of 3/9/69.

The story of Oursler's interview with Madame for *Liberty* is from Pakula, *The Last Empress*.

Donald watching air attacks from Purple Mountain is sourced from Sues. The attacks on Nanking are also described in articles written by Donald for the *Sydney Morning Herald*, 24/9/37, and Sydney's *Daily Telegraph*, 22/9/37.

Sues' project with the ministry of propaganda is told primarily from Sues' memoir, *Shark's Fins and Millet*.

The car accident with Madame and Donald near Shanghai is drawn from Fenby, *Generalissimo*, Sues, Selle, *Donald of China*, and Thompson, *Shanghai Fury*.

Tang's futile defence of Nanking and the departure of the Chiangs and Donald from the capital is drawn primarily from Fenby, *Generalissimo*. Donald's pessimistic visit to the US consulate just before is from McHugh's memo, 6/12/37.

McHugh's comments on the changed nature of his friend are sourced from the McHugh report of 20/1/38. Donald's request for medicines is in his letter of 19/4/38.

Donald's new life in Hankow is from Fenby, *Generalissimo*.

The activities of Patterson are from Pakula, and of Pawley from McHugh's report of 20/1/38, his letter of 16/2/38 and Seagrave.

McHugh's dinner with Rogers and the banker's subsequent meeting with Donald are sourced from McHugh's report, 20/1/38 and McHugh, *The Unknown Era*.

The trap for Japan in Tai'erhchwang draws from Fenby, *Generalissimo*.

Donald's comment on the Chinese army's new spirit is in his letter of 2/7/38.

The German ambassador's presentation of the Japanese peace feeler is drawn from Donald's letter of 23/1/39 and Fenby, *Generalissimo*.

Soong's meeting with the Italian ambassador is from the McHugh memo, 26/2/38.

The departure of von Falkenhausen is told in Donald's letter of 2/7/38. The German ambassador's question of whether the Japanese would prefer China had Russian advisers is told in a Howe memo of 7/11/37.

Donald's visit to the ministry of information in Hankow is from Farmer, *Shanghai Harvest.*

Donald's recovery of his health in Kunming draws from McHugh's letters of 28 and 29/8/38. His interrupted return to Hankow is from Donald's letters of 15/1/39 and 30/12/38.

The departure of the Chiangs and Donald from Hankow is drawn from Fenby, *Generalissimo*, Tong, *Dateline: China*, Pakula, and Guo, '1938, letter from Donald to Timperley'.

McHugh's daily crossing of the upper Yangtze is sourced from Pakula.

Christmas with the Chiangs in Chunking is sourced from the Donald letter of 15/1/39.

Donald's assessment of visiting Western businessmen is in a letter to Hornbeck, 21/1/39.

Hahn's approach to Madame Chiang to write a book about her and her sisters is drawn from Hahn, *China to Me*.

Clark Kerr's re-evaluation of Donald is in his letter of 13/2/41.

May-ling turning on Donald is from Fenby, *Generalissimo*, although the same anecdote is told in other sources with different reasons for her reaction and with it taking place at different times. The strongest consensus is on her line. The level of corruption in the Kung family is outlined by McHugh in his 20/1/38 report.

The story with Donald's line, 'Madame keeps me in cake', was told by Votaw, 27/3/74. Donald told McHugh he was at the end of his nervous strength in a 25/5/39 letter. TV Soong's claim that the minister of finance is Chiang's dog is from Seagrave.

Donald's trip to Madagascar is drawn from his letter of 9/9/39. His itinerary is outlined in the Chan letter of 8/7/39.

The description of *Mei Hwa* is in a Donald letter to Peter Rathvon, 13/7/36, in the Hoover Archive.

Cripps' tour is drawn from Estorick, *Stafford Cripps*. His discouragement by Madame Chiang is in that book and in Cripps' report of 29/4/40.

Donald's correction of May-ling's speech is told in the Clark Kerr letter of 13/5/40 and an undated clipping in the Lewis papers, 'Last Days of Chiang Kai-shek's Private Adviser'.

Chapter 14 Escape and Capture

Ansie Lee's description of herself is quoted in a Lewis letter, 10/11/77.

Donald's arrangement with the bureau is from his letter of 1/5/40.

The talk given by Donald in Rabaul is drawn from an unsourced clipping in the Lewis papers, 'Morale of China at High Pitch'.

Donald's exchange with Tulagi customs is sourced from his letter of 30/10/40.

Madame Chiang's conversation with Clark Kerr is noted in the Clark Kerr memo of 6/11/40.

The contacts from May-ling while Donald was in the Pacific are from Selle, *Donald of China*.

Donald's explanation for abandoning his book is quoted in Thompson, *Shanghai Fury*.

Bond's finding of a flight from Honolulu for Donald is drawn from his letters of 3/9/69 and 2/7/71.

Donald's experience at Sulphur Springs is related by Chapman in a letter, 24/4/70.

Life in the Santo Tomas internment camp is drawn from the Chapman logs, Lucas, *Prisoners of Santo Tomas*, the Arthur Perkins diary, and Thompson.

The *kempeitei* visit to Santo Tomas is drawn from a *Sydney Morning Herald* report of 9/2/45 and Thompson. The report of Donald held in the Philippines in the *Sydney Morning Herald* of 5/8/43 is noted by Thompson.

Life in Los Baños is drawn primarily from the Manning report of 13/12/44.

The temporary departure of the Japanese from Los Baños is told in Heichert's 'Record of Events'.

The various contacts with Filipino guerrillas before rescue is outlined in Heichert and Grey's 'Summary of the Events'.

The liberation of internees from Los Baños is drawn primarily from Lucas, Stahl, *How We Took It*, Armamento, *The Indomitable*, Heichert and Grey, and the Moat letter of 21/2/70.

Donald learning that he is to be repatriated to the US is told in Moat's letters of 21/2 and 7/4/70.

Details of the voyage to San Francisco is drawn from a Lewis interview with Tierney, 1/12/74.

Chapter 15 Yesterday's man

Donald's presence at the San Francisco Conference is described from his letters to Chapman, 20/6/45, and Muriel, 18/6/45. His comment about the conference was made in his letter of 25/5/45.

MacArthur headquarters comment on Donald's press release is sourced from Bertram, *NZ Listener*, December 1946.

Donald's dental problems are drawn from his letters to Chapman, 25/5 and 20/6/45, and Muriel, 19 and 20/6/45.

His reminiscences about New Rochelle are in his letters to Helen Rathvon of 1/10/24 and 3/3/25, in the Hoover Archive.

Mary and Muriel's circumstances are drawn from the Nunneley letter, 10/5/75. Donald's advice to Muriel is in his letter of 15/9/45.

Donald meeting May-ling in New York is drawn from his letter of 23/8/45 and Thompson, *Shanghai Fury*.

Donald's stay in Tahiti is from his letter of 7/12/45. His fluoroscope test is sourced from Bertram.

Dr Ethridge's test on Donald and his work with Tong to enable his patient to be transferred to Shanghai is drawn primarily from his letter of 12/3/70, with support material from Donald's letter of 10/3/46, and Bertram.

Selle's meetings with Donald are drawn primarily from Selle, *Donald of China*, with additional observation from Ethridge's letter. While I don't regard Selle's book as a very reliable source of Donald's life, that's principally because I don't regard Donald as a reliable source at that time—if he ever was. Selle's reliability regarding his own activity is less contentious, although I have added to it in the context of Donald's changing attitude to him revealed in Donald's letters to others, most notably his letter to Chapman, 2/7/46.

Donald's departure from Honolulu and arrival at Shanghai is from Ethridge's letter, as is Madame's decoration of Donald's room in the Country Hospital. His farewell by the Selles is from Selle.

Donald's wish to discontinue the book is from his letter of 2/7/46, his explanation for wanting to do so is quoted from his letter of 18/4/46. Madame Chiang's efforts to curtail the book are sourced from Selle's letter of 8/3/69.

Chiang's visit to Donald is sourced from an unsourced newspaper clipping in the Lewis papers, 'Last Days of Chiang Kai-shek's Private Adviser'.

The proceeds of the sale of the Peking house are in the Donald letter of 12/10/46.

Donald's final day in the Country Hospital is drawn from Trivett, 'Treatise', the clipping 'Last days . . .', and another clipping, 'Donald's Last Moment Told By His Doctor'.The funeral is described from the *North China Daily News*, 11/11/46,Trivett,'Treatise' and Trivett's letter of 24/4/70.

Epilogue

Mary Donald's reaction to Selle's book is shown in her letters to Selle, 7/8/49, and to Lewis, 9/3/71. Legal advice to her came from the Nassau letter, 30/6/48.

Details of Donald's estate are in his earlier will of 2/8/38, updated in his letter of 1/4/46. The outcome is in Hall's letters of 7/7/48 and 16/4/49, and Nassau's letter of 3/2/49. Hall's comment about pressing Madame Chiang for money is in his letter of 29/11/47.

Mary and Muriel's health problems are outlined in Mary's undated letters to Croucher in the Lewis papers.

Dinner with the Chiangs in Taipeh is told by Warner in his letter of 17/6/70.

INDEX